T0330723

Regulating Water and Sanitation
for the Poor

Regulating Water and Sanitation for the Poor

Economic Regulation for Public and Private Partnerships

Edited by Richard Franceys and Esther Gerlach

Routledge
Taylor & Francis Group

LONDON AND NEW YORK

First published by Earthscan in the UK and USA in 2008

For a full list of publications please contact:
Earthscan
2 Park Square, Milton Park, Abingdon, Oxfordshire OX14 4RN
711 Third Avenue, New York, NY 10017

Routledge is an imprint of the Taylor and Francis Group, an informa business

First issued in paperback 2015

Copyright © Richard Franceys and Esther Gerlach, 2008. Published by Taylor & Francis.

All rights reserved. No part of this book may be reprinted or reproduced or utilised in any form or by any electronic, mechanical, or other means, now known or hereafter invented, including photocopying and recording, or in any information storage or retrieval system, without permission in writing from the publishers.

Notices
Practitioners and researchers must always rely on their own experience and knowledge in evaluating and using any information, methods, compounds, or experiments described herein. In using such information or methods they should be mindful of their own safety and the safety of others, including parties for whom they have a professional responsibility.

Product or corporate names may be trademarks or registered trademarks, and are used only for identification and explanation without intent to infringe.

ISBN 978-1-84407-617-8 (hbk)
ISBN 978-1-138-99717-2 (pbk)

Typeset by MapSet Ltd, Gatesehad, UK
Cover design by Susanne Harris

A catalogue record for this book is available from the British Library

Library of Congress Cataloging-in-Publication Data has been applied for

Currency conversion rates in this book are based on purchasing power parity, unless otherwise stated, and expressed in US$. Purchasing power parity is a method of expressing the purchasing power of different currencies in their home countries for a given basket of goods, rather than market exchange rates. The calculations in this book have been made using the EconStats economic database.

Contents

List of Figures, Tables and Boxes

FIGURES

TABLES

BOXES

Preface

This book is about enabling better, cheaper water and sanitation services for poor households in the rapidly growing cities and towns in lower- and middle-income countries. It investigates the possibility that regulation, primarily economic regulation, might act as a driver for improvement of those services.

The monopoly utilities providing formal piped services are overwhelmingly under public ownership and management, notwithstanding the 'privatization decade'. The services delivered are usually of poor quality, for limited periods during each day, at a price well below the actual cost.

This attempt to subsidize water services for overall public benefit usually fails in that poor people, who benefit most from good cheap water, are generally not connected to the formal piped network. The public services usually reach the poor, if at all, only through the expensive intermediation of vendors, neighbours and water carriers. Paying between five, ten or even one hundred times more for water than the connected 'rich', on a volumetric basis, it can be argued that it is the poor who gain least benefit from a public supplier.

Economic regulation can be simply described as providing a partially independent but informed view on what might be acceptable costs and appropriate prices for water services relative to desired standards. Such regulation has developed particularly in the context of the need to ensure that new private operators do not abuse their monopoly position in the drive for additional profits.

However, it can be argued that it is the overwhelmingly predominant public sector, presumed to be managed for the public good by public managers, that has abused its monopoly position, though by default rather than any intent. It is the poor who suffer most from the limited hours and bad quality of water supplied because low-income households cannot easily afford the coping strategies of higher-income groups that are the household storage, treatment and pumping systems.

This lack is exacerbated in the informal housing areas, the slums and shanties that are home to an estimated billion people. Having to afford the increased supply costs of hand carriers, carters and other vendors where there are no pipe networks forces low-income consumers to pay too much of a limited household budget to access water (often at the cost of failing to pay school fees or achieve adequate nutrition or health care). Poor households equally pay the additional cost of lower quality water and limited amounts of it through poor hygiene and health.

Improving services to the poor requires a 'good enough' utility that has been facilitated not only to move towards sustainability through viable tariffs and better management of water losses but also to be creative in recognizing presently indirectly served low-income consumers as potential revenue generating customers, for the benefit of all.

This book, based upon research in ten countries, funded by the UK's Department for International Development (DFID) and undertaken through partner organizations around the world, investigates how economic regulation can act as a stimulus to the public providers to deliver better services to the lowest-income groups, in the context of both public and private provision.

However, the researchers recognize that the challenge of achieving 'good enough' economic regulation on behalf of the 'average' customer is in itself an ongoing process often yet to be achieved. Extending regulatory performance for the explicit benefit of the poor, particularly in a setting of limited economic wealth and governance, may be expecting 'too much, too soon', a point that is explored in the reported case studies.

The principles of economic regulation are clear, particularly with regard to a private sector operator. Regulators, with a reasonable level of independence or autonomy, determine a maximum water price (or total revenue that might take into account external subsidies) required to pay for a desired level of outputs at a reasonable level of (ideally, incentive-derived) efficient costs. The failure to allow utilities to set viable tariffs, often in the name of 'ensuring access to the poor', has contributed significantly to the failure of those utilities.

Prices in high-income countries have tended to increase faster than inflation as society demands ever higher standards. Prices (even including subsidies) in lower-income economies have usually been significantly lower than costs and desperately need to rise, particularly to fund ongoing serviceability as well as service enhancement and, most importantly, to fund service expansion to the poor.

The total income requirement, particularly in low-income countries, need not derive only from consumer revenues but may also be supported through general taxation where cross-subsidies within the tariff structure cannot realistically support the desired level of service and sustainability. If the world wants to accelerate that process further, i.e. to achieve the Millennium Development Goals, it might well require support through 'international taxation', that is donor funds. There is therefore a further role for economic regulation in ensuring fair use of any such external support.

In incentive-based regulatory systems service providers are encouraged to out-perform the regulatory assumptions and, where private companies are involved, are allowed to retain any efficiency savings achieved within the price or revenue cap for a period. This is a mechanism to generate even higher efficiency before the benefits are shared with customers in reduced prices or enhanced standards for the future.

BOX 0.1 THE REGULATION GAME

If regulation is the impartial referee in the football match between the government/policy-makers and the utility direct providers (agreeing fair prices in return for societal desired standards), with the customers in the stands expecting a good performance, and the customer forum/customer committee as the biased linesman shouting 'offside' whenever the game seems to be going against customer interests. ... at present the poor are perhaps playing a different game altogether, on the dusty waste ground outside the main stadium – playing a game between the poor and their alternative providers with no referees/regulator and government. Our challenge as a sector is to ensure that the poor are invited to join in the main match, perhaps standing on the hill at one end rather than sitting in the main seats – but definitely part of the experience. And to stretch the picture perhaps way too far, with the alternative providers also now in the stadium, selling drinks and ice creams to all the crowd!

Source: Developed by Richard Franceys from the original analogy of Clive Wilkinson and Will Dawson, previously Chair and Regional Manager of Central CSC, OFWAT, UK

This model of economic regulation has been adapted around the world usually in the context of a 'public–private partnership'. The 'fashion' for formal private sector involvement in the water sector in low-income countries has now passed, due to its rejection by society as well as by the losses incurred by many of the international private operators. By one analogy (and a less than agreed perspective) the international private sector represented a 'heart transplant' – powerful and effective but quickly 'rejected by the body'. However, the regulators live on and this study investigates whether an appropriate level of economic regulation of public providers could deliver similar mechanisms for financeability and efficiency as well as being a prerequisite for developing effective pro-poor urban services. If the 'heart transplant' has failed perhaps a 'pacemaker' of a regulator could make a difference? It is not yet clear how the public sector might be incentivized by being able to retain out-performance benefits, except as an, easily misused, direct return to staff.

This DFID-funded research project however is not about economic regulation itself but rather sought to investigate how regulators are interpreting and acting upon any requirements to ensure services to poor consumers and how this might be enhanced. It seeks to give newly established regulators the necessary understanding to require the direct providers to work under a universal service obligation, to ensure innovative service to the poorest, even in informal, unplanned and illegal areas, acknowledging the techniques of service and pricing differentiation to meet and promote effective demand.

Looking to achieve early universal service, the research also considers how the role of small-scale, alternative providers, including community-based and non-governmental organizations (NGOs), can be recognized in the regulatory process, harnessing their 'closeness to the customer' skills while minimizing the delivery costs. Customer involvement, at an appropriate level and part of the necessary transparency in information, is seen as the third key aspect of this approach. The research investigated mechanisms for poor customers, and most importantly potential poor customers, to achieve a valid input to regulatory decision-making to achieve better water and sanitation (watsan) services within the context of social empowerment and sustainable livelihoods, always prerequisites for lasting development.

Although this study is concerned with ensuring the delivery of 'effective water and sanitation for all', the focus on economic regulation leads to a focus on monopolistic network suppliers that in practice in low-income areas usually means water-only services – the sewers rarely reach the slums. Good on-site sanitation solutions supplied through a competitive local market of masons and latrine builders and NGOs achieve the desired convenience and public health benefits while minimizing water consumption and costs. Limited further discussion of sanitation in the text therefore does not indicate any devaluing of its importance – it simply does not need significant input from regulators (though it does from others!) at the present level of economic development in the slums.

Acknowledgements

The financial support of DFID of the UK Government is gratefully acknowledged: Department for International Development Knowledge and Research Contract R8320. This document is an output from a project funded by DFID for the benefit of developing countries. The views expressed are not necessarily those of DFID. The findings, interpretations and conclusions expressed in this document are entirely those of the authors.

The research work reported was dependent upon the willingness of many people to contribute: householders responding to questionnaires and sharing in focus groups, utility staff and government officials answering specific questions, and NGO partners sharing their concerns and experience. We acknowledge with thanks that dependence and recognize especially the interest and support at the commencement of the research programme (recognizing that some may have subsequently moved from these posts) of: Andrea Vink, Programme Coordinator, Banda Community Development Programme; Charles Ibanda, Chairman, Community Health Concern; Charles Odonga, Chief Manager, National Water and Sewerage Corporation, Uganda; Eugene Larbi, NGO Trend; E. Martey, Water Sector Restructuring Unit; Ruby Beecham, Ag Chief Director, Ministry of Works and Housing; Stephen Adu, Regulator, Public Utilities Regulatory Commission, Ghana; S. Satyanarayana, Chairperson, Ramagundam Municipal Council; M. Gopal, Managing Director, Hyderabad Metro Water Supply and Sewerage Board; Rajeswara Rao, Project Coordinator, Andhra Pradesh Urban Services for the Poor; Srinivasa Chary, ASCI, Hyderabad, India; Inpart Engineering and Manila Water Company, Philippines; C. Chipulu, Managing Director, Lusaka Water and Sewerage Corporation, Zambia; Benny Chatib, Chairman of Customer and Community Communication Forum, Jakarta; Achmad Lanti, Chairman, Regulatory Body of Jakarta Water Supply Provision, Indonesia; Osward Chanda, Director, National Water Supply and Sanitation Council, Zambia; Claudia Vargas, Ministry of Housing and Basic Services, Bolivia; Eng. M. Abubakar, Federal Ministry of Water Resources, Abuja, Nigeria; Eng. Munther Khlaifat, Secretary General, Ministry of Water and Irrigation, Jordan; country research adviser Dr Ziad Al-Ghazawi; Dennis Mwanza, Managing Director, Water Utility Partnership for Capacity Building – Africa; Alain Mathys, Manager of 'Water and Sanitation Solutions', Suez Environnement, France; Barry Walton, Consultant; and Andrew Nickson, IDD Birmingham, UK.

The advice, review work and contributions of Joe Morris and Andy Narracott, Cranfield University and Peter Robbins, Open University are also noted and appreciated. Special thanks to Barry Walton for his contributions to the Buenos Aires work on customer involvement and service to the poor. We would like to thank Barbara Evans for reviewing an earlier version of this research report and providing helpful comments. The involvement of Eng. Gerald Osuagwu, Federal Ministry of Water Resources, Abuja, Nigeria, who not only attended both the Workshops but also contributed significantly to the Latin America Study Tour, has been highly valued.

The involvement and contributions of participants at the Inception and Research Review Workshops are also gratefully acknowledged, particularly our invited speakers: Philip Fletcher, Chair, Water Services Regulation Authority, England and Wales; Sir James Perowne, Chair, Consumer Council for Water, Central and Eastern; and Stuart Braley, CEO, Auriga, the trading company of Severn Trent Trust Fund. We also owe a considerable debt to Severn Trent Water and South Staffs Water. They undertook their task of educating the customer representatives on Central CSC about the realties of public water provision and regulation – a task all water providers face with, as always, only partially aware customer representatives – with commitment and patience.

List of Contributors

EDITORS

Dr Richard Franceys leads the Water and Society programme at Cranfield University having undertaken research and consultancy in over 40 countries, focusing upon capacity building, institutional development, tariffs and financing to serve the poor. He is a long-standing member of the Consumer Council for Water in England and Wales.

Dr Esther Gerlach is a post-doctoral researcher in the Water Management Group at Cranfield University, with an interest in the social, economic and institutional dimensions of the urban water sector.

CONTRIBUTORS

Alizar Anwar is an independent consultant, presently working with the Jakarta Water Supply Regulatory Body, following many years working with PAM Jaya, the earlier water provider for Jakarta, Indonesia.

Urmila Brighu is a reader at Malaviya National Institute of Technology, Jaipur where she focuses upon issues relating to asset management planning and change management in the Indian water supply sector.

Lyn Capistrano is Executive Director of the Philippine Center for Water and Sanitation that actively promotes community participation and encourages local initiatives for sanitation efforts and the protection and conservation of water resources in the Philippines.

Marion Gessler was a researcher at Cranfield University when undertaking this study and now works for United Utilities, UK

Dr Peter Howsam provides input to teaching and research projects, addressing the legal framework for the subjects covered in a wide range of Cranfield postgraduate programmes.

Dr Sam Kayaga is a researcher at WEDC, Loughborough University where he specializes in sustainable urban water management systems, institutional, financial and management issues, following many years working for National Water and Sewerage Corporation, Uganda.

Dr Kwabena Nyarko is a lecturer in the Department of Civil Engineering, Kwame Nkrumah University of Science and Technology, Kumasi, Ghana, specializing in the management of water supply and environmental sanitation and water resources engineering and management.

Dr Samuel Odai is a senior lecturer in the Department of Civil Engineering, Kwame Nkrumah University of Science and Technology, Kumasi, Ghana, specializing in water resources engineering and management.

Kevin Sansom is a programme manager at WEDC, Loughborough University, specializing in institutional development, contracting out services, public sector reform, NGO engagement with government and services to the poor. He is also a Director of Delta Partnership management consultants.

Dr Andrew Trevett undertook this research while a Lecturer at Cranfield University. He is now the World Health Organization's Environmental Health Advisor in Bangladesh.

List of Acronyms and Abbreviations

AISA	Aguas del Illimani
AMP	assessment management plan
AVRL	Aqua Vitens Rand Ltd
BPL	below the poverty line
CAS	Comité de Asistencia Social Comunal
CBO	community-based organization
CCCF	Customer and Community Communication Forum
CCWater	Consumer Council for Water
CPS	Customer Protection Society
CSC	consumer services committee
DEFRA	Department for Environment, Food and Rural Affairs
DENR	Department of Environment and Natural Resources
DFID	Department for International Development
DWD	Directorate of Water Development
EMOS	Empresa Metropolitana de Obras Sanitarias
EPA	Environmental Protection Agency
ETOSS	Ente Tripartito de Obras y Servicios Sanitarios
FEJUVE	Federacion de Juntas Vecinales
GNI	gross national income
GTZ	Deutsche Gesellschaft für Technische Zusammenarveit GmbH
GWCL	Ghana Water Company Ltd
HDI	Human Development Index
IBT	increasing block tariff
IDB	Inter-American Development Bank
JBIC	Japanese Bank for International Cooperation
JDA	Jaipur Development Authority
JICA	Japanese International Corporation Agency
JMC	Jaipur Municipal Corporation
JWSRB	Jakarta Water Supply Regulatory Board
LCC	Lusaka City Council
LDR	less-developed region
LGU	local government unit
LWSC	Lusaka Water and Sewerage Company
LWWG	Lusaka Water Watch Group
MDG	Millennium Development Goal
MDR	more-developed region
MIDEPLAN	Ministry of Planning
MoE	Ministry of Environment

MoH	Ministry of Health
MoWLE	Ministry of Water Lands and Environment
MSE	Ministry of Science and Environment
MWH	Ministry of Works and Housing
MWI	Ministry of Water and Irrigation
MWSS	Metropolitan Waterworks and Sewerage System
NARUC	National Association of Regulatory Utility Commissioners
NEDA	National Economic Development Authority
NGO	non-governmental organization
NRW	non-revenue water
NWASCO	National Water Supply and Sanitation Council
NWRB	National Water Resources Board
NWSC	National Water and Sewerage Corporation
OFWAT	Water Services Regulation Authority
O&M	operation and maintenance
OS	obligatory service
PHED	Public Health and Engineering Department
PMU	Programme Management Unit
PPP	public–private partnership
PSO	public service obligation
PSP	private sector participation
PURC	Public Utilities Regulatory Commission
RCA	Restated Cooperation Agreement
RDC	resident development committee
RHB	Rajasthan Housing Board
RO	Regulatory Office
RUIDP	Rajasthan Urban Integrated Development Programme
RWSSC	Rajasthan Water Supply and Sewerage Corporation
RWSSMB	Rajasthan Water Supply and Sewerage Management Board
SEC	State Enterprise Commission
SERNAC	Servicio Nacional del Consumidor
SIRESE	Sistema de Regulacion Sectorial
SISAB	Superintendencia de Saneamiento Básico
SISS	Superintendencia de Servicios Sanitarios
SSISP	small-scale independent service providers
TPJ	Thames PAM Jaya
ULIGWU	Urban Low Income Group Water Unit
USO	universal service obligation
WAJ	Water Authority of Jordan
watsan	water and sanitation
WCC	water customer committee
WD	water district
WLE	Ministry of Water Lands and Environment
WRC	Water Resources Commission
WSSA	Water Supply and Sanitation Act
WWG	water watch group

Water and Sanitation for the Urban Poor

Richard Franceys

Regulation is how the incentive to ensure service delivery at lowest cost is built into reforms and how the cost savings from the incentives are shared with the users. Effective regulation requires effective regulatory tools and effective skills. (Estache, 2005)

WATER AND SANITATION FOR THE URBAN POOR IN LOWER-INCOME COUNTRIES

Progress is being made in ensuring clean water supply and safe sanitation for the poorest. However, this progress is not fast enough to meet the goals of the world expressed through the United Nations-sponsored Millennium Development Goals (MDGs), particularly with respect to the need for improved sanitation. Urban water and sanitation fall under MDG Goal 7, which aims to 'ensure environmental sustainability'. Within that goal, Targets 10 and 11 specifically state that the international community aspires to halve, by 2015, the proportion of people without sustainable access to safe drinking water and hygienic sanitation (from a 1990 base year) and, by 2020, to have achieved a significant improvement in the lives of at least 100 million slum dwellers. Water supply and sanitation also implicitly contribute to Goals 1 (eradicating extreme poverty), 3 (promoting gender equality), 4 (reducing child mortality) and 6 (combating HIV/AIDs and other diseases) (UN, 2006).

Figure 1.1 illustrates the ever-increasing challenge of providing large unserved or under-served rural – and now, ever more predominantly, urban – populations with adequate water supply and sanitation services. While presently an estimated 85 per cent of the people without access to improved water sources worldwide live in rural areas, rapid expansion of cities and urban sprawl creates large concentrations of water demand with more limited access to traditional sources, a situation exacerbated by the high potential for pollution of those sources. 5 billion people are expected to live in urban areas by 2030 (up from 3 billion today). The number of slum dwellers in the world, presently estimated at approximately 1 billion, can be expected to double within the next 25 years under a 'business as usual' scenario (UN-HABITAT, 2003a). The annual growth rate of slum populations in sub-Saharan Africa has been 4.5 per cent (UN, 2006), which implies a 'doubling time' of less than 20 years – very much a case of water providers needing to run even if they are only to stand still. And over half of all 'new urbanites' can be expected to be poor (UNFPA, 2007). In sub-Saharan Africa it appears that almost 100 per cent of new urbanites are poor as the present and predicted growth in slum populations almost exactly matches the growth in urban populations.

The ongoing lack of safe water and sanitation (and other 'preventable environmental causes') in the rapidly expanding urban areas, as well as in the rural, is believed to lead to 'at least 1.6 million children dying each year'. 2.6 billion people are reported to be without access to adequate sanitation, 1.1 billion without access to safe water at the beginning of the (second) water decade (WHO and UNICEF, 2006).

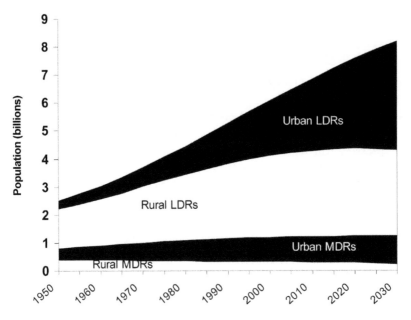

Note: LDRs are less-developed regions that comprise all regions of Africa, Asia (excluding Japan), Latin America and the Caribbean, Melanesia, Micronesia and Polynesia; MDRs are more- developed regions that comprise Europe, Northern America, Australia/New Zealand and Japan.
Source: Author's analysis of DESA (2006)

Figure 1.1 *Rural and urban population growth*

For urban areas, the focus of this study, the service improvement challenge should be more straightforward than in rural areas, even though coverage at present remains significantly dependent upon national wealth as illustrated in Figure 1.2. The UN (2006) already reports that city dwellers in sub-Saharan Africa are twice as likely to have safe water as those living in rural areas. A likely explanation is that this improvement will have been driven by absolute necessity. Alternative sources of supply, vaguely potable streams and rivers, hand-dug wells and springs, for example, are simply not an option in most urban areas. But there is another critical issue regarding the rural–urban divide in the context of economic regulation of services. Urban water supply is very 'capital intensive' but where invested appropriately that capital investment can deliver good quality water at a low volumetric cost. Where the price charged, that is what consumers actually pay, is significantly below even that low cost, as has been usual without economic regulation, then cities continue to siphon off most of the capital available nationally for urban rehabilitation as well as some expansion, all at the expense of developments in the rural areas. As the cities grow ever larger, and therefore more powerful, they should not be allowed to drink at the expense of much more limited water accessibility in rural areas.

By getting the balance of investment, service and tariffs correct, the task of economic regulation, most urban water services could be made to be sustainable through reasonable, affordable user tariffs. Extending those services to the poor is a different task. For one of the particular challenges the water and sanitation sector faces is, perhaps surprisingly, limited demand from the prospective beneficiaries. It appears that outsiders are much more aware of the benefits that

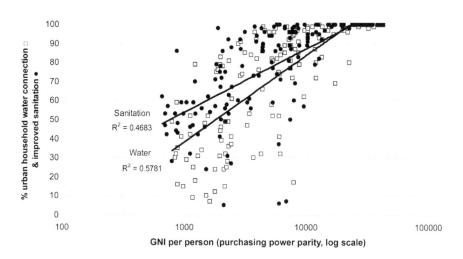

Note: GNI = gross national income.
Source: Author's analysis of World Bank (2007) and WHO and UNICEF (2006)

Figure 1.2 *Significance of wealth to water and sanitation coverage*

can be derived from clean water and effective sanitation than consumers. Everybody already has some form of water supply; otherwise they could not live in that location. Everybody could (and many have to) excrete in the open, close by their home, whether in nearby rural fields or urban slum streets. Good promotional 'social marketing' campaigns can affect this limited demand for a while but without continued inputs normal patterns tend to resume. Medical bills, school fees, food, perhaps even electricity and cable television in some slums (and definitely mobile phones, though recognizing the gender bias in these products) are often seen as more important, within the context of limited household incomes. They are definitely seen as more important than allowing tariffs to rise to ensure capital maintenance of a water system or latrine that 'only' provides welcome, but apparently too expensive, convenience. Particularly when the rhetoric of the sector often encourages a belief that the absolutely vital human right to water also means that it should be free.

A key approach to serving the poor therefore is not only social marketing of health- and hygiene-type ideas but actual marketing of lowest possible cost services for water and sanitation in urban areas. Developed and discussed in an earlier DFID study (Sansom et al, 2004), the concept of service and pricing differentiation to meet the specific interests of different customer segments, that is marketing, is a critical component that economic regulation has to recognize and harness, requiring such pro-poor activities from the providers.

To date, the capital-intensive technologies that are most effective in the networked water sector have not been delivering, particularly to slums in urban areas, because of institutional and organizational weaknesses allied to the pricing challenge described. These weaknesses may be in terms of appropriate competences (as always, based upon incentives) in the service providers, particularly in adapting service delivery modes appropriately. But these weaknesses may be equally a reflection of the socio-economic conditions, perhaps also of the institutional capital within which they must operate. Experience suggests that these issues can only be addressed effectively through long-term support to appropriate organizations, particularly service providers but also to the ever more required economic regulators, ideally within the context of a growing economy.

Without effective reform of water sector governance and capacity building for the various organizations in order to channel additional resources over the long term to bridge the affordability and willingness-to-pay gap (though smaller than often assumed) it will not be possible to achieve the world's water and sanitation goals. Reform requires both resources and institutional drivers, not only to deliver that reform but also to maintain it for long enough to limit the tendency to revert to a restricted service, particularly a service that fails to serve the poor. Economic regulation, some level of independent judgement over reasonable prices and services, is seen as a potential driver for reform and maintenance of that reform in the context of public utility services.

URBAN WATER SUPPLY: INSTITUTIONAL REFORM
AND PUBLIC–PRIVATE PARTNERSHIPS

Various approaches have been attempted to accelerate the provision of sustainable services over the years since the first water decade in 1980, promoting, without necessarily realizing it, the development of 'institutional capital'. Following the demise of international training programmes and technical assistance, there then followed fashions for community management, social marketing, demand-responsive approaches, public–private partnerships and now public operator partnerships. Most of these efforts could be considered to have been inadequate in their effect, usually because of poverty linked to limited national economic resources and the institutional inadequacy referred to earlier. Governments and donors have usually not been able to overcome these weaknesses, tending to commit only to initial capital investment type projects for short periods before moving on to the next 'good idea'.

It was the new 'good idea' of the 'privatization' approach to institutional reform that delivered the initial impetus for regulatory development. 'Privatization' was quickly reborn as 'public–private partnerships' (PPPs) perhaps to stress that the approach was never about the private ownership of any water resources, perhaps to make it sound more acceptable to the sceptical. Other terminology was developed to similarly confuse the uninitiated, referring to private sector participation, disinvestment, capitalization, demonopolization, equitization, opening of capital, peopleization, ownership reform, disincorporation, all in different countries at different times. Regulation does not appear to have needed such rebranding, perhaps because it was never seen as a threat, perhaps because it is rarely understood.

All of the PPP terms refer to some level of involvement of the private sector to a greater extent than had been common in that setting previously. In some countries it referred to having staff vehicles maintained by an external garage rather than having all work undertaken by the public provider workshop (Sansom et al, 2003). This cannot be seen as a significant threat to world water, but all such private sector involvement was targeted during the powerful and successful international campaign against any private involvement in water supply. In other settings PPP refers to the responsibility for all operations being transferred to a private company, though one that employs 90 per cent of the existing staff and where all the assets, not to mention control of water resources, remain under government control and ownership. Only rarely did the PPP concept mean selling off all the assets to a private owner (or more usually selling shares in a renamed public provider, maintaining existing management and staff).

This spectrum of private sector involvement, reflecting different levels of risk and potential reward, is usually reflected through the labels given to different types of private involvement: service contracts; management contracts; design, build, operate contracts; build (own), operate and transfer contracts; leases; concessions and divestiture. Described in more detail elsewhere (Weitz and Franceys, 2002), it is worth noting that all such contracts need provision for adjustment through negotiation and arbitration should conditions and requirements change. The longer the contract, the more certain it is that conditions and requirements will indeed change. Economic regulation is, in effect, simply a sophisticated form of arbitration but one where more stakeholders are involved because it affects the prices charged direct to customers and takes place within a national and international concern over service delivery and the environment.

The presumption has often been that 'private' refers only to large-scale international operators. Although initially true of the sorts of concessions and divestitures that demanded economic regulation, there is another reality in that the majority of the poor in particular have long been served by private providers. As already mentioned, the small-scale vendors and carters, the neighbours on-selling from their tap or private borehole, are all private. Perhaps more contentiously, in many countries NGOs are equally seen as private though perhaps of a 'not for profit distributing' variety. All these small-scale alternative providers tend to operate in a multi-provider competitive market ideally not requiring any economic regulation – and perhaps most importantly not being seen as a threat to existing vested interests. These other private providers may not need to be regulated, in fact ideally not if they are selling in a potentially competitive environment, but they do need to be recognized in the overall process of serving the poor. Where the reality has been that the poor have found themselves at the mercy of an unregulated but 'mafia captured', and therefore very uncompetitive, market then a more direct form of regulation of small-scale providers is necessary. But we recognize that those small-scale providers have generally been meeting a need that the public utility has been failing to serve and that a reasonable profit margin is the price that must be paid for reasonably efficient service delivery.

The promotion of large-scale international private sector involvement as a means to deliver service reform was partially driven by the initial expectation that the private companies would deliver, from private sources, the finance necessary to upgrade water and sanitation services. However, with a few exceptions, the private equity markets were not convinced enough to invest their money in pipes buried in the ground in low-income economies and, in hindsight with good reason, not daring to trust any regulatory system (or perhaps more importantly the host government) to protect that investment. What the new private operators did deliver was increased technical competence and expectation, particularly in increasing efficiency, but also of commercial viability through enhanced service provision and tariff collection. This convinced the multilateral donors to lend through them and, for a while, unlocked many billions for investment. It has been cheaper for consumers to accept a reasonable level of profit for those more efficient, lower-cost, private companies than to

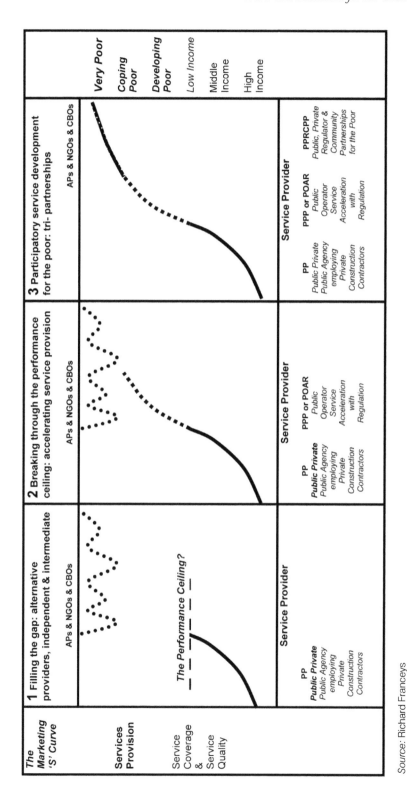

Figure 1.3 *The marketing 'S' curve related to services providers, improvement and partnerships*

Source: Richard Franceys

continue to pay the costs, limited in financial terms but high in economic terms, of the failing public sector.

Earlier work for the Asian Development Bank (Weitz and Franceys, 2002) also suggests that the best of the private operators were learning how to serve the poor living in the slums and shanties. Looking at urban service delivery through the lens of the marketing 'S' curve (see Figure 1.3) it is suggested that the conventional public providers reach a 'performance ceiling' in service coverage that very much equates to their societies' economic and institutional environment or expectations. The performance gap, that is service to the rest of the population, was being met by a mixture of self-service coping strategies, independent and intermediating vendors, community-based organizations (CBOs) and NGOs. The research in ten Asian countries found that the best international private operators were able to break through that performance ceiling through conventional upgrading approaches – and that where they were working in partnership with civil society, NGOs and CBOs they were then able to reach the most difficult part of any 'S' curve, the late adopters, in this case the slum and shanty dwellers.

This analysis is important in the present context because it demonstrates that it is possible to accelerate service development beyond the normal socio-economic trend line, as illustrated in Figure 1.4, with the correct approach and suitable drivers for change. Figure 1.4 illustrates that although water and sanitation provision remains very significantly dependent upon economic growth, the poorest countries now have a higher coverage ratio than was previously the case at similar levels of wealth. Economic regulation could be part of the driver for utility change. Please note with interest the almost vertical dashed line in Figure 1.4 showing an approximation towards the change in mobile phone coverage between 1990 and 2007, relative to the change in water coverage. Ability to pay is higher where demand is facilitated, a point we return to later.

However, in the context of the supply-side PPPs, this 'unfreezing' of the existing socio-institutional situation, following the terminology of Lewin (1997), was, as is normal, quickly followed by the response of the 'restraining forces', that is the vested interests for whom the existing situation provided all that they needed (which did not include water supply to all). Whether it was politicians perceiving a loss of patronage and power over tariff setting or trades unions wanting to protect unduly the privileged positions of their elite members (elite in the sense of having a formal job in an economy where the informal predominates) or civil society groups finding a cause that resonated, the PPPs have been rejected by society. Interestingly this rejection has been more complete in poorer societies or countries where the need for improved water has been greatest and therefore perhaps where the significance or implications of any change are highest.

Similarly, many governments were not sufficiently convinced to allow 'foreign control' of their monopoly public water supplies, a reluctance that was again most marked in the poorer countries where governance can be weak and

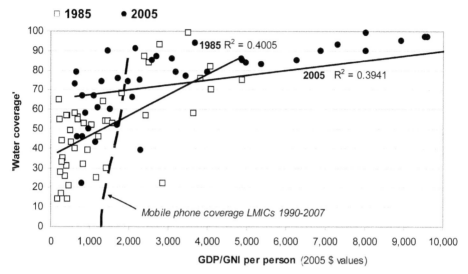

Source: Author's analysis of WASH (1992), World Bank (2007) and WHO and UNICEF (2006)

Figure 1.4 *Change in significance of wealth to coverage over a 20-year period*

governments need to be cautious about being taken advantage of by foreign suppliers, a caution based on hard experience.

The result has been that international private water companies have made headlines mainly in relation to the number of depressingly early contract endings rather than their significant (though rarely reported) contributions to developing workable alternatives to serving poor urban communities. Society, having rejected many of the forms of PPP, has to recognize the fact that the excellent NGO- and community-led water schemes face resource constraints (both financial and environmental, for example access to water) that prevent them from scaling up to match the needs of a growing and increasingly impoverished urban population. Where successful, NGO scaling-up invariably encounters the same problems currently faced by conventional utilities.

The end result of this PPP experiment is that the upper middle-income countries, using an analysis from the Cranfield PPP database (Franceys, 2008), appear to have embraced private sector involvement to a similar extent to the high-income countries – approximately one third private, two-thirds public. Although this does not represent a balance within (most) individual countries it appears to show a governance need for the private sector to be present to at least act as a comparator by which public providers can be judged, and incentivized, between countries. Each pattern, public or private, we would argue needs the spur of comparative competition and the potentially cheaper public sector can become extremely inefficient without the spur of private sector comparators.

However, the recent reluctance of both governments and the private sector to work together in lower-income economies, where the public health benefits of clean water and sanitation are highest, had led to private sector involvement reaching just about 10 per cent urban involvement in lower middle-income countries and only perhaps 5 per cent now in low-income countries. This might well be seen to disadvantage the poorest the most. Why should the poorest not be able to benefit from the challenge of private sector comparators that the rich appear to value? But recognizing that time has passed, the task now is to use appropriate levels of economic regulation to promote service to the poor through increasing the pressure on the public providers, while fully supporting those public providers through long-term capacity building.

Overall there has been a failure of governments and/or their regulators, as well as the private companies, to deliver on their promises to be in anything like the oft-proclaimed 'partnership' that demands 'acting together' and 'deciding together' by some definitions. It was always unrealistic to expect too much of a partnership with such unequal partners – a massive multinational against a city-level client or, as an alternative perspective, a sovereign government against a temporary foreign visitor. Both views illustrate such unequal levels of power relationships that it is hard to see how they could ever be called partnerships. But some level of working together and deciding together remains critical if service delivery to the slums is to out-perform economic growth.

There is now a movement towards the greater empowerment of national operators, the public operator partnerships, and smaller-scale service/management contracts models. It is therefore even more important to ensure that the needs of the poorest are met where there are not the comprehensive requirements of an all-embracing concession with clear and demanding service targets, and where there is no automatic built-in mechanism for sharing best practices around the world, as was the case with the largest international operators. Which perhaps leads to an even greater need for empowered regulation of public as well as private providers to achieve water for all?

WATER FOR LIFE: WATER FOR ALL

'Without water, it is all just chemistry, but add water [to the catalogue of genes and the proteins they code for] and you get biology' (Franks, 2006, cited in Matthews, 2006). The simple fact that the human body, on average, contains 60 per cent of water should be enough to convince that access to water is an absolute necessity – and as such is already achieved by all people in one form or another. There is good reason for declaring that 'water is special, water is life!', as the slogans continue to remind us.

It is the safety, regularity, convenience and, above all, price of this access – in terms of distance to point of consumption, variability of supply and water quality – that are now the main cause for concern. However, water is also highly valued in productive uses, supporting various livelihood activities including household livestock and gardens, even in urban areas. Water is therefore an economic good as well as a basic need, critical for health and social welfare. WHO estimates that US$1 invested in water and sanitation would give an economic return of between US$3 and US$34, depending on the region. Achieving the global targets would require an estimated additional investment of around US$11.3 billion per year over and above current investments. The benefits would include an average global reduction of diarrhoeal episodes of 10 per cent and a total annual economic benefit of US$84 billion (WHO, 2005).

Similarly, excreta disposal in its most rudimentary form involves nothing more than the edge of a field, a rubbish tip or an empty plastic bag discarded into the street. However, sanitation refers to the process of ensuring that excreta disposal is safe and does not lead to disease in other people or cause harm to the environment. People prefer comfort and convenience in excreta disposal and many cultures value privacy. Hygiene and hand-washing ensure that any possible link between the pathogens in human waste and the ingestion of those pathogens through food and water (the faecal–oral route) is broken.

Water and sanitation provision is therefore a complex amalgam of behavioural issues, development issues, health issues, economic and societal issues. Gender issues have equally been recognized as important in development work, and are emphasized especially in the water and sanitation sector. Women are now encouraged to participate in water projects and decision-makers show a commitment to increasing gender equity.

Given the inability of public authorities and their agents very often to provide sufficient safe and accessible water and sanitation facilities that respond to actual and expressed needs, deteriorating service levels tend to reinforce social exclusion. By one definition 'social exclusion happens when people or places suffer from a series of problems such as unemployment, poor skills, low incomes, poor housing, high crime, poor health and family breakdown' (Social Exclusion Unit, 2006). This is a UK definition included to demonstrate that serving the poor is not just a low-income country challenge but also needs to be recognized as part of the responsibility of all regulatory systems, a point developed further in the case study of economic regulation in England and Wales (Chapter 7). Understanding powerlessness, further discussed below in the context of understanding poverty, is critical in 'making sure mainstream services deliver for *everyone*'.

Considering how economic regulation might enable water providers to serve the poor better with these life-critical services in the context of social exclusion it is necessary to acknowledge that poverty comes in many forms, with different characteristics, over a 'spectrum of poverty'.

There are descriptions such as the 'income poor' (those living on less than US$1–2 per day); the 'health and education poor' (where limited incomes either deny access to health and education or leave families utterly vulnerable to the costs of the next sickness episode or school fees demand); the 'housing poor' (for those living in multi-family occupancy of a room or small dwelling in tenements and in slums or the other names given to informal or unplanned

Table 1.1 *Characterizing poverty*

Category of poor	Characteristics
Lower middle-income households 'vulnerable non-poor'	Often employed at low wage levels by government or the formal private sector, living in conventional housing, are susceptible to unexpected financial shocks, particularly ill-health or family expenses. Conventional water and sanitation tariffs are normally affordable but may need to be structured in a way that allows for delay in payments in exceptional circumstances so as not to disrupt household finances and push the family into poverty.
'Developing poor'	Can be characterized as a household in a slum or informal housing area that has sufficient income to be able to invest in permanent (semi-permanent) materials for their own housing, with a fairly regular income from at least one semi-skilled member of the family.
'Coping poor'	Describes households with perhaps a single daily employed unskilled earner living in what we could call a temporary shelter (but that might be used for many years), perhaps rented from a slum landlord.
'Very poor'	Might be characterized as a single parent family, very possibly female-headed, sharing a one- or two-room temporary shelter with other families with very irregular or seasonal employment.
'Destitute'	Refers to the street sleepers and the street children with no fixed living space.

and/or illegal housing areas); and most importantly the 'powerless poor', characterized by 'insecurity and vulnerability, bad social relations, low self-confidence and powerlessness' (Narayan et al, 1999)

To these descriptions other characteristics can be addressed: the unemployed, the underemployed, the randomly employed as in daily paid (and employed) labourers, the over-borrowed, the single parent, female- or child-headed household, the disabled, the chronically sick, the elderly and the street kids.

Reflecting on these descriptions and a number of different sources (particularly Plummer, 2002a) the researchers developed the 'segmentation' below as capturing a minimum number of poverty segments that have to be recognized by a watsan provider and their regulatory environment if they are to be effective.

Facilitating water and sanitation services to the urban poor requires recognition of these different levels of poverty that might each require a different approach by the service provider, whether technical, financial or spatial. The goal is to reach as many people as possible with the lowest-cost formal piped supply that can significantly reduce average household spending on water. However, although achievable for most of the 'coping poor', conventional supplies may not be possible for many of the 'very poor' and probably not at all for the 'destitute'. For many in these segments of the population water stand posts or kiosks, which do not add the transaction costs of the stand post to the cost of water charged, may be more appropriate as a temporary (short- to medium-term) solution. Any regulatory approach has to recognize the importance of the technology of service delivery in addition to the need for inclusion and empowerment – an ever more challenging task.

It is now widely recognized that genuine demand-responsive approaches produce better outcomes in terms of access and effective use of services and are more sustainable than the supply-driven approaches, which had long dominated the water sector. Giving local stakeholders and ultimately service recipients a voice and a choice in basic service provision was emphasized in water projects that centred on community management in rural areas. In the urban/networked context, consumer involvement is taking longer to establish but is receiving attention within partnership approaches (see www.bpdws.org and www.wsup.com) and practical participation is being explored as a vital component of consumer protection. The 'S' curve of Figure 1.3 can only be completed through the involvement of people in a quite different way than is normal for a conventional engineering-focused utility.

Many water sector reforms have missed the opportunity to introduce stakeholder involvement from the beginning in the formulation of sector policy. Reforms are often designed without stakeholder consultation and rarely accompanied by timely and broad communication and information campaigns. Where consultation and stakeholder participation feature in national policies, the legal framework often fails to specify the necessary instruments to facilitate interaction between institutional actors and consumers.

Fortunately, the international consumer movements have discovered and added public utility services to their portfolio, noting that 'when consumers cannot vote with their feet, forms of involvement become even more crucial as a means of assessing quality, delivery and value for money, and of shaping the service to match consumers' needs' (NCC, 2002). In the developing economy context, 'consumers' must not be understood to refer only to those already receiving a service, but should be interpreted to include those who potentially could (and, for the various reasons discussed earlier, should) become formal customers of water services.

Urban water supply: Finance and tariff reform

Understanding the needs and potential of poor customers is vital but, in the end, sector reform is dependent upon tariff reform to ensure adequate revenue flows for financial sustainability. The importance of achieving financial (self-)sustainability for the sector cannot be overemphasized. Tariff reform is a critical and always politically sensitive element of water sector reform that is clouded in many myths and misconceptions. In summary, sustainable water and sanitation costs much more than is generally acknowledged in terms of investment and capacity building but equally customers are generally able to contribute far more to those costs, when spread over a 'maintainable' and affordable longer term, than is usually recognized – with the notable exception of the 'very poor' and 'destitute'. A key challenge in terms of pro-poor service delivery is to harness the enormous financial resources that are currently diverted into the informal sector (to the various vendors and resellers that serve the majority of low-income households without a utility water connection) at the level of the 'developing' and 'coping poor'.

There remains the need to recognize the difference in potential for cost-reflective tariffs between the various levels of country wealth and also in geographical situations, often between regions within a country. What can be achieved in lower middle-income countries (or provinces for example with bountiful and accessible water resources) is quite different from what can be achieved in low-income countries with declining water availability. In fragile states it is unlikely that tariff reform can be achieved and alternative sources of revenue will have to be provided to utilities – though some form of regulatory oversight might well remain beneficial in promoting efficiency through benchmarking.

The tariff structure should allow the service provider to comfortably recover the costs of everyday operations and ongoing capital maintenance, as well as, ideally, generating revenues that enable debt servicing and capital invest-ments. The technicalities of accurately determining and fairly allocating the costs of service provision are complex in the context of urban and networked water services. There are several design objectives for water and sanitation tariffs that frequently conflict with each other. There is no consensus on optimal tariff structures, though many developing countries have favoured increasing block tariffs with a low 'lifeline' block designed to safeguard affordability – very proba-bly as a result of donor advice. These complicated tariff systems are now believed to confuse rather than assist but it is notable in the case studies how often they are used. Experience has begun to indicate that single rate volumetric tariffs may well be more manageable as well as fairer to the poor (though England is now moving in the opposite direction). A frequent problem is the confusion over the difference between willingness to pay and ability to pay. This often leads decision-makers to respond to public outcry over any increase in tariffs or indeed public disapproval of the whole concept of charging for something that is perceived as 'free' or 'a gift of God'. There is a great need for raising awareness about the need to contribute financially to a water *service*. While water remains 'free' when collected from springs and rivers or harvested as rain, piped water undergoes a series of collection, transportation and storage, as well as necessary treatment and purification processes. Piped water conveniently delivered into the customer's home thus becomes a relatively costly product, without even counting in the administrative overheads associated with running a modern, customer-friendly service. This is another reason for recognizing the role of customer involvement.

Where there are genuine and valid concerns over affordability problems for lower-income segments of the population, special pricing and service arrangements may be developed to meet the needs of the poorest. There is a growing consensus that the present broad subsidy schemes, including most increasing block tariffs, tend to bypass poor households, and subsidies are captured by the middle- and higher-income classes who are much more likely to be connected to networked services. Recent research (Franceys, 2005a) has shown that in many instances high initial connection charges, rather than the relatively smaller ongoing usage fees, present the real bottleneck. The challenge for regulators is thus to reconcile cost recovery and social protection objectives as well as developing subsidy mechanisms that explicitly and transparently target people in need. Some countries successfully operate means-tested subsidy schemes (see for example the Chile case study, Chapter 7) though they have been criticized for high administrative costs. Another difficulty lies in defining suitable eligibility criteria, particularly among 'non-recognized' communities or slums.

Networked sanitation, that is sewerage, is an expensive form of sanitation that is very appropriate to commercial centres and high-income housing areas. Generally costing at least as much again as piped water supply (120 per cent with safe sludge disposal), when the resulting wastewater is necessarily treated before discharge, there is a tendency in many cities to add on just 20–30 per cent to the water bill for sewerage. Removing this subsidy to the rich, along with the other inherent subsidies, is a necessary part of utility reform. Variations such as condominial sewers or reduced cost sewerage are examples of how technology can be used at a lower price to meet the needs of richer low-income urban customers – technical variations that regulators need to be aware of.

It is worth noting that financial assistance with ongoing water bills as well as initial connections to water services is not just a 'poor country' phenomenon. Examples can be found in many comparatively rich nations, with UK water companies as examples of private and public utilities that, as suppliers of an essential public service, have begun to accept their share of the responsibility in dealing with the affordability problems experienced by their customers.

ECONOMIC REGULATION

To achieve all these goals requires a subtle, perhaps impossible, balancing act from any regulatory agency as illustrated by the traditional and much used triangle diagram (see Figure 1.5). The example in Figure 1.5 is adapted from the 'key relationships of power' (World Bank, 2003) but in this variation places the citizen customer at the top, as the 'keystone'. Meeting the needs of citizen customers is after all, the goal. However, the triangle diagram is, not surprisingly, too simplistic to represent the actual process of regulation where there are many more stakeholders involved and where the key balancing act is to achieve the outputs desired by customers and society as against the inputs that customers and governments are willing to contribute.

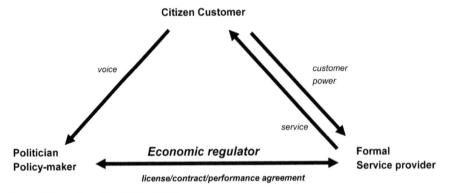

Source: Adapted from World Bank (2003)

Figure 1.5 *The role of economic regulation*

The *World Development Report 2003* (World Bank, 2003) describes a 'long route of accountability through the State, politicians and policy makers' with a 'short route through client power between citizen clients and providers'. It is the experience of the researchers through contacts with many utilities in many countries that the long route has tended to become so distorted that an adequate voice has never reached the service providers. Similarly the short route tends more towards illustrating the powerlessness of an individual customer in the face of a monopolistic technocratic provider. Experience from South Asia illustrates that customers have become so trained in accepting poor service that customer power has made no difference in situations of just one or two hours of water supply every other day or even once a week. One story is that only when the service frequency reached one or two hours *once in every two weeks* did customer power begin to have an effect. But that was of course when the storage capacity affordable to middle-income customers had been exceeded. The silent poor had been suffering far more for longer.

Hence the authors see the need for an 'empowered route' for customer power through customer involvement with the price and service setting economic regulator. The additions to the triangle diagram in Figure 1.6 therefore include a mechanism for customer involvement in the regulatory process. We have also added, in the context of focusing upon serving the poor, the necessary recognition of the informal or indirect customers – indirect in that they may be purchasing the formal service provider's water through vendors and neighbours on-selling, informal in that they might be bypassing that service altogether, accessing water through non-networked wells and boreholes. Those alternative providers are also illustrated as having links with the formal service provider, perhaps as tanker drivers buying water in bulk, but also possibly entirely separate and therefore needing their own lines of communication with the regulators, along with all the other stakeholders illustrated.

The regulators are placed in this diagram as the adjudicators, the referees between the politicians and policy-makers and the service provider. Many are

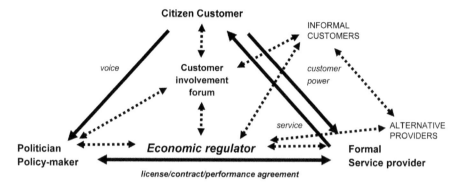

Figure 1.6 *The extended role of economic regulation and customer involvement*

surprised that this is the key relationship that needs 'regulating' in the face of a monopoly supplier, assuming that the role should be to adjudicate between the customer and the provider. Some element of this may be required on the (should be) rare occasions that the process required by the regulatory system breaks down. The overwhelming task of regulation is to mediate between the high expectations of society, as filtered through the politicians and policy-makers, with the equally high reluctance to allow a reasonable price. The result has traditionally been that the provider does not have the revenue and consequent access to finance to operate effectively and to enhance and expand service according to need and demand – and all too common where the poor suffer most as a result.

INTRODUCTION TO THE CASE STUDIES

It is this framework that the authors and researchers have used to undertake the fieldwork research as described in the case study chapters. Each case study attempts to explain the context in which service provision is being attempted, recognizing the institutional and legal framework in addition to the economic conditions. There is a description of the performance of the service provider and the way in which economic regulation has been operating. The focus of this study is, however, not on private provision of services, though it is necessarily described where appropriate, or on the efficacy of economic regulation as a whole. This work attempts to 'drill down' to the level whereby economic regulation is, maybe, having an effect or could be enabled to have a greater effect on service to the poor.

We have used the terminology of a 'universal service obligation' (USO), explained in detail in Chapter 3, to describe the requirement to serve poor consumers for their benefit and for the benefit of society as a whole. Some see a USO as synonymous with a 'human right' to water and in many ways it is. We have used the USO description because we believe that in the interests of long-term sustainability of services to the poor the focus has to be on establishing a viable formal service provider. There is no other means of delivering the capital investment that in the end translates into the economies of scale that deliver the cheapest water to all in urban areas. Therefore the focus on a service obligation also attempts to communicate the necessity that such service has to be paid for. Notwithstanding the limited apparent demand for water described earlier, the willingness to pay for mobile phones, particularly in the slums, has demonstrated that there may well be a higher level of affordability than often assumed. Translating that affordability for water into revenue for the formal provider by all but the very poorest is necessary for service sustainability.

However, the research recognizes that this is a goal unlikely to be achieved in the short term and for that reason we have investigated the alternative service providers to get a better sense as to whether they need to be simply recognized or perhaps incorporated into the regulatory approach – but all with the long-term view of gradually transferring their business to the formal provider. If that formal provider can be enabled to work more effectively why should the poorest have to pay the intermediation costs or the diseconomies of scale of the alternative providers? Such an approach does not necessarily destroy the livelihoods of all alternative providers; it simply encourages them to move out beyond the provider efficiency frontier (explained further in Chapter 10) to the new peri-urban developments so characteristic of the rapidly growing urban areas.

The final part of the fieldwork was to investigate the present approaches to customer involvement, again with a focus on the involvement of poor customers, direct or indirect and to capture the views of some of those consumers relative to the researchers' opinions on regulation and service delivery. Not surprisingly they do not always coincide. In that process the researchers also tried out adaptations of a simple focus group, participatory appraisals with groups of slum dwellers, to investigate and to demonstrate to regulators the level of feedback and customer involvement that could be achieved and that could be drawn upon in regulatory decision-making.

The case study locations were selected through the common approach of attempts at rigour necessarily limited by pragmatism, significantly influenced by where regulators were known to be in place and by where the research partners were based. The cases can be separated into four main groups:

- unregulated (except by the traditional government oversight);
- regulation of public providers;
- regulation of management and concession contracts;
- regulation of 'divested' water utilities.

There is a clear bias in the cases towards services in capital cities. It is in such cities where private sector involvement, and therefore regulation, has initially taken hold, perhaps because it is where governments have felt most required to do something about service delivery. It is also where the slums are normally largest. The researchers believe that the approaches described later are very scalable to secondary cities and towns but that is a process that is dependent upon economic growth as well as governance extension.

The order of case studies as they are reported here also reflects the length of the practice of economic regulation in that setting. This could be useful in building up an ever-deepening understanding of service to the poor based on the presumption that it is reasonable to expect more regarding service to the poor from those with longer experience. This approach recognizes that getting economic regulation to work for the average, majority, customer is necessarily the initial and primary goal. Equally the length of regulatory involvement might show there is no such correlation with pro-poor service.

Information on country-level statistics is included, national wealth per person for example, poverty levels and the 'Human Development Rank Index', as the reader might like to consider the extent to which such factors affect economic regulation and in particular regulation for the poor. Governance, institutional capital and economic wealth are recurring themes in enhancing service delivery.

The initial fieldwork for this research was undertaken in 2004 and 2005. Although much has changed since then in terms of the names of the owners of some of the private providers, and on occasion the role of any private providers (Ghana has gained a management contract, Bolivia has lost a private concession as examples), the completion of this publication has not uncovered any significant change in the pattern of regulation and, most disturbingly of all, little change in service to the poor.

The fieldwork researchers have a stimulatingly varied understanding or perspective on regulation and services to the poor. Several were deeply suspicious of the role of any privatization and regulation, some had worked for utilities, one is working partly for a regulator, one for an NGO and there are several academics with a background in teaching and researching infrastructural service provision from a management and engineering perspective. The lead researcher has taken a view on the effect of regulation in England and Wales from the perspective of working (very part-time) for the consumer body for water, initially linked to the regulator – a participant observer approach in research terms. We should also explain that the fieldwork in Latin America was much more limited than in the other locations, particularly so in the case of Buenos Aires where because so much has changed and so much remains disputed we have omitted the formal case altogether, though we have included references to that situation where it seemed appropriate. We have tried to capture these different perspectives in the overview while ensuring the individual viewpoints of the researchers are reflected in the individual cases (see Table 1.2).

Table 1.2 *Case studies*

	India	Uganda	Zambia	Ghana	Indonesia	Jordan	Bolivia	Philippines	Chile	England
Human Development Index rank*	128	154	165	135	107	86	117	90	40	16
Population living on <US$2/day (%)	80.4	–	87.2	78.5	52.4	7	42.2	43	5.6	–
GNI per capita (US$, 2006)†	3800	1490	1000	2640	3950	6210	2890	5980	11,270	35,580
Country population (millions)	1110	30	12	23	223	6	9	85	16	60
Urban population (%)	29	13	35	49	50	83	65	64	88	90
Urban population growth rate 2005–2010 (%)	2.3	4.8	2.1	3.4	3.3	2.5	2.5	2.8	1.3	0.4
Urban water coverage (%)	95	87	90	88	87	99	95	87	100	100
Water supply by household connection (%)	47	7	41	37	30	96	90	58	99	100
Improved urban sanitation coverage (%)	59	54	59	27	73	94	90	80	95	–
Research focus location	Jaipur	Kampala, Jinja	Lusaka	Accra, Kumasi	Jakarta	Amman	La Paz, El Alto	Manila	Santiago	Midlands
Research focus population (millions)	2.75	1.3	1.1	2.4	10	2.2	1.4	11	4.7	8.5
Service provider at time of fieldwork	PHEED & JMC	NWSC	LWSC	GWCL	PJ & TPJ	LEMA	AISA	MWSI & MWCI	AA	SVT, SST
Regulator			NWASCO	PURC	JWSRB	PMU	SISAB	MWSS-RO	SISS	OFWAT
Regulatory start date			2000	1997	2001	1999	1999	1997	1990	1989

Notes: * out of 177 countries. † Implied purchasing power parity conversion rate to US$ (in case study introductions) from EconStats. The researchers believe it is only possible to judge any pro-poor regulatory effectiveness against the scale of the challenge, that is the poverty level of the urban unserved in the context of the urban growth rate, while recognizing the limitations of social, economic and institutional capital as evidenced by the HDI ranking and gross national income (GNI) per capita. However, so as not to distort the cost and price of water supply, in the case studies we have used national currency to US$ conversion rates at purchasing power parity based upon the rates quoted in EconStats (www.econstats.com/weo/V023.htm accessed 1 February 2008).

Source: Human Development Index (HDI) data from UNDP (2008); poverty and income data from World Bank (2008); urban population data from UNFPA (2007); water and sanitation coverage data from WHO and UNICEF (2006)

2

Economic Regulation

Esther Gerlach and Richard Franceys

> *You cannot privatize without regulation but you can regulate without privatization.* (interview with regulator)

In view of the enormous challenge for regulation in the global water and sanitation sector, this chapter aims to examine the situation from an academic research perspective. The existing body of knowledge on the subject of water utilities regulation has been reviewed and the chapter presents key concepts and regulatory developments in high- and lower-income countries in the field of economic regulation and the social responsibilities it has taken on. Works of academics and practitioners have been included, mapping out different perspectives and contentious issues. Much in the same way that the review informed the research at the planning stage and continues to inform its analysis, it now introduces the reader to the 'regulatory challenge' ahead.

Why economic regulation?

Because of the capital intensity of networked water and sanitation it is only viable to have a single, monopoly provider. All monopolies tend to be captured by vested producer interests over time, whether through 'professional hobbyism', trades-union protectionism or political opportunism. Incentive-based economic regulation can limit monopoly abuses, ensuring that customers are not disadvantaged by having to pay excessive prices to an inefficient supplier where there is no competition. Water supply (again, sanitation less so), although a 'private good' in economic terms (rival and excludable) also carries considerable 'externalities', that is benefits to society over and beyond the initial consumption, both in limiting common water resources depletion and in protecting receiving waters from wastewater disposal. Therefore government has a wider societal, public health and environmental benefits interest in water supply in addition to ensuring that citizens receive an important basic needs product at a fair price.

To achieve this overall goal, regulation of water supply incorporates aspects of water quality regulation, environmental regulation, particularly of water abstraction and wastewater discharges, and economic regulation to oversee a monopoly provider. This research is based on an understanding of economic regulation as the process of acting as an 'impartial referee', balancing, judging, adjudicating and refereeing the various stakeholder interests, not the writing of 'regulations'. However, that is the role of the drinking water and environmental regulators who have much more of a role in setting and monitoring standards rather than the 'balancing act' that the economic regulator has to deliver.

Water (and sewerage, but not on-plot sanitation) is the most capital intensive of all the networked industries, compared with electricity and gas for example. Ensuring that these necessary capital assets can be financed and maintained adequately, necessarily incorporating quality improvements and service expansion, is a key role of economic regulation. The level of capital investments in England and Wales is shown in Figure 2.1. Of particular concern to the water industry is the implication of the increase in investment from 1950 onwards. There is a growing proportion of 50-year old assets that are reaching the end of their reasonable lives and will soon begin to require replacement or significant overhaul. The alternative to capital maintenance, practised in many systems, has been termed 'inter-generational transfer, whereby a failure to pay costs now is simply transferred to future generations through failing assets. This approach has been demonstrated in London where, until very recently, one third of pipes were reportedly 150 years old and half were approximately 100 years old. An anecdote from 1988, just before privati-

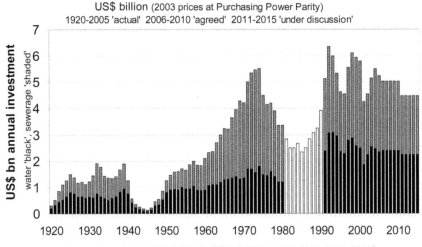

US$ billion (2003 prices at Purchasing Power Parity)
1920-2005 'actual' 2006-2010 'agreed' 2011-2015 'under discussion'

Source: Richard Franceys' analysis of IWES (1977); OFWAT (1996, 1999, 2003, 2004, 2007f)

Figure 2.1 *Water and sewerage investment, England and Wales, 1920–2015*

zation and regulation, reports that in one part of London new plastic pipe house connections were being connected into the original wooden elm water mains. Capital maintenance is a challenge to all service providers. Where such long-term maintenance is not undertaken, the result is excessive leakage and poor quality service to customers, particularly during periods of drought, or in low-income country experience it results in ongoing intermittent, and therefore health challenging, supplies.

Defining 'regulation'

The growing academic interest in the theory of regulation and regulatory developments is reflected in the growing body of literature available on the subject. The term 'regulation' is used at different levels of generality and its precise definition differs from discipline to discipline. Usually it is understood to refer to different forms of government intervention into society or, more specifically, market-based activities to induce or curtail certain types of behaviour. The latter corresponds to economists' narrower interpretation of the meaning of regulation as being mainly concerned with economic actors and firms in particular. Standard textbooks also define regulation as the promulgation of specific rules to be monitored and enforced by a public body. The broadest definition offered includes all forms of social control by public or private agents with regulatory effects, whether these are the result of deliberate intervention or merely chance occurrences (Baldwin and Cave, 1999).

Regulation of economic activities has a long history in the US, where early and groundbreaking theories of regulation originated. Regulatory reform (or deregulation), now underway worldwide, and the privatization of the British utilities added further perspectives and have widened the academic discourse. Many observers have commented on the conceptual confusion arising from different interpretations and usage of the term 'regulation' by academics and practitioners from different backgrounds (Prosser, 1997; Black, 2002; Jordana and Levi-Faur, 2004). Jordana and Levi-Faur (2004) assert that there is little use and sense in searching for an authoritative and consensual definition. They also make the important point that the various interpretations reflect the changes in the socio-economic context of regulation. It is not the aim of this book to review the many and varied theories of regulatory development and conceptualization that have emerged from economics, law and political science. For the purposes of this review it will suffice to note that definitions of regulation range from narrow interpretations of regulation relating to economic activities to all-encompassing views that include issues of governance, legislation and social control under the heading 'regulation'.

Economic regulation, which broadly refers to government interventions into the market (Posner, 1984) is particularly relevant to the utilities. The lawyer sees economic regulation as the area of interventionist law that addresses instances of inadequate competition and natural monopoly (Ogus, 2001), which is particularly relevant to water services and hence water utilities regulation. The legal rules, however, are not sufficient to achieve regulatory objectives, as Majone (1997, quoted in Jordana and Levi-Faur, 2004) points out. Regulation, he asserts, 'requires detailed knowledge of, and intimate involvement with, the regulated activity'. There is indeed a tendency to associate 'regulation' with the activities of utility regulators, as noted by Baldwin and Cave (1999) in the case of post-privatization Britain, where regulatory decision-making has become increasingly influenced by social policy objectives. The gradual shift in emphasis from 'pure' economic regulation to a greater level of social regulation has generated a substantial literature. This review proceeds with an examination of the current 'state of the art' of utilities regulation in industrialized countries, including its social and economic rationales, as well as regulatory principles and best practice. The next chapter turns to the specific challenges found in developing-country settings.

Utility regulation: Rationales

Generally, the motivations for introducing regulation are manifold, but instances of 'market failure', where regulation is deemed necessary to safeguard public interest objectives, top the list of rationales presented in the literature (for example Ogus and Veljanovsky, 1984; Armstrong et al, 1994; Bishop et al, 1995; Baldwin and Cave, 1999; König et al, 2003). Of the various types of market failure, the prevention of monopoly abuse is seen as the main justification for regulation of utilities and infrastructure. Ogus (2001) here emphasizes situations of natural monopoly, where economies of scale are such that the competitive potential is almost reduced to zero and the market is supplied at lowest cost by a single firm (Baldwin and Cave, 1999; Parker, 1999). Regulation, König et al (2003) argue, is then required to control profit-seeking behaviour of private providers or to protect customers from inefficient (or low service standard) public monopolies. The authors identify customer's lack of access to adequate information regarding the services they receive, wider societal concerns and 'essential' qualities of certain services as additional forms of market failure that may require regulatory intervention. Ogus (2001) sees an economic justification for what has become known as 'social regulation' in such information asymmetries and externalities. Armstrong et al (1994) point out the low demand elasticity associated with most utility services, where allocative inefficiencies threaten to cause substantial losses in welfare.

History shows how utility regulation is intrinsically linked with the wider political and social framework. Black (2002) reports a shift in the normative goals of regulation towards an inclusion of social goals. The UK privatization experience, which involved a drastic reorganization of ownership and regulatory structures, serves as an illustration of these developments. Beginning with British Telecoms in 1984, the Thatcher government ended an era of public ownership by implementing a large-scale privatization programme of its utilities.

Within less than a decade, telecoms, electricity, gas and water services had changed into private hands. Dedicated industry regulators were appointed for each sector to prevent monopoly abuse by the newly created national or regional private monopolies (Bishop et al, 1995). The transition of public policy from the traditional welfare state with state-coordinated service provision towards private provision (and sometimes ownership) under regulatory supervision is often referred to in the literature as the 'rise of the regulatory state' (Minogue, 2002; Cook et al, 2003).

Parker (1999) summarizes the rationales for this combination of privatization and state-directed regulation: in the absence of a competitive market, regulation was premised to act as a price control mechanism and a driver for efficiency improvements. The primary duties of the newly established regulators were to ensure the satisfaction of reasonable consumer demand and the financeability of service provision or, in other words, the ability of companies to finance their activities in terms of service maintenance and investment programmes. Reviewers of the privatization process frequently comment on its negative side-effects. Young (2001) reports how achieving social equity was soon proving a challenge in a competitive market and resulted in a heated public debate as rising consumer debt stood in stark contrast to perceived excess company profits and managerial pay. Waddams Price and Young (2003) present evidence that some vulnerable groups were adversely affected by the changes following privatization. Access inequalities to utility services, described as a 'necessary condition of participation in a modern society', resulted from the erosion of cross-subsidies inherent in the nationalized public services and entrenched the social exclusion suffered by large sections of society. Graham and Marvin (1994) claim that utility sector privatization entailed a complete change in service ethic with an overriding profit motive. Social dumping of marginal users, which often correspond to poor domestic customers, could be observed as a simultaneous trend toward 'cherry-picking' as utilities concentrated their operations on the more lucrative market segments. Affordability problems were particularly marked in the water sector, where heavy capital investment was required and prices continued to rise in response to new environmental and quality standards. Controversies centred on disconnection of water services. Within three years of creation of the regional monopolies the number of disconnections had risen sharply to an annual 21,000 households, prompting fears for public health with this loss of universal access (Graham and Marvin, 1994; Prosser, 1999). At that time, Graham and Marvin (1994) called for stronger state protection of universal access to basic utilities services and strong regulators to safeguard equity principles. Prosser (1994) equally criticized the disregard of the social dimension in the utilities regulation debate. He alleged an overemphasis on economic principles that neglected the social considerations he perceived as becoming 'absolutely central to regulatory credibility and performance'.

Ugaz and Waddams Price (2003) see the UK experience as proving the relevance of distributional concerns, which they contend were given little attention upon privatization, to public perception. Social concerns sparked a new wave of government involvement to tackle access, equity and distributional aspects of the essential utility services, reinforced by the 2000 Utilities Act, which included explicit social obligations for gas and electricity regulators. In the case of water and sewerage services, disconnection of residential services for non-payment reasons was banned in 1999 along with prepayment metering options. The 1999 Water Act also introduced vulnerable charging schemes to assist certain customer groups, while its latest revision specifically instructs the regulator to consider the interests of the disabled or chronically sick, pensioners, those on low incomes and residents in rural areas (HMSO, 2003, 39, 2C). Nevertheless 20 per cent of the population found themselves obliged to commit an unreasonably high proportion of household income to water bills in 2003, and thus experienced 'water poverty' as defined in Fitch (2003a), while findings of a review by Narracott (2003) confirmed an under-representation of vulnerable customers' interests in the regulatory system. The National Consumer Council (NCC, 2002) attributes this marginalization to their being 'pigeon-holed as being "hard-to-reach"'.

A far more elaborate social security system than in other countries that have experimented with utilities privatization and liberalization and virtually universal connection levels has not even prevented utilities regulation from becoming highly politicized in the UK, as Ugaz and Waddams Price (2003) point out. In addition to its primary goal of maximizing economic efficiency, the remit of regulation has been extended over the years to include social dimensions (Prosser, 1999). There is now a greater emphasis on distributional and other supplementary aims compared with a purely economic view of market failure correction. Much of the contemporary regulatory debate has been confused by the failure to distinguish between the economic and social rationales for utilities regulation, Prosser (1997) argues. He distinguishes three types of regulatory tasks with different regulatory rationales. Monopoly regulation, which aims to increase allocative efficiency in the absence of effective competition, and regulation for competition both find their justification in purely economic reasoning. Social regulation, in the case of utilities, is founded on the belief that services should be made accessible to the widest possible range of social groups.

Having explored the 'why' and 'what' questions of utilities regulation, the next section looks more closely at regulatory design and procedure. There is a vast literature on 'how to regulate', ranging from economic analysis of various regulatory approaches to critical evaluations of appropriate institutional arrangements. As regulation of household water services is the subject of primary interest, the focus of this review is on conduct regulation rather than regulation of market structure, seeing that the nature of the industry is such that there is little scope for introducing competing networks.

Principles of economic regulation:
Incentive regulation, driving efficiency

The standard textbook identifies efficiency and cost reduction as the major objectives of regulation (Baldwin and Cave, 1999). In the absence of information asymmetries, economic regulation would be a simple matter of calculating optimal prices, determining cost reductions to be achieved by a firm and issuing instructions to this effect. This statement implicitly underlines the crucial role information plays in the regulatory process as recognized by the New Regulatory Economics (Armstrong et al, 1994). Due to their informational advantages over regulators, firms have to be given incentives to reveal their efficiency potential and implement cost reductions. The key design issue for incentive regulatory systems lies in achieving the right balance between incentives and the distribution of efficiency gains, or profit, between shareholders and customers (Vass, 2003a). Baldwin and Cave (1999) discuss the relative advantages of the two available alternatives, rate of return regulation ('cost-plus pricing') and price capping.

'Rate of return regulation' was the original form of economic regulation before Professor Stephen Littlechild, reportedly following the 'Austrian School' of economics, adapted it for the newly privatizing UK utilities. The principle is that government (the regulator) fixes a rate of return on capital allowed to the provider that is then included in the tariff along with agreed operating and capital expenditures. Any over- or under-recovery of this return is managed through an adjustment to the price in succeeding years. The rate of return approach, practised mainly in North America, is understood to cost capital at around 4–5 per cent on average (in nominal terms). In practice most public utilities around the world are also operating under a 'rate of return', primarily with regard to servicing borrowing, though the assumed return might be nominal or, in practice, even negative.

Rate of return regulation has three disadvantages: it gives regulated firms an incentive to maximize the amount of capital employed, as the return in cash terms is based on capital expenditures. Thus it pushes regulated firms towards 'gold-plated' investment (three back-up systems rather than one), over-design of hardware, early replacement of computers, vehicles and so on, and, third, firms regulated under this system have little incentive to improve technical and price efficiency.

The degree to which a company will be compelled to improve long-run efficiency is determined by the rewards offered. With a fixed rate of return a company benefits little from improved efficiency, therefore rate of return regulation is considered a low-powered incentive mechanism.

Incentive-based regulation sets prices for a period, in the case of England and Wales for five years. Ten years was specified initially but found to be too long when situations and EU legislation are changing requirements within a shorter period. These prices include an assumption as to the cost of capital but allow any out-performance by the companies to be retained as additional profit until shared back with customers at the next price review.

This has proved to be a powerful mechanism to improve efficiency. Although called a price-cap approach, until fairly recently it has in practice in England and Wales been a revenue cap due to the very limited extent of metering. For the regulator to ensure that the companies can finance their operations and capital investment 'he' has to ensure that the total revenue is sufficient. Therefore any adjustments of tariffs, reductions for the poor for example, within the 'tariff basket' (the overall revenue requirement) necessarily lead to increases in tariffs for others. As the average metering penetration now passes 30 per cent in England, the regulator is proposing to formally change to a revenue cap, one which will be reviewed (and reimbursed where deemed necessary) at each five-yearly price review. By this means the regulator can ensure the revenue vital to ensure financeability while limiting the need to forecast not only the next level of metering take-up (which can reduce demand and thus revenue) but also the implied need to forecast weather for the next five-year period. Water consumption changes significantly in dry periods, with consequent effects on revenue and profits.

RPI-X, the best-known variant of the price cap that has become the most distinctive feature of UK utility regulation (Armstrong et al, 1994; Rees and Vickers, 1995), provides higher-powered incentives for out-performing efficiency targets. Efficiency gains are retained as economic profit by the company for a certain period of time and passed on to customers at regular price reviews, when price controls are set for the next regulatory period. This 'regulatory lag' is described as the key feature distinguishing RPI-X from rate of return regulation (Armstrong et al, 1994). When it was first introduced, RPI-X was perceived as the superior alternative due to its greater inherent cost-efficiency incentives and operational simplicity. After two decades of RPI-X regulation, it has proven more complex and problematic than anticipated. Rather than being gradually replaced by the introduction of competition as expected, it had to be supplemented with quality controls (Armstrong et al, 1994; Rees and Vickers, 1995). For all its successes, RPI-X has failed to eliminate the fundamental problems of regulation, which are discussed below. With the recent proposals for 'menu regulation' as well as revenue guarantees (OFWAT, 2007c) and the promise of a lower cost of capital, it may be that incentive-based regulation is achieving not its demise but proof of the law of diminishing returns.

Box 2.1 Price setting in England and Wales

Price cap = RPI + 'K' where RPI is the price of a weighted basket of goods, that is, an indicator of annual inflation, and K = – P0 (a sharing of past efficiency gains) – X (an estimation of future efficiency gains) + Q (environmental quality enhancement in water supply and/or wastewater) + V (security of supply) + S (improvements to service levels)

Regulatory risk

In addition to the information asymmetries, the economics of regulation is complicated by problems of policy commitment and regulatory capture by other interests (Armstrong et al, 1994; Rees and Vickers, 1995). Determining a company's efficiency potential and setting a price cap accentuates the information problem. While operating costs should be observable from published company accounts, information relating to capital expenditure, the value of existing assets, cost of capital and projected productivity and demand is not readily available. In his discussion of the RPI-X mechanism, Vass (2003a) exposes the problems of inconsistent or underdeveloped methodologies for resetting price controls. While perceived 'excess' profits have undermined confidence of the British public, relationships between regulators and investors have become strained following a series of 'unnecessary' disputes. Appeals processes can substantially add to the cost of regulation, which is often cited as an important factor.

The commitment problem primarily relates to the danger of opportunistic behaviour on the part of the regulator. Specifically, it refers to ex post opportunism, the temptation for regulators to break the 'regulatory contract' after a firm has made capital expenditures by tightening policy such that the company will find itself unable to recover the investment. This exploitation of the sunk cost nature and irreversibility of infrastructure investments bears the risk of underinvestment as investors expect guarantees of a 'fair' return on investment and an increase in the cost of capital where uncertainties persist (Armstrong et al, 1994; Rees and Vickers, 1995). But the commitment problem is not exclusively connected with regulatory discretion, as Rees and Vickers (1995) point out. A change of government may involve a change of regulatory policy with similar results. Baldwin and Cave (1999) cite 'windfall taxes', which can and have been employed to recapture large industry profits during initial regulatory periods, as an example of political intervention that may reduce incentives if regulated firms suspect that the tax will be repeated.

The literature also warns of making the premature assumption that regulators will always choose to act as guardians of the public interest. Armstrong et al (1994) trace the evolution of 'capture theory' back to the Chicago School economists, who considered the option of regulators becoming aligned with the industry to the extent that they act in the interest of incumbents rather than consumers and potential competitors. Laffont and Tirole (1991) develop the early capture theories further to include other interest groups who would compete in the 'market for regulatory decisions'. Armstrong et al (1994) find evidence in favour of limiting regulatory discretion where there is risk of capture, but conclude that the literature offers little insight beyond the implied need to balance authority and incentives for regulatory authorities – as well as companies – to maximize social welfare.

Institutional structure of regulation

The stability of the 'regulatory bargain' depends as much, if not more, on the structure and behaviour of regulatory and political institutions as on the form of regulation adopted (Rees and Vickers, 1995). Much debate has centred on the independence of regulators and how to establish and maintain arm's-length separation between government, operators and regulators. In the UK, individual regulators specializing in a single industry were expected to allow quick and non-bureaucratic decision-making (Baldwin and Cave, 1999). König et al (2003) see personal accountability and predictability of decisions as advantages of UK-style individual regulators. Fast professional development is cited as an additional benefit of single-industry regulators by Parker (1999), who also provides arguments in favour of multi-industry regulators. Cross-sector knowledge transfer can improve efficiency and effectiveness, economize on regulatory expertise as well as provide a more consistent approach across the various regulated industries. Without stating a preference, König et al (2003) provide arguments in favour of regulatory commissions. Spreading decision-making power among several members reduces the risk of capture and can provide different perspectives on a given problem. The authors also see the potential of greater stability and continuity in the event of changing governments, as discussed previously. The more practically oriented publications such as König et al further discuss institutional design issues such as appointment of regulators and funding arrangements, which otherwise receive comparatively little mention.

Relative to the large body of literature on the various aspects of regulation, there are few published accounts of sector-specific research. The UK water regulator OFWAT (Water Services Regulation Authority) generally features strongly in the literature on UK regulatory reform, and there is an emerging literature describing regulatory experiences in developing countries, which will be the subject of the next chapter. The basic approach to water utilities regulation shares many of the principles already discussed, with quality issues assuming greater significance in the water industry than in other infrastructure sectors. Klein (1996) maintains that regulatory mechanisms – within or independent of government – can be found in all countries to counterbalance the monopoly elements inherent in piped water systems. He emphasizes the paramount importance of regulating and monitoring performance standards relating to service quality aspects. There he distinguishes health and safety issues arising during the production process (environmental impacts) and service provision (water quality) as well as the quality of customer service.

In the UK, regulatory responsibilities are divided between several agencies. Strict environmental and quality regulation is exercised by the Environment Agency and the Drinking Water Inspectorate respectively, influencing OFWAT's regulatory decisions, which lie in the economic domain. The preceding section has already hinted at the link between price and quality regulation, which is reflected in the water industry's price cap, RPI+K. The K factor reflects the scheduled increase in real prices. Armstrong et al (1994) identify investment as a crucial determinant of K, as companies need to be enabled to meet statutory environmental and quality standards. The peculiarities of the water industry have influenced regulatory procedure. In response to the limited potential for competition, OFWAT has placed greater emphasis on refining benchmarking techniques. Armstrong et al mention the opportunities for yardstick competition, i.e. efficiency comparisons between the regional water monopolies. Klein (1996) suggests a possibility of generating such yardstick information across different countries. OFWAT publications set out the regulatory approach to encouraging investment 'at the right level and at the right time' (OFWAT, 2004). In consultation with stakeholders the regulator has established clear procedures regarding the determination of the 'unknowns' discussed above to ensure financeability but sharing the benefits of greater efficiency with customers.

Several concerns regarding regulatory performance and regulatory conduct have transpired during the discussion of the literature so far. Authors have commented on the effectiveness and efficiency of regulation in correcting market failure and achieving social equity objectives under different regulatory arrangements. Some have questioned regulatory authority and legitimacy of decision-making. Regulatory discretion and the various monetary and non-monetary costs of regulation have been the subject of debate. The majority of authors have implicitly and explicitly suggested regulatory principles such as credibility, independence, accountability, trustworthiness, competence and commitment as well as transparency, fairness, consistency and predictability of decision-making. These attributes of 'good regulation' have occupied a host of academics, consultants and government advisers, and this section discusses some of the literature that has been produced.

Regulatory performance and legitimacy tests

Berg (2000) identifies three elements that determine the effectiveness of regulation. A regulatory agency must be provided with a well-defined legal mandate and adequate organizational resources to successfully carry out its duties. The agency itself then needs to develop a set of core values or operating principles that are consistent with its policy objectives. He acknowledges that newly created agencies are likely to deviate to a greater or lesser extent from this ideal case, and the factors typically evolve over the lifetime of a government agency. The legal mandate serves as a basis of regulatory authority, while circumscribing the boundaries of regulatory jurisdiction divides responsibilities between the line ministry and the regulator. Berg (2000) argues that explicit legal statements regarding the regulator's functions are desirable, and the provision of appropriate instruments facilitates the achievement of regulatory objectives. Agency values play a crucial role in establishing the legitimacy of the regulator in the eyes of the other stakeholders involved in the regulatory process.

This question of regulatory legitimacy or 'worthiness of public support' is central to the effectiveness of regulatory systems. It has also elicited debates on the justification of regulatory discretion and the extent to which it should be limited. Prosser (1997) summarizes the argument with respect to the economic and social rationales of utilities regulation: whereas regulators derive legitimacy from their technical expertise in increasing allocative efficiency, which requires rational and non-arbitrary decision-making, distributive concerns (i.e. the social rationale, which is of key importance to utilities) involve choices that some parties prefer should rest with government holding the democratic mandate. Baldwin and Cave (1999) suggest that regulatory performance is best evaluated against five key benchmarking criteria, a suitable combination of which can be argued to legitimize regulatory arrangements or decisions. First, the legislative mandate satisfies the need for authorization by a democratically elected body but does not solve the problem of discretionary decision-making as legislation is often framed in ambiguous terms. Second, accountability of the regulator to a democratic institution can act as a substitute for imprecise mandates. Third, fairness, accessibility and openness of regulatory procedure are the basis of the 'due process' argument, which calls for stakeholder participation in regulatory policy. Fourth, decisions may further be justified by the level of regulatory expertise, but this criterion relies on public trust in the reliability of expert judgements and may fail to satisfy the accountability criterion. Last, efficiency, both in the implementation of the legislative mandate (productive efficiency) and the production of desirable outcomes (allocative and dynamic efficiency) can be used as a claim for legitimacy. However, in addition to being difficult to assess objectively, efficiency of utility regulation is entangled in Prosser's (1997) argument regarding regulatory rationales. König et al (2003) concur with these five 'key tests of regulatory legitimacy', but seem more realistic regarding the trade-offs involved in attempting to improve regulatory performance on all counts simultaneously.

Principles of good regulation

Baldwin and Cave (1999) claim that their five benchmarks are consistent with the principles of regulation highlighted in the regulatory debate. This debate has been driven by the practical need for well-designed and balanced government interventions, and is thus not confined to theoretical academic discourse. According to the five 'principles of good regulation' endorsed by the UK government, regulators should aim for proportionality of interventions relative to the risk and costs of compliance. The accountability principle demands that regulators should be able to justify their decisions and remain open to public scrutiny. Consistent application of rules is expected to heighten predictability and relieve uncertainties among the regulated. Transparency involves effective and timely stakeholder information and consultation, and targeting of interventions allows for flexibility in meeting clearly defined targets and systematic review of the effectiveness of specific regulations (Better Regulation Task Force, 2003). The Australian counterpart task force (quoted in Berg, 2000) identified the following best practice principles: communication and consultation to promote stakeholder information and participation, consistency and predictability of decision-making, flexibility in the selection of policy instruments and their adaptation to changing conditions, independence to remove undue political influence, effectiveness and efficiency, accountability and finally, transparency of the regulatory process. Berg (2000) takes the international experience so far as evidence that these principles (or agency values, in his terminology) are required to support regulators in their activities. Quoting Stern and Holder (1999), Berg (2000) then separates the principles of good regulation (or good 'agency governance') into those relating to agency design and those relating to the regulatory process. Good agency design hinges on clarity of roles, autonomy and accountability, whereas participative, transparent and predictable processes enhance the legitimacy and effectiveness of newly established regulators vis-à-vis other non-government stakeholders.

Researchers have approached the issue of implementing good regulatory practice from different angles. A number of authors have highlighted the effect of discretionary decision-making on companies' investment decisions as well as the cost of capital, both of which ultimately influence consumer prices and quality of service. Armstrong et al (1994) merely raise this issue of regulatory risk in their discussion of RPI-X, whereas Vass (2003b) directly links the problem with the question of regulatory independence. His conclusion is that both regulatory and ministerial discretion should be constrained to protect regulatory objectives from individual interests, whereby independence of economic regulation serves to control the dangers of political interference. In his view, this approach to risk minimization has the additional benefit of promoting public confidence, which becomes a central concern as contemporary regulatory regimes attract criticism for a perceived lack of accountability and transparency, as much of the literature confirms.

Minogue (2004) examines the accountability and transparency principles and draws attention to the variety of instruments that can be employed to satisfy public demand for more 'openness' in regulation. He shows that increased transparency of regulatory systems and accountability of actors are not goals per se, but instead fulfil the purpose of maintaining an equilibrium state of regulatory objectives and outcomes for regulatory regimes that are embedded in the prevailing administrative doctrine and are thus predisposed to certain policy instruments. The 'traditional' public administration approach prefers a more legalistic approach to regulation, in which expert review is expected to provide justification for regulatory decisions and thus accountability. Under the 'consumer sovereignty' doctrine, information is emphasized as a means to improve consumer choice, and finally, 'citizen empowerment' advocates maximum public scrutiny through direct involvement of informed citizens.

Each scenario draws on a different combination of the four 'transparency tools' (voice, choice, representation and information). Minogue (2004) also shows that certain trade-offs are associated with the pursuit of accountability and transparency, and how the holding to account of all activities may result in an increasingly rigid regulatory system.

Vass (2003b) directly comments on the British principles of 'better regulation' as they relate to the utilities sector. With regard to the transparency principle, he argues that a clear statement of policy objectives ought to be supplemented with the promotion of clear expectations among customers and the general public. The ubiquitous negative portrayal of 'profit', for instance, is counterproductive for confidence in an incentive-based regulatory system. Targeting, he explains, is related to the cost-effectiveness of regulatory interventions, and the consistency principle should not be mistaken for rigidity. Consistency relates to the objectives of regulation and does not preclude a level of regulatory discretion to adapt rules flexibly in the light of new information and accumulated experience.

Regulatory organization

There is no single model of regulatory organization and the emphasis given to OFWAT says more about the experience and location of the authors than anything else, noting that Chile established its own regulator, SISS, coincidentally in the same year as OFWAT, in 1989.

Every country has to adapt the principles of economic regulation to suit its own structure of governance. There can be regulation by government department, regulation by performance agreement, regulation by contract, regulation by competition or fair trading authorities, advisory regulators, expert panel regulators as well as quasi-independent regulators along the Chile and England and Wales approach. Although the proclaimed ideal is an independent regulator, if the governance reality in any country is such that the independence is more myth than practice then it would be more useful to develop adjudicating capacity within a government department than to waste resources ('cherrywood desks') on yet another ineffective organization.

A survey by Asian Development Bank (2005) found that less than 40 per cent of East Asian infrastructure regulators described themselves as even nominally independent. The study suggests that it is critical to ensure that regulators are not given more discretion than the political culture can absorb: 'New regulators should rely much more on transparent rules than on discretionary power, and some responsibilities should be delegated to outside experts ... hearings should be public, contracts and licenses should be also wherever possible' (Asian Development Bank, 2005).

In high-income countries as well, governments have demanded that regulators submit to political demands – as in the case of the UK where government reportedly 'threatened' the Rail Regulator with immediate legislation to curb his powers if he dared to upset their plans to move against (in effect renationalize) the then private Railtrack, the company responsible for the railway infrastructure.

Economic regulators have been established as national entities, as provincial entities and surprisingly often as (capital) city-level entities. The costs and professional capacity required would seem to rule out city-level entities but they have been developed to service city-level concession contracts, usually in advance of private sector involvement in the rest of the country. For the sake of efficiency and best use of scarce professional resources several water regulators are part of multi-utility regulators or indeed have dual responsibilities themselves. Bolivia had developed an overarching regulatory system within which all the sectoral regulators were located.

Regulators have also been established to referee the activities of the public sector, notwithstanding the focus on private companies in this chapter. As described further in the case studies, established in expectation of private sector involvement (though not always forthcoming) there are economic regulators of public providers in Ghana and Zambia, the regulator in Bolivia oversees a large number of public and cooperative providers and there is even a regulator of public services within the UK. The Water Commissioner, Scotland, although only advisory in a price-setting role, has had a significant effect on the prices allowed for new investment. In a much poorer country, the Water Supply Authority in Lao PDR is using comparative regulation to promote improvements of the public water providers of the main towns (some fairly small) of the country. League tables and 'naming and shaming' utilities when they fail to submit data on time are reportedly delivering results as they strive to produce on time for subsequent reports. They have a vision for 'A first class water supply infrastructure that delivers the highest service possible that represents best value to customers now and in the future' and a mission 'To regulate in a way that provides a potable, sustainable and affordable water supply for all by 2015' (WASA, 2005). By such approaches, economic regulation can begin to facilitate improved services for the poor.

3

Regulating for the Poor

Esther Gerlach

In much of the developing world, low-income households do not enjoy access to safe, convenient and reasonably priced water services at the same level as their wealthier counterparts at home and abroad. Over the past two decades governments have implemented infrastructure reforms, usually involving neo-liberal economic strategies as promoted by international financing institutions (Cook et al, 2003; Nickson and Franceys, 2003). Although the policy changes in the water sector are now less markedly inclined towards private sector participation, utility ownership, operation and oversight functions have become redefined in attempts to improve water utilities performance. The various models of regulation that have been experimented with and the very specific challenges to regulation that have emerged in developing-country settings are the subject of this chapter.

Before moving on to the workings of utilities regulation in lower-income economies, the first section takes a step back with the intention to familiarize the reader with the 'local realities' in the target countries. The literature is reviewed to gain a basic but sound understanding of the problem of urban poverty (considering the literature in more depth than the introduction in Chapter 1) and the fragmented water markets that serve low-income households, which constitute an important aspect of the operating context for water regulators in the developing world.

The concept of urban poverty

The concept of 'poverty' revolves around various aspects of deprivation. Hossain and Moore (2002) suggest that poverty reduction strategies driven by international organizations have resulted in an overemphasis on quantitative definitions of poverty, often in highly narrow economic terms. Friedmann (1996) distinguishes four major approaches to conceptualizing 'poverty'. The bureaucratic approach prefers precisely defined absolute and relative poverty lines, which usually measure the lack of financial resources and are essentially political definitions according to Friedmann. The moralistic approach, referring to the 'destitute', 'indigent', 'deserving poor' or popular classes, for instance, implies moral judgements. Academics speak of 'structural poverty', 'exclusion' and 'marginalization' and tend to associate poverty with external conditions, such as the prevailing socio-economic order. Finally, the disempowerment explanation, founded in social activism of poor communities, includes social, political and psychological dimensions, such as lack of access to resources, lack of voice in the political process and lack of self-confidence. Hossain and Moore (2002) argue that in policy terms poverty is a matter of perception rather than simple facts, and with this perception the conceptualization of poverty varies over time. The definition of poverty has now shifted from classical poverty lines to including non-monetary criteria such as health, education, lack of voice and power. The multiple dimensions of poverty, which encompass aspects of insecurity, vulnerability, indignity and repression, are now widely recognized by practitioners as well as academic researchers, who acknowledge the significance of social exclusion in assessing the origins and implications of poverty (Courmont, 2001; World Bank, 2001).

A study of the literature on water supply and sanitation services shows that the urban poor are normally assumed to be slum dwellers, squatters or occupants of multi-tenancy buildings of a substandard quality, and vice versa residents of such areas are assumed to be poor. However, some researchers specifically refer to the expanding urban fringe and peri-urban areas rather than the slums as the locations where they expect to find poor urban communities. The diversity of the poor is now being emphasized (Plummer, 2002a; UN-HABITAT, 2003a), but there remains the practical problem of incorporating measures of security, empowerment and opportunities into the standard measures of poverty. Some broad classifications are needed to define the beneficiary target group for this research, i.e. which urban poor communities can reasonably be expected to benefit from the economic and social regulation to be introduced. Plummer (2002a) explains how the degree of poverty affects household priorities: while the 'very poor' have no money at all to spare for water services, the 'middle poor' prioritize water over sanitation, while the 'better off poor' cut back on service expenditures only in emergencies. The micro-finance literature, which distinguishes the 'destitute', 'extremely poor' and 'very poor' from the 'moderately poor' and 'vulnerable non-poor' who are at risk from marginalization and deprivation, offers a further useful starting point (for example Cohen and Sebstad, 1999; Hasan, 2003; Simanowitz, 2004) from which the proposed segmentation in Chapter 1 was derived.

Water services for the urban poor

Problems with assessing the adequacy of water services have long been recognized, but are still subject of review and debate. The often-quoted *Global Water*

Supply and Sanitation Assessment 2000 Report only refers to 'improved' access to drinking water, providing its own definition of what is considered an 'improved source' (WHO and UNICEF, 2000). Satterthwaite (2003) gives a passionate account of how 'nonsense statistics' obscure the true level of urban poverty and the extent of the challenge that lies ahead in providing water to all those who are presently unserved or under-served. He challenges reports from various countries that report high service coverage achievements, when in fact large proportions of the population rely on the classical 'poor people's solutions' such as standpipes and kiosks.

Even where 'adequate' supplies are on the increase in absolute terms, official coverage statistics are often found to be misleading as they 'confound growing numbers of connections with growing population' (Foster and Araujo, 2004). Webb and Iskandarani (1998) introduce the concept of household water security, which draws upon existent theory relating to the concept of food security and combines aspects of availability, access and actual water use on a macro-scale, suggesting that poor households are particularly water insecure. Although the paper neither exclusively nor specifically addresses the issue of urban water supply, the underlying concept of considering water as a resource, an economic commodity and a human entitlement provides interesting ideas for developing a corresponding concept of 'urban household water security' that could replace the purely technical notion of 'adequate access'.

Poor urban communities face various problems in accessing networked water services, many of which are related to water companies' perceptions. Slums housing large urban communities have been described as the 'water engineer's nightmare' (Katakura and Bakalian, 1998). Reasons other than distance from existing networks and accessibility problems explaining the operators' reluctance to connect residents of slums and shantytowns include the perceived problems of affordability and non-payment and the lack of security guarantees for pipelines and connections installed on land of insecure or disputed ownership (McPhail, 1993; WaterAid, 2001; Almansi et al, 2003). Almansi et al (2003) show that frequently access is delayed, if not denied, by cumbersome administrative procedures. A detailed literature review on the 'connection charge barrier', which according to Clarke and Wallsten (2002) will continue to 'make a mockery of any policy intended to connect the poor', has been carried out for this research programme's sister project. It was found that the issue of 'charging to enter the water shop' had not been addressed in any systematic way in the literature (Gerlach, 2004). The results of the research confirmed the suspicion that connection costs in many cases are not only too high, but also lack predictability, thus seriously hampering service access for the urban poor (Franceys, 2005a). Alternative options of accessing water services are examined in the next section, which establishes current knowledge on actual and existing water markets in developing-country cities.

Urban, developing-country water markets: Coping with inadequate services

There is widespread agreement on the fact that the continuous pressures of rapid population growth and rising poverty levels far exceed the capabilities of conventional public service provision, which more often than not suffers from inadequate infrastructure networks, historic underinvestment and managerial inefficiencies. Service failures occur on a multitude of levels, and service for poor people is usually equivalent with poor quality service (Brocklehurst, 2002; World Bank, 2003). Official service coverage statistics often mask the extent to which households, and in particular the poor and vulnerable, rely on costly or time-consuming coping strategies and alternative means of securing drinking water supplies (Zérah, 1997; UN-HABITAT, 2003b). As attention focused on the centralized monopoly providers and their various shortcomings, there was only occasionally note of the widespread occurrence of water vending in the literature (Zaroff and Okun, 1984), and alternative providers were not 'rediscovered' until the late 1990s. Today there is growing interest in the irregular and fragmented urban water markets where a variety of agents occupy the many gaps left vacant by the utilities, and in particular (but not exclusively) cater for lower- and lowest-income households where there are no options for self-supply. Many case studies have examined the nature of alternative providers (for example Solo, 1998; Collignon and Vézina, 2000; Conan, 2003; Llorente and Zérah, 2003), and governments, donors and advisers acknowledge their role in terms of the number of people they serve and their ability to successfully match services with the needs of a diverse and often financially and socially disadvantaged clientele (Brocklehurst, 2002; McIntosh, 2003; Plummer, 2003; UN-HABITAT, 2003b; World Bank, 2003; Stallard and Ehrhardt, 2004).

Though many of the alternative providers' businesses are not officially registered, cases of illegal distribution of utility water have also been reported (WPEP, 2000; McIntosh, 2003). The definition of an alternative provider becomes somewhat ambiguous, with blurred boundaries between local entrepreneurs operating within the informal economy and those engaging in outright theft and fraud.

Stallard and Ehrhardt (2004) advise private sector participation (PSP) projects to cooperate with alternative providers on account of their ability to serve customers beyond the reach of conventional projects and their ability to cater specifically for the poor through innovation, flexibility and economical solutions. Alternatively, community management is portrayed as an option allowing for extensive household participation in designing and delivering services, albeit not without certain capacity and sustainability problems (Mitlin, 2002).

The lack of official recognition of alternative providers' functions and their ambiguous legal situation are presented as a core problem by Plummer (2002b). Communication with public authorities is likely to be non-existent and the attitude of formal (private) monopoly providers, protected by exclusivity clauses in their concession agreements, may range from tolerance to outright hostility (Collignon and Vézina, 2000). The ambiguous operational framework increases alternative providers' business risk to the extent that it becomes virtually impossible to raise money for investments from commercial banks. Without access to public subsidies and conventional financing, independent small-scale businesses invest family savings and are consequently forced to achieve full recovery of all costs (Solo, 1999). Insecure investments severely restrict planning horizons, with typical amortization periods ranging from less than three months in the case of vendors and resellers to approximately three years for independent suppliers (Drangaert et al, 1998; Troyano, 1999; Conan, 2003). Recent study results indicate that profit margins are lower than presumed and operators are surviving on modest incomes (Collignon and Vézina, 2000; Vézina, 2002; Conan and Paniagua, 2003). The particular role of alternative providers within a regulated approach to ensure adequate services to the poor is explored further in Chapter 8.

Regulatory rationales in developing countries

The beginnings of utilities regulation in developing countries are usually associated with post-privatization reforms under the guidance of foreign advisers. Incentive regulation based on England and Wales' OFWAT model has become a popular export to developing countries (Parker, 1999; Nickson and Franceys, 2003). However, some authors have voiced their disapproval of such policy transfer experiments, the sparse literature on which suggests that 'blueprints are borrowed, but honoured in the breach more than the observance' (Cook et al, 2003). Many see the reasons for regulatory failure in the failure to address the local realities described above. Minogue (2003) detects a disparity between regulatory 'best practice' as promoted by donors and existing (and different) administrative, political, legal and economic conditions in the developing countries under reform. Laffont (2005) finds unsurprising the initial reliance on conceptual frameworks borrowed from the Western world, noting that there is a distinct lack of theoretical understanding of economic regulation in developing countries. Academic researchers are only beginning to build the foundations for a theory of regulation that recognizes the constraints and objectives of economic regulation in developing economies (Parker and Kirkpatrick, 2002; Laffont, 2005). Parker and Kirkpatrick (2002) suspect this theory may be substantially different to the accepted theory that originated in high-income nations.

In view of the major service gaps commonly found in developing countries it is now becoming clear that regulatory rationales necessarily differ from those in developed countries. Widespread poverty pushes social objectives higher onto the political – and hence regulatory – agenda. Practitioners state the challenge more boldly as finding 'reasonable ways to improve substantially and on a large scale the service provision for the poor' in an environment that is characterized by inefficient social redistribution systems and a large share of the population surviving at or below the poverty line (GTZ, 2004). Minogue (2003) argues that regulating for development and poverty alleviation may require a higher degree of political intervention on behalf of the poor than conventional models of independent regulation permit, even if such independence should be aspired to. Together with Cook (Cook and Minogue, 2003), he proposes to think of regulation as the 'bridge' between often conflicting efficiency and welfare objectives. What under the conventional 'fixed bridge model' would amount to regulatory capture, is simply making allowances for the special circumstances of developing countries in terms of the scale of the need and institutional and capacity deficits under the suggested 'flexible swing bridge' model. This notion is supported by Stern and Holder (1999), who emphasize the need to reach clarity about regulatory objectives and requirements while retaining flexibility and creativity with respect to optimal institutional set-ups for each country and industry.

Regulatory failures and constraints

Nickson and Franceys (2003) note that experiences with water regulation remain limited. Nevertheless the literature is full of anecdotal evidence of regulatory failures, mostly relating to some form of capture. Shirley and Ménard (2002) suggest that it was the bureaucratic and legal institutions' susceptibility to political interference and corruption that ultimately weakened regulators in Latin American and African case study countries. Trémolet and Browning (2002) demonstrate that not even autonomy necessarily protects against overrule of regulatory decisions by political interests. Esguerra's review (2002, cited in Mitlin, 2002) of the world's largest water concessions in Manila reveals that the (under-)bidding private companies subsequently tried to influence the regulatory process to rule in their favour. Instances of undue intervention on the part of regulators, effectively leading to 'micro-management' of the service providers' operations, have also been observed (Nickson and Franceys, 2003). Nickson and Vargas' (2002) analysis of the perhaps most spectacular failure of PSP identifies weak regulatory capacity as one of the decisive factors in the termination of the Cochabamba concession following the high-profile water conflict in Bolivia. In spite of attempts to create an appropriate regulatory framework, the conflict was characterized by almost continuous political intervention and pressure on the regulator to endorse predetermined government decisions. Regulatory budget constraints, lack of qualified staff, an ambiguous legal framework and the lack of consumer participation exacerbated the problem.

The above evidence only confirms earlier warnings about constraints that political and economic environments impose on the new regulators. In 1999, Parker summarized the prerequisites for UK-style regulation as political commitment to regulatory independence and a 'reasonably stable' economy. He fully acknowledged the need to beware of trying to copy a system that has achieved many benefits for consumers and investors in its home country into a setting where the right balance of regulatory independence and accountability may be even more difficult to achieve. Anticipated problems include the continuation of customary political appointments, which undermine the credibility of regulators and thus investor confidence, recruitment problems and a high risk of political intervention, intensified by the lack of vocal parliamentary opposition and free press (Parker, 1999). A more recent review identifies the lack of regulatory capacity as a major challenge to successful regulation in developing countries (Cook et al, 2003). Cook et al add the limited potential to recruit skilled regulatory personnel, a problem that is further complicated by low civil servant salaries, to Parker's above list. Developing countries, they argue further, are predisposed to 'gaming' because the potential lack of government integrity, independent media and judiciaries allow for greater exploitation of the information asymmetries inherent in the regulatory process. Under these circumstances, further research needs to focus on understanding and addressing information asymmetries, appropriate regulatory instruments, institutional aspects of regulation such as incentives, regulatory structures and capacity building, and how the principles of 'good regulation' can realistically be incorporated into regulatory reform in developing countries (Cook et al, 2003).

What these papers fail to note is the fact that the sequence most commonly observed is that regulatory arrangements follow after negotiations for private sector involvement have begun (Nickson and Franceys, 2003). Not surprisingly, early regulation efforts have focused on contractual arrangements, where price-sensitive contract deliverables, at least initially, take precedence over other considerations (Halcrow, 2002). In McIntosh's (2003) view this reduces newly created regulatory bodies to contract administrators. The Asian Development Bank (2001) confirmed that regulation in the region had indeed not evolved significantly away from mere contract administration. McIntosh (2003) claims that most developing countries have only implemented regulation by contract over the past decade. Halcrow management consultants (2002) use the terms 'regulator' and 'contract supervisor' interchangeably, which opens up questions regarding foreign advisers' understanding of the nature of regulation in developing countries. The problem of sequencing and inequalities between negotiating partners in terms of experience thus becomes acute (Mitlin, 2002; Budds and McGranahan, 2003). Johnstone et al (1999, cited in Mitlin, 2002) note that the high level of concentration in the international water market may tip the balance in favour of private companies 'who know a lot more about regulatory options and their potential consequences than the regulators themselves'.

Privatization, regulation and the poor

Although some authors continue to blame the World Bank for neglecting the effects of service privatization on low-income households (Bayliss, 2002), a growing interest in the impact of privatization on poverty can be detected in the literature (Estache et al, 2000; Brocklehurst, 2002; Clarke and Wallsten, 2002; Weitz and Franceys, 2002; Budds and McGranahan, 2003; Gutierrez et al, 2003). Irrespective of the views on dangers and benefits of private sector participation in service provision expressed by the authors, the critical issues converge: affordability problems associated with tariff rises, cost of connections and widespread elimination of illegal connections, and the challenge of achieving universal service coverage feature in the majority of accounts. Critics and champions agree that adequate regulatory structures need to be in place for privatization to have the desired effect of connecting and protecting the urban poor. Where privatization has been successful, Cook (1999) argues that the largest gains have been achieved by effective regulation rather than privatization itself. Plummer (2002b) adds that the regulatory framework is 'perhaps the most critical aspect of the external operating context for the success of all PPPs'.

At the same time, the privatization literature dispels some myths, which are neatly summarized by McIntosh (2003): blaming private operators for tariff increases, convenient as it may be especially where international water companies are involved, is a case of confounding causes and effects. PSP is no miracle cure for decades of mismanagement and underinvestment. Tariff increases, McIntosh argues, are absolutely crucial to finance ambitious connection targets. Poor households' alleged low willingness and ability to pay has merely been used to conceal government's reluctance to charge. The consistently higher prices paid to alternative providers prove this point. In line with the findings of privatization critics (Budds and McGranahan, 2003; Gutierrez et al, 2003), McIntosh (2003) concedes that without explicit directions, PSP will not solve the problem of serving the urban poor. Laurie and Crespo (2002) put some of the benefits of the Bolivia privatization experience, reported for instance by Barja and Urquiola (2001), into perspective, arguing that in the case of the La Paz–El Alto concession, the achieved service expansions have been overemphasized, obscuring 'significant anti-poor elements' that are rooted in regulatory weaknesses and a lack of democratic participation.

In recognition of the fact that PSP and its associated efficiency gains do not automatically deliver benefits for the urban poor, donor initiatives are now developing 'pro-poor' PSP strategies (Brocklehurst, 2002; Stallard and Ehrhardt, 2004). Early lessons from privatization experiences indicate the importance of pro-poor contract design and the supporting policy and regulatory frameworks. Komives (1999) concludes that the typical concession contract performs better if tangible objectives are formulated, these are supported by financial incentives to serve the poor, policy barriers are eliminated, and services retain a high degree of choice and flexibility. Exclusivity clauses and strict technical service specifications are examples cited as counterproductive by restricting or eliminating options available to poor households. Subsequent research commissioned by development banks initially focused on pro-poor transaction design and contract preparation, covering key elements of sector reform ranging from appropriate legal frameworks to tariff structures and subsidy allocation (Brockelhurst, 2002), but is expanded upon in a more recent report by Stallard and Ehrhardt (2004). The regulation literature followed suit and, in line with the findings of 'pro-poor PSP' studies, elaborated on regulatory strategies designed to turn poor services into services for the poor.

From poor regulation to pro-poor regulation: Establishing the poverty focus

Trémolet (2002) notes that regulatory agencies are rarely mandated to protect poor consumers, a complex task requiring specialist skills and dedicated resources. Smith (2000) emphasizes that an effective pro-poor regulatory strategy must prioritize service expansion and cost minimization in order to remain sensitive to the affordability concerns of the poorest. The broad consensus in the literature is that the key to meeting the challenge lies in matching customer needs and preferences with relevant and accessible services. Stallard and Ehrhardt (2004) compare this first step of developing the necessary understanding with market research. Attention should be paid to the characteristics, attitudes, expectations, aspirations and financial circumstances of the poor. Trémolet and Browning's (2002) report linking regulatory frameworks and tri-sector partnerships provides excellent arguments in support of early involvement of multiple stakeholders to create a flexible and innovative environment of mutual support and recognition of interests and constraints. Smith (2000) as well as Stallard and Ehrhardt (2004) acknowledge the role of partnerships in performing broader regulatory functions such as assessing the needs of poor customers. The latter advise against relying on frequently inaccurate official statistics and see local partners as potential contributors to community surveying.

Regulatory mechanisms: Price and service differentiation

Smith (2000) advocates more pragmatism in regulatory controls on pricing and service quality. Tight price regulation may actually remove incentives to serve the poor, who may be more costly to serve, and high technical, health, safety and environmental quality standards may come at a price that turns the poor away from regulated services. In response to these affordability concerns, Baker and Trémolet (2000) propose to allow an 'acceptable relaxation in quality' of services to ease access of the poorest. They note that stricter enforcement of quality standards can add significant costs to the service, though enforcement is generally weak. The authors admit that optimal quality standards are difficult to determine, which speaks in favour of Smith's (2000) model of nurturing competitive markets, where choice reveals consumer preferences. There is a general agreement that minimum standards tend to be oriented at first world standards rather than acceptable standards that meet the basic needs of the poor, and specifying the technology to be employed can stifle innovation and adaptive low-cost solutions. However, a slightly more prescriptive approach may be preferable as far as performance targets are concerned. Stallard and Ehrhardt (2004) suggest that coverage targets, for instance, should be specifically tied to locations rather than statistical figures, with built-in flexibility to respond to circumstances. Outcomes should take precedence over input standards, Baker and Trémolet (2000) concur. They also emphasize the role of publicizing quality information, in which community organizations could play a role as a cheap and effective means to address the problem of information asymmetries, as long as a suitable balance can be maintained between public education and interest group lobbying. Stallard and Ehrhardt (2004) propose that above the required minimum standards, public information campaigns could actually replace regulatory oversight, while still promoting quality improvements. Sansom et al (2004) go into considerable detail in investigating and reporting on practical techniques for service differentiation that are in use around the world and might have potential for adaptation within a regulatory framework.

Tariffs and subsidies

The design of appropriate tariff systems is a critical regulatory task, which goes hand in hand with subsidy allocation. It has become an established fact that subsidies more often than not have bypassed their intended beneficiaries. Clarke and Wallsten (2002) find that only in Eastern Europe have monopolists used subsidy schemes to promote access to infrastructure services for the poor. Many authors give reasons and examples of how the prevailing tariff and subsidy systems entrench social exclusion. Tariffs are generally set too low to turn poor households into attractive potential customers, and subsidy schemes are plagued with high errors of inclusion (subsidies are captured by the non-poor) and exclusion, i.e. subsidies fail to reach the – often unconnected – poor (Boland and Whittington, 2000; Whittington et al, 2002; McIntosh, 2003). While there is no scope for debating appropriate pricing mechanisms within this review, it is essential to note that even consumer organizations support the view that the poor stand to gain from raised tariffs (Simpson, 2002). Only an increased revenue base can stimulate much-needed network expansions and service improvement.

Trémolet (2002) makes the explicit link between pro-poor tariff and subsidies required to meet cost-recovery levels. She highlights the need for innovative delivery mechanisms for subsidies. To date subsidies are usually incorporated into the tariff designs in the form of cross-subsidies. Boland and Whittington's (2000) critical evaluation of objectives and considerations governing tariff development reveal some of the limitations and even negative impacts associated with cross-subsidy schemes. They find no evidence to support the assumption that increasing block tariffs (IBTs), originally devised to assist low-income households in developed countries through below-cost first blocks without introducing overall revenue distortions, increase the likelihood of households connecting to the system or encourage poor households' water use. IBTs promote public health no more than uniform tariffs with built-in rebates, nor do they achieve equity or resource conservation. Boland and Whittington provide convincing arguments that in spite of their widespread popularity, IBTs have wrongly been promoted as the most suitable choice in developing countries. IBTs also penalize shared connections, which are commonly found among connected low-income households, a point also raised by several others (Inocencio, 2001; Weitz and Franceys, 2002). Many authors support the 'access priority', maintaining that subsidizing new connections should be prioritized over actual consumption subsidies (Brocklehurst, 2002; Simpson, 2002; Weitz and Franceys, 2002; Whittington et al, 2002; McIntosh, 2003). Some authors assert that subsidies should never cover the full cost of provision (Brocklehurst, 2002; Stallard and Ehrhardt, 2004).

Regulators not only face the challenge of balancing competing objectives in developing tariff structures, but also have only limited control over subsidy levels, as Trémolet (2002) points out. However, Chisari et al (2003) demonstrate that the choice of regulatory system (i.e. price cap or rate of return regulation) influences the choice of technology and hence the level of investment (and hence subsidy) likely to be required. Subsidies often are used as political instruments, as Boland and Whittington's (2000) observations confirm: subsidies reflect subjective notions of fairness rather than objectively promoting equity. The main purpose of tariffs is to cover revenue requirements (Boland and Whittington, 2000), but there are uncertainties surrounding government commitment to agreed levels of subsidy (Trémolet, 2002). The problems of administering subsidies and monitoring performance become more complicated when subsidies are directly linked with service provision (for example, through output-based aid mechanisms), and when subsidies are allocated to small-scale alternative providers (Trémolet, 2002). Stallard and Ehrhardt (2004) suggest that subsidy payments should be linked with specific services but remain technology and provider neutral. Subsidy payments in the form of direct transfers to customers are generally favoured as the economically best solution (Trémolet, 2002; Chisari et al, 2003), with cross-subsidies rated second-best. Chisari et al (2003) introduce a universal service fund as an alternative option to finance USOs, where these have been introduced by the regulator.

Incorporating alternative providers

While it is now almost an undisputed fact – supported by international development agencies (Brocklehurst, 2002; Stallard and Ehrhardt, 2004) – that regulation should encompass both utilities and alternative providers, very few tentative suggestions can be found in the literature as to what these future regulatory arrangements should look like. Insufficiently flexible solutions are a major concern, feared to destroy effective and original solutions (Troyano,

1999). Collignon and Vézina (2000) warn that an overemphasis on technical standards and formal procedures can prove counter-effective by increasing overheads with associated price rises and service deterioration, ultimately forcing independent providers out of business before satisfactory substitutes can be offered. The literature identifies price, water quality, market entry and market share as main aspects of regulation (Baker and Trémolet, 2000; Plummer, 2002b). Plummer (2002b) recommends relaxing performance standards and exclusivity rights given to utilities, supporting alternative providers in securing legal contracts, revising tariff regimes, addressing land tenure issues and disseminating a 'spirit of inclusion' among the incumbent large-scale service providers. Most authors agree that a healthy level of competition should be encouraged to promote service extensions to poor households, with alternative provider licences providing a degree of formality. Baker and Trémolet (2000) raise the point that relaxed rules should be a temporary measure. Self-regulation by provider associations has been proposed as another option (Stallard and Ehrhardt, 2004), as positive experiences are reported in the literature (WPEP, 2000; Conan, 2003; Plummer, 2003). Trémolet and Browning (2002) propose replacing costly 'traditional' regulation through price and quality standards with making performance data publicly available, thus relying on the regulating effects of reputation.

Customer and civil society involvement

The centrality of information has received frequent mention in the preceding discussion of pro-poor regulation. Brocklehurst (2002) emphasizes needs-responsiveness as a central feature of regulatory design. Stallard and Ehrhardt (2004) advocate continuous engagement with the beneficiary communities from the project design stage through to establishing feedback mechanisms allowing for interaction between customers, operators and government/regulators. They emphasize the need for cultural sensitivity and an understanding of the special challenges facing the poor. A host of participatory and surveying techniques are available for consumer consultation and gathering site-specific information. Establishing accessible and inclusive regulatory processes is a more difficult challenge, as Foster (2003) reports from Latin America, where the failure to create mechanisms for interaction within the legal framework nurtured a negative public perception of regulation. She finds that regulators in the region have developed creative ways of improving the 'opaque, technocratic and non-participatory' image of the regulatory process, engaging the public in capacity-building activities and public consultations. Permanent interaction in the form of customer representation remains the exception, but has been imple-mented in Buenos Aires, where representatives of consumer associations form an advisory body to the regulator. The regulator in Jakarta has introduced customer representation modelled after England and Wales' WaterVoice, but so far this has not been evaluated in the literature. As Simpson and Shallat (2004) report, consumer organizations are currently participating in informal sector regulation, such as water vending (Kenya) or community-managed cooperative water systems (Philippines). More formal arrangements include membership in regulatory boards in some African countries and membership in the water company's board (Senegal).

Within formal regulatory frameworks, customers currently enjoy a very limited level of influence and there are few, if any, reported attempts of including poor or unconnected households in the process. Smith (2000) sees poor access to transport and communication links as an impediment for the poor to become involved. Extreme poverty seriously limits participation as daily wage-earners lack time and financial resources and perhaps education and confidence to participate meaningfully. Although these issues are little discussed in the regulation literature, they can be gleaned from discussions on accountability and consumer voice (Ear-Dupuy, 2003). Smith (2000) insists that stakeholder engagement must go beyond formal hearings. Regulators should take a proactive stance and reach out to the disadvantaged by visiting communities, establishing consultative and advisory bodies, and educating citizens about their rights under the regulatory system. Ugaz (2002) regards the involvement of consumer associations as an indication of attempts to incorporate the voice of the poor. She presents a basic set of considerations that affect the design of consumer involvement. Decisions need to be taken regarding which participants are to join the system, how to encourage, train and empower them to overcome knowledge barriers and transcend unequal power relations between the various actors involved.

Service obligations and the concept of universal service

This section introduces the various types of obligations that governments have sought to impose on service providers in order to protect public interest objectives. among these, the concept of 'universal service' frequently appears in the literature on networked industries. Much of literature provides justifications for the introduction of USOs in the context of monopoly services or, more recently, and mainly in the telecommunications sector, in a competitive environment. Choné et al (2000) introduce the underpinning notions of 'equal access' and 'affordable tariffs', as well as some of the constraints related to USOs. Ubiquity, the provision of service connections in all locations, and non-discrimination, which refers to the same tariff irrespective of customers' location and cost of connection, form the geographical component of USOs. The relatively sparse literature with a developing-country focus tends to emphasize welfare aspects or the social component of USOs (for example Gasmi et al, 2000; Clarke and Wallsten, 2002; Chisari et al, 2003). The water sector is notably under-represented in the discussions, according to which the main challenge for regulators consists in correcting the market distortion introduced by the USO and, as Choné et al (2000) explain, in 'determining optimal rules for allocating and funding those USOs'. The section examines the current understanding of the concept of universal service, contrasting its present meaning with its historical origins as well as applications in developed and developing countries.

Simmonds (2003) develops a comprehensive definition of the contemporary universal service concept in her evaluation of service obligations imposed under EU legislation. These obligations emerged in the course of European market liberalization as the express commitment of the Union to protect certain 'general interest services' that are deemed essential in economic and social terms. The Commission here distinguishes between universal and public service obligations (PSOs). Public services, it is emphasized, do not necessarily have to be provided by the public sector, nor does the term imply public ownership of the service infrastructure. Community legislation further states that universal service, designed to guarantee 'access to certain essential services of high quality at prices [everyone] can afford, is an evolutionary concept, which is shaped by technological innovations, changing general interest requirements and users' needs' (The European Parliament and The Council quoted in Simmonds, 2003). The political use of terms, Simmonds argues, has thereby caused some confusion. In the strictest sense, PSOs refer to any type of government obligation imposed on service providers for public interest purposes, and encompass both USOs and specific PSOs, which do not include the element of universality. Simmonds' concept of universal service is based on a very broad definition of access, which includes notions of equity and equality. It is centred on consumers' needs and expectations with regards to access, service quality, choice, security of supply and appropriate mechanisms for redress and compensation, but also considers wider societal interests, such as environmental concerns and the protection of vulnerable groups. Independent scrutiny and stakeholder consultation, Simmonds argues, are vital to ensure openness in management, price setting and funding. To accomplish this 'societal idea' of universal service, she recommends a set of regulatory instruments, designed to promote socially conscious service delivery.

In the context of telecommunications, the origin of the term 'universal service' has been traced back to the early 1900s. Mueller (1997), in his account of the development of telephone networks in the US demonstrates that universal service at the time did not have the connotations of affordability and non-discriminatory service for all that it has today. The AT&T Bell Laboratories' slogan 'One system, one policy, universal service' effectively intended to preserve AT&T's monopoly profits. The term 'universal service' thus arose from fierce market access competition, with 'universal' implying everywhere, rather than extending services to everybody (Verhoest, 2000). Verhoest's discussion of the 'myth of universal service' illustrates with reference to the EU telecoms sector that even in the European context the concept of universal service was basically market-related, and not necessarily a result of deliberate social policy. This fact is often obscured by the political use and misuse of a term with a dual economic and social meaning. Historically, the concept of universal service clearly developed with reference to the market, and Mueller (1997) defies conventional wisdom by demonstrating that it was not a result of regulatory intervention by government.

As the concept of universal service has significantly evolved away from its early economic roots, it is interesting to note that in Europe service obligations are not consistently imposed on all public interest services. There is a notable scarcity of references to the water sector in both the academic literature and existing laws and regulations, compared with an extensive literature evaluating and analysing universal service in, for example, telecommunications. Under current EU legislation, USOs apply to the telecoms and postal services, and PSOs are imposed on the gas and transport sectors. Simmonds (2003) notes that although the Community recognizes water as a service of general economic interest, it is mainly environmental considerations that have driven the regulation of the sector. The US National Association of Regulatory Utility Commissioners (NARUC), in contrast, recognizes the financial implications of maintaining safe drinking water supplies in view of environmental threats. NARUC perceives a national commitment to household affordability as essential and recommends a national 'universal water service' policy to protect 'high quality drinking water at affordable rates for every American' (EPA, 1998).

As previous chapters have clearly shown, there is a tremendous need for improving access to affordable water services in developing countries. However, authors discussing universal service in these settings have tended to focus on the funding implications of extending service obligations to include under-served rural areas and the urban poor (for example Clarke and Wallsten, 2002; Chisari et al, 2003). They do, nonetheless, provide some insight into the understanding of the universal service concept. Chisari et al (2003) note that service obligations or connection targets have often been used in the context of PPPs as policy instruments to accelerate access to utility services for the poor. The authors discuss USO and obligatory service (OS) as the 'standard tools' available to governments, which have been used by regulators in the Latin American countries under review and are projected to remain a feature of utility services, notably in the water and sanitation sector. Both USO and OS are described as subsidy mechanisms, the implications of which need to be considered in the light of the regulatory objective of ensuring financeability of operations. OS is defined as compulsory service to all households wishing to connect under the existing tariff structure, whereas affordability concerns feature in the USO. The USO thus extends the notion of 'universal access', which is supported by OS, with an ambition to promote socially desirable consumption levels through tariff control. The authors further raise the issue of unidirectional and bidirectional service obligations (obligation to serve and obligation to use), highlighting water and sanitation service as a likely candidate for the latter. While OS is deemed appropriate for services with geographically variable supply costs and where availability fails to reach socially desired levels, USO would be the chosen instrument for essential products or services, which some consumer groups find difficult to access unless tariffs take into account their ability to pay, possibly further excluding them from other markets. Clarke and Wallsten (2002) see the justification for universal service policies in externalities associated with service uptake, 'merit good' qualities of services and political or development goals. Any combination of these factors may induce governments to provide subsidies to poor or rural consumers. Water and sanitation services qualify because of the public and environmental health benefits associated with adequate consumption levels. The authors point out that the 'merit good' argument begs the question why some services are mandatory and others, arguably more important, are not legislated for.

The ultimate regulator: Customer involvement

Consumers as service recipients are arguably the best monitors of service quality and reliability. As they are directly affected by regulatory decisions, they should be informed and consulted about planned changes (Plummer, 2003). So far communication between utilities and poor communities has been suffering serious shortcomings, where it has not been neglected altogether. The UK National Consumer Council (NCC, 2002) deems customer involvement essential to 'design and deliver goods and services that meet people's needs, improve standards, identify problem areas, and provide value for money'. In the case of developing countries with their often 'uninspiring track record' in public service provision, Burra et al (2003) emphasize that urgently needed, practical solutions must be rooted in the experiences of those who have to live with the problems. Isolated, bureaucratic approaches are best avoided by opening the policy-making and regulatory process to external groups who bring in fresh perspectives (Berg, 2000). Engagement of all stakeholders, including (potential) customers, does not only improve the quality of decisions, but can also improve the legitimacy of regulation (Smith, 2000; Foster, 2003). Additional benefits of involving consumers mentioned in the literature include reduced risk of regulatory capture and increased accountability (ECLAC, 2003). McIntosh (2003), echoing ideas expressed in the *World Development Report 2004* (World Bank, 2004b), suggests confronting the governance crisis through a civil society that demands accountability of policy-makers. He emphasizes the role of NGOs as advocates of the unserved and under-served poor and in monitoring policy implementation. Especially for the poorest, consumer and/or community engagement can make an important contribution to empowerment.

There are special challenges in involving the poor, and regulators wishing to establish customer representation will have to proceed in a proactive way. Even the UK experience shows that domestic customers are in a weaker position compared to the resources and lobbying power of commercial customers (NCC, 2002). People may be unaware of their rights and the assigned tasks of regulators (Berg, 2000). Again, this is not exclusively an issue in developing countries, as the same ignorance has been reported among applicants to a UK water charity: fearing disconnection of their water supply, they sought help with their rising water debt not knowing that disconnections had been banned by the government some years ago (Fitch, 2003a).

In view of the social disadvantages and serious time limitations that restrict the participation of poor people, formal mechanisms of customer representation and involvement may not prove feasible. Hanchett et al (2003) warn of unrealistic expectations for establishing inclusive ('mixed') customer committees. As the poor are excluded from formal service provision in many instances, creativity will be needed to give due consideration to their special circumstances and concerns when incorporating them into the regulatory process.

Customer involvement, perhaps traditionally viewed as some form of customer representation, may initially take the form of information, but will have to extend into a real dialogue between customers, providers and regulators. Arnstein's ladder of citizen participation is the classical measure for the level of influence over decisions granted to the public (Arnstein, 1969). Whatever level of involvement is decided to be appropriate, it is important for authorities to clearly state the objectives and conditions of participation to avoid false expectations (Drafting Group, 2002). There is a vast literature available on the theory of participation, and resource books detail the various methods that have been tried over the years. Abelson et al (1995, cited in van Ryneveld, 1995) provide a concise set of principles for evaluating the different approaches, and particularly explore the usefulness of deliberative methods in recognition of the need for a two-way dialogue and consensus building among all participants of the debate. Citizens' juries, consensus conferences and the like have become increasingly popular and may stimulate broader and more meaningful participation than traditional methods such as surveys and focus groups have done in the past. Further research will be required into participatory methods that can accommodate the poorest.

A parallel examination of arrangements in the England and Wales regulatory system is appropriate as currently 20 per cent of the population are experiencing 'water poverty', defined by Fitch (2003b) as a 'situation faced by householders who are obliged to devote an unreasonable high proportion of their income to paying for water'.

Although there is evidence of regulators in developing countries trying to set up customer representation mechanisms, there is little to be found in the published literature. Several authors attribute public opposition to water sector reforms to a failure on the part of the regulators to defend consumer interests (Foster, 2003) and adequately engage them in the regulatory process. While Shirley and Ménard (2002) report that in none of the cases they reviewed consumers were involved in the regulatory process, Foster (2003) finds that Latin American regulators are demonstrating 'significant creativity in developing mechanisms for interaction with civil society'. Public consultations modelled after US-style public audiences are most widespread, as are capacity-building programmes. Contrary to Shirley and Ménard's findings, she cites the Buenos Aires regulator ETOSS (established in 1999, only six years after the concession contract started) as most advanced having a 'Consumers Commission', which gives members an opportunity to review Board decisions. Given the total lack of reference to any kind of formal or official involvement of low-income households, it can be suspected that so far none of these attempts have included the poorest.

As mentioned previously, formal hearings may not prove appropriate in a developing-country setting. Regulators will have to proactively pursue customer involvement objectives. Smith (2000) suggests visiting communities and perhaps establishing specialist consultative or advisory bodies. However, to make customer representation meaningful, whatever type of involvement is chosen, consumer bodies must be truly representative and able to speak for those without the power and resources to ensure their voices are heard. There are different tools and techniques outlined in the literature, but it is pointed out that it may take time before consumer involvement has evolved into an active partnership between all interested parties (for example Berg, 2000). Troyano (1999) notes that while it is important to guarantee stakeholder participation, this should not happen at the expense of operational efficiency. Finding an optimum strategy for each case will much depend on local factors, but certain organizational options for customer bodies are worth considering. In the UK utilities sector, for instance, Simmonds (2002) distinguishes between two types of arrangement: in the integrated model, customer representatives are affiliated with the regulatory office, whereas independent consumer councils are external, as their name suggests. Accounting for the regional characteristics of the water industry, customer representation in the UK to date has had a regional structure and focus as opposed to the single national body which exists for other utility sectors. Independent consumer councils have attracted criticism as they are feared to duplicate the regulatory task of consumer protection, potentially adding an unnecessary level of bureaucracy and threatening to induce rivalry between regulatory bodies and consumer bodies. Detached from regulatory staff, independent consumer bodies might struggle to gain access to vital information and receive due recognition from companies (Simmonds, 2002).

4

Monitoring Public Providers
for the Poor

Following the introduction to regulation and water and sanitation services to all, the first two case studies consider service providers where there was no existing proclaimed economic regulation. However, in the case of India, it had been decreed that all states should establish a water regulator (a requirement since withdrawn) and in Uganda there is a level of performance monitoring which was, perhaps, as good as a regulator might achieve. The fieldwork researchers first investigated the sectoral organization for water supply, the legislative framework and the operational and any regulatory performance for the conventional service. They then examined in detail to what extent that service was reaching the poor, whether there was a role for alternative providers, independent or intermediate, and how customers, particularly poor customers, were involved in the process, beyond payment that is. To complement that investigation the researchers convened participatory discussions, focus groups, within a selection of poor communities to hear first hand the challenges those consumers faced and to gain a better understanding of how any regulatory system might incorporate their views in the future.

CASE STUDY 1: JAIPUR, INDIA

Marion Gessler and Urmila Brighu

The water sector and institutional framework

The Government of Rajasthan, the largest and most water-scarce state in the Indian Union has adopted a State Water Policy that outlines a framework for sustainable development and efficient management of the water resources of the state. With respect to drinking water the state requires: the gradual increase of water rates to support the urban and rural water supply piped schemes, increase of the budget allocation for upgrading the domestic water supply, ensuring water quality and encouraging private sector participation. State owner-ship of all the water resources within the state and the introduction of abstraction licensing are also foreseen in the State Water Policy as well as the introduction of necessary legislation to cater for the needs of the economically weaker sections of the population.

Even though the State Water Policy articulates the need for reforms and states the policy objectives, a cause for concern is that these have not been trans-lated into action as yet. This study therefore represents a 'pre-regulation' study and, from experience prior to this study, is believed to be fairly representative of the unregulated public providers.

As per the Constitution of India responsibility for water is vested with the states. According to the 74th Constitutional Amendment (Municipal Act) the particular responsibility of urban water supply and sewerage should be trans-ferred to urban local bodies. However at present, in Rajasthan the Public Health and Engineering Department (PHED), a department of the state government, continues to hold full responsibility for providing water supply and sewage treat-ment (sewerage being the responsibility of local bodies).

The PHED has the full responsibility for the water supply sector, for planning, implementation (design and construction), service provision and operations and maintenance of water supply projects in Rajasthan. However, the PHED, being a department of the state government, does not enjoy full auton-omy and so does not have a mechanism for setting water tariffs.

The role of policy planning and formulation rests with the Government of Rajasthan. The body responsible for urban water supply in the central govern-ment, the Ministry of Urban Development and Poverty Alleviation, plays an advisory role by providing guidelines for developing policies and programmes to facilitate the efforts of the state and municipal governments.

The PHED is overseen by the Rajasthan Water Supply and Sewerage Management Board (RWSSMB), which controls, supervises and guides the PHED on behalf of the Government of Rajasthan in policy, financial and technical issues. RWSSMB is not an independent entity but an extended arm of the government.

INDIA KEY FACTS	
• Human Development Index rank	128 out of 177
• Population living < US$2 per day	80.4 per cent
• GNI per capita at purchasing power parity (2006)	US$3800
• Country population	1110 million
• Urban population	29 per cent
• Urban population growth rate 2005–2010	2.3 per cent
• Urban water coverage	95 per cent
• Water supply by household connection	47 per cent
• Improved urban sanitation coverage	59 per cent
• Research focus location	Jaipur
• Research focus population	2.75 million
• Service provider	Public Health Engineering Department and Jaipur Municipal Corporation
• Contract form	Direct public department provision
• Exchange rate to US$ at fieldwork	INR43.8
• Implied purchasing power parity conversion rate to US$	INR9.4
• Implied undervaluation ratio	4.66

In contrast to water supply, operation and maintenance of the sewerage systems is undertaken by bodies such as the Jaipur Municipal Corporation (JMC) but sewerage charges are levied and collected by the PHED and given to the local bodies in order to operate and maintain these systems. Responsibilities in sewerage and sewage treatment for Jaipur City are as follows:

- PHED designs some sewerage systems and all sewage treatment installations, owns the assets created for the existing sewage treatment work and is responsible for operation and maintenance (O&M). PHED has to ensure the proper design and execution of all sewerage works carried out by other agencies.
- JMC designs and constructs sewerage systems falling within their area and carries out all the sewerage O&M in Jaipur City.
- The Jaipur Development Authority (JDA) designs and constructs the sewerage systems for new areas of Jaipur City falling under the JDA area.
- The Rajasthan Housing Board (RHB) designs and constructs sewerage systems for new housing estates.
- JDA and RHB also execute water supply projects in new housing areas. After completion the assets are turned over to PHED for O&M.

Overall, it can be seen that many agencies are involved in planning, developing and operating the water supply and sanitation system in Jaipur. This multiplicity and overlap of responsibilities is a bottleneck and is partly responsible for ineffective and poor performance. Clear demarcation of responsibilities and mandates of these agencies are desperately needed.

Operational performance and regulatory practice

The National Water Policy 2002 (Government of India, 2002) has accorded topmost water allocation priority to drinking water. The Tenth Five Year Plan (2002–2007) of the Government of India envisages 100 per cent coverage for drinking water supply and 75 per cent for sewerage and sanitation in Class I cities (>1 million). At present Jaipur City is far from meeting these goals.

At present 84 per cent of the population of Jaipur is supplied water by the PHED: 76 per cent through individual connections, 5 per cent through hand pumps and 3 per cent through public taps. The total number of PHED Jaipur employees is around 3000, which gives an average of about 11.5 employees per 1000 connections (SAPI, 2004).

2007 data provided by PHED Jaipur City state a production rate of 156 litres per capita per day. This number, calculated by dividing water production by population connected, includes losses. Hence the adjusted value would be less.

There can be wide variations within the city in quantity and quality of water supplied. The coverage figures do not indicate the actual functioning of the system. Breakdowns may deprive the consumers of water for several days. Coverage figures also do not reveal the regularity or limited duration of supply, the varying year-round performance (such as even more limited water availability in summer) and the number of hours of supply in the case of household connections (two to three hours per day), and for public stand posts, the distance, time taken to collect water, number of users of each stand post and so on. Most importantly, the coverage figures say nothing about the equity of distribution. It is likely that poorer areas are provided with less water whereas the influential rich obtain a more satisfactory service to complement their coping strategies. The poor households that are not connected end up paying higher costs in terms of collection time and health-related costs from drinking contaminated water. Wealthier households have better possibilities to cope with this situation. Installing roof tanks and (additional) supply from privately owned boreholes improve their situation.

Therefore official statistics of coverage and figures of quantity of water supplied tend to hide various realities regarding both the operations of the system and the experience of consumers. Alternative statistics suggest there are upwards of 20,000 boreholes in the city, the majority of them private and some delivering water quality well outside the prescribed limits.

There are no service standards set with respect to duration or quantity of water supply. A set of guidelines exists with specific time limits for operations such as redress of consumer complaints and application procedures for new connection. But even these procedures are not subject to any form of monitoring and there is no way to enforce compliance.

Estimates speak about at the best 60 per cent (in terms of area) of Jaipur being connected to the sewerage system. Not all the sewage is treated before being discharged into natural watercourses and 20 per cent of the wastewater generated in 2000 was reportedly not collected at all (SAFEGE, 2000).

The residential zones where there is no sewerage have on-site sanitation installations. Many dwellings, including almost half of the slums, have no sanitary facilities and so open-air excretion is common.

The price for urban water supply is constant throughout Rajasthan. The current tariff has not been revised since 1998. Generally tariffs are very low. Over a period of 30 years the tariff for minimum consumption increased by 300 per cent but from a very low base. Average monthly bills for 10 cubic metres (m^3) have been INR30 (US$3.2) and INR60 (US$6.4) for 20m^3 per month. However, with a recent amendment in September 2007, consumers in six selected cities (Jaipur included) will have to pay an 'infrastructure development (water) surcharge'. There is no surcharge if monthly water consumption is less than 15m^3. If water consumption is between 15–40m^3 the surcharge is 25 per cent and if water consumption is more than 40m^3 the surcharge is 35 per cent of the total amount of water billed.

The increasing block tariff is structured into three consumption blocks. 31 per cent of domestic consumers fall within the lowest block, the one that should be subsidized. Lowering the first block to the level of lifeline consumption (6m^3) would help to target subsidies more effectively. Industrial tariffs are substantially higher than domestic rates, but with only a marginal share of the revenue collected from industrial consumers, cross-subsidization becomes irrelevant. Charging industry more than the actual cost tends to drive them to self-provision. System performance has to improve significantly before it might possibly 're-attract' industrial customers and households that are now privately served.

Only 3 per cent of consumers pay flat rate tariffs. Since 1990 all new connections have been metered, such that 92 per cent of customers now have metered supply, but around 50 per cent of the meters do not work.

The connection charge of INR200 (US$21.3) does not seem to be a big hurdle. For selected economically weaker sections of the population in Jaipur, for example people living below the poverty line (BPL), this charge could be partially paid by the government in form of a direct subsidy. The process of identifying BPL households is very slow; the women in focus groups conducted for this study reported: 'They have been here, we filled in some forms and we have never seen them again.'

Sewerage tariffs are 20 per cent of the water tariff, where a household is connected to the PHED network. Otherwise the rate is INR1365 (US$145.2) as a one-off payment or in monthly rates.

The very low tariffs do not send the right signal, i.e. that water is scarce and must be treated as a valuable commodity. As there is no existing licensing practice to regulate abstraction, people can abstract any amount of water for free without any bar.

Tariffs are determined by the PHED. The initial proposal is put forward by the department to the RWSSMB. Upon approval by the Board, the tariff proposal is put forward for approval by the state cabinet, the final decision-making authority for tariff setting. This means 'tariff decisions are not based on financial data analysis and reasonable planning, but purely on political impera-tives i.e. making popular decisions to win the next elections'. Consequently tariffs and revenues from water charges are too low and 'the PHED is a bottom-less pit for government's subsidies', a clear indicator of the need for a move towards more independent economic regulation (quotations from fieldwork interview, June 2004).

An analysis of the most recently available financial information (2004–2005 financial statements and previous) suggests a negative return on fixed assets oscillating between 30 per cent and 50 per cent over the past ten years (including an unrealistically low allowance for depreciation), an operating ratio of over 200 per cent and a days receivable ratio usually higher than one year.

In the light of this financial performance, local and state governments necessarily provide funds not only for investment in new schemes but also for O&M through their annual budget. Monetary help in the form of loans is provided by institutions like the World Bank, Asian Development Bank and Japan Bank for International Cooperation (JBIC). Projects being undertaken with the support of JBIC include conditions for reforming the water sector in Rajasthan. Any sustainable change, other than technical upgrading, has still to be proven.

The Rajasthan Water Supply and Sewerage Corporation (RWSSC) has been involved in raising funds from financial institutions that are then handed over to PHED divisions. Originally RWSSC was formed in line with an agreement with the World Bank while negotiating for a water supply and sewerage project. RWSSC was supposed to exercise wide-ranging powers and receive assets, liabil-ities, obligations for service provision and staff from PHED. None of this has yet happened.

Service to the poor and a universal service obligation

The most recent data produced by the Rajasthan Urban Integrated Development Programme (RUIDP) in 2000 show that illegal unplanned poor settlements (so-called *katchi basties*) have settled on a large scale along the foot of the hills towards the north and the east of the city, with a few located in other parts. Any additional information, other than location of the slums, was not available. Visiting these areas, the researchers found out that there is no 'standard' slum area and that different categories concerning legal status, water, sanitation and infrastructure services can be defined.

The researchers focused their fieldwork with consumers in four areas, the first of which might be described as representing the 'developing poor', the second 'coping poor' and the third and fourth 'vulnerable non-poor'.

The Balmiki Nagar settlement with 5000 inhabitants is a regularized slum that has existed for 12 years. The inhabitants own their houses and do not need to pay rent. The average household size is 5–6 people. The family income ranges from INR1500 up to INR4000 per month (US\$159.6–425.5). Most men and women have employment in the solid waste collection business. They are employed by JMC but they now fear privatization and the likelihood of being employed by private contractors.

The water supply situation is generally satisfactory. The area is served with six public stand posts that deliver a 24-hour water supply, one PVC tank (volume 4m3), filled up twice per day in the morning and evening). An estimated 25 per cent of the households have their own piped connections. They are supplied 30 minutes each day and receive only 4–5 buckets of water at very low pressure, so they also have to use the public stand posts. The households with their own water connections reported having been on flat rate earlier, but since meters were installed their bill increased rapidly. They pay INR30– 50 (US\$3.2–5.3) per month.

Not all households have electricity connections. Some live without electricity, others shared connections. Illegal connections are not possible any more with new cables. The average monthly bill for electricity is between INR300 (US\$31.9) for shared connections and INR350 (US\$37.2) for households that have their own connection.

Average consumption is estimated to be three buckets per person per day (180 litres per household per day or 6m^3 per month). Mainly women and children are involved in the process of collecting the water and spend an average of 1.5–2 hours collecting water. Water is collected as per the need. Queuing time is approximately 10 minutes each turn. Water is stored in drums and cement tanks inside the house. Water quality seems to be satisfactory. Generally household treatment is not necessary. In terms of reliability, the women reported problems during recent years where there was no water at all for approximately one day each month during the summer. People are satisfied with the water service because it is free so they do not complain.

All the women were illiterate and not all of them could afford to send their children to school because they claim that school dress and learning materials are too expensive. Every two weeks they meet with the local school teacher and learn how to write their signature.

The sanitary situation is quite good as there are open drainage canals in the newly constructed streets and pit latrines or pour flush latrines in every household.

In Kunda Basti water is the most prevalent problem. The area is not connected to the PHED pipeline that is 1 kilometre away from the area. Until 2004 the water supply relied on hand pumps. An alternative source outside the area in a factory half a kilometre away was used to collect water for free. When the hand pumps became dry the PHED installed three 4m^3 tanks in the area.

Time for water collection was then reduced from up to 3 hours per day to 10 minutes for each turn. The PHED tanks are normally filled once per day but on a very irregular basis. Water is stored in buckets and drums in the houses. People have no complaints about water quality, they do not treat the water and do not report any water-related diseases. Water quantity is a big issue and the slum wants to have a stand post connection soon but PHED states that there are technical problems.

Sanitation is very poor in Kunda Basti. The area is not connected to the sewer system, so open drains are used. People do not even have latrines in their houses and have to defecate in the open field.

The unregularized area of Nirmaan Nagar is now 20–25 years old, and it comprises of about 800 households with an average size of 7–8 members. Women are mostly housewives and men have regular jobs with the government or private employers. 50 per cent of the women are literate and all the children go to school. Family incomes are quite good and range from INR3000 to INR15,000 (US$319.1–1595.7). Around 50 per cent of the households rent their homes and pay INR500–600 (US$53.2–63.8) in rent per month. All the houses have electricity connections and pay INR300–750 (US$31.9–79.8) per month for electricity. In recent years prices went up from INR400 (US$42.6) but the service did not improve; however, generally people are satisfied with the electricity service.

In contrast water supply was the major issue in the area, which was not connected to a PHED mainline and did not have even a public stand post supply. Hence a private supply system was installed. All of the households received water from a private tubewell, receiving water from the private supply for 5–10 minutes twice per day in the morning and evening. They paid INR150 (US$16) per month to the private supplier, but the service was not good. Within the last nine years prices have risen by 300 per cent. The water connection fee is INR2000 (US$212.8).

The area is not connected to the sewer system. Open drainage is also perceived as a problem. Most households have pit latrines. Only 5 households out of 120 still have to defecate in open areas.

In Lunka Puri Basti, a settlement of 15,000 people that has been in existence for around 25 years, family incomes vary from INR1500 to INR3000 (US$159.6–319.1). Women are mainly housewives and men are employed on an irregular basis as rickshaw drivers and construction workers. Most of the households have a shared or their own electricity connection. Monthly bills range from INR800 to INR1000 (US$85.1–106.4). Over recent years their bills increased by at least 300 per cent.

Around 40 per cent of the area, the sections at higher altitude, have piped connections. Their monthly bill is around INR30–40 (US$3.2–4.3). People reported problems with meter reading as 'meters do not work for most of the time'. The majority are served by two hand pumps and a public stand post from a PHED tubewell. The service is said to be quite reliable and the quality good. Average consumption is 2–3 buckets per head per day.

At a first glance it seems that this poor area is very well served by PHED, but not deliberately it appears. The tubewell in the centre of Lunka Puri was built to supply a water reservoir for surrounding better-off areas. The public stand post was only a side-effect.

Clear signs of increasing water scarcity and decreasing quality will make the situation, so far only caused by bad management, even worse. Connection procedures are unclear. The technical reasons stated by PHED for not connect-ing the areas are not plausible. The approach for developing the supply network could perhaps be better described as chaos management or 'fire fighting'.

In contrast, the electricity services are satisfactory in all survey areas. Connection rates are high, billing procedures clear and efficient. The Kunda Basti area was recently connected to the grid, which is a clear sign of improve-ments in the sector. The reduction of illegal connections is a sign of good management, the same as price increases that have to be paid for better services. Faced with the choice between water and electricity at the same costs INR200 (US$21.3) people in Kunda Basti would chose electricity, believing they would still be able to organize water somehow without paying. The reported prices from private water suppliers were much higher than the existing PHED tariff.

Alternative providers

Although water and sanitation services can be considered weak in Jaipur, services to the slums are, in context, effective. The alternative providers do not have a business serving the poor – their work is in providing boreholes to higher-income households (resulting in groundwater overexploitation) and providing tankered (including camel-powered cart) supply to the peripheral areas of the city, though not necessarily to poor peri-urban areas.

Consumer involvement and perceptions of low-income consumers

Within the existing framework, customers of PHED in Jaipur are not at all involved in any process of price setting. There is no mechanism for any planned consultation with consumers and no formal hearing procedure yet in place. Customers cannot express their needs and priorities to the decision-making parties other than through political votes. There is a complaints process, usually related solely to a failure in piped supplies but non-response to complaints is a grievance that is expressed by consumers.

Focus groups were held as part of the research to investigate the expressed needs of poor consumers to ascertain to what extent existing systems of monitoring and complaints registers delivered and could be enhanced through a regulatory framework.

In Balmiki Nagar, women complain about lower salaries, hard work and competition for getting jobs. The majority belong to scheduled castes and they work as sweepers cleaning sewer lines and in municipal solid waste collection. These people have difficulty even getting washing and cooking jobs in households.

The major everyday problem of these women does not seem to be water but finding employment and making money for their living. That is why they all fear any further increases in costs. Their experience of price rises in electricity bills frighten them. Their willingness to pay for improved water services is very limited at a maximum of INR50–100 (US$5.3–10.6), but preferably nothing as they can cope with the current situation.

In Kunda Basti, the consensus is that their willingness to pay for a household connection amounts to INR50 (US$5.3) per month. For shared connections or a stand post they do not want to pay anything. Having asked them about their preferences, they say that given that both water and electricity cost INR200 (US$21.3), they would rather pay the electricity bill as they think they could manage to organize an alternative water supply. People in Kunda Basti struggle to survive. They are used having to cope with very bad conditions and are not used to voicing their grievances.

In Nirmaan Nagar, the PHED also supplies water through hand pumps and tankers. However, out of six hand pumps only two work 'but not properly and were about to fall dry'. Water from hand pumps was not used as drinking water. The water tanker supply started in June 2005 (after complaining to their member of the Legislative Assembly). The tanker comes once a day on a more or less regular basis. Water consumption is 4–5 buckets of water per head, with water stored in drums, buckets and cement tanks. Water for non-drinking purposes can be stored up to three days. The women spend 1–2 hours per day collecting water. The water quality of the private supply and the tankered supply 'is good, treatment is necessary'. The women said that 'they are not happy to walk down the road to collect water from the tanker'. Their willingness to pay for an improved water supply (own connection) was INR150 (US$16) per month. In 2007 a PHED water supply was established in Nirmaan Nagar.

In Lunka Puri Basti, ten women took part in discussions. Lunka Puri's inhabitants really want their settlement to be improved with new roads and water connections. Their willingness to pay for a water connection is a maximum of INR50 (US$5.3) per month.

It was found that the water situation in the 'regularized' slum (government recognized) is best. A good, reputedly 24-hour stand post water supply (taken from a borehole to overhead tank main), proper roads and a functioning drainage system make for reasonable living conditions. Slum dwellers reported that the piped water supply is generally unreliable and insufficient; an additional source is always needed. A public stand post supply is stated as the minimum requirement. However, the researchers noted that there were above-ground pipe supplies to one of the slums, provided by the PHED, who had also undertaken a local campaign to enable households to connect to this supply.

People are used to getting water for free and would prefer to continue to do so. For improved water services the stated willingness to pay ranges around the affordable 3 per cent of the household incomes. The percentage of income spent on water services is generally below 1 per cent. This figure also shows that low-income groups pay twice as much in relative terms as high-income groups, a clear sign that subsidies are not targeted well.

Regulating water and sanitation for the poor

The public provider is delivering a barely adequate service, however limited outsiders might perceive that to be. For this service slums dwellers pay very little or nothing. There is a real concern that prices for water supply will rise. Unlike the majority of urban slum dwellers around the world, they do not have to pay exorbitant amounts to vendors. Government is subsidizing this service through general taxation in an effective, though inefficient, manner.

Economic regulation is desperately needed to address the inefficiency of the overall supply that is leading to dramatic falls in groundwater levels due to the 20,000 household boreholes sunk as a result of the failure of the public provider. Ultimately the changes that a reformed service provider could deliver will be beneficial and would need a driver such as independent regulation.

The central government, through the Jawaharlal Nehru National Urban Renewal Mission of the Ministry of Housing and Urban Poverty Alleviation, has suggested that the establishment of a state-level water regulator would become a requirement to enable future access to central government funding. During the course of this study this requirement was dropped with the, perhaps more politically acceptable but less effective, requirement for 'modern and transparent budgeting, accounting, financial management systems, designed and adopted for all urban service and governance functions' with 'local services and governance … conducted in a manner that is transparent and accountable to citizens' (JNNURM, undated).

Considering the potential for economic regulation of water, during the past decade the power sector in Rajasthan has been given an economic regulator. The Rajasthan Electricity Regulatory Commission (RERC) was established in January 2000 following tariff reforms and rationalization in November 1999. The Rajasthan State Electricity Board was subsequently restructured in July 2000 into five companies: one generation, one transmission and three distribution companies (discoms) in Jaipur, Jodhpur and Ajmer.

In 2001, the Rajasthan Electricity Regulatory Commission in turn instituted the Commission Advisory Committee with 21 appointed members representing the interests of commerce, industry, transport, agriculture, labour, consumers, NGOs and academic and research bodies in the energy sector. The Consumer

Unity and Trust Society, an NGO, was nominated to this committee to represent the interests of domestic and agricultural consumers. The Trust advocates consumers' concerns and at grassroots level tries to establish a network for consultation.

However, reform with regulation and transparency has yet to deliver improved performance. In the period from 2000 to 2004 the distribution losses of Jaipur Discom remained at the very high level of 40 per cent. This level of losses is totally unsustainable and RERC warns of financial collapse of the companies (RERC, 2004) if no substantial improvements can be achieved.

Similarly, the picture drawn from Jaipur's water utility portrays extreme inefficiencies, lack of customer involvement and representation, lack of effective pro-poor water policy and consequently the urgent need for reforms. In the midst of this there has been some good pro-poor work in the form of above-ground pipelines in some slums along with household sanitation from an NGO. The Government of India and the foreign lending institutions are exerting pressure on the State of Rajasthan to bring about change. The framework for reforming the water sector is set but at present there appears to be nobody willing to carry out the necessary steps. It seems that the restraining forces continue to overwhelm any drivers for change. The political parties and the government administration appear to be unwilling to give up control over pricing decisions and believe that they somehow benefit from the arrangements as they are at present.

Independent economic regulation without political interference on tariff decisions remains a distant goal. At least one can hope that consumers will learn how to use their power and voice and start pushing for improvements from below as the pressure from above is insufficient. The experience from the electricity sector shows that introduction of the regulatory process, potentially strengthened by the customers' voice due to enhanced consultation and engagement, has delivered the necessary price increases. However there is a real fear that this increase in energy prices would be replicated in water if 'cost-reflective' regulated tariffs became the target, again without any resulting improvement in services.

Today in India the state exerts too much control in too many areas. Being owner, policy-maker and manager of the water sector at the same time, the state is involved in too many tasks and is not able to concentrate on the essentials. An enabling state which allows others to do what they can do best would be for the benefit of the whole country. To bring about real change, Shourie (2004) proposes 'institutional revolution' is necessary rather than reform. Society has yet to agree with this prescription.

CASE STUDY 2: KAMPALA, UGANDA

Kevin Sansom

> *The company has eliminated middle men who constantly sold a jerry can of water at almost three or four times the normal rate, through making water more accessible with free connections, sensitisation of water usage and supply of water through protected springs or boreholes.* (NWSC, 2008)

The water sector and institutional framework

Uganda, East Africa, has a low proportion of its population living in urban areas. Although it is a low-income country, in recent years the government and its providers of infrastructure services have proactively pursued new public management approaches including corporatization and PPPs with an emphasis on improved accountability and transparency.

As part of the reform of the urban water sector in Uganda it was envisaged that a substantial PPP, some form of lease contract, would be introduced following the initial two successive water management contracts in Kampala. This would be accompanied by the creation of an independent regulator and an asset holding authority. Though these reforms have been delayed, perhaps due to changes in the international water market, the government is intent on progressing change within the sector, with the aim of supporting either public or private sector management.

In the urban water sector the National Water and Sewerage Corporation (NWSC) manages the 22 of the larger towns. Management of water services for the remaining smaller towns in Uganda is the responsibility of the town councils as part of the government's decentralization programme. The municipal councils receive support from the Directorate of Water Development (DWD), which is part of the Ministry of Water Lands and Environment (MoWLE). DWD coordinates the letting of management contracts by local municipal councils to local operators in 40 towns. The initial outcomes of these contracts are encouraging, but it is acknowledged that there is scope for improvements in investment planning and regulation of services.

The MoWLE in Uganda has wide discretionary powers for economic regulation under the Water Statute 1995, and these are subject to fairly flexible interpretation. DWD is responsible for technical standards. These agencies are to some extent limited by capacity.

The Ministry of Finance through its privatization unit has substantial informal powers on matters such as reform and tariff policy. Some level of economic regulation has evolved through performance contracts between the Government of Uganda and the NWSC. This is a form of 'regulation by

---

UGANDA KEY FACTS

•	Human Development Index rank	154 out of 177
•	GNI per capita at purcahsing power parity (2006)	US$1490
•	Country population	30 million
•	Urban population	13 per cent
•	Urban population growth rate 2005–2010	4.8 per cent
•	Urban water coverage	87 per cent
•	Water supply by household connection	7 per cent
•	Improved urban sanitation coverage	54 per cent
•	Research focus location	Kampala, Jinja
•	Research focus population	1.3 million
•	Service provider	National Water and Sewerage Corporation
•	Contract form	Publicly owned corporatized utility
•	Regulator	Performance review board
•	Exchange rate to US$ at fieldwork	UGX1870
•	Implied purchasing power parity conversion rate to US$	UGX326
•	Implied undervaluation ratio	5.74

---

contract' that is commonly used as the 'French model' of regulation, but in this case the contract is between government and a public utility. Performance is meant to be monitored by a quarterly committee comprising senior civil servants from the MoWLE and the Ministry of Finance as well as the Chair and Managing Director of NWSC, without any external involvement.

A multi-sector regulator was proposed for the water, power and possibly communications sectors. This would reduce the financial burden on the water sector and allow for the most effective allocation of scarce resources. However, the establishment of a regulator for the power sector was not followed by the setting-up or inclusion of water regulation.

Similarly, an asset holding authority had been envisaged to hold the water and wastewater assets of the large towns grouping on behalf of government. The holding authority was to have been 100 per cent government owned, set up as a limited liability company governed by a board of directors. DWD, acting on behalf of government, was to enter into a concession contract with the authority, which would be fully responsible for all infrastructure investment planning and execution. The asset holding authority would also have monitored the performance of the proposed private operator. The performance of the authority itself was to be monitored by the regulator. None of this has happened to date and with the ongoing excellent performance of NWSC it is unlikely to be needed in the near future.

The legal framework

Service providers

The MoWLE is the main ministry with responsibilities for water supply and sanitation provision in Uganda. Within the ministry these responsibilities lie with the DWD. To support these responsibilities the Water Statute 1995 (and the National Water and Sanitation Corporation Statute 1995) provides MoWLE and DWD with wide discretionary regulatory powers (economic and technical respectively). This situation supports the call for an independent regulator.

The NWSC is responsible for water supply and sanitation provision in the large towns (15 in number). The regulatory process operates via performance contracts (known as Internally Delegated Area Management Contracts), both between NWSC and the government and between NWSC and the actual utility or service provider, whether private or public.

In smaller towns (51) a number of private operators, overseen by town council-based local water authorities, provide the services – as established under the Local Government Act 1977 and the Water Statute 1995.

The activities of service providers are also governed by secondary legislation arising from the Water Statute 1995 and relating to standards, permits and procedures.

One perception of this situation is that an adequate regulatory framework is in place but its application is poor and the organizational set-up contains some duplication and contradictions; furthermore the political will to enforce compliance is not good.

To some extent these problems have been recognized by the Ugandan government in the revised Performance Contract between themselves and NWSC. They accept that amendment of the 1995 Water and NWSC Statutes, involving separation of the asset management, operations and regulation functions, may be necessary.

Service recipients

Service recipients are not clearly defined in the legislation. 'The urban water sector in Uganda is broadly defined to cover all towns with populations exceeding 5,000 people, together with all gazetted town councils' (MoWLE, 2003).

There is no explicit USO in Uganda, although there are various references to 100 per cent coverage:

- the 'government acknowledges its obligation to provide social services including water to the entire population' (MoWLE, 2003);
- the government has stated that 'it intends to ensure universal access to safe water supplies (100 per cent coverage) in urban areas by the year 2010' (MoWLE, 2003);
- the government has stated that their overarching objective under the National Water Policy is 'to extend the use of safe water supplies and appro-

priate sanitation services to 100 per cent of the urban population', but that this objective is not expected to be achieved until 2015 (MoWLE, 2003);

- MoWLE (2003) gives as one of its goals 'sustainable, adequate and safe water supply and sanitation facilities within easy reach of 80 per cent of the urban population by 2005 and 100 per cent by 2015';
- the Water Statute 1995, section 4(b) provides that one of the objectives of the legislation is 'to promote the provision of a clean, safe and sufficient supply of water for domestic purposes to all persons'; and
- the 1995 Constitution states 'The State shall endeavour to fulfil the fundamental rights of all Ugandans to social justice and economic development and shall, in particular , ensure that … all Ugandans enjoy … access … to clean and safe water'.

There are in the Constitution a number of other provisions that are relevant: '21.(1) All persons are equal before and under the law in all spheres of political, economic, social and cultural life and in every other respect and shall enjoy equal protection of the law' and '39. Every Ugandan has a right to a clean and healthy environment'.

As in most countries, many of those not provided with adequate water supply and sanitation are the poor living in informal settlements. These are regarded by authorities as illegal and are typically unplanned and unserviced.

Operational performance and regulatory practice

Compared with many utilities in Africa, NWSC is showing spectacular improvements in the commercial aspects of its business against a number of key indicators. Such improvements lead to greater revenue generation that provides more resources for investment in services to low-income and unserved consumers.

Managing Director William Muhairwe (2006) reports on the efficiency gains between 1998–2006: increase in operating profit from a loss of US$400,000 to a profit of US$4 million; unaccounted-for water reduced from 60 per cent to 27 per cent; staff productivity increased from 36 to 7 staff per 1000 connections; service coverage increased from 48 per cent to 70 per cent; and new connections increased from 3000 to 28,000 per annum.

The increase in service coverage has been driven by the phenomenal rise in the number of active pipe connections in urban Uganda from 43,000 in 2000 to 132,000 in 2006 (MWE, 2006).

The very recent increase in connection numbers explains the WHO and UNICEF 2006 figures of 7 per cent of households (19 per cent according to the Uganda Household Survey, 2000) with their own pipe connections, with just 6 per cent of the poorest 40 per cent of the urban population having their own connection.

The positive trend in NWSC's profitability is partly driven by debt write-offs by central government and supported by European Development Fund (EDF) and International Development Association (IDA) grants, reportedly counted as revenue. The return on fixed assets values show a similarly positive trend, achieving a positive value of 1 per cent in 2002–2003 but again this includes grants from various sources (NWSC data to researcher).

This has occurred due to NWSC improving the performance of its own staff, but also through engaging with the private sector. A three-year management contract for operational services in Kampala with Ondeo Services Uganda Ltd (following an earlier contract with Gauff) had been in operation for two years but was terminated in early 2004 when the revised contract terms were deemed to be too expensive. However, a key benefit has been the contract management experience gained by NWSC staff, which they have found useful in developing and managing internal area performance contracts with each of the area offices.

The contracts contain significant incentives for their staff and demonstrate the government's commitment to improving the commercial performance of the utility. Also relevant is the provision of generally reliable water services for which NWSC charge relatively high water tariffs in comparison with other utilities in the region and NWSC's emphasis on developing the capacity of their staff. Many of their staff are well educated, with significant numbers of staff having postgraduate qualifications.

In recent years an NWSC priority has been to increase the number of connections by extending water mains into peri-urban areas. There has been less emphasis on providing new connections in informal settlements.

NWSC, with assistance from GTZ (Deutsche Gesellschaft für Technische Zusammenarbeit, a federally owned international cooperation enterprise for sustainable development), reviewed their tariff structure in June 2003 as part of a 'rebalancing' exercise so that commercial customers are not unfairly overcharged and to ensure that revenues from domestic customers do not diminish over the years. NWSC, under the supervision of its board, has the authority to implement automatic annual inflation adjustments (ARD, 2005). The guiding principles for changes to the current tariff structure were: no overall tariff increase, no substantial revenue reduction, simplicity and 'pro-poor' with a reduction of cross-subsidies. It was agreed that cross-subsidies could not be eliminated totally and that the reduction would have to come as a gradual process.

The proposals were not adopted by NWSC whose current policy is to rebalance some of the price differential between commercial and domestic customers and to seek to subsidize connection costs. This could be done by having a flat domestic tariff and providing a lower tariff rate to registered customers with yard connections or water kiosks in low-income areas. This should encourage more on-selling of water to neighbours. The average tariff at present is UGX1100/m^3 (US$3.37), with a charge in 2004 of UGX400/m^3 (US$1.22) at standpipes, UGX693/m³ (US$2.14) residential and UGX1264/m³ (US$3.87) for more than 500m³. These are significantly high by world averages.

What is striking is the absence of any mention of government involvement as regulator in this planning although it is understood that all parties remain very aware of the social and political implications of their considerations.

The Ministry of Water and Environment in Uganda has wide discretionary powers for economic regulation, which are subject to fairly flexible interpretation. The DWD is responsible for technical standards. Other agencies have some specialized technical responsibilities such as the Ministry of Health and the National Environmental Management Authority. Each of these agencies is to some extent limited by capacity (MoWLE, 2003). The Ministry of Finance through its privatization unit has substantial if informal powers on matters such as reform and tariff policy.

The economic regulation system in force is not defined in detail; however, it includes the powers of the Minister and Director of Water Development under the Water Statute 1995. Economic regulation has evolved through performance contracts between the Government of Uganda and NWSC and between NWSC and town area offices or management.

Following the success of the first performance contract (2000 to 2003) between the Government of Uganda and the utility NWSC, a second performance contract was signed for the period 2004 to 2006. This document was developed by the Utilities Reform Unit in the Ministry of Finance in conjunction with NWSC. The parties responsible for administering the performance contract are the permanent secretary of MoWLE, the permanent secretary of the Ministry of Finance, the board chairman of NWSC and the managing director of NWSC. This sub-committee should meet every quarter to consider progress, but at the time of the fieldwork there had only been one meeting. This cannot be considered to be the most independent or proactive form of monitoring as a substitute for economic regulation. It has, however, delivered the required outcomes.

The stated purpose of the second performance contract is to: 'further increase efficiency by consolidating and enhancing the financial and commercial sustainability of the operations of NWSC and to prepare the Corporation for the transition towards a higher level private sector participation mode' (Utilities Reform Unit, 2003). This financial and commercial emphasis is reflected in the tables of performance against key indicators at the back of the performance agreement. These tables show the actual performance against each indicator during the first contract (2000–2003) and targets for 2004–2006. The reward structure for the NWSC top management team includes a performance incentive element of 25 per cent of basic salary. The board will decide on the appropriate bonus to be paid each year.

The second performance contract included some provisions for serving the poor such as introducing a new social connection policy along with a connection fund. It also modified the customer charter to cater for the poor, defining who the 'poor' are by measures such as volume consumption bench-marks or geographical area. There was also the requirement to develop a roll-out plan to study the needs of poor consumers and to propose a social mission programme and negotiate with the government on a possible subsidy to serve the poor.

There are no actual indicators or targets for serving the poor in the contract. There are, however, a number of provisions and targets for improving customer services. The reluctance to make commitments to serve the poor is exemplified by one clause that states: 'Investments imposed as a social mission should be implemented as separate units in order not to impose a financial burden on NWSC' (Utilities Reform Unit, 2003).

It is not surprising therefore that there is no evidence that the performance contracts have enhanced the prospects of serving the poor. Indeed the commer-cially based incentive payments for senior managers could inhibit progress in this area. However, the government and NWSC have declared that they want to place more emphasis on serving the poor – a more proactive regulatory approach is likely to be required if substantial programmes are to develop.

Opportunities for independent examination of targeted interventions are very limited because the review committee meets infrequently. An independent regulatory authority would enable more detailed assessment of targeted inter-ventions such as services to the poor.

Service to the poor and a universal service obligation

The key problems and coping strategies of the urban poor related to water service provision, as perceived by the urban poor, include: low service levels, long average distance to safe water (around 0.5 kilometres when more than 0.1 kilometres means a higher health risk), high cost of water from stand posts or kiosks (five times more than houses with their own tap), and high average time to collect water with the challenge that alternative sources may be contaminated (focus group findings).

However, the range of water sources made possible by Kampala's 'seven hills', particularly the spring sources, means that the 'very poor' and 'destitute' can access the water they need, albeit at a distance and with potentially poor quality. A cleaner and more accessible piped source that requires a cash contri-bution might be desired by the 'coping' and 'developing poor' but not necessarily by the poorest. In this context, while there is no definitive USO for urban water services in Uganda, it is worthwhile examining both the ministry's water sector targets and the service level assumptions made for future invest-ment calculations.

The target that most resembles a USO is: 'the percentage of people within 0.2 kilometres of an improved source' (MoWLE, 2003). The problem with such an indicator is that people may be within this distance of an improved water source but may still not use the source for a variety of reasons such as cost or functionality. Also, the 'improved sources' referred to by the indicator include non-utility sources such as protected springs. None of the present indicators relate specifically to serving the poor, but the new 2004–2006 performance contract with NWSC includes some pro-poor provisions: the introduction of a new social connection policy, a new connection fund, new measures for social inclusion, and new proposals for a government subsidy programme. Indicators or targets have yet to be set.

The sector goal as defined in the MoWLE's *Urban Water and Sanitation Strategy Report* (MoWLE, 2003) is: 'sustainable, adequate and safe water supply and sanitation facilities within easy reach of 80 per cent of the urban population by 2005 and 100 per cent by 2015'.

While this may sound like a USO, terms like 'adequate', 'safe' and 'within easy reach' are too vague for this to be an appropriate USO. The water service-level assumptions for the future investment requirements in the same MoWLE report are: 'a basic service to provide piped water to 80 per cent of the urban population with the remaining 20 per cent being served by point sources (40 per cent private connections and 40 per cent standposts)' (MoWLE, 2003).

It is useful that the precise service levels are stated in this assumption statement, which could correlate with a potential USO. However, the reliance on stand posts or water kiosks is surprising when, for example, many are disconnected in Kampala, essentially because the water vendors cannot earn sufficient income because of the easy availability of alternative sources. When the government considers agreeing a USO, it will need to assess current service levels in specific areas and how to overcome the common barriers to serving informal settlements. Investment plans to achieve an agreed USO should also be based on assessments of consumer demand.

The vast majority of households in informal settlements who do not have access to the piped network have been paying high unit costs for public stand posts and vended water. The subsidies inherent in the tariff mechanisms do not reach users who are not direct NWSC customers. Hence the NWSC water tariff subsidies do not really benefit the residents of informal settlements.

The prices paid by stand post or water kiosk customers are often ten times the amount paid by consumers with private connections for a given volume. By way of coping, water quantities consumed by kiosk users are much lower than in the case of consumers with direct access to piped services. The current commercial/industrial tariffs chargeable to vendors have a rising block tariff structure with the first $500m^3$ being subsidized and customers paying more for water when they consume more than $500m^3$ per month. This disadvantages the poor in cases where residents in low-income areas sell water to their neighbours and exceed the $500m^3$ per month limit and incur the higher rate.

Rather than seeking to subsidize the consumption of water, it would be better to subsidize access to the piped network by reducing connection costs and to subsidize less convenient service options. This could be done by having a flat domestic tariff and providing a lower tariff rate to registered customers with yard connections or water kiosks in low-income areas. This should encourage more on-selling of water to neighbours.

Connection charges have been lowered recently by NWSC to encourage more connections but still all the costs need to be considered. A complementary study (Franceys, 2005a) found that to gain a working connection householders had to fund costs before approval of application, including on-site surveying expenses and the official connection fee with possible 'extra' payments before approval, then road-cutting costs, materials costs, transport costs (materials and inspectors and pipe workers), trenching and plumbing costs and charges for a meter, in addition to the opportunity cost of the householder in managing this process. Overall it was found that the average cost for a new water connection was UGX626,400 (US$1920), equivalent to 150.6 months of average billing for a household, though this figure is distorted by the long pipe lengths required for some new low density peri-urban middle-income connections.

In the light of this evidence and other experience, NWSC has dramatically changed its policy, now providing 'free connections' (excluding the cost of the meter) for those within 50 metres of service pipelines to new applicants. However the question remains as to whether this can really be deemed to be pro-poor because the poor usually, necessarily, live much further from the water mains.

NWSC (2008) now claims that it has 'eliminated the middle men who constantly sold a jerry can of water at almost three or four times the normal rate, through making water more accessible with free connections, sensitisation of water usage and supply of water through protected springs or boreholes, account-ing for almost 100–150 litres of clean water usage per person in Kampala'.

Alternative service providers

Before the recent upsurge in household connections, the alternative providers had a substantial share of the water market. It is not yet clear to what extent this market has actually been eliminated. In Kampala the most commonly used alter-native modes of water supply include water kiosks, water carriers and springs (unusually common in this urban area due to the topography of Kampala, a city 'built on seven hills').

With regard to the regulation of the use of springs, a water quality study in Kampala found that only 46 per cent of samples complied with standards, the remainder were contaminated with *E. Coli* (Government of Uganda, 2004). While it may be tempting to close the contaminated springs, many poor people in urban areas often use a combination of sources, such as spring water for cleaning and kiosk water for drinking. If alternative supplies to springs are very expensive or not available nearby, closures would not be acceptable. Public health campaigns could, however, be organized to raise awareness about the use of water from contaminated springs and the need to find other sources for drinking purposes.

The first step in effective support and regulation of alternative service providers is through some form of government recognition of the legitimacy of their activities. Water quality is a valid aspect for regulation, either in terms of regulating groundwater extraction, or water quality checks at water collection points, although enforcement of non-use of sources where contamination is found can be very difficult if good alternative supplies are not available.

Water vendors often charge high water prices, so it is tempting to try and regulate their prices. However, it would be impractical for a regulator to study and take into account all the varying costs of a wide range of water vendors in a city and then regulate them on a fair basis. A more promising option is for a utility/regulator to publicize the price of water that the vendors pay at the location where they collect their water, so that their customers know the vendors' price mark up.

The best long-term solution to high water vendor prices is to encourage competition. The utility can either compete with the vendors themselves by improving services to those areas, or encouraging other alternative service providers to operate. The utility has a clear comparative advantage because of the economies of scale associated with having large piped networks. Encouraging fair competition, such as ensuring that existing and potential alternative service providers are not unfairly excluded from the market is an important role for those responsible for regulation.

Regulators and utilities should have 'serving the poor' as part of their remit. But it is not feasible to compel private vendors to provide good services to the poor. Vendors often provide services to the poor because there is a gap in the market that they exploit.

Consumer involvement and perceptions of low-income consumers

NWSC have implemented a number of measures to improve services for customers in recent years, including reducing the average time to deal with complaints, using Geographical Information Systems-based customer records and introducing and publicizing a customer charter. In terms of initiatives to capture the voice of the poor, NWSC has appointed a community development officer in its commercial and customer services department. There are currently no other staff or committees for capturing the voice of the poor.

Some of the results of focus group discussions related to water services, conducted in a number of areas in Kampala with direct and indirect customers, are captured below. The communities questioned can be characterized as 'coping poor' and 'developing poor'. Note that the problem ranking varies significantly between direct and indirect customers. Direct (connected) customers saw the main issues as the cost of connection (including the challenge of being on the 'wrong side' of the road – where 'road-cutting charges' to access the water main on the other side of the road add very significantly to the cost of connection), the cost of reconnection (having failed to pay bills for a period) and the cost of the water itself. Irregular supplies, low pressure and the billing system were also ranked high. For indirect customers, the declared issues were the high cost of water (significantly higher than for direct customers), the perception that 'water causes typhoid', the high cost of connections (keeping them as indirect customers) and the irregular supply.

Where are the poor people located?
'Our whole zone is comprised of poor people. Our expenditure is high but with low incomes leading to poverty. We suffer a full brunt of social problems in this community' (Women in a focus group in Lufula zone LCI, Bwaise II Parish Kampala).

'The poor normally prefer living in wetlands for example Kasanvu in Wabigalo. This is a wetland in which plots of land are cheap as UGX30,000 [US$92] for a twentieth of an acre. People have put up housing units in these plots and the area is very crowded that one wonders how life goes on' (consumer, Wabigalo Makindye).

What are the current issues/problems of poor consumers in the selected informal settlement?
'Sometimes big boys or men harass girls or ask for sexual favours and in return making sure they filled their jerry cans for them' (Kasubi focus group about the Kiwunya well).

'The cost of water is so high and varies from vendor to vendor but usually ranges between UGX25–33 [US$0.08–0.010] [per container] which limits the amount of water the poor can purchase' (Wabigalo focus group discussion).

'Meter readers connive with some customers and we do not know how but they end up paying low prices to them. Consequently they charge very low prices to the customers at our expense hence we lose customers' (men in a focus group discussion, Nakulabye Rubaga Parish).

What are the barriers and constraints to improving water services to the poor?
'The main water pipe is far from reach. It is across the road yet KCC is hesitant to allow digging up the road when one wants to access water (be connected)' (women in a focus group discussion, Bwaise II Parish).

'Most of these people in this area are tenants and they find it hard to install water in the premises. There is a case where Jane S's landlord refused her to have water in the premises of Mr Kaye S' (women in a focus group in Nakulabye, Rubaga division).

How could utilities support local small-scale providers?
One suggestion was the introduction of prepaid water services: 'They can give us cards. You pay for the water amount, which is equivalent to the money you have. Just like air time cards when your air credit is over, you pay again. This will minimize corruption in the water sector, promote fairness and ease' (men in a

focus group discussion, Wabigalo Parish).

What are the common coping mechanisms?

'It is easier to store water in tanks such that when it is scarce, then people can buy and I make profit to be able to afford the NWSC bill' (vendor in Bwaise II).

'At her home one woman said that they use a set of plates for lunch then she keeps them unwashed and uses another set at supper and then washes the whole lot thereby saving water' (water consumer, Wabigalo Parish).

Regulating water and sanitation for the poor

NWSC, the national water utility, has achieved significant improvements in their commercial performance but there had been only limited initiatives to serve the poor at the time of the study fieldwork. This is probably due to a perception that a big commitment to serve the poor could threaten achieving the commercial targets and staff incentive payments that are specified in the performance contracts. If the government is to see substantially improved services to the poor, future reforms will need to set out targets clearly, with funding and incentive payments for improving services in specified low-income areas.

Recent conversations with NWSC senior staff indicate that they well understand and have recognized and responded to the challenge to serve the unserved – at some level recognizing that they had to be able to deliver a viable utility before they could effectively reach out to the unserved.

Meanwhile the proposed multiplicity of entities, regulators and asset holding authorities and private operators has not, to date, been realized. Similarly NWSC's attempts to float itself on the stock market have not been successful. What is most impressive is NWSC's progress in developing as a fully functioning, government-owned utility with internal management contracts providing the incentive for increasing service performance.

Some level of regulation by performance contract in the Ugandan urban water sector has shown that the regulatory functions such as performance monitoring of the utility's commercial activities and promotion of operating efficiency can be done by this approach, if only partially, because they relate to business activities where performance can be confirmed by financial audits.

To set tariffs and assess value for money in a thorough manner that secures effective water services for the poor an independent regulatory authority(s) is required to develop a sound regulatory process based on comprehensive performance monitoring.

Potential priorities for a new independent water regulator, or a revamped performance monitoring committee, in Uganda would include agreeing a USO based on differentiated service levels, a performance monitoring system that captures service levels, coping strategies and consumer preferences in specified low-income areas, establishing a consumer consultative committee, and, as ever, critical to the regulatory task, ensuring agreed targets are financeable.

5

Regulating Public Providers
for the Poor

The second two case studies investigate two national economic regulators who, at the time of the fieldwork, had been established in the expectation of international private involvement in at least the capital city. However, the regulators were in fact trying to regulate weak public providers and also a number of secondary towns with various organizational arrangements.

CASE STUDY 3: LUSAKA, ZAMBIA

Sam Kayaga

> *Regulatory activities should be extended to independent alternative service providers, who currently serve over 50 per cent of the peri-urban areas in Lusaka.* (Zambia Case Study Report)

The water sector and institutional framework

Zambia is one of the most urbanized countries in sub-Saharan Africa. High rural–urban migration in the period from 1980 to the early 1990s culminated in about 40 per cent of the population living in urban areas. Coupled with dwindling income levels, this led to a proliferation of informal, unplanned settlements where it is estimated that 60 per cent of the urban population live.

In 1993, the Government of Zambia instituted water and sanitation sector reform with the objective of separating the roles and functions of policy-making, service provision and regulation in order to provide cost-effective, equitable and sustainable water supply and sanitation services. This reform process culminated in the establishment of the independent economic regulator, the National Water Supply and Sanitation Council (NWASCO), assisted by enactment of the Water Supply and Sanitation Act No. 28 of 1997. The NWASCO Board was appointed thereafter, and management structures were put in place in time for the regulator to become operational in the year 2000. The Act clearly spelled out the roles, functions and institutional set-up of the regulator, the obligations of local authorities and the rights and powers of the service provider. However, the rights of the consumer were not mentioned in the Act. By 2006 NWASCO had 14 staff to serve the country, funded by a 2 per cent levy on service provider's turnover (increased from an initial 1 per cent).

Based on this legal framework the regulatory administration, rules and structures were established. The regulator has issued guidelines for the benefit of service providers on licensing, minimum standard levels, business planning, financial projections, investment planning, tariff development, corporate governance, report writing, services to the urban poor, human resource management strategy and water quality monitoring.

Service providers, public or private, are granted ten-year licences by the regulator, following agreements on required minimum service levels to be achieved in a specified timeframe. By the end of 2003, 21 service providers had been granted ten-year licences, while 26 providers had been given one-year long provisional licences, pending the processing of baseline data. The service providers are required to provide data regularly on specified service indicators from which the regulator compiles quarterly reports to the national parliament,

ZAMBIA KEY FACTS	
• Human Development Index rank	165 out of 177
• Population living < US$2 per day	87.2 per cent
• GNI per capita at purchasing power parity (2006)	US$1000
• Country population	12 million
• Urban population	35 per cent
• Urban population growth rate 2005–2010	2.1 per cent
• Urban water coverage	90 per cent
• Water supply by household connection	41 per cent
• Improved urban sanitation coverage	59 per cent
• Research focus location	Lusaka
• Research focus population	1.1 million
• Service provider	Lusaka Water and Sewerage Company
• Contract form	Publicly owned corporatized utility
• Regulator	National Water Supply and Sanitation Council
• Regulatory start date	2000
• Exchange rate to US$ at fieldwork	ZMK4650
• Implied purchasing power parity conversion rate to US$	ZMK3082
• Implied undervaluation ratio	1.51

as well as annual Urban Water Supply and Sanitation Sector Reports. These reports are also used to benchmark performance across utilities. The regulator makes inspections to check the authenticity of the provided data. The service providers pay one-off application fees at the time of registration/renewal and monthly licence fees, at rates prescribed in the Act. The shortfall of the regulator's budget is filled by allocations made by the parliament.

The Lusaka Water and Sewerage Company (LWSC), wholly owned by Lusaka City Council (LCC), is the formal service provider in the capital, with an estimated service coverage of 34 per cent. It offers a range of service options, differentiated in tariff structure, which include individual house connections, yard connections, communal standpipes, bulk water for household tanks and household sewerage connections.

Regulation, however valuable, faces an additional challenge in regulating public providers. Recent reports suggest that LWSC has not produced a business plan for four or five years and the regulator will not approve tariff increases until LWSC improves its performance on unaccounted-for water and other indicators.

The legal framework

The urban water and sanitation sector is grounded in the following major legal instruments.

Local Government Act No. 22 of 1991 gives local authorities the responsibility and an obligation to provide water and sanitation services to all areas within the local authority. They are also empowered to make by-laws and set standards and guidelines for provision of services.

The National Water Policy of November 1994 is oriented to providing adequate, safe and cost-effective water supply and sanitation services with due regard to environmental protection. The policy recognizes peri-urban areas as legal settlements, 'to be treated in the same manner as urban areas with regard to provision of water supply and sanitation facilities'.

The Water Supply and Sanitation Act No. 28 of 1997 specifies how local authorities may provide urban water and sanitation services, and establishes NWASCO as the regulator for the urban water and sanitation sector. Local authorities may provide services through their departments, or through commercial utilities licensed and regulated by NWASCO.

The Town and Country Planning Act (Cap. 283) regulates physical planning and development throughout the country. Local authorities are delegated to act as planning authorities and to enforce planning control in their areas of jurisdiction. The Housing (Statutory and Improvement Areas) Act provides for regularization of the unplanned settlements that are not covered by the Town and Country Planning Act.

Other legal documents of importance to water and sanitation provision to peri-urban areas are the Water Act (Cap. 312) that controls the development and management of water resources in the country; the Environmental Protection and Pollution Control Act of 1990, which deals with environmental protection and pollution control; the Public Health Act (Cap. 295) and the National Health Services Act of 1995, which deal with the regulation and management of public health in the country.

Service providers

Under the Water Supply and Sanitation Act (WSSA) No. 28, 1997 a 'Service Provider' means any person who provides water supply or sanitation services. Responsibility for water supply and sanitation provision rests, through the Ministry of Local Government and Housing, with local authorities: 'Notwithstanding any other law to the contrary and subject to the other provisions of this Act, a local authority shall provide water supply and sanitation services to the area falling under its jurisdiction, except in any area where a person provides such services solely for that person's own benefit or a utility or a service provider is providing such services' (10(1) s.10, Part III of the Act).

Part III of the Act (s.9) provides for the establishment of a utility: 'A local authority may resolve to establish a water supply and sanitation utility as a company under the Companies Act (1994) as follows:- (a) as a public or private company; (b) as a joint venture with an individual or with any private or public company; (c) as a joint venture with another local authority or several other local authorities.' The requirements of the Companies Act 1994 and Water Supply and Sanitation Act 1997 are apparently such as to preclude many small-scale service providers from gaining licences to operate. They currently operate informally, which means they have no legal status and are not regulated, having no formal statutory duties or any protected rights.

Water supply and sanitation provision and therefore all service providers, including commercial utilities, are regulated by NWASCO, established under section 3 of the 1997 Act. The legal obligations of a utility are set out in 'a) Service Level Agreement (between the utility and the regulator), to which the mandatory Guidelines on Required Minimum Service Level 2000 apply and b) Service Contract (between the utility and a customer)'.

There is no explicit USO in the legislation, or in the operating guidelines, agreements or contracts, but it is considered that with some modification the required minimum service levels could in effect constitute a USO. This is supported by the National Water Policy (1994), which in section 2.6 states: 'tariffs must be based on principles of fairness and equity which entail: (among other things) providing a minimum level of service to persons who are unable to afford the full costs'.

In the event of non-compliance with legal obligations, the regulator can serve an enforcement notice, impose financial penalties, suspend the operating licence and ultimately cancel a licence.

The 1997 Act not only imposes duties on, but also provides powers (Part VII) to, a utility or service provider (i.e. in relation to access to, or acquisition of, land for water supply or sanitation provision purposes, reduced service levels in the event of drought or other disasters, disconnection and so on). In the case of disconnections this is only allowed where someone has not paid the bill for the services provided or where someone has damaged/interfered with the installations belonging to the service provider.

Service recipients

Although the Zambia Constitution (Art. 112, 1996) requires that the state shall endeavour to provide clean and safe water, neither service recipients nor their entitlements and rights are clearly defined in the legislation (Act 27, 1997). In the absence of a formal USO this is important. The National Water Policy 1994, issued by the Ministry of Energy and Water Development, does state that 'The overall national goal shall be: universal access to safe, adequate and reliable Water Supply and Sanitation Services' (section 2.4) but this applies only to the rural population. With regard to the urban population, while referring to the problem of the 'proliferation of illegal settlements' it only goes on to state: 'However, peri-urban areas considered to be legal settlements by Government shall be treated in the same manner as urban areas with regard to the provision of water supply and sanitation facilities' (section 2.5).

The Act 28, 1997 requires providers to ensure efficient, affordable and sustainable water supply and sanitation services within service areas. These requirements are clarified to some degree by the regulator in their *Guidelines on*

Required Minimum Service Levels (NWASCO, 2000). The service provider is tied, under its licence to operate, to achieve minimum standards. However, achievement is a phased process with the Guidelines specifying working towards 75–90 per cent coverage in the licensed service area.

In practice individual customers sign a contract with the service provider and this defines the rights and obligations of both parties. This service contract (between utility and a service recipient) sets out the duties, powers and entitlements of the two parties. The primary duty of the consumer is to pay the appropriate fees for the services provided.

The rights of an individual are protected via the regulator by checking that a utility meets its licence obligations and by water watch groups, where they have been set up. A water watch group is comprised:

> *of volunteers from the community whose main objective is to represent consumer interests in the sector and provide information to consumers on service delivery. They have delegated powers from NWASCO to follow up outstanding consumer complaints by bringing them to the attention of the service providers and ensuring they are resolved. Should the Water Watch Group's intervention fail, NWASCO is then called upon to take it up with the utility. At this stage, the utility risks being penalized and the matter publicized by the regulator.* (NWASCO, 2006)

Operational performance and regulatory practice

LWSC is a private liability company wholly owned by LCC. However, according to an interviewed official of LCC, LWSC was created out of political pressure from the central government and the local authority has limited authority over its strategic and tactical direction, although several members of LCC sit on the utility's board. As an example, loans to LWSC are secured and guaranteed by the central government, and tariffs are approved without LCC's input. LCC can only protect the residents through enactment and enforcement of the by-laws. According to NWASCO's 2003 records, LWSC employs 482 permanent staff and produces an average of 76.2 million cubic metres of treated water in a year, which it supplies to 34,514 water supply connections. With a target population of 1,120,000 people in Lusaka, LWSC's overall service coverage is estimated at 34 per cent.

There are two major hindrances to extension of distribution mains by LWSC: insufficient water supply in the system and inadequate funds for carrying out the extensions. However, LWSC continues to fund establishment of new public tap stands in the peri-urban areas. To reduce capital costs associated with extension of services, LWSC runs small diameter pipes to service public tap stands. Furthermore, unlike individual household yard tap connections that incur a deposit of ZMK20,000 (US$6.50), public tap stands do not attract a deposit.

The disconnection/reconnection procedures for public tap stands are subject to different regulations than those for a private household connection. For public tap stands, assistant community development officers of the LWSC Peri-Urban Unit are fully involved in the process. If it is noticed that there is inadequate revenue from a particular communal tap, the community development officers discuss the situation with the tap attendant, community leaders and/or communities, if need be. If the trend is not reversed, the tap is disconnected. The assistant community development officers then hold community sensitization meetings to explain the importance of clean water, reasons for cost recovery and the consequences of the disconnection. Once there is reassurance that payment will be made, the supply is reconnected for free.

LWSC is overstretched by the expansion of the peri-urban areas to the extent that service coverage at the time of the fieldwork was estimated to be 34 per cent of the 1.12 million people resident in Lusaka. In order to bridge the service gap, international NGOs such as CARE, Irish Aid and JICA (Japanese International Corporation Agency) have set up alternative water supply systems in peri-urban areas.

LWSC operates a rising block tariff structure, which may be difficult to operationalize given that the metering coverage was estimated at 32 per cent in 2003. The situation is worse in the peri-urban areas where it is estimated that less than 1 per cent of the connections have functional and well-serviced meters. It is therefore not surprising that LWSC, with an unaccounted-for water rate of 58 per cent in 2003, was ranked by NWASCO as the second worst utility in Zambia in that respect. However, LWSC is not keen on improving metered coverage because of the high level of vandalism of meters and other fittings in peri-urban areas and the high administrative costs in terms of reading/maintaining meters, writing and distributing bills.

Billing in peri-urban areas is therefore exclusively based on flat rate charges. Individual yard taps pay ZMK1400 (US$0.45) per month, while households drawing water from public tap stands pay ZMK3000 (US$0.97) per month for an estimated 200 litres per day per household. For those households who are able to pay, the monthly water bill is usually paid as a lump sum in advance. Otherwise, poorer households are allowed to pay in weekly instalments of ZMK750 (US$0.24).

The regulator, NWASCO, licenses all the commercial operators, the majority for ten years with several of the smaller operators on temporary one-year licences. To date, political interference in tariff setting, a key value of economic regulation, has been kept to a minimum, and NWASCO has so far displayed a high degree of independence. A good indicator is when NWASCO was able to raise the tariffs by about 100 per cent during the year of general elections.

Appointment of Council members, who are the executive arm of NWASCO, together with the technical and financial sub-committees, has been institutionalized. The first three-year term of office expired at the end 2002. New Council members were nominated and appointed at the beginning of 2003.

The management structure has been in place since the end of 2000, and positions duly filled with technical staff. However, a representative of the international donor community interviewed pointed to the inadequacy of NWASCO in terms of human and social science skills.

Since its institution, NWASCO has come up with key guidelines on service provision for the benefit of the utilities and other service providers. In addition, NWASCO has held training workshops for the key staff of utilities and other service providers on the application of these guidelines. Further support has been provided in technical and human resources for a few service providers with critical deficiencies.

One of the key guidelines developed is the reporting format expected of the service providers. Initially, a simple and inexpensive information system was developed and introduced to the service providers. This system has since required improvement and increased sophistication to respond to the growing complexity of required information.

The regulator has been prepared to impose penalties for poor performance, as in the case where the operating licence for Kafue District Council was suspended and LWSC was appointed as statutory manager to provide services in the interim period. The suspension was only lifted after service provision stabilized under LWSC and the officials of Kafue District Council committed themselves to improvement in service provision.

Service to the poor and a universal service obligation

Over 60 per cent of Lusaka's population live in 33 peri-urban areas around the city. With a population of over 100,000 Kanyama is one of four peri-urban areas working under a water trust system. CARE International supplied all necessary infrastructure and empowered the community to manage all aspects of service delivery. As residents previously paid nothing to obtain their water, a major objective of the project was sustainability and cost recovery. Education and empowerment exercises followed and ultimately mobilized the community into constructing the system. The management team was appointed through a competitive and transparent process. Legal ownership was transferred to LCC, though the community retains symbolic ownership.

The water is delivered through 101 water vendors who staff the metered water points at times throughout the day. ZMK100 (US$0.03) is charged per three 20-litre containers. New household connections are a recent addition to the network and are already meeting operational costs. The project also installed water-flushed toilets in central areas that were passed over to LCC for management (interview with Cathyrn Mwanamwambwa, CARE International, July 2004).

It is in this context that a national policy and action plan for service delivery to peri-urban areas was developed. In response, LWSC developed a new policy that culminated in a new Peri-Urban Unit with the objective of improving efficiency and effectiveness of services to peri-urban areas. It is a section wholly responsible for provision to an estimated 540,000 people in 78,000 households living in the peri-urban areas served by LWSC.

As part of the sector reforms, the Peri-Urban Water and Sanitation Strategy document specified the overriding goal as achieving improvement of sustainable and effective service provision to all areas of LCC. For this purpose, the peri-urban areas, which form a large portion of the city, were identified by a number of criteria, namely those areas:

- where infrastructure had been planned as low-cost or which were informal;
- that were informal but have been upgraded after their legalization;
- that do not have essential services;
- where infrastructure fails to meet urban standards;
- where poverty is more prominent, though the areas are not inhabited exclusively by the poor.

Performance of various service providers is monitored against agreed service levels. Incentives for good performance include positive considerations during tariff reviews and allocation of investment funds from the special Devolution Trust Fund, an independently managed fund dedicated for enhancement of services to the urban poor. The government has established the Devolution Trust Fund for the purpose of redressing the imbalances in service levels in the peri-urban areas of the country. This fund was initially managed fully by the regulator, but changes are now being made to make it an independent entity with a high input from the regulator.

Another incentive is the good corporate image portrayed by good benchmarks in the annual Urban Water Supply and Sanitation Sector Reports. Penalties for poor performance range from financial fees and suspension of a service provider, to cancellation of a licence.

Service provision to the urban poor in Zambia is highlighted at policy level, as evidenced by the formulation of the National Peri-Urban Water and Sanitation Strategy, and the appointment of senior officials, at deputy director level, to oversee its implementation. This policy was replicated at corporate level in LWSC, with the Peri-Urban Unit, with the right balance of human resources, set up in the mid-1990s and that has since been instrumental in service provision in the peri-urban areas of Lusaka. However, this research has found that with increases in population of the peri-urban areas, the service provider has not matched the increased demand with the required volume of resources. As a result, the service levels in the peri-urban areas have been declining. This information was provided by key informants and was corroborated through focus group discussions held with consumers in the peri-urban areas.

Alternative service providers

Even though LWSC does not have the capacity to serve the majority of the city's residents there is hardly any vending of water in small containers, a common occurrence in low-income areas of cities in many low-income countries. The lack of small-scale service providers in Lusaka could be explained by a high number of agencies that have been involved in water service provision to peri-urban areas. The institutional framework for service provision has been complicated by the scope and number of agencies involved.

In order to bridge the service gap, international NGOs such as CARE, Irish Aid and JICA have set up alternative water supply systems that use groundwater to meet the required demand. Many of these water systems are managed by local CBOs, either independently or under a franchise of LWSC, the legally recognized service provider in the whole of the Lusaka City area.

However, LWSC does not have the capacity to monitor and ensure that services provided by these alternative providers conform to the required minimum service levels as prescribed in the operator's licence. Neither has NWASCO carried out any inspections to ascertain the level of service received by residents being served by these alternative service providers, resulting in exclusion of those affected from the benefit of the regulatory regime.

Alternative service provision in Lusaka can be through piped water supply provided by the utility but managed in partnership with the community and/or a private concessionaire and LWSC; a borehole initially provided by international aid, now managed in partnership with the community and/or a concessionaire; a combination of these two approaches with the same management structure; or a borehole initially provided by international aid with a completely separate water trust formed to manage the system.

Consumer involvement and perceptions of low-income consumers

To provide a channel for the customer's voice into the regulatory process, a water watch group (WWG) was formed in Lusaka and has been operational since 2002. Two other WWGs have since been set up in other cities. Membership is voluntary but openly competitive and usually advertised in the national press. The members, who are selected on the basis that they are knowledgeable and motivated by the interest of working in the water sector, are required to serve a two-year term. The WWGs sensitize consumers on their rights and solicit their complaints and views, acting as intermediaries with the service provider. The WWG is facilitated by the regulator to carry out sensitization rallies in peri-urban areas.

Lusaka Water Watch Group (LWWG) has a temporary office at NWASCO headquarters where members meet every two weeks and liaise solely with the public relations officer of NWASCO. In addition to basic training to help them carry out their functions, NWASCO provides LWWG members with stationery, transport and other logistical support. LWWG also meets with a representative of LWSC Customer Services to discuss the complaints they have received. A member of LWWG and the LWSC Director of Marketing and Customer Services who were interviewed alluded to the good working relations between the utility and the consumer representatives.

Member retention was also identified as another challenge facing the sustainability of the watch groups, given that members do not receive an allowance for their contribution. The level of 'limited expenses' was suggested as a reason that members would be more likely to 'move on' if another more beneficial opportunity were to arise. At the time of this study, three members had had to resign with only four remaining out of the seven volunteers. They had initially joined for a term of two to three years, being interested in serving the community.

Customer complaints are collected in LWSC collection boxes situated at LWSC headquarters and at general post offices around the city. An earlier review found that the use of complaint boxes has not generated as many complaints as expected. LWWG has now diversified into other channels of communication to include the use of letters, telephone contacts and consumer general meetings (usually organized during market days), which has resulted in an increased number of registered consumer complaints. LWWG members use civic members in the informal settlements as points of contact into the community and its members. LWWG members also meet with resident development committee (RDC) members (elected civic leaders of informal settlements) and/or market management committees prior to holding consumer meetings. Venues for consumer meetings are prioritized according to the number of complaints received from an area.

WWG members were investigating a sample of complaints, often oral complaints heard directly and not on appeal after utility investigations, as other similar groups prefer.

As a result of this combined intervention, initial evaluation shows that consumers are increasingly receiving a better response to their complaints. However, a number of challenges remain. The level of funding received from NWASCO is inadequate compared to what the work demands, to the extent that the consumer group was unknown to most people interviewed in the low-income settlements. An increase in funds would increase both their geographical coverage and the intensity of their mobilization activities.

Functions carried out by the WWGs include:

- receiving and validating unresolved complaints from consumers, and presenting them to the service provider;
- collecting information on service levels that feeds into the performance measurement of the service provider;
- informing NWASCO on the effectiveness of the regulations;
- sensitizing consumers on proper use of water and their obligations towards the service provider;
- educating the consumers on the role and function of NWASCO.

As part of the case study research to investigate and confirm levels of customer awareness and interest, focus group discussions were held in four locations of peri-urban areas of Lusaka City at the end of July 2004. These discussions were held in Ng'ombe and Garden compounds and in Baulen and Kamanga compounds. The purpose of the focus groups was twofold: to capture the experiences, perceptions and opinions of low-income consumers on key issues and problems, and to evaluate the suitability and acceptability of use of a focus group discussion methodology by the regulator for capturing the voice of the urban poor.

The sites were selected in order to reflect diversity in service levels and management options. Although all the selected areas are legally recognized as peri-urban settlements, each compound had peculiar characteristics.

Bauleni (population of about 45,000) is supplied by boreholes constructed and managed by different organizations, namely LWSC, JICA and Irish Aid. Garden compound (estimated population of 50,000) is supplied through LWSC distribution mains. However, the supply is insufficient, to which CARE International has responded by drilling a borehole to boost the water supply. This borehole is to be handed over to LWSC upon commissioning. Kamanga's (estimated population of 10,000) borehole water supply was constructed by Irish Aid and handed over to be managed by the community. However, the system collapsed after only a year of mismanagement but was rehabilitated with the assistance of the City Challenge Fund. The condition for obtaining the grant was community management in partnership with LWSC. Finally Ng'ombe compound (estimated population of 37,000) is supplied by LWSC through a mains pipeline and a borehole. This area is also prone to inadequate water supply.

In all the four locations where focus group discussions were held, water to these areas is supplied through projects funded by various international funding agencies. These are JICA, Irish Aid and CARE International. All the projects had similar policies on connection of individual households. Most participants draw their supply from communal standpipes and did not know the system in place. The charges were ZMK2500 (US$0.81) for obtaining the application form and ZMK75,000 (US$24.33) for the connection charges. Connection materials are provided by the applicant. Someone from the project visits the applicant's residence and advises on the materials to be bought. Most participants said LWSC procedures for new connections are well publicized and well known.

Many participants expressed the desire to acquire individual household connections. However, most participants were aware that currently LWSC has put a ban on new connections, which is a result of inadequate water supply. Furthermore, many participants pointed out that the cost of extending water connections to individual houses is high and out of reach for the majority of the residents in their locations. Others felt the procedures were long and cumbersome. One participant claimed that it took him one year to get his application processed.

Most participants were not confident about the quality of the water supplied to their locations. They attributed the deterioration of water quality to frequent pipe bursts and the high level of contamination of the groundwater table, which is the main source of supply to the water schemes in the peri-urban areas. The participants suspect that rubbish littered all over the catchment areas of the boreholes is contaminating the water sources. Other suspected sources of contamination are the pit latrines constructed upstream of the boreholes. The participants pointed out that their suspicions are confirmed by advice given by the service provider to boil or chlorinate the water collected from the borehole schemes.

Most participants pointed out that there was an inadequate quantity of water, as supply is currently being rationed between different parts of the service areas. Similarly, most participants find the supply unreliable. Public taps are opened a few hours in the morning and a few hours in the afternoon. Residents must collect all the allocated water in the given time slots. In one location, residents are not able to receive services on Sundays because the tap attendants go to religious services. The pressure on most taps is perceived to be inadequate, mainly due to inadequate water supply, but sometimes due to pipe bursts.

When asked about the utility's response to leakages and bursts, most participants were dissatisfied with the reaction time to these maintenance problems. As a result, the community leaders in some locations have collected maintenance funds and managed them, which have been used to train community-based plumbers, purchase tools and provide the plumbers with bicycles to carry out maintenance work in the locations. Some communities have instituted neighbourhood watch groups to identify and report leaks and bursts to the community-based plumbers.

There were mixed perceptions about the water tariff. Participants in two of the four locations felt that the water tariff is fair, while the rest thought they are being overcharged. This anomaly may be explained by the different levels of mobilization for cost recovery done by different projects. All participants know that LWSC sets the tariff, which ranges from ZMK14,000–15,000 (US$4.54–4.86) per month for individual households and ZMK2500–3500 (US$0.81–1.13) per month for households fetching water from communal standpipes. The price varies depending on the guidelines set by the funding organization. In addition each household is expected to purchase a scheme membership card worth ZMK500 (US$0.16) per year, which is paid to LWSC cashiers.

Mechanisms for payment of bills vary from one location to another, depending on the guidelines provided by the funding agency and the management system in place. The payment system in compounds where LWSC is managing the service provision is uniform. Previously, RDCs used to receive payments on behalf of the service provider. Currently, only the LWSC cashiers can receive payment, which is normally collected once a month in advance. Recently, LWSC has been flexible in terms of receiving smaller instalments such as for a minimum of one week. In the other compounds wholly managed by community leaders, some RDCs have instituted flexible payment methods: consumers can either make advanced monthly payments on flat rates or volumetric rates when people fetch water from the standpipe.

In one location where focus group discussions were held, some participants raised their concern over lack of accountability for funds collected by the tap attendants. They called for more strict monitoring systems to ensure that all the money collected is registered by the RDC office and used in the O&M of the water supply scheme.

There were few participants with individual connections. Most participants pointed out that LWSC normally provides notice of intention to disconnect individual household connections and communal taps. It was pointed out that LWSC staff showed some flexibility in effecting disconnections. If the consumer committed himself/herself to paying the outstanding bill in instalments mutually agreed upon, the disconnections would be stayed. Participants from two locations said that water to their communal taps had never been disconnected. This was confirmed by the fact that the participants did not know what the reconnection fee was.

According to the participants in the focus groups, some residents of the peri-urban areas normally use alternative water sources such as hand-dug wells mainly because they are unable to afford the costs or unwilling to pay for water services. However, many other residents who normally use piped water revert to these hand-dugs wells when there is a shortage of supply, or in the case of disconnection. A few participants attributed use of alternative water supply to the limited number of communal taps, leading to congestion and long queues.

During the discussions, it was pointed out that there are a number of challenges and problems associated with the use of alternative water supplies. There is the need to chlorinate the water at the point of use, which introduces the problems of costs and application of the chlorine. Furthermore, in some instances, particularly during shortages of piped water supply, consumers are charged up to ZMK200 (US$0.065) per 20-litre container of water drawn from shallow wells.

It was also reported that long periods of time spent looking for water by some housewives generate suspicion of infidelity among their husbands, sometimes leading to the break-up of families. Cases were cited where women and girls in search of alternative water supply during odd times have been raped or even killed in road accidents.

Most participants pointed out that they currently do not have a good mechanism through which they can effectively channel their complaints and concerns to the water utility. They claimed that community members are never consulted on issues concerning service delivery in their area. Participants from three out of the four locations expressed concern over the long periods taken by LWSC to respond to their complaints.

Other than RDC leaders in one of the four compounds, most participants expressed ignorance about the existence of the regulator or the LWWG. For instance, one group of participants claimed that they first heard of the regulator when the research team brought a letter of introduction from NWASCO. One participant said he had read about LWWG in a newspaper. Even the few who said they had heard about NWASCO denied knowledge of the purpose and functions of NWASCO. A number of suggestions were made to improve the voice of the consumers: LWSC should improve the level and scope of consultations with the community; RDC members could be utilized to interface with the community members through zonal development committee members and the neighbourhood watch groups; NWASCO should educate the community on its policies, roles, functions and activities; and the activities of LWWG should be scaled up to cover all the compounds, in consultation with the RDCs.

Regulating water and sanitation for the poor

Government, through the enactment of the Water Supply and Sanitation Act (1997) and its associated statutory instruments, has provided a good legal framework for establishment of a regulatory regime. The NWSSC and management structures have subsequently created a valid regulatory administration with good structures and rules with systems in place to make the regulator accountable to the executive.

The operating environment is conducive for the regulator to make independent decisions, without interference from the Executive – in the short time he has operated, he has managed to establish some considerable level of legitimacy among many stakeholders, managing to be fairly consistent and transparent in the period. It is notable that NWASCO was able to implement significant tariff increases during an election year.

Good progress has been made in targeting of interventions but there is room for accountability to the consumers to be further improved. The creation of LWWG, though still on a learning curve, has already paved the way for the customer voice to feed into the regulatory process and created benefits for the consumer through the reduction of the service provider's response time to consumer complaints. A focus group approach could be refined and utilized by the WWGs to make cost-effective rapid assessments of consumer perceptions.

Service provision to the urban poor is a priority of the government of Zambia as evidenced by the policies and structures put in place. This position is replicated at the service-provider level, although not with the same enthusiasm and priority of purpose. The setting-up of the Devolution Trust Fund, a fund that is meant to redress the imbalances of service levels in the peri-urban areas, has been a step in the right direction. It is important that its management is carefully worked out to ensure that the subsidies are not hijacked, but are well targeted to benefit the most vulnerable members of society.

The service provider in Lusaka is grossly overstretched by the increasing population in the peri-urban areas, where the service gap is currently filled by alternative service providers, largely funded by international NGOs. However, the consumers serviced by these alternative service providers are excluded from the benefits of the regulatory regime.

The major recommendations of this case study are that the rights and obligations of the consumers, the major stakeholders in the water sector and the major beneficiaries of the regulatory regime, should be made explicit in any future revision to the Water Act. The regulator's guidelines and annual reports should include targets on, and progress towards, enhancement of services to the peri-urban areas, and criteria for allocation of the Devolution Trust Fund should be informed by these statistics. Adequate information about the regulatory systems should be disseminated to low-income consumers to empower them and make them active partners in the regulation process. This information should be in a form that is simple, understandable and accessible to the target audience.

Collaboration between WWGs and the elected community leaders should be explored as a way of scaling up the activities of the WWGs in the peri-urban areas in a cost-effective manner. Guidelines for 'required minimum service levels' should be precise about what is considered as 'secure alternative resources', with particular reference to water quality parameters. The guidelines should also harmonize the targets on minimum service levels between small and large towns, and make explicit what the USO is, in order to focus the service providers on planning for the achievement of universal service provision.

CASE STUDY 4: ACCRA AND KUMASI, GHANA

Kwabena Nyarko and Samuel Odai

> *PURC is committed to the development and delivery of the highest quality of utility services to all consumers and potential customers.* (PURC, 2005c)

The water sector and institutional framework

Ghana's public provider of urban water services has been the subject of continual public sector reform since early structural adjustment reforms began in sub-Saharan Africa. However, the proposed options, and present practice, of private sector involvement continue to be hotly debated. An independent regulator, responsible for economic and service quality regulation, was formed as part of a move to attract international investment and protect the interests of the utility customer. The urban poor of Ghana rely on vendors or tankers who charge 3–15 times the normal utility price. Low-income, multi-occupancy tenement housing or 'compounds' make up 70 per cent of housing in urban areas. The poor and vulnerable live in slums or illegal, unplanned areas that lack almost all basic infrastructure.

The Water Resources Commission (WRC) is responsible for the regulation and management of all water resources. It is responsible for water allocation and granting of water rights, particularly for Ghana Water Company Ltd (GWCL), which pays WRC for the raw water it uses. The Environmental Protection Agency (EPA), under the Ministry of Science and Environment (MSE) is charged with environmental regulation. The EPA ensures that human activities do not pollute the environment. The Ministry of Finance is responsible for negotiation and approval of credit facilities (loans) in the water supply and sanitation sector.

At the time of this study, the state-owned GWCL was the lead organization responsible for urban water supply, operating 82 urban systems serving a population of about 8.2 million. GWCL is under the oversight of the Ministry of Works and Housing (MWH), which is responsible for water policy formulation and also providing some level of oversight of GWCL's activities. Some progress was being made in developing the performance of the public company before the introduction of the present 'performance-based management contract' with its international operator partners from The Netherlands (Vitens-Evides International Ltd) and South Africa (Rand Water Services, Pty) to form Aqua Vitens Rand Ltd (AVRL). GWCL retains asset management and asset development responsibilities. The researchers believe this case study remains valid, as a commonly held view is that the management of urban water supply operations in Ghana will default back to GWCL sooner than the five-year contract would indicate.

GHANA KEY FACTS

• Human Development Index rank	135 out of 177
• Population living < US$2 per day	78.5 per cent
• GNI per capita at purchasing power parity (2006)	US$2640
• Country population	23 million
• Urban population	49 per cent
• Urban population growth rate 2005–2010	3.4 per cent
• Urban water coverage	88 per cent
• Water supply by household connection	37 per cent
• Improved urban sanitation coverage	27 per cent
• Research focus location	Accra and Kumasi
• Research focus population	2.4 million
• Service provider	Ghana Water Company Ltd (at time of study)
• Contract form	Publicly owned corporatized utility
• Regulator	Public Utilities Regulatory Commission
• Regulatory start date	1997
• Exchange rate to US$ at fieldwork	GHS9000
• Implied purchasing power parity conversion rate to US$	GHS1685
• Implied undervaluation ratio	5.34

Since 1997, the independent regulator, the Public Utilities Regulatory Commission (PURC), provides the economic and quality of service regulation for the sector. It operates alongside the State Enterprise Commission (SEC), which is responsible for regulating all state-owned enterprises including GWCL with whom SEC signed performance contracts since its establishment in 1989.

The key tasks and responsibilities of PURC, the regulator, are to:

- provide guidelines for rates to be charged for the provision of utility services;
- protect the interest of consumers and providers of the utility services;
- examine and approve water rates;
- monitor and enforce standards of performance for provision of utility services;
- promote fair competition among public utilities;
- receive and investigate complaints and settle disputes between consumers and public utilities;
- initiate and conduct investigations into standards of service quality given to consumers.

MWH sees the achievement of a USO as its mandate. For PURC, the achievement of a USO as a primary duty is not so easily acknowledged even though it is seen as an important goal. PURC currently has no working definition for universal service obligation nor explicit strategies with key milestones to ensure its early achievement; there are no incentive mechanisms for the parties, the regulator and the service providers to drive service delivery to everyone; and there are no guidelines or strategies to ensure its achievement in general and especially for the urban poor.

They do, however, now have a Social Policy and Strategy for Water Regulation that has a 'working definition of the urban poor as those (i) without direct access to regulated pipe supplies, (ii) who depend on secondary and tertiary suppliers and (iii) who buy by the bucket' (PURC, 2005b). Although not in the legislation, PURC sees itself as having 'a primary concern to address the interests of the poor' (PURC, 2005b).

The legal framework

The act that established the GWCL, Act 310, instructs GWCL to provide service to all inhabitants in the supply area. The Constitution of Ghana, Article 35(3) states a legal obligation for the provider to promote 'just and reasonable access by all citizens to public facilities and services' (Government of Ghana, 1992). GWCL responds to this legal requirement by pointing to its three levels of service delivery designed to accommodate all housing types: the house connection, yard connection and standpipes.

The PURC Act, 1997 (which established PURC), Act 538, to regulate the water and electricity services in Ghana, under Section 11, Duty to Provide Adequate Service requires: 'A public utility licensed or authorised under any law to provide utility service shall (b) make such reasonable effort as may be necessary to provide to the public service that is safe, adequate, efficient, reasonable and non-discriminatory.' There is no other requirement or explanation with regard to serving the poor, though there interestingly is a requirement to ensure use of up-to-date technology.

The Constitution (Article 17) permits Parliament to make 'different provision for different communities with regard to their special circumstances' though it is unclear if this is an obligation. As with the non-discrimination requirement in the PURC Act it does perhaps pave the way to promote service provision to its unserved areas by collaborating with alternative providers. Assuming PURC protects this entitlement for all citizens to gain access to services and facilities, as stated above, then they would be legally bound to enforce this legislation if it continues to be breached.

However, the current legislation appears only to authorize the service of the formal provider and does not encompass the role of alternative service providers. Legislation does exist to allow independent operators to function by way of abstraction licences, though it is not known whether they are granted (or even enforced) in a formal operator's catchment area.

The PURC Act also grants the power to make regulations that are necessary for the implementation of its mandates. The commission has so far issued two regulations. These are: the Public Utilities (Termination of Service) Regulations 1999 and LI 1651 that sets out the circumstance under which utility service consumers may be terminated (disconnected); and the Public Utilities (Complaints Procedure) Regulations 1999 and LI 1665, which specifies the procedures by which any person (utility or consumer) may lodge a complaint with the Commission.

Section 31 of the Act allows for the establishment of consumer services committees (CSCs): '(1) There may be established by the Commission in such areas of the country as it considers necessary consumer services committees. (2) The Commission shall by legislative instrument prescribe the membership and functions of a consumer services committee'. As described later, CSCs have yet to be established.

Service providers

The main service provider at the time of the study was GWCL. Previously a public utility (Ghana Water and Sewerage Corporation), GWCL has operated as a limited liability company since 1999 – under the Statutory Corporations (Conversion to Companies) Act No. 461, 1993. However, its key objectives did not change. The Ghana Water and Sewerage Corporation Act No. 310, 1965 requires GWCL to supply water to all inhabitants in its supply areas.

MWH, responsible for water policy formulation, is also the part of government with primary responsibility for water and sanitation. However, more day-to-day control is exercised through PURC, which provides the economic and quality of service regulation; and SEC, which is responsible for regulating state-owned enterprises, such as GWCL, which operate under a performance contract. There is provision in both cases for financial penalties if targets are not met.

Under Section 4 of Act 538, 1997, PURC is an independent body and is not subjected to direction or control of any authority in the performance of its functions. It operates by setting performance targets linked to incentives/disincentives with tariff levels set against achieving a number of agreed targets.

PURC, for administrative purposes, falls under the Office of the President, but is essentially an independent body that has the responsibility of approving tariffs (previously set by GWSC), promoting fair competition and monitoring quality of service standards. Ultimately, under the Public Utilities Regulations (Termination of Service), Legislative Instrument 1651, 1999, PURC has the power to determine termination of service.

PURC has been funded directly by the government but there have been attempts to replace that source with a regulatory charge to ensure continuing independence in regulation. In its *Social Policy and Strategy for Water Regulation*, PURC states its vision 'To become a model institution which ensures the delivery of the highest quality services to all consumers at fair prices' (PURC, 2005b).

The service provider has various powers, including the right to enter any land for water supply and sanitation provision purposes (under Legislative

Instrument No. 1233, 1979) and the right to disconnect (14 days notice is required before disconnecting a customer).

Other service providers exist but these largely operate informally (i.e. they are not legal entities) serving the unserved and under-served. They include domestic vendors (neighbour on-sellers); street vendors (supplying from carts) and tanker operators. The last of these have formed associations in Accra and operate more formally under a Memorandum of Understanding with GWCL. Typically all of these providers obtain their water for supply from GWCL. Those who do not (i.e. independent service providers) are required, as is GWLC, to have a permit (from WRC under Act 522: Water Resources Commission Act, 1996) to abstract water from a source for supply. Regulations also exist to prevent pollution of water sources, including controls on wastewater and effluent discharges. In this case the regulator is the EPA under the MSE.

The service provider had until recently operated without any binding duties with respect to its customers. However, a Customer Charter was in preparation to spell out the rights and obligations of both the service provider and its customers. For the alternative service providers there is no formal relationship.

Service recipients

Service recipients do not appear to be clearly defined nor are their rights, although some duties, such as the obligation to pay for services received, are defined.

There appears to be no explicit reference to a USO. However, under the No. 538 Act, 1997, the service provider is required to make reasonable effort to provide a safe, adequate, efficient and non-discriminatory service. Furthermore the Public Utilities Regulations (Termination of Service), Legislative Instrument 1651, does include some measures for the protection of residential consumers. The Public Utilities Regulations (Complaints Procedure), Legislative Instrument 1665 provides a mechanism for recipients to complain and gain redress and the new Customer Charter should help make GWLC customers aware of their rights. Note that those served by alternative service providers do not, and will not, benefit from such provisions.

Operational performance and regulatory practice

GWCL is responsible for urban water supply and at the moment has about 80 systems serving a total population of some 6 million. As of 2004, urban water coverage was estimated at 59 per cent and is expected to reach 85 per cent by 2015 (PURC, 2005b).

Analysis of the 1996–2003 PURC data (2005a) indicates a 7 per cent increase in water produced over the eight-year period at a time when the urban population could have increased by approximately 30 per cent, resulting in an average water supply of 40 litres per person per day. During the same period the analysis shows an 89 per cent increase in total operating costs, a 128 per cent increase in the unit cost paid for water (real), a 146 per cent increase in average tariffs (real), a 23 per cent reduction in the ratio of collection to billing, a 0 per cent increase in revenue water but a 103 per cent increase in collections (real). GWCL losses are regularly in excess of 50 per cent and in 2002 reached 58.54 per cent of the water produced.

It is PURC's policy to 'undertake a major tariff review every five years' while monitoring on a quarterly basis the performance of the service provider and any needs for an interim review of tariffs 'taking into account inflation, exchange variations and any extraordinary changes in the operating environment' (PURC, 2005c).

It was the declared intention of PURC to move from a five-yearly assessment of the performance of the service provider to an annual review. However, there have been no published annual assessments since this statement was made in 2005.

PURC has a well-thought-through aim to move tariffs from their present 94 per cent recovery (2003 data in PURC, 2005b) of operations and capital maintenance to a gradual recovery of the costs of capital:

> *This approach shall also incorporate reasonable expectations of improvements in operating efficiency. It was projected that GWCL could over a period of five years reduce losses from leakage and illegal connections from 50 per cent to 40 per cent of water produced and increase the collection of money from 77 per cent to 95 per cent of charges billed. The transition to full cost recovery is expected to take five years.* (PURC, 2005b)

> *National pricing policy for essential services, including petroleum products and electricity, calls for uniform prices throughout the country. The PURC believes that water supply should be no exception to this rule and a uniform price structure is supported. Although not a reason for adopting this policy, there is the added advantage of cross-subsidisation from larger population centres, where incomes are higher than average and the cost of service is low (through economies of scale), to those centres where incomes are lower but the cost of service is generally higher.* (PURC, 2005c)

While GWCL was required to submit its investment and asset management plans (AMPs) to PURC, they were not in any way linked to a specific requirement to serve a number of the urban poor. Even though the utility acknowledges this importance, its view is a common one: that the current tariff levels were set too low and were insufficient to increase the network into unprofitable areas. Some interviewees for this research saw GWCL as 'very hostile to PURC – seeing them as a biased referee'. PURC had reportedly not received audited financial statements from GWCL for several years at the time of the fieldwork.

The new tariffs approved by PURC, now seen by some as 'part of the water company', are 0.66 new cedis/m^3, equivalent to 6600 old cedis/m^3 (US$3.92) for the first 20m^3 per month, also the rate for public stand posts.* Consumption above 20m^3 is priced at 0.66 new cedis/m^3 (US$5.4) with industrial and special commercial rates of US$6.53/m^3 and US$12.1/m^3 respectively. Regulation is clearly making a difference in the move towards cost reflectivity.

Service to the poor and a universal service obligation

Overall pro-poor orientation and consciousness has evolved significantly in recent years. As attempts to implement PPPs were continually stalled over at least a ten-year period, preparations by the government for their arrival continued with concerns for the poor and vulnerable leading the agenda. The Ghana Urban Water Project is the most recent urban water improvement project. Promised funding is about US$130 million for the sub-sector with about US$10 million earmarked for pro-poor activities. At least two years into the successor management contract that promised funding was still not being adequately accessed and utilized.

According to PURC and GWCL, pro-poor water supply is recognized by the use of lifeline tariffs and the provision of public standpipes for informal areas and urban poor neighbourhoods where house connections may not be available. The lifeline tariff, the first step of an increasing block tariff, has recently been extended from 10m^3 to 20m^3 for all domestic customers, irrespective of income level or type of neighbourhood. As many of the poor share connections, either living in multi-occupancy compounds or tenement blocks, they end up paying higher prices for their water than the rich households. Moreover, cost recovery and economic efficiency objectives are unlikely to be reached because middle- to high-income households may never consume beyond the first subsidized consumption block.

A possible source of funding for future infrastructure improvements could come from the Social Investment Fund. Devised as part of the Ghana Poverty Reduction Strategy, the fund provides 75 per cent of capital cost, while the District Assembly pays 15 per cent and the beneficiary community 10 per cent. Since to date there is little or no collaboration with the relevant urban water supply stakeholders, it seems unlikely that this will provide an efficient and effective means for tackling water-related poverty issues.

Meanwhile there is continuing poor targeting of subsidies. A study (Nyarko et al, 2004) on domestic water pricing for households with direct connection to the piped network in Kumasi revealed that the low-income households in multi-occupancy houses with single meters, or in compound houses, were paying 20

---

* The new version of the cedi (Ghanaian currency) was introduced on 3 July 2007 as the equivalent of 10,000 'old cedi'. Since the ISO currency code GHS does not distinguish between the new rate and the old one, for clarity we have used the terms 'new cedi' and 'old cedi' throughout this book.

per cent more than the high-income users per unit volume. The study also revealed that the low-income households were using 56 litres per person per day while the high-income households were using 120 litres per person per day (Nyarko et al, 2004).

Of particular interest in Ghana is the prevalence of compound housing where many households live in single rooms in one compound owned by a landlord. Reportedly 70 per cent of households in urban areas live in such rooms in compound houses (Ghana Statistical Service, 2000). Consumers do not yet desire pipe connections to their rooms ('there no space'), but describe how they were 'paying too much' for their water from the landlord's standpipe: 300 old cedis per 17 litre bucket (US$10.50/$m^3$) when the official stand post rate was 100 old cedis per bucket (US$3.50/$m^3$) and the metered rate for their landlord's private connection was US$2.90/$m^3$.

The regulatory protection is there to limit the differential between the standard price and the stand post price. There is a need to monitor these regulated on-selling prices more effectively or perhaps promote competition by tertiary 'flexible' low-cost distribution lines through the compounds to enable easy connection by tenants, thereby challenging landlords to reduce their on-selling price. As is commonly noted, competition can often deliver lower prices faster and more beneficially (for customers) than any regulatory process.

In parts of Accra there is a demand for extensions of water mains and the distribution network to unplanned housing as it advances into cheaper land on the periphery of the city. The understanding of a USO developed in this study does not require early service provision to such conventional developments. Service extension has to be based on a commercial decision of the water provider based on probable growth in housing density and the growth in the likely demand. However, major settlements in such peri-urban areas of low-income residents might necessitate earlier service coverage due to the immediate demand and economic and public health benefits – but this would not necessarily extend to existing villages being gradually absorbed into metropolitan areas.

Deputy Minister, MWH, Hon Dr Charles Brempong-Yeboah, in a presentation to a workshop on 'PSP and the Urban Poor' describes how the government has been trying to involve the private sector since 1992/3: 'the current problems with urban water supply have come about in large part due to the inability of the public utility company, GWCL, to improve its efficiency'. The Minister is personally very committed to ensuring service to the poor and a body provisionally termed the Urban Low Income Group Water Unit (ULIGWU) is being established within the Ministry to identify the poor so that they can be targeted for assistance. In addition, the project management unit handling the investment requirement of GWCL has a key person with responsibility for ensuring environmental compliances and promoting the interest of the urban poor.

Alternative service providers

For the poor and vulnerable dwellers in the informal and illegal settlements, alternative service providers were found to be the only available option because the number of public standpipes was woefully inadequate.

Ghana has several mechanisms for delivering water that complement the formal water supply network. There are water vendors (including neighbours who on-sell water), tanker operators and small-scale independent operators (who may also supply the vendors and tankers, aside from supplying individual customers). All these alternative providers are not directly regulated by the PURC but instead are left up to the open market. This research has found that the majority of the poor rely on these alternative providers.

Water vendors are a common part of the low-income communities. Despite being largely unrecognized, there is a requirement that they must obtain written permission from the formal provider before vending can commence – causing many to operate illegally by ignoring this requirement. Conversely, tankers, which are usually the property of entrepreneurs, service unserved and under-served areas in collaboration with the formal service provider. An agreement has been made with the tanker associations, which stipulates roles and responsibilities and sets a special tariff, sanctioned by PURC, that recognizes the intention of selling to the unserved and under-served areas. This tariff is made known to consumers through prominent sign boards at filling stations.

Tankers were for a long while 'stealing' water to sell to the unserved areas of the city. A Memorandum of Understanding between the network provider and tanker associations was formed, which has seen a number of service improvements to the unserved and under-served areas. Despite costing users up to ten times more than water from a formal connection, it benefited the consumers by stipulating that tankers could only be used for transporting potable water, thus maintaining improved levels of water quality. However, monitoring procedures have yet to be put in place to enforce this requirement.

An independent producer and provider in Kumasi indicated his desire to extend pipes to interested customers to increase coverage (and benefits) to the community. However he pointed out his fear of what could happen to his investment in the future, for instance, when the proposed PPP comes. Independent providers, who source from groundwater, operate outside of the regulatory framework. Water quality data could be made easily available and abstraction licences, though required by law, are unmonitored and unenforced.

Though in the past it has been neglectful of these users, PURC has also been taking further steps to improve the service offered by water tankers. One initiative includes increasing the number of filling stations used by the tankers, with the eventual aim of passing on the savings in fuel to the end user. This is because the majority of the water cost is due to the high price of fuel for haulage. Plans are also said to be underway by PURC to prepare guidelines for the tanker operators. Some of the considerations are:

- price comparisons between areas and regions;
- handling of complaints against operators either by GWCL or the tanker association;
- mechanisms to prevent the formation of cartels;
- mechanisms for monitoring and ensuring water quality.

Many consumers also buy drinking water in 300 millimetre sachets, that is sealed plastic bags, from private businesses for US$0.60, about 1000 times the unit cost of piped water. Those who can further afford larger quantities buy bottled water.

Consumer involvement and perceptions of low-income consumers

The Draft Water Supply Policy states the government policy of empowering the general public and civil society through consumer involvement (MWH, 2004). In particular, it aims to make the utility more accountable to its customers by increasing awareness of consumer rights and obligations, and providing mechanisms for consumers to participate in decision-making about the level of service. In response, PURC has taken steps towards the formation of CSCs, similar to those formed in England and Wales, where the CSC would be able to represent the concerns of the customers to the regulator and the utility. The plan has yet to be implemented and is reportedly stalled due to a lack of available funds. Other reports point to a concern that such committees might be hijacked for political ends, becoming 'too powerful on the ground'.

However, a system that seems to show initial success is the use of residents' associations that are being used by PURC to collect customer feedback. Communication is also being made with established consumer groups and in public hearings where, for example, new tariff proposals or other related water supply issues are discussed. The media is also used both by the regulator and by customers. The regulator has used a combination of radio, TV and print media to create awareness on certain issues. Customers have also increasingly used local radio to complain about service levels, putting pressure on the provider in new and innovative ways.

Such mechanisms were failing to reach the majority of the urban poor since, according to one interviewee, 'it is only existing customers who have clear channels to complain and make their voice heard'. A study conducted by the regulator found that nearly all poor urban respondents were unconnected to the network and instead relied heavily on alternative service providers. It was revealed that given a problem with their water supply, they had no appropriate avenues to direct their complaints.

By ignoring the alternative water supply sector for too long, the regulator was failing to meet the needs of the poor. The beginning of good customer involvement is being pursued for those already connected to the network, but it is the unconnected, indirect customers, the urban poor, who remain vulnerable by being allowed to fall through the regulation gap.

The government is aware of these issues. The Deputy Minister, MWH, Hon Dr Charles Brempong-Yeboah described how 'at a recent meeting with all the stakeholders the ministry [MWH] offered to "open its doors as widely as possible", even to invite all stakeholders including those currently kicking against the idea of implementation of any form of privatisation whatsoever to even participate in the contract documentation preparation so that their respective fears with regards to the performance of the ultimate contract will be addressed' (quotation from fieldwork interview).

To understand the reality of consumer interests relating to water, 50 residents (of which 68 per cent were female) in poor communities in Kumasi were interviewed on accessibility to waters supply services. The communities visited were Ayigya, Emmena and Anloga. The main objective was to investigate the sources of water supply, the cost and the perception of the customer on the service and their desired improvements.

Ayigya Zongo is a densely populated Muslim community of more than 5000 people. Most of the adults are artisans and traders and the government employs a small percentage. It could be characterized as 'vulnerable, non-poor'. Almost all the community members have access to water supplied from GWCL through standpipes, which are privately owned. The walking distance to the standpipes is not more than 50m.

Emmena is a typical peri-urban community, often being the forgotten element of piped water supply and regulation. Most adults in the community are farmers and the settlement can be described as incorporating a mixture of 'developing poor' and 'vulnerable, non-poor'. It is in the urban fringes of Kumasi. Generally, the members of the community depend on water from GWCL, which is supplied through a standpipe owned by the community. The distance from individual houses to the standpipe can be more than 60m. The price per bucket of water is GHS200 old (US$0.12), which is paid to a committee in charge. The water supply from GWCL is not regular, about eight days in a month, and many of the residents depend on the four hand-dug wells in the community owned by individuals. This is sold in most cases at the cost of GHS100 old (US$0.06) per bucket.

Out of the 50 respondents in Ayigya zongo and Emmena, 5 had house connections, 1 relied on a public standpipe and 44 were relying on neighbours. 19 respondents indicated that they had previously had a house connection but were disconnected because of non-payment of the water bills. The majority of the disconnections took place within the previous year. However, some of the disconnections had occurred 'about ten years ago'.

Those without a house connection were paying vendors 1.4 to 3.6 times the lifeline tariff enjoyed by those with a connection. The respondents without house connections were paying for water at a cost of 100 old cedis to 250 old cedis per 18 litre bucket (US$0.06–0.15). 30 respondents were buying at 100 old cedis a bucket, 14 respondents at 150 old cedis a bucket and 1 person was buying at 250 old cedis a bucket (US$0.06, US$0.09 and US$0.15).

In case of water shortage, a majority (49 out of 50) of the respondents were relying on hand-dug wells within their areas; 39 respondents were getting the service at no cost, 6 were paying 100 old cedis per bucket, 1 was paying 150 old cedis per bucket and another 200 old cedis per bucket (US$0.06, US$0.09 and US$0.12).

Only 25 per cent of the respondents had heard of PURC. A majority (over 90 per cent) indicated that they have no one to report to on issues related to water supply services. A few, however, indicated that they have reported issues affecting water supply to their assemblyman before. When asked about their preferences for water supply, respondents indicated house connection (40 per cent), yard connection (28 per cent) and standpipes (32 per cent).

Another example, this time from a metropolitan area, is Sodom and Gomorrah, an informal settlement in the City of Accra located in the central business district. It was temporarily allocated to refuge seekers from an ethnic conflict in the northern part of Ghana. Since then most of the rural–urban immigrants, especially from the north, have settled in Sodom and Gomorrah. The city authorities have made temporary provision of services such as water and electricity, and GWCL was asked to provide some standpipes when the area was allocated for settlement.

Over the years the various coping strategies of the residents have developed into a web of livelihoods within the community. There are mechanics who repair the trucks that bring yam from northern Ghana. There are local restaurants ('chop bars') and there are various water points (private vendors), bath houses and telecommunication centres to provide service to the inhabitants. During the daytime, the settlement resembles a market where a lot of things are sold. At night it turns into a community that provides shelter for most of the immigrants in Accra, who sell items along the streets.

Although plans are far advanced to remove the settlement by the government and city authorities (and had been for some time), water supply to Sodom and Gomorrah is mainly through standpipes owned or manned by private individuals. It is likely that there are a number of illegal connections. Water is sold at 400 old cedis (US$0.24) a bucket and the cost for having a bath in the private bath house is also 400 old cedis, inclusive of water. GWCL claims they were asked to provide a number of standpipes initially when the city authorities made the place a temporary area for resettling migrants.

In the 'old township' part of Accra, the majority of respondents indicated that by the nature of their accommodation, where they have only one room, a house connection with inside plumbing is 'obviously out of the question'. The alternative of a yard connection was deemed to be 'okay, but the price should not be high'.

Most were buying water at 200–400 old cedis a bucket (US$0.12–$0.24) in areas where GWCL water flows regularly. The source of water was mainly from vendors, including those with yard connections. Most of the landlords were selling the water at 400 old cedis per bucket to the tenants and other neighbours to supplement their income. At the 'worst' end of the spectrum, in areas where the reliability of water was a problem such as Teshie, some residents were buying water at 500–1000 old cedis per bucket (US$0.3–0.6 or up to US$35/m^3).

Regulating water and sanitation for the poor

An analysis of this case study suggests that the existing regulatory mechanisms are inadequate to deliver services to the urban poor in a sustainable and equitable manner. Achievement of the USO is not a primary duty for PURC, even though it is recognized as very important. Both PURC and MWH do not have a working definition for a USO and there are no mechanisms in place to require, monitor and ensure early achievement of a USO.

The MWH sees the achievement of a USO as its duty but does not have clear programmes and mechanisms in place to achieve it. Business as usual would therefore result in an increased proportion of the poor without an improved water supply. The activities of the alternative service providers, currently serving the majority of the urban poor groups, are not regulated by PURC. The regulatory framework is also not facilitating the activities of the alternative service providers for the benefit of the service recipients, as the regulatory framework lacks the mechanisms to issue a permit or licence to the independent producers.

The existing level of customer representation and involvement is low and virtually non-existent for the unserved poor.

Since the fieldwork for this study was completed, PURC has issued a *Social Policy and Strategy for Water Regulation* (PURC, 2005b). This states that PURC will insist that public utilities include pro-poor criteria when undertaking water supply projects and will promote cooperation between utility and secondary providers in safeguarding the quality of service. This is a very significant step forward in regulating for the poor. There is no information publicly available, three years on, as to any progress in implementing these excellent proposals.

Based on the study conclusions and the subsequent release of the Social Policy a number of recommendations can be made.

Clear guidelines and mechanisms for reducing the proportion of the poor without access to improved water services should be developed by PURC/MWH, enabling the strategy to be implemented within a reasonable time. The government should reconsider whether PURC should have the achievement of a USO as a complementary primary duty and therefore prepare a working definition of the USO that will form the basis to require, regulate and monitor its achievement by service providers.

MWH should be proactive in sourcing funds to address pro-poor concerns. Pro-poor aspects clearly have a direct link to poverty alleviation. For example some of the highly indebted poor countries' relief, could be earmarked solely for pro-poor water supply.

The services of the alternative services providers should be well acknowledged and their efforts facilitated to ensure more inhabitants have access to improved water supply services. MWH and PURC should develop guidelines and modalities for the operations of the independent producers and should develop procedures for registering or licensing these alternative service providers, informing them directly of the role and obligations they have to the various relevant agencies as well as the customers.

There is a need to have explicit mechanisms to empower customers so that their needs will be adequately addressed by the regulatory framework. Customer representation should be particularly mindful of the urban poor and the vulnerable. It is recommended that PURC uses a focus group methodology or suitable participatory methodology to consult with the urban poor on a regular basis to incorporate their voice and concerns in the delivery of water supply services.

6

Regulating Management and Concession Contracts for the Poor

The four case studies in Chapter 6 consider economic regulation of a variety of PPPs, ranging from a limited form of concession in Jakarta, Indonesia, full concessions in Manila, the Philippines and La Paz and El Alto in Bolivia to a much shorter management contract in Amman, Jordan. The main service providers have subsequently changed in each of these cities. This has been due to non-renewal at the end of the contract in Amman, cancellation of the concession in Le Paz and El Alto and changes of ownership in one of the two concessionaires in Manila (following failure of the national 65 per cent partner) and Jakarta (a withdrawal from international business by the operator). However, the role of regulator has continued and the need for services to be extended to the poor remains equally strong.

CASE STUDY 5: JAKARTA, INDONESIA

Esther Gerlach and Alizar Anwar

> *Regulating means not only approving.* (Achmad Lanti, Chief Regulator, JWSRB)

The water sector and institutional framework

About half of Jakarta's residents do not have access to the municipal water supplied by the private operators. This figure drops further when public stand-pipe customers are discounted. The overwhelming majority of the urban poor are relying on an unregulated private water market. Constrained to a minimal level of discretionary powers initially, the Jakarta Water Supply Regulatory Board (JWSRB) made early progress towards establishing good relations with the public and sees the improvement of the situation of non-connected households as a priority. The regulator also shows an interest in exploring alternative options in view of the generally accepted fact that service extension to all residents of Jakarta, under existing arrangements, is unlikely to be achieved even by the end of the concession contracts in 2022. Sanitation coverage by sewerage is very low in Jakarta, less than 2 per cent, and since the unregulated water market relies on groundwater there is regulatory concern that the groundwater may have been heavily polluted by sewage.

In 1997, PAM Jaya, the provincial water provider with responsibility for the city's water supply, entered into contracts with two companies to provide water to the city of Jakarta. With increasing demands on existing infrastructure from rampant urbanization, the government invited private funding to maintain, improve and expand the already stressed infrastructure, while making monetary gains in efficiency that only the private sector would offer.

The special capital region of Jakarta (DKI Jakarta) was divided into two parts with the initial intention of generating competition and creating yardstick information between the two. The eastern half was contracted to a joint venture between, at the time of the fieldwork for this case study, indigenous PT Kekarpola Airindo and Thames Water International from UK (PT Thames PAM Jaya, or TPJ) and the western part to a joint venture between Indonesia's biggest conglomerate, the Salim Group, and Lyonnaise des Eaux-Dumez (France) (now PT PAM Lyonnaise Jaya, or Palyja).

Since Indonesian law lacked provision for private sector participation in basic services, the regulatory framework existed only in the regulation-by-contract approach. PAM Jaya was thus reduced to an asset holding authority with monitoring and coordination duties to oversee the agreements. Central government's role existed only in guidance on tariff setting and water quality, also being responsible for national water resources and policy setting.

<table>
<tr><td colspan="2" align="center">INDONESIA KEY FACTS</td></tr>
</table>

• Human Development Index rank	107 out of 177
• Population living < US$2 per day	52.4 per cent
• GNI per capita at purchasing power parity (2006)	US$3950
• Country population	223 million
• Urban population	50 per cent
• Urban population growth rate 2005–2010	3.3 per cent
• Urban water coverage	87 per cent
• Water supply by household connection	30 per cent
• Improved urban sanitation coverage	73 per cent
• Research focus location	Jakarta
• Research focus population	10 million
• Service provider	Palyja and (during study) Thames PAM Jaya
• Contract form	Concession
• Regulator	Jakarta Water Supply Regulatory Board
• Regulatory start date	2001
• Exchange rate to US$ at fieldwork	IDR9230
• Implied purchasing power parity conversion rate to US$	IDR2600
• Implied undervaluation ratio	3.55

Amid an economic crisis afflicting the region, the contracts were later renegotiated to address imbalances in their division and to address failing investor confidence. The Restated Cooperation Agreements (RCAs) initiated a new period whereby an independent regulator was established alongside PAM Jaya.

JWSRB commenced operations in November 2001 with limited powers. For a provisional period of three years (subsequently extended), JWSRB agreed to:

- monitor and enforce compliance of contractual performance levels;
- develop mechanisms to resolve outstanding customer complaints;
- propose tariff adjustments to government on behalf of the operators;
- arrange coordination between relevant government agencies to aid in implementation of the contract agreements.

The legal framework

Currently the legal framework is undergoing reform, with local parliament set to empower the regulator by law with the ability to make jurisdictionally independent decisions to meet specified objectives in public health, economic sustainability, transparency, fairness, reliability, quality and affordability. Legitimacy is to be derived from this legal mandate, which will render JWSRB directly accountable to the public, instead of being answerable to the governor.

The 2005 Governor of DKI Jakarta Regulation No. 54 appears only to adjust the existing situation rather than transfer legitimacy. Article 3 'Status, duties and authorities' describes how 'The Regulatory Body shall have the status as an independent and professional body that is free from the influences and power of other parties including the First Party and the Second Party in the Cooperation Agreement. In its capacity the Regulatory Body shall be able to issue decisions in terms of regulation, mediation, and arbitration with regard to the drinking water management and service in the DKI Jakarta Province based on transparency.'

However, Article 5 states that 'In implementing its functions, the Regulatory Body shall ... submit the proposed water tariff complete with basis of calculation and supporting reasons for each category of customer including those subsidized consumers to the governor for tariff determination.' The vital regulatory function of tariff setting thus remains out of bounds for the regulator.

Service providers

The Indonesian Constitution provides for state control of water resources and usage with the objective of providing for the well-being of the people. This provision is incorporated in the new Water Act No. 7, 2004. While this could imply universal service delivery is a goal, it is not translated into an explicit legal obligation on either the primary authority or the secondary service providers (in Jakarta Palyja, an Ondeo partnership and the then TPJ, a Thames water partnership). The latter, however, are required to meet service standards in their defined service area.

The legal framework for water supply and sanitation provision is being reformed to permit both private sector and community service providers.

At present there is no single national regulatory body, independent of government. The model until now, as exemplified by the establishment of JWSRB, is one of regulation-by-contract (Cooperation Agreements). It is understood that the new Water Act No. 7, 2004 will address this issue via the introduction of new by-laws.

In addition aspects of water service provision are regulated under different pieces of legislation by four different institutions: the Ministry of Health regulates drinking water quality (Decision Letter No. 907, 2002); the Ministry of Environment regulates water quality of drinking water sources (Regulation No. 82, 2001); the Ministry of Public Works regulates raw water availability and water and sanitation development (Water Act No. 7, 2004); and the Ministry of Home Affairs regulates the relationships between the local authority (public), which has the primary responsibility for water supply provision, and any private service provider (Instruction Letter No. 21, 1996).

A comprehensive Indonesian national policy framework for the water sector is under construction. The forthcoming Water Resources Act contains provisions to guarantee minimum access rights for every citizen, giving regard to the protection of economically weak sections of society. Institutional management guidelines for local water providers are expected to form part of a three-tier approach for urban, rural and fringe areas. Pro-poor development was cited as one of the basic principles of the forthcoming national policy, but none of the laws contain any explicit statements regarding service provision to the poor.

The governor's Regulation 54 states that 'The objective of establishing the Regulatory Body shall be able to ensure the provision and distribution of drinking water that meets quality standard, quantity, and continuity economy and affordability of the people'. There is no other mention of pro-poor aspects.

Service recipients

Article 33(3) of the Constitution of the Republic of Indonesia, while giving the state the power to control water resources, also gives it the responsibility to ensure that such control of water usage provides for the well-being of the people. This could be interpreted as providing a legitimate expectation by each citizen to be provided with, or have access to, water to satisfy their needs.

Under Local Act No. 11, 1993 the people of Jakarta could again have a legitimate expectation to receive drinking water because the governor has the responsibility exercised through PAM Jaya (now delegated to private operators) to distribute drinking water for the people of Jakarta. But the same Act by describing service recipients as individuals or institutions that fulfil conditions as water customers in accordance with prevailing rules and regulations, means that some people are excluded.

Service recipients are obliged to pay for the service they receive and the service provider has the right to disconnect in the case of prolonged non-payment. Recipients have the right to receive a continuous water service that complies with water quality standards in sufficient quantity and a sanitation service to ensure community and environmental health (new Water Act No. 7, 2004). It is reported that in practice some customers have taken informal (and technically illegal) action and not paid their bills and that this action did not resulted in disconnection.

In Jakarta the service providers have no explicit USO. Service recipients do have some recourse under the responsibilities accorded to the JWSRB, which is required to monitor implementation of the cooperation agreements, particularly with regard to water service delivery to water customers, and to develop, determine and decide concerning dispute resolutions with water customers. The service provider has set up a complaints hotline and a water customer advisory committee has been set up but this in effect is an NGO with no statutory basis/authority. Law No. 8, 1999 was intended to provide a legal framework for consumer protection, but a national body for consumer protection has yet to be established.

The government has provided some water terminals/public hydrants to service poor communities in slum areas but without proper controls on use so that in practice some of them are operated by 'water mafias'. Another significant means of gaining a supply of water is from illegal connections, which the police are meant to control.

Service provider performance and regulatory practice

Service coverage ratios for Palyja and TPJ were 52.9 per cent and 62 per cent respectively (self-reported figures, July 2004), assuming 7.6 persons per connection and water supplied to public hydrants (from where water is sold on by vendors). At an assumed 380 persons per hydrant these contribute a large fraction of 'coverage'. Operator- or central government-owned 'water terminals', represent the 'standpipe equivalent' in the remaining unserved areas, to which city water is supplied via water tankers.

Tariff setting is carried out in accordance with Ministry of Home Affairs guidance dating from 1992. The guideline explains that the structure of the water tariff should adopt a progressive tariff system, with the water companies being able to finance their operations, making reasonable gains from their investments, and that cross-subsidies should be implemented to achieve social objectives. A pro-poor pricing policy has ensued. The charging scheme allows for significant reductions for occupants of low-income housing with a simple flat rate charge for those obtaining water from public hydrants. Jakarta is unusual in using incremental block tariffs that vary according to the housing standard as well as the institutional or commercial use. With an initial rate in 2004 of IDR500/m^3 (US\$0.19) up to 20m^3 per month for stand posts and 'very simple housing', the tariff rises to IDR2250/m^3 (US\$0.87) for up to 10m^3, IDR3000 (US\$1.15) for 11–20m^3 and IDR3500 (US\$1.35) for more than 20m^3 per month for 'very basic housing'. Luxury housing was paying between IDR4750 and IDR6750 (US\$1.83–2.60) and commerce and industry IDR9100/m^3 (US\$3.50) as a flat rate for all consumption.

A steady increase in subsidies since the concessions were issued has culminated in consistently low tariffs for the low-income customers. This is in contrast to other wealthier income groups who have seen a marked increase in their water tariffs. The increase in tariffs to the poor were 16 per cent at the beginning of the concessions, with no increase in March 2001 and a 17 per cent increase consecutively in April and December 2003. This is in contrast to average water prices, which rose by 18 per cent in July 1998, 35 per cent in March 2001, 40 per cent in April 2003 and 30 per cent in December 2003.

The decision letter regarding the most recent revision of water tariffs for Jakarta was issued by the governor in August 2006. It is reported that 'although it is automatically adjusted each semester, in reality it is not yet adjusted' 18 months on. When (if) it is implemented the water rates for the lowest-income consumers will have risen significantly, by 90 per cent for the poorest, but by just 24 per cent for commerce and industry: IDR950/m^3 (US\$0.37) for up to 20m^3 per month for stand posts and for 'very simple housing', IDR3260/m^3 for up to 10m^3, IDR4280 for 11–20m^3, and IDR4990 for more than 20m^3 per month for 'very basic housing' (US\$0.1.25–1.92). Luxury housing will be paying between IDR6200 and IDR8850 (US\$2.38–3.40), and commerce and industry IDR9100/m^3 (US\$4.36) as a flat rate for all consumption. Regulation is playing its part in trying to ensure that tariffs are more cost-reflective – these now have to be implemented in a way that enables the poor to get better quality water at lower overall cost.

Service to the poor and a universal service obligation

The concession agreement specifies that service coverage in Jakarta should reach 75 per cent by 2007 from the starting level of 70 per cent in 1997 and to achieve 98 per cent by 2017. The most recent information indicates that connection numbers had increased by 63 per cent in the Palyja area, and 31 per cent in the TPJ area by the end of 2005. However, there is very little evidence that these new connections are being accessed by the poor.

There are various barriers that prevent presently unserved low-income households from accessing networked services and associated subsidies:

- operators will not connect to illegal housing areas without a licence; local regulation prohibits connection to the network;
- connection fees remain elusively high, currently at about IDR500,000 (US$192); payment in instalments is only an option in the western part of Jakarta;
- networks frequently do not reach low-income housing areas, particularly in the north;
- some households prefer not to connect as municipal services are perceived as unreliable and of low quality.

Central government is taking steps to alleviate water poverty among the urban poor via the 'Energy Subsidy for the Poor' (SE-AB) assistance programme. Following hard-hitting increases in the price of fuel, the scheme aims to assist water-supply projects in low-income areas. Project funding is supplied to construct small-scale water systems, make household connections or help finance an increase in water tankers.

Groundwater pumping schemes from deep wells have been initiated in the past, often with donor assistance. In North Jakarta, where shallow wells are saline, communities of up to 50–60 households participate in the scheme, paying a tariff to meet both operational (electrical) and maintenance costs.

Public baths are prevalent in the city, making up the shortfall for those without bathing facilities at their house. Using groundwater from a private well or an existing network connection, their private operators complain of making little money.

The poorest rely on steadily deteriorating 'traditional' water sources. Residents in illegal settlements, who could be more accurately described as illegal residents occupying government-owned land near landfills, underneath flyover bridges, along railway tracks or riverbanks, rely almost exclusively on alternative sources, such as shallow wells, except where city water is obtained illegally or through intermediaries (vendors).

Women in a number of communities complained of bearing the brunt of water shortages when their husbands, as head of the household, were responsible for supplying water. One respondent described how 'in times of drought, only one or two wells are available to use. The community has to split themselves into two groups; one group can queue for water in a two-hour period in the morning and the other in the afternoon. Each family had to pay IDR15,000 (US$5.77) per month to the well owner to cover electricity costs'.

The concession contracts are arguably pro-poor in that the companies are shielded from the commercial risks involved in serving low-income customers as revenues are divorced from water tariffs. Operators receive remuneration dependent on volume delivered, which is multiplied by a fixed 'water charge'. At the same time there are no contractual requirements to serve the poor, and the financial imbalances that have arisen force the introduction of connection quota, which favour the better-off. PAM Jaya as the First Party to the concession agreements is now pressuring the private operators to seek a 'balanced composition of connections', limiting water sold to the poor at below-cost prices and seeking an increase in new connections to high-income and commercial customers.

It was asserted that all registered residents of Jakarta are entitled to government assistance with basic services; the key to eligibility, however, lies in holding a valid municipality identity card. This automatically excludes immigrants, and Winayanti and Lang (2004) report complications arising from the fact that the card cannot be obtained without a formal address. As an introductory letter from a registered neighbourhood association is required to apply for an ID card in the first place, this prevents illegal settlers from obtaining full resident status and denies them citizen rights.

The companies have put effort into increasing the number of stand post connections (53 per cent: Palyja, 1998–2005) and coverage has increased from 32 per cent to 50 per cent in the west and from 57 per cent to 66 per cent in the east, still a long way from the desired 75 per cent by this stage (though equally calls into account the 'starting position' of 70 per cent). It appears that the alternative providers are still getting most of the business of the poor.

Alternative service providers

Water vending remains a thriving business in Jakarta. With a lack of available alternatives, whether because of the large distance to a water connection or the poor quality of groundwater, the water vendor has been allowed to flourish.

The majority of mains-connected public hydrants are managed by private individuals, who are often reselling the subsidized water at market prices via a number of water carters. Where distance to the network is great, private water tankers deliver municipal water to a number of terminals, where it is distributed in the same way.

These vendors operate without regulatory control and with no significant enforcement of price and quality controls. Price developments of formal and

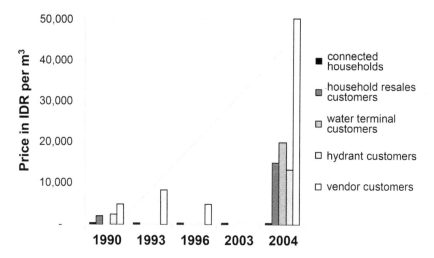

Note: Trend lines fitted to demonstrate steep increases of 'poor people's solutions' compared with the modest tariff rises seen by connected households.
Source: Author's compilation from own research data and 1990 North Jakarta water expenditure survey (Crane, 1994), average vendor prices reported by Lovei and Whittington (1993) and in the 1996 survey conducted by Kjellén et al, quoted in Kjellén and McGranahan (1997)

Figure 6.1 *Price developments of water supply options typically accessed by low-income households*

informal water supply options over the past 15 years are shown in Figure 6.1. The figures reveal steeply rising water costs from sources available for the poor.

Various measures have been introduced at different times in an attempt to curb excessive vendor prices. In 1990, to initiate self-regulation through increased competition, the resale of city water was legalized so long as it was distributed through an approved water meter. Early evaluations of this deregulation measure indicated positive and significant effects both in terms of prices paid and quantities consumed by low-income households (Crane, 1994) but the scheme was soon abandoned. It is speculated that this was due to pressure from standpipe operators who saw on-selling households as a threat to their trade.

Consumer involvement and perceptions of low-income consumers

Chief Regulator Achmad Lanti initiated a mechanism for customer involvement only three months after coming into office. Customer involvement, he argues, is essential to comply with the customer protection mandate given to him in the governor's decree. The Customer and Community Communication Forum (CCCF) was established as a formal communication platform, consisting of water professionals from government, the operators and the research community, as well as NGOs and community representatives.

The CCCF was later strengthened with the addition of water customer committees (WCCs). Set up to act as independent NGOs in the five municipalities of the city, the WCCs carry out public information campaigns via a quarterly newsletter and a website. Approximately 14 per cent of the JWSRB budget, about IDR200 million (US$22,000), is allocated to the WCCs, reflecting the high priority given to customer involvement.

Meeting every quarter, the CCCF handles macro-scale issues on behalf of customers, tackling demands from communities for network expansion or taking steps to help educate customers and providers alike.

The WCCs liaise with communities, companies and local government on customer complaints, lobbying for service improvements on behalf of underserved communities, but also assisting the operators in reducing illegal connections.

The WCC membership is open to all customers, but presently members are mostly politicians. Despite attracting some criticism, this benefits the WCC by being able to take advantage of existing links within the administrative system.

The current arrangements, however, do not effectively target the poor. Most of those surveyed had never heard about the WCC, hardly surprising when the urban poor are the wrong target audience for a JWSRB newsletter and website. If, as the survey showed, in times of water scarcity women are suffering most, their representation is not being effectively made when only 2 of 52 WCC members are women.

To aid in collecting information regarding perceived performance levels of the operator, a system was devised utilizing key stakeholders. Monthly meetings are held by the five municipal WCCs to address levels of service using key performance indicators: continuity of supply; quality of water at house taps; water pressure at house taps; response to complaints; meter reading; and billing (such as accuracy, promptness and easy access to payment points).

A household survey was conducted among low-income customers and non-connected residents of selected slum areas. Individual households were interviewed by a team of surveyors according to a predefined questionnaire, and priority concerns of the community were verified in focus group discussions. The aim of the survey was to gain an overview of the accessibility of water supplies with the associated implications for household expenditure, convenience and overall water consumption for different types of household.

A range of communities was included in the household survey to reflect the complexity of the situation from the point of view of the poor. The majority of respondents find employment in the informal sector, with household income not exceeding IDR1.5 million per month (US$577); these are the 'coping poor' and the 'developing poor'. This can fall as low as IDR180,000 per month (US$69), as observed in the case of scavengers living near a municipal landfill site, characterized as 'very poor' and 'destitute'. The lowest-income settlements consisted of temporary dwellings made of discarded plywood, corrugated metal sheets, cardboard and canvas. The sample included residents in the highly water-stressed areas of North Jakarta as well as areas with good groundwater access further south. Similarly, a selection of customers and non-connected consumers within the eastern and western parts of Jakarta were included to adequately represent both private operators' service areas.

There is a clear north–south differential with regard to consumer's reliance on piped water, as groundwater quality decreases on approaching the coast. The TPJ network reaches the densely populated north-eastern areas near the harbour, but due to low water pressure low-income customers are frequently forced to resort to alternative supply methods. Higher-income customers rely on storage tanks and install suction pumps to increase the meagre flows. Communities in the north-west (Palyja service area) are entirely reliant on self-supply (usually groundwater pumping schemes with or without donor assistance), or water supplied to water terminals through the central government's energy subsidy programme. Depending on their location with respect to the network, traditional *kampung* (slum areas) are more likely to have access to a formal household water connection. Residents in illegal settlements rely almost exclusively on alternative sources, except where city water is obtained illegally or through intermediaries (vendors). Privately owned public baths exist in many areas, including those notorious for crime and prostitution. Tenants of (semi-) permanent, multi-occupancy buildings near the city centre were found to be either connected to the water network through a formal water connection or reported to have access to a public bath provided by their landlord. Rainwater collection and the use of bottled drinking water, both observed during the survey, had not been previously reported in surveys.

Among the households surveyed, there were no complaints about the current water tariff. Affordable tariffs, considered a major pro-poor measure among policy-makers and service providers, are of less concern to poor households, as discussed below. Much more important are affordable options to connect to the piped water supply in the first place. Connection fees, currently charged at IDR474,000 (US$182) for a pipe connection for customers in the K1 and K2 (social) categories are unaffordable for many low-income households.

Water quality complaints were exclusively related to frequent and lengthy supply interruptions and low pressure in the distribution network experienced by customers in many low-income areas. Non-connected consumers showed initiative and ingenuity in developing simple but effective solutions to groundwater quality problems. The frequently high iron content, for instance, was removed by means of simple filtering techniques using easily available and replaceable materials. In the south of Jakarta where groundwater is available, it was perceived as superior in quality to city water by some respondents. Those unwilling to connect to the network also cited the unreliability of piped water as a major concern. Bottled drinking water is purchased at an estimated monthly cost of IDR85,000 (US$33) per family – a considerable burden on the poor with the alternative being similarly costly. Stakeholders across the sector confirmed that boiling water before drinking was common practice among all customers.

Regulating water and sanitation for the poor

The regulatory framework in Jakarta needs a clear separation of policy-making, implementation/operation and regulatory functions and an allocation of an appropriate balance of powers and responsibilities to each actor. Further integration of regulatory controls regarding raw water provision for formal operators as well as price and quality of alternative sources and suppliers would be desirable. JWSRB would benefit from establishing clear regulatory procedures, while PAM Jaya's involvement (and hence scope for interference) should be minimized.

Loopholes created by framing legislation in general terms without detailed objectives, the means by which they are to be achieved and penalties for failing to achieve them, benefit only politicians seeking to retain control over sensitive aspects of infrastructure services.

The private operators could be directed by a mission or strategy prepared by DKI Jakarta, detailing the envisaged developments in the urban water sector, and particularly with respect to service provision for the poor.

Priorities need to be re-examined in the light of the aspirations of customers and those presently unserved. Is it reasonable to require drinking water quality by year ten of the contract, if similar investments could drive network expansion into new areas, retaining the 'clean' water standards Jakarta residents have become accustomed to?

Research findings have shown how creative and innovative even the poorest households can be in overcoming water quality problems, using simple and effective techniques, making a strong case for differentiating service standards.

The link between investment requirements and convenient but affordable services must be made. It has been suggested that Indonesian water suppliers should be able to access direct government subsidies intended for the poor as central government assistance experiences targeting problems and fails to reach the neediest recipients.

The complex and complicated tariff policy of cross-subsidies is failing to fulfil its intended social objectives. The problem is mainly attributed to the very large price differentiation between customer groups, encouraging commercial users to find cheaper alternatives with negative impacts on the environment (groundwater overexploitation) and operators' revenue bases. There are also ingenious ways for middle-class customers to find their way into lower tariff categories. Customers with shared connections are penalized by the progressive tariff structure. Meanwhile, high connection fees and illegal resident status are preventing the poor from accessing formal water supplies.

Community-managed systems in areas beyond the reach of the network prove the workability of alternative solutions. JWSRB is exploring ways of encouraging such systems in order to shut out 'water mafias', but again political support is needed.

Strong leadership and political commitment are crucial to achieving the universal service objective in Jakarta. At present, water suppliers are caught in the middle of contradictory policies from government, requiring cost recovery on the one hand, but heavy subsidies to the poor on the other. An overhaul of the policy framework, clearly stating objectives for operators with respect to their social and economic functions and responsibilities, is long overdue, but unlikely to be achieved under the current water-sector reform programme.

CASE STUDY 6: AMMAN, JORDAN

Esther Gerlach

> *Our vision is to be leaders in the transformation of water and sanitation services throughout the Kingdom and to see in place more responsive customer-focused business-oriented utilities that are economically efficient and sustainable.* (PMU)

The water sector and institutional framework

Jordan has made remarkable progress towards achieving a universal service for its urban population, engaging the private sector in a drive towards efficiency and customer-focused service improvements. Notwithstanding exceptionally high connection rates and a tariff policy that was designed to ensure affordability to all citizens, there remains considerable scope to address the link between water and poverty from an institutional perspective.

Conditions of extreme water scarcity, a resource of vital importance for the Kingdom's socio-economic development, have precipitated the increasing centralization of the Jordanian water sector. According to official statistics, Jordan's then population of 5.5 million has been growing at an average annual rate of 2.8 per cent (Department of Statistics, 2004). This increase is putting high pressure on the country's limited and vulnerable water resources, but Jordanian authorities have been successful in providing a household water connection to almost 100 per cent of the urban population. Available supplies, however, have steadily declined to a present annual per capita share of approximately $160m^3$ (GTZ and MWI, 2004). This places the Kingdom in the category of absolute water scarcity (defined as $<500m^3$/capita/year, according to the water stress index (Abdalla et al, 2004), and has rendered water shortages a permanent feature of domestic water supply.

Growing municipal, industrial and tourism water demand is in strong competition with the traditional stronghold of irrigated agriculture, creating a large deficit. According to latest projections, demand outstrips available supplies by 30 per cent. Freshwater resources are fully committed and the country is paying the price for the overexploitation of groundwater aquifers with deterioration in water quality (MWI, 1997a). Once a number of outstanding augmentation projects have been completed, Jordan will be reliant on non-conventional measures to meet its rising demand. Desalination and wastewater reuse are becoming increasingly attractive options. Currently an estimated 51 per cent of the population are connected to wastewater treatment systems (GTZ and MWI, 2004).

The Water Authority of Jordan (WAJ) administers the municipal water supply and wastewater sector under the umbrella of the Ministry of Water and

JORDAN KEY FACTS	
• Human Development Index rank	86 out of 177
• Population living < US$2 per day	7 per cent
• GNI per capita at purchasing power parity (2006)	US$6210
• Country population	6 million
• Urban population	83 per cent
• Urban population growth rate 2005–2010	2.5 per cent
• Urban water coverage	99 per cent
• Water supply by household connection	96 per cent
• Improved urban sanitation coverage	94 per cent
• Research focus location	Amman
• Research focus population	2.2 million
• Service provider	LEMA (at time of study)
• Contract form	Management contract
• Regulator	Programme Management Unit
• Regulatory start date	1999
• Exchange rate to US$ at fieldwork	JOD0.71
• Implied purchasing power parity conversion rate to US$	JOD0.3
• Implied undervaluation ratio	2.36

Irrigation (MWI). MWI holds the overall responsibility for the formulation of water strategies and policy, water resource planning, research and development and coordination with donors. The Ministry of Health (MoH) is vested with the primary responsibility of drinking water quality monitoring to ensure compliance with public health requirements. Water resource protection against pollution is the stated role of the Ministry of Environment (MoE).

In the wake of PSP in water sector projects, MWI created a Programme Management Unit (PMU) in 1997 to act on behalf of WAJ in facilitating the implementation of the Greater Amman Water Sector Improvement Programme. In 1999, municipal water services in Greater Amman were delegated to a joint venture of Lyonnaise des Eaux (now Ondeo, France), Montgomery Watson (US) and Arabtech Jardaneh (Jordan), known as LEMA, under a management contract in effect at the time of the case study fieldwork, which expired at the end of 2006.

In the Amman Governorate municipal water supply to Greater Amman through the LEMA contract, which has no coverage targets, is overseen for WAJ by PMU, with PMU established under a Charter of Operations that sets out its mandate, objectives, powers and duties and specific functions.

The mission of the Jordanian regulator, PMU is as follows:

> *Our mission is to obtain efficiencies in investment in infrastructure and improve the management of water and sanitation services. We will achieve this through promoting changes to develop the institutions and resources available*

for the provision of water and sanitation services, and by creating appropriate mechanisms to ensure the interests of consumers are protected at all times. (PMU, 2002)

Established as a semi-autonomous body, PMU was expected to assist in:

* the administration of the Amman Management Contract;
* the restructuring programme of Amman's water supply system; and
* knowledge transfer, especially with regard to PSP in the water sector.

PMU operates under supervisory control of an Executive Management Board, which is headed by the minister. The Board receives advice from the Delegation of the European Commission in Jordan. PMU is funded through a number grants and loans from US and European development partners. Government counterpart contributions include the provision of office space within the WAJ/MWI building.

Although PMU has progressively been awarded additional responsibilities, the Unit's regulatory functions remain limited to sector monitoring with a focus on performance improvement and asset management. Decisions of a financial nature are perceived as politically sensitive to the extent that tariff decisions require the approval of the Cabinet, limiting even the decision-making powers of the minister to recommendations.

The legal framework

Service providers

In Jordan the MWI, created in 1992, holds the overall responsibility for the formulation of water strategies and policy, water resource planning, research and development and coordination with donors.

A single body is responsible for providing municipal water supply and wastewater services in Jordan and that is the WAJ. It is an autonomous corporate body and carries out its functions in accordance with the Water Authority Law (No. 18 of 1988, as amended). The law provides for the establishment of water departments within each of the Kingdom's 12 governorates.

It is reported that the establishing legislation has resulted in overlaps between the roles of WAJ and MWI and that clarification is needed. Despite this it is considered that existing laws 'are strong enough', but 'the application of the law has been unsatisfactory'.

Primary responsibility of drinking water quality and monitoring rests with the MoH, which is authorized to prevent the distribution of water declared unsafe.

A USO is not explicit .The policy in Jordan is to achieve reasonable domestic use (100 litres per capita per day is recommended). The policy is that this is achieved by expanding the role of private sector service providers. With respect to wastewater services the policy is to prioritize expansion of wastewater services in urban areas already served and where users are willing to pay for services.

According to one interviewee, 'The majority of residents are supplied according to a rotational rationing programme, on average receiving water once or twice per week. LEMA's major contribution to improved service has been to regularise rationing days.'

Small-scale private service providers operate where LEMA fails to provide a service. Tanker operators usually source water from privately owned wells that have to be licensed to sell potable water. They must register their trucks and obtain a licence in order to operate as a service provider. WAJ, under Law No. 18, is supposed set the price of water sold via tankers, but in practice this is only used as a guideline and there are no penalties for exceeding price limits. However, as for other service providers, public health aspects are well regulated and enforced by the MoH.

Service recipients

The rights of service recipients are not clear. People in informal settlements are supposed to be entitled to 'normal municipal services', but often squatter status means that individuals are unable to provide the documentation required to obtain a connection. The Constitution while asserting that all Jordanians are to be treated equally before the law makes no explicit reference to water rights or the 'right to life'.

Law No. 18 (Art. 23(2)) provides for water councils within the water department in each governorate. The purpose is 'to allow citizens and local authorities to participate in deciding priorities regarding water and wastewater projects and plan for their implementation'. In theory there is a mechanism for citizens to report problems to WAJ but it is reported that in practice this does not operate in Greater Amman. It is reported that LEMA has, however, made progress with customer consultation.

The duty of recipients to pay for services is much clearer. LEMA has the responsibility and powers to deal with illegal use from the system it operates. Persistent offenders and those who do not pay the required charges face legal action in the courts.

Service provider performance and regulatory practice

Diminishing water availability, historic underinvestment and rapid, unnatural population growth following several waves of refugees and migrants had created a challenging operating environment with persistently high non-revenue water (NRW) levels (in the range of 45 per cent). During the period of its management contract, LEMA made significant progress towards turning Amman water supply and sewerage services into a profitable and customer-focused business. Profitability levels increased such that revenues comfortably covered both operational expenses and the management fee and generated modest profits for WAJ/MWI.

The majority of residents in Greater Amman are supplied according to a rotational rationing programme, on average receiving water once or twice per week. LEMA's major contribution to improved service has been to regularize rationing days. Surveys show that customers value this reliability as it allows them to structure their time around the availability of water, but 33 per cent of low-income families wished for an increased duration of their weekly supply.

Water rationing is intimately linked with operational difficulties, as the periodic surging of the network causes a high rate of pipe failures and meter malfunctions. In November 2004, continuous supply was introduced to 26.5 per cent of LEMA's customers, reportedly based on these technical considerations. It is worth noting that the winter rationing programme did not receive direct government approval but was instead met by silence. The decision was not made public.

Universal service in terms of full network coverage and equal treatment of customers irrespective of social or income status had been accomplished in Greater Amman, even prior to the introduction of PSP. In spite of these achievements, protection of the poor is presently not part of the regulatory process, leaving scope for the evolution of a USO to eliminate present inequalities.

The National Water Strategy setting out long-term strategic goals for the sector recognizes the intense population pressure on the country's vulnerable water resources. Nevertheless, the Government of Jordan expressed its commitment to 'securing water services at affordable prices and acceptable standards' (MWI, 1997b) and extending services to unserved areas. The policy target consumption level is set at 100 litres per capita per day, with reasonable domestic use awarded priority over competing water demand.

PMU as the quasi-regulatory agency seeks to safeguard consumer interests, but at a practical level is mostly concerned with technical issues surrounding the improvement of service provision. Service to the poor and the protection of vulnerable groups could not be ascertained as stated policy goals and references to social objectives do not appear in PMU's Charter of Operations (MWI and WAJ, 2001).

Social considerations, however, have traditionally played an important role in determining water tariffs. A lifeline allowance of $20m^3$/connection/quarter affords an average-sized household in Amman (5.7 members) a modest allowance of 40 litres per capita per day at JOD3.47/quarter (US$11.60) in 2005. When the World Bank pushed for tariff reform, the Government of Jordan defended the heavy subsidies into the water sector, citing the low ability to pay of the Jordanian consumer (World Bank, 1997).

The legal situation in Jordan currently leaves up to the consumer the choice of whether or not to connect to the network (though interestingly not in the case of wastewater services), and some large consumers have reportedly made alternative arrangements. By incorporating minimum storage requirements in the revised Building Code, the government effectively endorses the practice of shifting part of the water infrastructure cost onto the customer.

Although connection rates approach 100 per cent within the service area, customers have had to learn to live with the inconvenience of water rationing. As a consequence, customers are obliged to invest in storage facilities. These mostly take the form of storage tanks installed on rooftops (99 per cent of low-income households have this facility), and can be backed up with ground and/or under-ground storage (used by 19 and 4 per cent respectively). The service provider's responsibilities regarding quality and safety of supplies end at the water meter and in spite of scientific evidence pointing to a potential public health risk arising from microbial contamination through prolonged storage (Evison and Sunna, 2001), household storage remains an entirely unregulated area.

Service to the poor and a universal service obligation

Until the economic recession in the mid-1980s, Jordan had enjoyed low poverty levels. By 1993, however, the proportion of households living at or below the poverty line had risen to 21 per cent, with 6.6 per cent living under the abject poverty line. The phenomenon of urbanization of poverty has also been observed: about two-thirds of the poor can be found in urban areas, where citizens benefit from the comparatively very high access to municipal water services. On the downside, 2001–2002 figures indicate that 23.8 per cent are lacking access to secure tenure (Ministry of Planning and UN, 2004). 'Very poor' households can dispose of an average monthly income is JOD70 per month (US$233), the 'developing ("coping") poor' earn up to JOD300 (US$1000).

With regard to the location of poor households within the city boundaries, very little accurate information could be obtained. Amman's business and commercial centres as well as wealthy residential areas are located in the west, and from informants spanning the range of administration to local residents it is evident that poverty is generally understood to increase eastwards from the city centre.

Low tariffs, including a 20m^3/quarter lifeline, were cited as the single pro-poor measure by key stakeholders. At present consumption levels, the price of municipal water is unlikely to generate affordability concerns for even the poorest families. Water rationing largely determines per capita water consump-tion for low-income customers with a higher than average number of household members and limited storage facilities (0.64m^3/person as the low-income house-hold survey revealed). The cost of storage and water treatment and the lack of financial means or *wasta* ('social connections') to access alternative water sources in times of scarcity generate access inequalities. Research has demonstrated that effective water prices rise to a level comparable to that paid by the highest users under the progressive tariff structure (Iskandarani, 2001) and surveying revealed that contrary to popular (and official?) belief the sharing of water connections is widespread. Only 60 per cent of low-income families report they have their own connection, with up to five households sharing in extreme cases – who experience an associated inflation of bills under the increasing block tariff.

Alternative service providers

The persistent insufficiencies in water supplied via the municipal network cause households to augment their supplies from the open private market. The researchers examined the private water market in Amman through a survey of 100 low-income households and a one-day tanker driver survey in June/July 2005.

According to Iskandarani (2001), the proportion of households in Amman choosing to obtain additional water reaches 30 per cent. Among the low-income segment, 49 per cent of households surveyed indicated they have used private tankers in the past (three times per summer on average), and 40 per cent have borrowed water from their neighbours during shortages. So-called 'water-stores' selling treated drinking water have also become increasingly popular in recent years; 18 per cent of the sample use them as their main source of drinking water.

According to WAJ figures, 1267 private tankers were registered in Amman Governorate in 2004, of which 289 are owned by industries and hospitals (Darmame, 2004). The remainder are owned and operated by individuals rather than companies. Tanker owners explained that water deliveries can be ordered over the phone (mobile) or at well-known tanker meeting points in the city (for example 6th Circle, Middle East Circle) where drivers park and wait for customers.

Government (WAJ) regulations set the selling price for water delivered via private tankers to JOD2.0/m^3 (US$6.67) in summer and JOD1.75/m^3 (US$5.83) in winter. Drivers obtain water from privately owned groundwater wells. Wells licensed for the sale of potable water incur a JOD0.25/m^3 (US$0.83) extraction charge (tax). In addition, well owners charge drivers a fee in the range of JOD0.05–0.6/m^3 (US$0.17–2.0), with seasonal variations reflecting water demand.

As far as consumer end prices are concerned, private tanker operations currently exist in a regulatory vacuum. Drivers are likely to exploit customers' ignorance of existing regulations and the lack of enforcement on the part of WAJ/MWI. There are no defined procedures to monitor prices, and penalties for overcharging do not exist. Water is sold to customers at JOD2.0–3.5/m^3 (US$6.67–11.67) (and JOD1.5/m^3 (US$5) in winter), with low-income customers paying the lower price range, but drivers made it very clear that, especially in summer, water is a market commodity. Selling prices of up to JOD7.5/m^3 (US$25) were noted during field observations in summer 2004.

Drivers quoted 2m^3 as the minimum for purchase, but indicated a preference for selling whole tanker loads. Tanker capacities range from 3–20m^3, with 6m^3 being the most common. Average delivery sizes varied between east (2–3m^3) and west Amman (6m^3), with poorer customers indicating an average purchase of 3.1m³ (within a range of 1–6m³). Some drivers insisted that the entire load must be paid in full, regardless of the delivery size. Only 27.1 per cent of survey respondents using private tankers were able to purchase entire loads. The majority (64.6 per cent) share a load with neighbours, while those negotiating a part load purchase were the exception (8.3 per cent).

Without access to formal complaints procedures and stricter price control, poor customers, who are unlikely to afford extensive household storage or are unable to secure top-up supplies from the service provider's 26-vehicle tanker fleet, are left most vulnerable. None of the households surveyed had ever received water from a LEMA-operated tanker.

There are further concerns about private tanker operations undermining the service provider's profitability and consequently reducing the government's revenue. In the absence of a legal obligation to connect to the municipal water supply, large consumers use tankers to increase their reliability of supply and exploit the economic advantages of lower water charges and estimated, as opposed to measured, sewerage charges. There are also unconfirmed suspicions that water stolen from the network may be illegally sold through private tankers.

Consumer involvement and perceptions of low-income consumers

Although stakeholder involvement has been included by the Government of Jordan in the Water Strategy as a principle of good practice, participation is at a premature stage. In the case of government agencies it has barely moved beyond information provision, while LEMA customers are being consulted to a previously unheard of extent on a wide range of service-related aspects.

In theory, concerned parties from government and the private sector are to be represented on water councils within the water department in each governorate. WAJ law (Article 23(2)) states that 'this is to allow citizens and local authorities to participate in deciding priorities regarding water and wastewater projects and plan for their implementation'. Certainly in the Municipality of Greater Amman this is not the case as the project management for the Greater Amman Development Strategy stated that sole responsibility for water services rests with MWI, and the municipality's role has been reduced to the provision of other infrastructure services, including rainwater drainage.

PMU has identified the need to promote its role in the wider community and is seeking to increase the level of recognition of its activities by stepping up efforts in public relations.

Customer consultation by LEMA in the form of regular surveys, focus group discussions and exit polls at customer service centres, carried out by an independent market research company, are used for routine monitoring of customer expectations and satisfaction. However, as results have been met with disbelief by government officials, these reports largely remain internal. The company prides itself for having built up an image of strength and fairness. In contrast to the 'normal' Jordanian official who shuns the media, LEMA has devised a proactive and transparent approach. Communication strategies include newspaper announcements, radio broadcasts and television appearances by the directors of LEMA's various departments.

When questioned about poor households, there were no indications that these create any more of a problem or are treated in a different way to wealthier customers. To the contrary, LEMA staff state 'we don't have a problem with the poor, we have a problem with the rich'. Members of staff unanimously indicate that no special efforts are made to address the needs of low-income households, although social responsibilities are part of the company's business philosophy.

In view of gathering customers' views, LEMA pointed out positive experiences made with focus group discussions, which were described as 'generally very useful tools'. However, less is known about suitable approaches towards the poor (presently consultations are not disaggregated by 'social class'). According to a member of LEMA, There is a general view that the lower-income people are more difficult to deal with because their educational standards do tend to be lower. 'Their knowledge and experience of the issues of water are less.' In response to this, the market research organisation employed to carry out LEMA's customer consultations declared this a common misconception, explaining that the toughest respondents are wealthier customers and educational level bears no relevance. Some adjustments need to be made for lower-income customers, especially in the case of women living in more remote areas, who prefer holding focus groups discussions in their homes.

In what appears to be a low-trust society, people tend to rely on their own experiences rather than believing statements made by government agencies. Interviewees rarely mentioned civil society organizations as pressure groups. Instead, parliament and journalists were cited as 'groups' trying to exert pressure. No NGOs involved in urban poverty alleviation and water supply issues could be identified, but there is a 1200-member Customer Protection Society of Jordan (CPS), which was also known to both WAJ/PMU and LEMA.

The CPS President described the society's objectives as 'satisfying consumer basic needs [and] protecting consumers from monopolies and high prices for some products and services'. Regarding the poor, the society concedes that prices are very low, but adequate quantities are not guaranteed.

Cultural attitudes and the local environment were cited as reasons why formal customer representation is unlikely to be established in the short- or medium-term future. Customer committees in the form currently used in the England and Wales WaterVoice model might be unsuitable. Interviewees stated, 'Who are the characters who could fill these positions here?' and 'People are unlikely to trust a selected few to represent the general public's opinion.' It was noted that committees would be seen as a welcome opportunity for citizens – but most likely as an opportunity for gaining personal advantages. However, PMU did show an appreciation of the benefits of using participation to make different viewpoints heard, such as women's rights for instance. PMU affirmed that 'bits and pieces' could be appropriate but with respect to the WaterVoice model, it would be its spirit rather than the structure that would be applied.

The independent consumer voice is currently overshadowed by self-selected pressure groups and politically motivated individuals, whose interests tend to differ from those of the average customer, while the views of low-income families are likely to be obscured by surveying strategies based purely on geographical location rather than household income. Cultural attitudes and apprehensions in what is described as a low-trust society are cited as a barrier to introducing more formalized customer representation under the regulatory framework.

To understand better the actual services received by low-income consumers, as well as their views, a 100-household survey in selected poor areas in Greater Amman was undertaken by a Jordanian field researcher on behalf of this study.

Results show that low-income households tend to be larger than the official average of 5.7 persons per household (Department of Statistics, 2004) in that 34 per cent of the households interviewed for this survey comprised eight or more members. Of the respondent households only 60 per cent had access to their own water connection, with nearly one fifth sharing a connection between three or more households. This rate of sharing is less than that reported in previous studies, which quote 40 per cent of 50 surveyed low-income households as having individual connections (Darmame, 2004). Nonetheless it contradicts widespread opinion among utility and water authority staff who perceive Jordan's progressive tariff structure as a natural incentive for households to obtain individual connections to access the low-cost lifeline, presumed to support low-income families in Amman. The lifeline allowance covers the water requirements of only a minor proportion of respondents (3 per cent), while the majority (46 per cent) pay up to three times the minimum charge and 14 per cent regularly pay more than ten times the cost of the lifeline. The average amount billed to a poor household was JOD17.4/quarter (US$58). Clearly a large proportion of house-holds are at risk of falling into higher consumption categories and having to commit larger shares of available household income to water bills.

Women in east Amman confirmed that the rationed supplies are not suffi-cient for their families of eight or ten members, even with the storage facilities, which are now required: 'the government makes everybody do it like that'. Supplementing provisions with water from private tankers was described as 'very expensive', and concerns were voiced about contamination of supplies. Sudden water cuts were frequently experienced during the summer months, resulting in 'serious problems'. It was confirmed that private tankers sold water by the tanker load, which households then shared. Water provided by LEMA tankers was described as 'difficult to obtain, unless one had "connections"'.

Although lower-income households are supposedly being supported through more frequent supplies (2–3 days per week), 19 per cent of the surveyed households received water only once per week. Storage capacity emerges as the limiting factor in household water consumption for low-income families. Few low-income households have access to additional ground storage and/or cisterns. Surveyed households had an average storage capacity of 640 litres per person (minimum 130 litres per person) at their disposal until the next supply day. The results indicate a correlation between household income and available storage; 4 per cent of the total sample has less than 30 litres per capita per day available to meet daily water needs, and 8 per cent no more than 50, unless additional supplies are bought in.

While increased supply is a major 'wish-factor', customers do show some appreciation for the difficulties faced by the service provider: 30 per cent believe that rationing is a result of water scarcity faced in the country, 49 per cent blame inadequate water allocation between different users – an issue that should be jointly addressed by providers and regulatory authorities – and 35 per cent think there are too many leakages in the pipe network. Only 6 per cent blame the company directly for mismanagement.

The overwhelming majority of households interviewed for this research (93 per cent) try to conserve their water, mostly through carrying out water-intensive activities (cleaning, laundry and so on) on the rationing day and generally limiting water use (though this does not amount to water conservation in the traditional sense of the word – it merely allows the household to start into the week with a full storage tank). Only a few households report being seriously affected by rationing to the extent that personal water use is restricted. However, confidence in water quality is low: 37 per cent of respondents believe some level of treatment is necessary to improve water quality or have switched to bottled water for drinking purposes. It is important to note that it is mainly, if not only, the poor who use tap water for drinking.

Reported coping strategies for lack of water through the piped network included buying water from private tankers (49 per cent of households), borrowing from neighbours (40 per cent), use of ground storage (13 per cent), storing water in the home (11 per cent), access to wells and springs (3 per cent) and purchasing bottled water (2 per cent).

The bottled alternative, unsurprisingly, is proving more popular with rising household income. Households using bottled water report buying an average of 31.6 litres per week at an average price of JOD0.042/litre (US$0.14). This corresponds to 24 times the price for water taken from the network. There clearly is a willingness and ability to pay over the odds for high quality drinking water even among 'the coping poor', though much less so among those representing 'the poorest of the poor'.

Surprisingly perhaps, quality and not price appears to be the main concern of tanker customers: of the 49 per cent of households using private tankers, 42.9 per cent noted water quality as a problem – while 18.4 per cent would rank water quality from private tankers similar to that of water supplied by LEMA – and only 6.1 per cent explicitly complained about extortionate prices. 20.4 per cent actually thought private deliveries were reasonably priced, and 44.9 per cent rated the service provided by tankers as 'good'.

Regulating water and sanitation for the poor

The case study shows that high connection rates cannot be the single measure of the achievement of sustainable access to safe drinking water for the poor. Failure to deliver a continuous supply has been established as a root cause of persisting access inequalities, as the system favours wealthy households who can afford large storage facilities and top-up supplies from the private market.

The present situation highlights two major issues pertinent to this research: a USO needs to evolve once the primary target of household connections across the city has been achieved and service improvements must be associated with capital investment requirements, a point strongly emphasized by the operator. An economic regulator is best suited to the task of ensuring the financial sustainability of services and driving continuous service improvements on behalf of all customers.

Key regulatory functions, such as tariff setting appear out of reach of an independent regulator in Amman within the foreseeable future. However, an agency with a certain (perceived?) level of independence could be formally introduced as a mediator between all stakeholders to promote openness and fairness in an environment in which political and economic uncertainties prevail.

Efforts should be strengthened to increase the legitimacy of regulation, no matter in which form it is envisaged in the future. PMU is advised to act proactively, increasing the information flow between stakeholders, including the public, and thus developing accountability that transcends the institutional hierarchy. There is evidence to suggest that customer consultations, disaggregated by social group, would give a more accurate picture of willingness and ability to pay for water services and service improvements, allowing appropriate decisions to be taken regarding tariff design and targeting interventions where needed. The case study household survey in ten low-income areas of Amman has revealed discrepancies between official statistics (and opinion) and the situation faced by poor families.

It is further recommended that the risk of increasing the size of PMU should be considered in terms of staff numbers, and consequently the cost of regulation, beyond a point where past inefficiencies are repeated.

In view of the long-term sustainability of services it is advisable to consider strong enforcement of regulations concerning the private market, including competition, which may threaten to undermine the level of subsidy available. There may be a case for a reciprocal USO in which customers would be obliged to join a network in much the same way as providers are obliged to provide adequate services to all consumers. Water storage facilities may be a better target for financial assistance rather than indiscriminate subsidization of consumption.

CASE STUDY 7: LA PAZ AND EL ALTO, BOLIVIA

Andrew Trevett and Richard Franceys

The water sector and institutional framework

Water and sewerage services to the twin cities of La Paz and El Alto were privatized in 1997 with a 30-year concession awarded to the Lyonnaise des Eaux consortium, Aguas del Illimani (AISA). At this time around 93 per cent and 83 per cent of their respective populations had access to some form of piped water. Over the first five years, AISA committed to install 71,752 new household connections, 'equivalent to 100 per cent coverage' in El Alto, the poorer of the cities. At the time of this case study, figures indicated that coverage had reached close to 99 per cent in La Paz and El Alto. However, the dispute as to the accuracy of this figure based upon differing interpretations of concession and municipal boundaries, contributed to the subsequent cancellation of the concession by the government in 2006.

The national water and sanitation regulator, Superintendencia de Saneamiento Básico (SISAB), had awarded 29 concession contracts at the time of this research, though only one was to a private company, AISA, following the catastrophic end of the Cochabamba concession, with the remainder going to municipal or cooperative companies. In an environment of political turmoil, SISAB was struggling to convince a sceptical public that regulation was a tool that could facilitate a sustainable and improving water supply service.

The overall regulatory framework in Bolivia was established in 1994 when SIRESE (Sistema de Regulacion Sectorial, or 'System for Sector Regulation') was created to oversee the activities of the transport, telecommunication, electricity, hydrocarbons and water sectors. The creation of SIRESE was a consequence of a reform process to Bolivian infrastructure that included the granting of concession contracts and liberalization of markets, which became known as 'capitalization'. However, it was not until June 1997 that the Superintendencia de Aguas (water regulator) was established. The following month a concession contract was signed with the Lyonnaise des Eaux consortium (55.5 per cent of AISA was owned by Suez, 37 per cent by local investors and 7.5 per cent by the International Finance Corporation (IFC) to operate water and sewerage services in La Paz and El Alto. Following a bidding process (in which a second anticipated bidder failed to bid at the last moment) the contract was awarded against anticipated service coverage to be achieved within four years, rather than the more normal bidding against reduction in tariffs.

The Law of Water and Sewerage Services No. 2029, passed in October 1999, redefined the terms of reference of the water regulator and led to the creation of SISAB. SISAB is an autonomous state entity that is associated with the Ministry of Services and Public Works from which policy, standards and strategies for the

BOLIVIA KEY FACTS	
• Human Development Index rank	117 out of 177
• Population living < US$2 per day	42.2 per cent
• GNI per capita at purchasing power parity (2006)	US$2890
• Country population	9 million
• Urban population	65 per cent
• Urban population growth rate 2005–2010	2.5 per cent
• Urban water coverage	95 per cent
• Water supply by household connection	90 per cent
• Improved urban sanitation coverage	90 per cent
• Research focus location	La Paz and El Alto
• Research focus population	1.4 million
• Service provider	Aguas del Illimani (at time of study)
• Contract form	Concession
• Regulator	Superintendencia de Saneamiento Básico
• Regulatory start date	1999
• Exchange rate to US$ at fieldwork	BOB7.9
• Implied purchasing power parity conversion rate to US$	BOB2.7
• Implied undervaluation ratio	2.93

sector are taken. The Vice-Ministry for Basic Sanitation serves as the formal link between SISAB and the Ministry of Services and Public Works. SISAB operates within an institutional framework that includes government ministries, municipalities, service providers, civil society, development agencies and international development banks.

SISAB awarded concession contracts to co-operatives, municipal companies, one public company, one *mancomunidad* (a collective of two or more service providers) and, until final contract rescission, one private company. The maximum concession period was 40 years with a minimum of two years' duration, though mostly contracts of between 15 and 25 years had been awarded. Concession contracts are only issued to service providers that operate in an urban environment and serve populations above 10,000. As part of the long-term strategy, SISAB grants licences and registers. Licences certify that service providers or municipal governments serving populations of less than 10,000 agree to follow requirements for tariffs, and are eligible to access government funding. Registers confirm that a service provider supplies water and sanitation to a community or association, and is eligible for government funding.

SISAB is entirely funded by the service providers who pay 2 per cent of their income (after taxation) to SISAB. In addition to this core funding SISAB has received support for its own institutional strengthening from the European Union, Sida, GTZ, the World Bank, the Inter-American Development Bank and the Andean Development Corporation.

The mission statement of SISAB states that it is to exercise the regulatory function for the provision of water and sewerage services within the current legal framework, protect the equilibrium of interests between users, service providers and the state, with a view to improving the population's quality of life. The principal functions of SISAB are to:

- award or renew concessions, licences and registers;
- monitor the correct service provision;
- review and approve prices and tariffs;
- record and act upon the complaints and demands of both users and service providers;
- promote a better relationship with civil society in order to improve customer service;
- comply and ensure compliance with standards and laws;
- promote the management capacity of service providers;
- control the management of quality and coverage of services.

The new government of Bolivia has subsequently been reported as planning to remove SISAB in favour of a more decentralized approach to regulation.

The legal framework

There are clear and unambiguous statements in the legislation that point to the duty of the regulator and service providers to work towards universal access to services. For example, Law No. 1600 that created SIRESE states under Article #1 that the objective of the regulatory system is to regulate, control and supervise sector activities such that they operate efficiently, contribute to the development of the national economy and enable all citizens to have access to said services. Under Law No. 2066, modifying Law No. 2029 governing water and sewerage services, Article No. 5 declares that the principles governing the provision of services are universal access to services. However, that aim of achieving USO is not reflected in any of the principal functions of SISAB or in the mission statement.

The 1992 National Regulations for Water and Sewerage Services in Urban Areas recognize only in-house service connections and sewers as acceptable long-term solutions. Thus, standpipes, tanker truck delivery and latrines are by definition unacceptable for service provision in urban areas. However, AISA felt pressured into providing standpipes and tanker truck supplies to unserved areas of the city. The regulations imply a requirement for water and sewerage service provision to a very high standard and therefore of a high cost. In recognition of this problem SISAB approved a pilot project to test condominial sewerage, which has since become an accepted technology, a good example of the role of the regulator mediating between the long-term goal of society – highest standards for all – and present affordability.

BOX 6.1 PRESS REPORTS ON POLITICAL INVOLVEMENT IN WATER AND REGULATION IN LA PAZ

Quotes from and about José Barragán, the Deputy Minister of basic services and public works, include:

> *Aguas del Illimani has completed its contract perfectly – that is what the regulator says – but if you accomplish something that is insufficient, it continues to be insufficient. ... The concession contract focuses on a limited service area, not allowing the company to satisfy the population's needs. ... The contract underestimated the areas of service in El Alto. ... There are many problems associated with coverage and access to services in El Alto that depend on the original contract that had terms that were not enough to provide for the needs of the population.*

> *The relationship between the [concession groups] and the government is going in a very wrong direction as the concessions are not only supposed to be business contracts.*

> *I cannot continue working with the regulatory troubles that we are having that promote situations like Aguas del Illimani. We did not need to have the riot in order to fix some issues in the contract.*

> *Barragán was an apolitical appointment and worked without political affiliation, but has become increasingly disenchanted with the government's political machinations that he says use the water sector to gain political capital. 'If we do not take the correct steps we are going to be sued very hard and are going to lose everything, and I do not want to be a part of that', he said.*

Source: *Business News Americas*, 31 December 2004 and 16 February 2005

Probably the most unsatisfactory issue with the concession granted to AISA has been the confusion over the agreed service area. In the contract itself, there is ambiguity over the concession area of the contract. In one clause the contract stipulates that the company had to provide water and sewerage services to all houses in the municipal areas of La Paz and El Alto. In another clause there is reference to the *área servida*, which is the existing served area requiring further provision of connections.

The then Deputy Regulator illustrated this challenge with a drawing that showed how it is the poorest in the hillside houses surrounding La Paz, areas not accepted by the municipality as being within their municipal boundaries, that might not be counted within the universal coverage target. This ambiguity has caused difficulties in agreeing expansion targets and is likely to have provided ammunition to the anti-privatization and anti-regulator lobby to strengthen their case that increasing coverage is not taking place, or at least not fast enough.

The legal framework

Law No. 1600 (1994) that states the principle objectives of the regulatory framework (development of the national economy so that all citizens have access to services – including water) puts increasing access to water is a primary objective of regulation in Bolivia.

Law No. 2066 (2000) (post-water wars) 'Ley Modificadora a Ley No. 2029 de Servicios de Agua Potable y Alcantarillado Sanitario' is also relevant, especially Article No. 5 (a) 'principal objective is the universal access of basic services' and Article No. 15.

Law No. 2066, 'Titulo VI, Capitulos 1 y 2, Articulos No. 53 al 62', establishes the tariff policy.

The 2004 'Ley de la Politica Financiera' (Law of Financial Policy) centralizes both national and international funds, loans and grants, that the service providers can access.

Service provider performance and regulatory practice

By 2003, figures showed that overall potable water coverage in the contract area had reached nearly 99 per cent in La Paz and El Alto, and the company claimed it had reached 100 per cent coverage in El Alto itself, expanding coverage by 50 per cent in seven years to 233,900 customers, up from 155,900. There had also been a high demand for sewerage connections in all income areas, and coverage had reached around 90 per cent in La Paz and 61 per cent in El Alto – this exceeding the contractual combined target of 53 per cent. The demand was partly explained by property values not rising quickly for those houses without a sewerage connection. This was reported to be an important concern for the population. A new target of 73 per cent by 2006 was established by agreement.

By 2005, as the political situation grew more difficult, AISA was claiming the highest coverage ratios of all water and sewerage utilities in Bolivia (98.9 per cent coverage in water and 78.9 per cent coverage in sewerage, according to data and benchmarks established by the Bolivian regulator). It also claimed it had the lowest tariff level (US$0.22/m^3) of all major Bolivian cities, stable in dollar terms since 1997, it had a resolutely pro-poor policy, structured by the contract and fully endorsed and implemented by the company, an important investment in infrastructure (US$63 million from 1997 until 2004) and an increase in population served of 373,000 inhabitants for water and 435,000 inhabitants in sewerage through 156,000 new water and sewerage connections (Suez, 2005).

The number of standpipes had been reduced to 60 from 240 during the AISA concession, and the contractual responsibility was to eliminate them altogether. However, they were still being provided outside of the network area in El Alto as a temporary measure because of social pressure. Consumption from standpipes is low, typically around 25m^3 per month, because of the lack of sanitary facilities. Households using standpipes pay approximately US$1 per month for a consumption of 1.5m^3.

The tariff charged to all residential category users at the time of the field-work (2004) was US$0.22/m^3 for the first 30m^3, then US$0.44/m^3 from 31–150m^3, with figures quoted in US dollars, as the tariff was linked to the dollar. The tariff was a combined water and sewerage tariff. It was intended that in the sixth year of the concession the tariff should increase to cover the cost of extending sewerage and developing wastewater treatment but socio-economic pressures prevented this from happening. Thus, customers who do not have a sewerage connection pay the same tariff as those who do. The substantial first block in the residential tariff means there is little cross-subsidy from wealthy to poor residential customers. Furthermore, there is also a high subsidy from commerce and industry to residential users. The commercial sector pays US$0.66/m^3 for the first 20m^3 and US$1.19/m^3 for 21m^3 and above, while industrial customers pay US$1.19/m^3 for all water consumption. According to one interviewee,'There is 99 per cent bill collection efficiency at 12 months. It is in the Indian culture to pay their debts.'

SISAB gave AISA an A+ benchmark rating for its operations in 2003, the highest of any water utility in the country. AISA commented that 'what is clear today, with the efficiency gains over the last years, we have managed balance cash flow, the maintenance and running the system at first world standards – but we cannot finance expansion. We need US$3–4 million per year for expansion of service coverage'.

Regulator SISAB describes its mission as 'to regulate the sector but search-ing for equity between three groups: consumers, companies and the state' with a key component of that task being to revise tariffs on a five-yearly basis – being 'the only entity responsible, this is very sensitive, very important. … The regula-tor (with a status similar to a minister in the government) is a far more independent person here, there are no links with the executive powers, unlike in Buenos Aires.'

Tariffs up until 2004 were revised through a methodology calculated under the contract negotiations, but in 2004 the Ministry was planning to approve its own methodology of tariff setting. Taking a slightly different view of regulatory independence, the Vice Minister of the Ministry of Services and Public Works stated that 'the tariff is a result of a mathematical process, based on discounted cash flow equations, which I give to them – financial sufficiency is the concept'.

On the SISAB payroll in La Paz and Santa Cruz there were 31 staff. Additionally there were seven staff/consultants in La Paz and four staff in Santa Cruz, paid for by the World Bank. SISAB was trying to obtain approval from the treasury to employ these staff plus one more (12 total) on a permanent basis, believing it had enough funding (based on a sliding scale charge on utilities regulated, from '2 per cent of annual revenues to 50 bolivianos per month') but there was 'no permission given' to employ those staff. Another indicator of regulatory independence.

The complaints most often heard by SISAB are with respect to paying a US dollar tariff that means the bill increases every month even though consumption is unchanged: 'The tariff was fixed in the bidding processes for the concession and is to continue unchanged until 2006 from the concession's start on August 1, 1997. There are no inflation increases in the tariff.' The government promised in 2005, before revoking the concession, to tie the water rates to the boliviano rather than the dollar.

Another view on the process was given by the General Secretary of ANESAPA, the national service providers association, who was 'very much in favour of regulation, in particular a regulatory system giving clear objectives to the water companies. Prior to regulation, companies could do what they wanted'. In response to a question about progress since privatization, the response was:

> *they have done some good work, they have made good progress, but they are unfortunate in that they no longer have any political influence. Unlike Cochabamba, Illimani inherited viable tariffs and didn't have to increase tariffs at a political cost when they took over. There was 80 per cent coverage so the coverage improvement has not been in new works, just extending the distribution network. They have been successful in keeping a good standard of service and in cutting staff. SEMAPA [the predecessor to AISA] had between 3.8 and 4 staff members per thousand connections. Aguas del Illimani now has 2.8 per thousand connections.*

Service to the poor and a universal service obligation

As demonstrated by the bidding process, the government's key objective in privatizing water and sewerage services in La Paz and El Alto was to increase coverage in poor areas. A requirement of the tender was for companies to state how many connections they would provide in El Alto, the poorest of the twin cities, by the end of 2001. The winning company, AISA, committed to providing 71,752 new in-house connections in El Alto. This number was estimated to equate to a 100 per cent service provision in El Alto. The concession required that AISA must then keep pace with population growth over the 30-year lifetime of the concession.

In preparation for extending service coverage, the incoming utility undertook a social mapping exercise as well as an anthropological study. This aimed to understand the challenges of serving the fast-growing (from 90,060 in 1976 to 405,492 in 1992) largely indigenous population of El Alto, whose main language is Aymara, in order to understand their perceptions of water and how they might wish to be served (Ramiro, personal communication, 1999). The target low-income population to be served includes the 'vulnerable non-poor' who are living outside the designated service areas but in conventional housing, particularly on the steep slopes surrounding La Paz, and the 'coping' and 'developing' poor in El Alto who have been able to take advantage of relatively easy access to flat land in El Alto but who have no title to that land.

With privatization, the process of connecting to the water and sewerage network became simpler and less bureaucratic. The connection process was less time consuming, less costly and offered flexible payment options. For example, AISA itself requested permission from the municipality to open trenches on behalf of groups of applicants (Komives, 2001) as opposed to the common practice in some countries of expecting applicants to apply themselves.

'Within weeks of taking over, Aguas del Illimani had moved all officials who had to sign off on applications into one room. Applicants then knew exactly where to go to apply for a new connection and could watch paperwork move from official to official' (Komives, 2001). The case study researcher attended a community meeting with the company where difficulties in obtaining new connections were apparently readily addressed. One of the subsequent challenges for the water utility is the remarkably low water consumption of newly connected customers, for some households as little as $1m^3$ per month.

As a pilot project, condominial sewerage connections were made available as an alternative to conventional sewerage connections, costing about 25 per cent less. Condominial sewerage, also known as simplified or backyard or in-block sewerage, achieves reduced costs by constructing shallow sewers, sometimes with rodding eyes rather than manholes, through the rear of plots where there is no likelihood of vehicular damage.

The company also developed the possibility for households to contribute their labour in order to reduce both the water and sewerage connection costs. The standard charges were US$196 for water and US$249 for sewerage. Through contributing labour and certain materials, households could reduce these costs to US$90 and US$10 respectively. Furthermore, connection charges could be paid over a 30-month period at favourable interest rates.

In addition, the utility used a development approach in the poorest areas, including micro-credit facilities for household sanitary facilities, technical assistance and 'community organization and training' to allow 'community members to reflect on their reality and how to solve their problems'.

With regard to the challenge of illegal tenure, 'it is a big problem', but the company declared itself to be:

> *flexible because the property problem is a big problem, 70 per cent don't have papers, the municipality building of El Alto was destroyed in the events of 2003 when all records were lost. We are only giving service to areas where the principality has approved the area for urbanization. Areas which are not approved for urbanization include the steep areas around La Paz where there is physical stability problem but where the domestic tariff is applied to stand posts.*

Alternative service providers

Given the already high coverage of water supply in La Paz and El Alto there is limited need for alternative service providers. In areas of the city where the population density does not meet the criteria of 50 inhabitants or 15 buildings per *manzana* (approx 0.7 hectares), AISA is not obliged to provide connections. In some areas of El Alto that are not served by the pipe network, the municipality provides a tanker truck service. It was reported that vendor-supplied water in El Alto costs around US$3.50/m^3 (as opposed to the US$0.22/m^3 domestic piped rate).

By law, the 1992 National Regulations for Water and Sanitation Service in Urban Areas, stated that individuals or entities that wish to exploit a private water source must obtain permission from the water utility holding the concession. In effect the utility has authority over water rights in the concession area.

Where the criteria do not yet require the utility to provide piped water it is permitted that an individual household or group of households can install a pipeline and connect to the main. In such cases the household(s) retain the right to charge other households a connection fee to access that main. After a period of five years, ownership of such pipelines was to transfer to AISA, who had a responsibility to approve the technical standards and construction quality.

Consumer involvement and perceptions of low-income consumers

There were no formal consumer groups but with approximately 60 per cent of the population being members of their local residents' associations, through the federation of residents' associations (Federacion de Juntas Vecinales – FEJUVE), there was easy access to civil society. The regulator SISAB was holding workshops around the country to 'train customers' as to their duties and rights and the good use of water, accessing customers through the 'head office' of FEJUVE. This was part of a national campaign by SISAB called *Consumidores al Dia* or 'consumers up to date' with their bill payment. SISAB is implementing this education campaign through one-day workshops with the presidents (or a delegate) of FEJUVE. Workshops have 80–100 participants and start with a questionnaire of a sample of participants to assess what people know about SISAB, how to present a complaint, what are their water service rights and other relevant issues. At the end of the day the questionnaire is repeated partly for self-evaluation. SISAB explained that this work is based on an agreement signed with FEJUVE: 'we are pioneers in approaching civil society in this way'.

Since 1998 SISAB has required that all the regulated service providers must provide a consumer office, known as an ODECO, with the broad aim of improving the customer-utility relationship. The specific functions of the ODECO include attending and resolving customer complaints concerning water and sewerage services; providing information with respect to the regulated services; and answering queries and being a focal point for emergency calls.

There are stipulated time periods within which the service provider must respond to customer complaints. These time periods vary according to service provider. For example, AISA had to respond to an emergency situation such as serious leakage within 24 hours. In the case of an unusually high bill, the service provider had 15 days to investigate and a further 20 days to take corrective action (if necessary). SISAB undertakes an annual audit of customer attention performance of each of the concessionaires. This visit is announced only one day prior to the audit. Where customers are unhappy with the response to their complaint they may appeal to SISAB to further investigate and there is a freephone number to call SISAB. However, customers must fill out a complaint form that is logged by SISAB, who in turn present each case to the service provider in a weekly meeting.

SISAB and AISA were also cooperating with FEJUVE to promote better a customer–utility relationship. There are around 450 individual neighbourhood committees in El Alto and 580 in La Paz. FEJUVE have legal recognition and are viewed as representatives of civil society. Each week the representatives of the La Paz and El Alto FEJUVE meet with AISA to discuss problems or explain procedures to individual neighbourhood committees. FEJUVE representatives, now well versed in service procedures, act as intermediaries between AISA and individual member committees in a manner similar to a trades union.

At a meeting with representatives of the national FEJUVE, members explained how they represented 7200 neighbourhood committees nationally, looking at basic services (electricity, gas, telecoms, water). FEJUVE has legal recognition under Law 1551, recognizing them as representatives of civil society.

FEJUVE members described how they 'have lived the two faces of regulation, with regulation, and without regulation' and commented that water supply has improved technically and administratively but that there was something to work on regarding tariffs and coverage. They believed that the proclaimed 100 per cent coverage in La Paz and El Alto was that within the concession area, there is only 88 per cent potable water and barely 50 per cent sewerage coverage:

> *We have a duty to call the workshops, they have the duty to call members to attend. They must tell us if complaints are not being investigated, it is all in the framework and having good results. We are making a deeper analysis of the results of regulation: there has been improved service to 24 hours when there used to be many cuts, it is an interesting relationship (not good or bad) between Aguas del Illimani and the Federation, we have the lowest tariffs in the country in La Paz. We have meetings with Aguas del Illimani, one week for El Alto and the second week one for La Paz.*

The committees report to SISAB as necessary, the regulator noting that they could not expect knowledgeable customers without this level of interaction.

The El Alto representative from FEJUVE commented that El Alto is a special city as the people are poor. There are 450 communities, each covered by FEJUVE: 'People don't have sewerage systems, the state is giving no subsidies, everything is from the people in tariffs, to get a connection you have to pay. Treatment of wastewater does not cover all the town, the capability is not there, we need another plant as the existing plant is overloaded.'

The La Paz representative, representing 580 communities, coordinated 'the work between the committees and Aguas del Ilimani. ... Each Monday we talk about problems and the problems are being resolved slowly. We understand that it is a process that takes time.' There are 500 families per zone in El Alto. The neighbourhood committees, representing between 300 and 1000 inhabitants each have 15 to 21 representatives, of whom all are working voluntarily. The first committee was established in 1898 in La Paz. The first federation was in 1916.

In discussion with the case study researchers, some national FEJUVE committee members were interested in the idea of becoming part of a formal customer committee that might assist in adjudicating customer complaints in addition to lobbying for better services.

One householder from a low-income area explained how he paid US$30 for water and US$200 for power, but that part of the energy cost goes to boiling water because 'people do not trust the quality'.

Regulating water and sanitation for the poor?

The water and sewerage regulator in Bolivia, SISAB, has since its creation had to function in an extremely volatile political situation. The regulatory system was established in Bolivia at a time of increasing privatization and structural adjustment policies. The trades unions and indigenous movements ousted President Gonzalo Sanchez de Lozada in 2003 after bloody protests left more than 80 people dead. Since then the country has undergone a period of economic paralysis with more than 700 strikes, road blocks and marches, followed subsequently by another change of government. Amid this turmoil SISAB struggled to demonstrate to the wider public that it was working for sustainable, improved water and sewerage services.

SISAB has been trying to establish itself as a credible institution and has found support among international agencies such as the World Bank and European Union to develop its own capacity to be an effective regulator. On examination of its publicly stated aims and objectives there is no indication that SISAB is striving for increased access to water for the urban poor. There is however a clear statement that addressing service quality is one of the principal aims of SISAB.

SISAB must walk something of a tightrope in deciding how hard to push water utilities to improve service coverage and quality. It is recognized that many of the municipal and cooperative companies have very limited resources for investment in their water systems. SISAB does impose fines but is clearly aware that to exert its full authority on the smaller companies would lead them to collapse. Even in La Paz a substantial increase in tariffs is not thought to be socially acceptable.

This means that the current absence of wastewater treatment in La Paz (untreated sewage is discharged into rivers running through the city), with only minimal treatment in El Alto) will remain unchanged. The service provider, before the termination of the concession, had made it clear that such an investment would be impossible without a significant increase in tariffs.

According to SISAB, service coverage and quality has improved in La Paz and El Alto. Representatives of FEJUVE also accept that certain aspects of service quality had improved under the AISA concession.

However, because of political pressure, in January 2005 the Bolivian Government announced that it would cancel the concession contract. This move was intended to appease the neighbourhood committees who threatened a city-wide protest over the water privatization. The claim against the company was that it had not fulfilled the contract obligations to provide water and sewerage services to around '200,000 people' in El Alto. This claim is disputed by the utility who argue they have met their contract obligations, a view that appears to be supported by SISAB's records. The company claimed that 'the number of people living outside the service area is closer to 30,000 and that it is not required to extend service to them'. They were also in the process of obtaining donor funds to extend services to nearby unserved areas, beyond their understanding of the service boundary.

The effectiveness of the protest against the privatization was strengthened through the neighbourhood committees' ability to link it with a series of ongoing national strikes in protest at the increase in prices of oil and the intended privatization of gas. The government's initial announcement to cancel the concession, perhaps a sacrificial pawn, was rejected by the committees who claimed that it was too ambiguous and set no date for the company's departure. Eventually a government decree re-established the La Paz and El Alto municipal water company to resume the management of water services.

Considering the concession before its termination, the partnership between society, as mediated by government through the contractual, regulated goals, and the private provider might well be seen to have been delivering universal service in an exemplary fashion. It could be argued that it was the innovative approach of the new service provider who developed these services, rather than owing to any particular input from the regulator. But this would be reasonable as it is the role of the regulator to oversee the goals, not to deliver them. It is the responsibility of the regulator to ensure that there is sufficient 'room to innovate' for the service provider within a legal framework that protects against monopoly abuse.

However, society rejected this approach even though it achieved services significantly in advance of countries with similar levels of economic wealth. SISAB could take some responsibility for this seemingly backward step for failing to convince people of the necessary costs of providing a high quality water and sewerage services but in the end it was simply overwhelmed by much bigger societal issues.

CASE STUDY 8: MANILA, THE PHILIPPINES

Lyn Capistrano and Esther Gerlach

The water sector and institutional framework

In 1997 the Metropolitan Waterworks and Sewerage System (MWSS) entered into concession agreements with Manila Water Company and Maynilad Water Services, who were allocated the eastern and western service areas of metropolitan Manila respectively after a selective bidding process. Each company had to have at least 65 per cent national ownership. The winning bidder for the eastern concession surprised everyone by bidding for a very significant reduction in price. MWSS remained as asset holding authority. By virtue of the contracts, a Regulatory Office (RO) was established to monitor the implementation of the concession agreements.

The initial contracts required the concessionaires to undertake phased extension of service areas to ensure service coverage to the poor. Learning from each other, as well as from the electricity providers, Manila Water and Maynilad developed innovative approaches to service delivery in the slums and shanties.

According to the law on urban water services, local government units (LGUs) in the Philippines assume responsibilities for water supply and sanitation systems through water districts (WDs). In the case of the 12 cities and 5 municipalities comprising Metro Manila, this responsibility was delegated to MWSS, which as a public corporation was awarded the jurisdiction, supervision and control of waterworks and sewerage systems within the National Capital Region and peripheral territories (Rizal province and part of Cavite province) in 1971. A nationwide water crisis in the mid-1990s prompted urgent calls for effective measures to tackle the situation, and government policy responses incidentally paved the way for PSP in water services provision.

From the start of the concessions the contract regulator MWSS-RO saw its role as balancing the interest of stakeholders: protecting consumers from high prices and poor services and providing incentives to concessionaires to invest, be efficient and earn a profit. The monitoring functions of MWSS-RO include: compliance with drinking water and wastewater quality standards; water supply, sewerage and sanitation development, programme repair and maintenance of assets; non-revenue water reduction targets; collection efficiency targets; customer service standards; operational cost efficiency; and, of particular relevance to this study, projects to attain required population coverage and the required year to attain targets. However, other than financial auditing, MWSS-RO does not conduct a regular and structured audit of data submitted by Maynilad and Manila Water. According to the case study field investigations, when the concessionaires submit a monthly progress report, MWSS-RO has on occasion validated the information only through random community visits and interviews with people.

```
┌─────────────────────────────────────────────────────────────────────┐
│                      PHILIPPINES KEY FACTS                            │
│                                                                       │
│  • Human Development Index rank        90 out of 177                  │
│  • Population living < US$2 per day     43 per cent                   │
│  • GNI per capita at purchasing power                                 │
│    parity (2006)                        US$5980                       │
│  • Country population                   85 million                    │
│  • Urban population                     64 per cent                   │
│  • Urban population growth rate 2005–2010  2.8 per cent               │
│  • Urban water coverage                 87 per cent                   │
│  • Water supply by household connection 58 per cent                   │
│  • Improved urban sanitation coverage   80 per cent                   │
│  • Research focus location              Manila                        │
│  • Research focus population            11 million                    │
│  • Service provider                     Manila Water and Maynilad     │
│  • Contract form                        Concession                    │
│  • Regulator                            MWSS-RO                        │
│  • Regulatory start date                1997                          │
│  • Exchange rate to US$ at fieldwork    PHP55                         │
│  • Implied purchasing power parity                                    │
│    conversion rate to US$               PHP 13                        │
│  • Implied undervaluation ratio         4.23                          │
│                                                                       │
└─────────────────────────────────────────────────────────────────────┘
```

Maynilad, the original concessionaire for the western region, attempted to renegotiate its concession agreement with MWSS, partly due to foreign exchange devaluation that was a particular burden, having been assigned 90 per cent of MWSS's debt in the original concession agreement. Currency exchange protection had not been a feature of the original contract and government was reluctant to be seen to be relaxing the contracts in any way. Maynilad had also found it extremely difficult to make any significant impact on the approximately 65 per cent non-revenue water levels that it inherited. Subsequent to this case study fieldwork, MWSS completed the resale of the western concession to national investors having, during the process, received expressions of interest not only from Manila Water, the eastern concessionaire, but also from Ondeo, the minority partner in failed Maynilad.

The legal framework

Service providers

The research confirmed significant overlap between administrative and regulatory functions of the various agencies and public bodies involved in the water sector: the National Water Resources Board, Department of Health (DoH), Department of Interior and Local Government, Department of Environment and Natural Resources (DENR), Local Water Utilities Administration, National Economic Development Authority (NEDA), Department of Public Works and Highways, LGUs, Department of Finance and most importantly Barangay Water and Sanitation Associations/Rural Water and Sanitation Associations which operate and self-regulate community water systems.

In the Philippines, the Public Works Department is a government body with national-level responsibility for water supply and sanitation. However, the government has a strong decentralization policy and in practice LGUs have the lead responsibility for the provision of water supply and sanitation services (Local Government Code, Republic Act No. 7160, 1991). The code allows LGUs to delegate service provision to third parties, including both communities and private entities.

In Manila the primary service providers are the Manila Water and the Maynilad corporations. These private sector corporations operate under Concession Agreements (1997) regulated by MWSS-RO. MWSS is a government body established under a Charter (Republic Act No. 6234, as amended), with powers provided for under the National Water Crisis Act, 1995 (Republic Act No. 8041). Its RO was created by virtue of the Concession Agreements.

The Concession Agreements do not impose a universal obligation on the concessionaires. They are required to 'offer' water supply services to all existing customers in the service area and to make at least sufficient connections (net of any disconnections) to meet the coverage targets. They are also required to meet reliability (continuity and pressure), and drinking water quality standards. The latter are specified by the Department of Health Administrative Order No. 26-A, 1994, that is, the Philippine National Standards for Drinking Water 1993, under 2.9 of Presidential Decree 856.

A failure by the concessionaire to meet any service obligation that continues for more than 60 days (or 15 days in cases where the failure could adversely affect public health or welfare) could lead to financial penalties (Art. 10.4). In the case of dispute, Art. 12 obliges both sides to abide by arbitration proceedings (using an Appeals Panel) in accordance with the arbitration rules under international law of the UN Commission on International Trade Law (Art. 12 has been invoked with respect to Maynilad's concession). The provisions of Art. 12 are meant to preclude recourse to the courts. However s.3(d) of the Charter does provide for MWSS to sue and be sued.

Under Art. 6.8 concessionaires must comply with all Philippine laws, statutes, rules, regulations, orders and directives of any governmental authority. For instance because all waters belong to the state, a permit is required to abstract water for supply from any natural water source (Water Code – Presidential Decree No. 1067, 1976).

The two concessionaires do not serve all the people in Metro Manila and a range of small-scale independent service providers (SSISPs) exist. While water service providers should operate under licence from the National Water Resources Board (NWRB) many do not, but they are tolerated because they provide a useful service. They have no formal legal status, whether they obtain their water supply legally or illegally, and are largely unregulated, which means that they have no legal obligations but neither do they have any legal rights. In the latter case they are ultimately vulnerable to the exclusive operating rights of the large concessionaires in whose service areas they operate.

The Concession Agreement (Art. 5.3) did allow for any service provider operating legally (i.e. under licence from the NWRB) at the time the concession was granted to continue operating with the consent of MWSS. The Agreement (Art. 5.3) also allows for new 'third party' service providers to gain licences to operate from NWRB, but only if approval by both MWSS and the concessionaire is given. However, these apply only to new developments, for a limited period (less than 10 years) and are subject to revocation (upon 60 days' notice) whenever the concessionaire is ready and wishes to take over provision of services in those areas.

Service recipients

The rights of service recipients are not explicit but may be implied from the responsibilities for water supply and sanitation assigned to the various government departments, public authorities or private entities. Such responsibilities as expressed in law do not explicitly establish a USO. With MWSS for example the legislation sets out its 'attributes, powers and functions' but no duties as such. The Philippines Bill of Rights (Constitution) makes no explicit reference to rights to water supply and sanitation, but it does provide for access to information (s.7) and access to the courts (s.11), together with speedy processing of cases (s.16).

The spread of responsibility for water-related issues (from the President's office, various government departments and authorities or agencies, NGOs, private companies to individual citizens) presents a confusing picture to the average domestic water user. Lack of confidence arises when bodies such as the NRWB, with many powers and responsibilities, operate without the resources to exercise them.

Those receiving water from one of the concessionaires must pay the required charges and are liable to disconnection if unpaid for longer than 60 days (Art. 6.6).

A review of the laws, policies and guidelines pertaining to water supply systems revealed that there is no specific mention of the poor, nor are there any references to pro-poor regulation. Specific documents or guidelines that directly address the needs of the poor seem unavailable. Clear lines of accountability cannot be discerned from the legislation, which may explain why the various agencies charged with regulatory functions are observed to be weak in enforcing existing regulations. Unclear responsibilities and overlapping functions are a cause of confusion and frustration to the public and discourage individuals from taking action if they do not receive their entitlement to water supply as a basic human right.

The Local Government Code brings to the fore greater autonomy and the need for enhanced skills and competencies of local government executives and staff. As such, businesses and NGOs may be able to work in partnership with LGUs to enhance water provision to the poorest. This Code could potentially provide an enabling environment for communities and civil society organizations to take part in the regulatory process.

Government policies of prescribing water supply services on the basis of a three-level classification and cost-recovery strategies have resulted in many of the poor accessing 'Level I' (point source such as wells and hand pumps) and 'Level II' (communal taps) systems, which place the burden of improving water quality on the household. 'Level III' (household water connections) systems, which often receive the largest government investments and subsidies (in capital and operational costs), serve mostly the non-poor. Thus, the inequality in low access of the poor to Level III services is compounded by the subsidy going to systems serving non-poor clients. While the sector strategy emphasizes full cost recovery for new systems, it is equally important to initiate measures to remedy inequities in existing systems, especially in terms of providing the poor with access to preferred Level III services.

Service provider performance and regulatory practice

Manila Water (2008) reports that the population served since the start of their concession in 1997 to the end of 2007 has gone from 4.6 million to 5.3 million, representing an increase in coverage from 58 per cent to 98 per cent, with an increase in average water availability from 16 to 24 hours per day (increase in the percentage of customers enjoying 24-hour water availability from 26 per cent in 1997 to 98 per cent at the end of 2006) and a reduction in non-revenue water from 63 per cent to 25 per cent, and staff per thousand connections from 9.8 to 1.7. Capital investment of approximately US$350 million has also ensured that water supplied has increased from 95 litres per person per day to 179, achieving 100 per cent compliance with water quality standards.

As a reminder of the cost of sewerage and wastewater treatment, although the company can claim that it has successfully rehabilitated its major plant at Magallanes, the capacity of this plant represents just 4.2 per cent of the volume of water supplied.

The company was able to declare a profit from 2001, achieving net income of US$55.3 million for 2006. The declared 'compounded annual growth rate' in revenues was 27 per cent per year between 1998 and 2006, with net income growth averaging 56 per cent in 2006 (Manila Water, 2008).

Maynilad, now owned by D.M. Consunji Inc. and Metro Pacific Investments Corp. (83.97 per cent) and Lyonnaise Asia Water Limited (16 per cent), reports serving 677,985 billed water services, equivalent to a population of around 6.2 million (77 per cent coverage by population), up from 464,644 service connections at the time of privatization, with a present staffing ration of 3.5 per thousand connections. With a quoted production of 2266 million litres per day in 2007 and based upon the often-quoted 65 per cent non-revenue water, it

---

BOX 6.2 VISION AND MISSION STATEMENTS OF **MWSS-RO**

Vision: 'Continuous supply of safe, reasonably priced water and environment-friendly sewerage system through effective regulation'.

Mission: 'To ensure that the quality and level of service provided by the Concessionaires meet global standards; and to balance the interests of the stakeholders'.

Source: www.mwssro.org.ph

---

appears that Maynilad is delivering approximately 135 litres per person per day but 'as of June 2007, 42 per cent of customers have a 24-hour, uninterrupted water supply, while 40 per cent have intermittent water due to low pressure, or no water at all'. In addition 'roughly 944,000 West Zone residents get their water from private water connections, deepwells, and water vendors' (Maynilad, 2008). Maynilad has one sewerage connection for every ten water connections.

Regulator MWSS-RO (most recent available report 2003) undertakes a 'rate rebasing' exercise every five years that includes a 'full review of business plans' but between these price reviews there can be annual adjustments for inflation, quarterly reviews and adjustments if needed of any foreign currency differentials and an annual extraordinary price adjustment for unforeseen events such as El Niño.

The price review resulted in significant price rises over the period of private sector involvement. The average basic rate at the start of concession in 1997–1998 was PHP2.32/m^3 (US$0.18) for Manila Water and PHP4.96/m^3 (US$0.38) for Maynilad (down from pre-privatization levels of PHP8.78/m^3 (US$0.68). By 2007 the average prices were PHP15.90/m^3 (US$1.22) and PHP22.47/m^3 (US$1.73) respectively (MWSS-RO, 2007) but noting the very significant devaluation in 1997–1998 for US dollar figures. The authors see the level of increase not so much as a failure of private sector involvement but rather a success for economic regulation in that the only way to ensure adequate services is to ensure financial sustainability. Although cross-subsidies from government are a very appropriate means of delivering service expansion and serviceability, experience has shown that it is often wiser to depend upon revenue from tariffs. The 2008 rate rebasing is reported by Manila Water to be giving them anticipated tariff increases over the next five years of 19 per cent, 14 per cent, 12 per cent, 10 per cent and 10 per cent. However, these increases have also to deliver water supply expansion to Rizal towns and Bulacan and most significantly and expensively, wastewater coverage increases from 10 per cent to 30 per cent in the next five years, sewerage coverage having risen to 10 per cent in 2006 from only 3 per cent in 1997 (Manila Water, 2006). There is a 'guaranteed return' of 9.3 per cent included in the water tariff.

By contrast Maynilad 'will be implementing a PHP1.30/m^3 (US$0.1) reduction in its tariff, which will amount to a reduction of about PHP20 (US$1.54) in the water bill of a family of five consuming an average of 30m³ of water per month' (Maynilad, 2008) from January 2008 due to downward movements in the 'Special Transitory Mechanism'. Maynilad plans to invest US$200 million in 2008 and a total of US$640 million over the next five years in order to provide 24-hour continuous water supply to 100 per cent of the concession area by 2012 (Maynilad, 2008).

Service to the poor and a universal service obligation

Universal water service coverage was not a stated target of the concession agreements, though a very significant increase in coverage over the lifetime of the concession, including a representative cover of different areas in the metropolis, was a requirement. Official coverage statistics claimed a connection rate of greater than 80 per cent (2002 figures), but evidence collected for this research suggests that 35 per cent of the population still relies on groundwater and alternative small-scale independent providers, including homeowners' associations and water vendors. The use of statistics also obscures the real service coverage. For instance, according to Manila Water figures, each connection covers 9.2 users, whereas the average household in Metro Manila counts 5 members. The concession agreement states that one stand post for 475 people in low-income areas counts as full coverage.

An estimated 35 per cent of Metro Manila's residents live in informal slum settlements, with more than 20 per cent surviving close to or under the poverty line. In response to the scale of the need, especially among urban poor communities, both concessionaires have implemented targeted programmes to extend services to the urban poor: Bayan Tubig (Maynilad) and Tubig para sa Barangay (Manila Water). Maynilad's Bayan Tubig programme works with urban poor neighbourhood associations in bill collection and maintenance. Since drinking water is piped straight into urban poor households, water costs have dropped by a third. Water consumption has risen significantly though it is reported that public health has only improved by a relatively small amount.

Manila Water's 'Tubig para sa Barangay' programme offers three options to urban poor communities: individual household connections, meter/connection per 4–5 households and thirdly a community 'mother meter'. This 'service differentiation', matching the service level to consumers' needs, appears to have been critical in extending services.

Maynilad, using similar approaches, in addition introduced TEMFACIL (temporary facility), also known as the 3-R: 'recover, reallocate and reuse'. The pilot project is in Tondo, Manila, where non-revenue water is high due to illegal connections. For this project, pipes are laid at ground level, embedded in cement and integrated in curbs and pavements. The project aims to minimize illegal connections and recover non-revenue water. People are forced to get new connections as old pipes, where they were connected illegally, are no longer used.

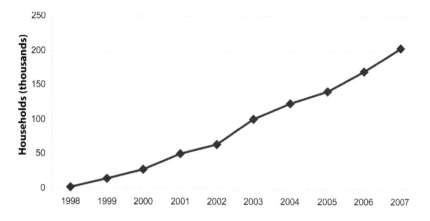

Source: Franceys' analysis of Manila Water Annual Reports

Figure 6.2 *Poor households reported as served through Manila Water's Water for the Community programme*

However, there is a belief that community initiatives to organize and manage self-supply and participate in the regulatory process are discouraged by the proliferation of regulatory functions spread across many agencies and the threat of political interference.

The water service providers studied for this research have internal policies and guidelines to get the poor connected. Maynilad has resorted to easy instalment payment of connection fees. Both Manila Water and Maynilad have enhanced the outreach activities of their customer relations units. They also try to act on complaints and enquiries as promptly as possible. The reconnection process has been made less tedious and less expensive.

Manila Water is now claiming that they have connected 204,000 poor households through their Tubig para sa Barangay or Water for the Community programme since 1997 (see Figure 6.2), representing more than 1 million people served (Manila Water, 2008), whereas Maynilad, most energetic in serving poor households in the early years, claim their Bayan Tubig programme, has benefited more than 102,000 households (Maynilad, 2008).

It was reported by one of the concessionaires that (many?) newly connected households were quickly increasing their consumption to the average level – implying that when the barriers to connection are overcome then serving the poor is a viable business – at least in Manila.

Alternative service providers

The other sources of water services unclassified by government policies are the SSISPs that can be grouped into:

- residential system operators who consist of real estate developers and homeowners' associations;
- mobile water truckers/water haulers; and
- local entrepreneurs who are engaged in constructing and operating independent water supply systems in communities (for example, water refilling stations), water co-operatives and also bottled water manufacturers.

Using a variety of water sources and delivery modalities, they provide water to needy communities at varying rates. They are driven, though, by a common enterprising mission to meet existing and potential demand at rates that reflect market forces, customer needs and varying preferences. To those sidelined by the public utility systems, these SSISPs provide an indispensable service and outreach.

There is no single central government agency regulating all the various types of SSISPs. Rather, there are several regulatory offices overseeing certain types of SSISP as well as responding to some components of regulation.

For example, Inpart Engineering, with its own boreholes, storage and distribution network, sells water to *aguadors* (water tenders) for PHP35.00/m^3 (US$2.7), which is equivalent to five drums. *Aguadors* sell one drum of water for PHP20.00 (US$1.54). A gallon of water (3.8 litres) is sold for PHP1.50 (US$0.11). In stores, various brands of bottled water are sold for an average of PHP30.00 per litre (US$2.3).

The non-recognition of SSISPs excludes them from the regulatory process and even prevents them from accessing loans to enable them to improve their services. In past instances water companies refused to sell bulk water to SSISPs. Local governments and neighbourhood associations can also make it difficult for SSISPs to operate in their jurisdictions.

To an SSISP like Inpart Engineering, Manila Water's Tubig para sa Barangay programme is one of the biggest threats to its existence as a business enterprise. SSISPs also perpetually lack capital to improve their operations. Instead of one, several regulatory offices oversee certain types but not all SSISPs. Improved policies and regulations can be created to address both the concerns of the poor and the SSISPs. It is the companies' stated objective to take over the areas served by the SSISPs with no compensation for the investment in piped distribution systems that some have made.

The apparent lack of price sensitivity by consumers of SSISPs – some of the neighbourhood association SSISPs also add on a local environmental improvement charge that is paid by poor households – indicates that the regulator could be more generous in setting tariffs for the two main utilities that would provide financing for a faster roll-out of lower-cost service coverage in poor areas.

One local entrepreneur, Inpart Engineering, has invested a considerable amount of money in establishing a local distribution system from the family borewell. Locally recruited plumbers act as agents for installing new connections and for collecting payments, little and often. This closeness to the customer brings many benefits in ensuring ongoing payments as well as sorting out complaints. For example, none of those interviewed in the focus groups was ever invited by Manila Water, Maynilad and MWSS-RO to attend any meeting or customer forum. However, those being served by Inpart Engineering were 'constantly consulted and informed', according to recipients of its service.

Consumer involvement and perceptions of low-income consumers

To promote customer involvement, MWSS-RO conducts public consultations before finalizing any petition for price adjustments. The involvement of the public, cause-oriented groups and consumers has been difficult but encouraging. The regulator is planning to expand the consultation process further, not only during price adjustments but also on matters involving performance of concessionaires on water service delivery. The effectiveness and independence of MWSS-RO has always been an issue for the concessionaires and consumers, considering that it was established under the jurisdiction of the MWSS Board of Trustees – one of the parties to the Concession Agreement. MWSS-RO has initiated reforms to strengthen its capability in monitoring the concessionaires' compliance with service obligation targets. In addition, it is also pushing for an independent regulatory body through legislation. Its proposed regulatory reforms include: adoption of key performance indicators and business efficiency measures, conduct of public assessment of water services, capacity building for MWSS-RO and the creation of a water regulatory commission.

Manila Water is required to meet customer services standards but nevertheless seems to have made significant efforts to improve communications and relations with its customers (with special consideration of the poor), and offers a customer hotline when problems with service provision arise.

The researchers talked with a total of 40 poor respondents in four separate communities served by four different water utilities, the communities being characterized as mostly the 'developing poor' with a few that could be categorized as vulnerable non-poor. Using story telling and pictures as sorts of 'discussion documents' to stimulate communication, the researchers helped the respondents articulate their views and recommendations. It was found that overall the majority of respondents were not aware of any customer forum or water associations existing in their locality. Even if they were aware, they had no knowledge about them or thought they could not access them, considering the time, cost and social connections required. Reasons cited for the arising issues and concerns were:

- the economic crisis and the lack of employment opportunities make it difficult for poor families to have water supply;
- political interference;

- illegal connections;
- communities are changing, they are beginning to assert their interests and work on their own issues, which is why there are now a lot of conflicts;
- lack of information;
- government and private sectors do not usually prioritize investments for urban poor communities;
- there is a perception that regulators protect water companies, not the consumers;
- absence of a person or group with harmonizing skills to take a lead and sustain efforts.

There is already an existing citizens' coalition for adequate, accessible and affordable water in the Philippines. Bantay Tubig, organized in April 2002 in response to the worsening water crisis in the country, monitors price increases, regulatory processes and the performance of water companies in Metro Manila. It started as a collaborative effort among civil society organizations. Bantay Tubig has organized public information campaigns on pricing and regulatory issues, mobilized against regulatory anomalies and concessionaire abuse, initiated Congressional enquiries on various aspects of water privatization, and pursued legal action against Maynilad. Bantay Tubig has no full-time secretariat. Members work on a voluntary basis, pursuing specific areas of the water issues according to their expertise.

This study used focus groups in low-income areas firstly to find out the actual situation of service to the poor under a regulatory system but also to test a focus group methodology to determine its potential as an ongoing tool of regulation, to enable the regulator to make better decisions regarding the balance of future investments, efficiency demands and pricing. Respondents described themselves as being 'often uneducated, afraid of authorities, lacking time and money to "voice" our opinions'.

Data gathered in the focus groups revealed the perception that:

- urban poor communities tend to be neglected in government development priorities;
- unaffordable connection fees as the 'passport to water services' act as a deterrent;
- water is not available 24 hours a day, households also experienced low water pressure;
- although there were few complaints regarding water quality, consumers tend to buy purified water for drinking; the prohibitive cost of medical care and hospitalization justifies this extra expenditure;
- the disconnection policy of the metropolitan water companies leaves the urban poor with no option but to pay the monthly water bill even if the water service is not efficient;

- utilities do not provide pipelines appropriate to the number of households and are perceived as reluctant to share water quality information with consumers.

With respect to water prices, common complaints included abrupt changes in monthly water bills, and water utilities' policy of charging the same tariff and other add-on charges to rich and poor households.

Suggestions were gathered from urban poor survey respondents on what would facilitate increasing access to mains water services:

- easy payment schemes for connecting; water utilities can best help the poor by setting easy instalment payment plans for low-income households to get connected;
- lower tariff rates or slightly reduced tariff structure for the poor;
- recognition of water vendors; when things go wrong with big utilities, water vendors can serve as a fallback and alternative;
- local governments must increase investments in sanitation, drainage and solid waste management in urban poor areas;
- water utilities must invest in extending the piped network to squatter areas. In terms of numbers, squatter families are greater than landowners. This is also good business for the utilities.

Wanting to know more about the technique of public performance assessment based on service quality indicators from utility and user data, an offshoot of the focus group process was designed to look into the system of feedback between Manila Water, Maynilad, the public and MWSS. The researchers took the participants from a community served by Manila Water and another community served by Maynilad to the respective local offices and head offices of both the water utilities to look into the 'performance corners', with a plan to have a focus group after assessing the information available. Both groups also visited the MWSS office to look into how the 'performance café' operates. These 'cafés' had been established with the support of the World Bank, managed by MWSS-RO, as places where customers might find out about the service and its costs. However, it was found that the performance cafés as well as the once-promoted performance corners in local utility offices were non-existent or no longer operational.

The researchers showed participants from both communities the MWSS website indicating the comparative performance of Manila Water and Maynilad in 1997 and from 2001 to the first quarter of 2003. The figures and the implications were explained to them. Afterwards, a focus group was held to get the reactions of the participants to the information they saw. The majority of the participants said that they did not find useful the web-based approach of communicating the service performance of the water utilities. The participants explained that they could not afford computers and internet connections, and they are not even literate in information technology. They suggested that the MWSS and the water concessionaires could work with NGOs, the local press and even parish offices to better reach the poor.

The householders thought that their concerns and problems can be overcome by:

- working together with everyone and involving each one with regards to community water concerns, considering the interests of the others;
- developing a spirit of trusting and collaborative relationships with utilities and regulators;
- having several utilities serving urban poor areas, instead of just one or two; it was hoped that private companies and also the government can become keen in investing in urban poor areas;
- penalizing corruption and inefficiency;
- regulators and water utilities disseminating more information, especially that is useful to the urban poor;
- reducing tariffs for households consuming less water than the prescribed minimum;
- not imposing add-on charges upon poor consumers.

The research showed that focus group discussions held with experienced facilitators can be a meaningful way of engaging local communities in the regulatory process. The urban poor asserted their interest in participating on a regular basis, provided that representatives from MWSS-RO and water providers take a proactive stance, participants receive adequate briefings and results are made accessible to community members. It was noted that some compensation for loss of earnings may be required to encourage the poorest of the poor who cannot afford the luxury of attending meetings instead of earning their daily living. According to one low-income focus group respondent, a better way for companies to communicate with customers is 'Text messages to the poor – we cannot afford computers or internet connections... send SMS text messages instead which are cheap, fast, very interactive and popular even among the poor'.

Regulating water and sanitation for the poor

The Philippines has an array of policies and regulations on water supply. However, despite these, the water sector is beset by issues that revolve around the reliability of the systems, availability and affordability of services, equitable delivery of services, sustainability and acceptable quality of water.

The roles of the many agencies undertaking regulatory functions remain unclear to the urban poor and are made more confusing by political interference. This discourages them from undertaking community initiatives to participate in the regulatory process. Where there are rules and regulations, it is unclear which agencies are accountable, making their enforcement impractical. Most of the urban poor respondents were unaware of the roles and responsibilities of the regulator.

The Local Government Code can potentially create opportunities for businesses and NGOs to work in partnership with LGUs to enhance water provision to the poorest. This Code could provide an enabling environment for communities and civil society organizations to take part in the regulatory process. However, it is necessary to conduct information campaigns to make people aware that regulators must support consumers and implement public policies on behalf of consumers. In this regard, regulators need access to information on water utilities as well as skills in communicating to the public their policies, plans and programmes.

Both regulators and consumers need support in legal aspects, public information, participatory monitoring and the collaborative involvement of all parties concerned. Regulators must initiate the process of calling all urban poor community associations in the locality and consulting on people's participation in the regulation process. This could then lead to the formation of an accredited consultative body. It would help to provide orientations and skills training on the regulatory process to key members. Urban poor representatives need to develop skills and confidence in communication, public speaking and writing.

The private sector in Manila has delivered a very significant increase in household water connections to the poor, but at a price that leaves many consumers uncertain as to who is receiving the greater part of the benefits.

The focus groups indicate that communities are changing. They are beginning to assert their interests and work on their own issues. Regulators and consumers need to work more actively with the media, civil society organizations and law-makers to promote pro-poor policies and put pressure on water utilities to perform better and extend service to even more poor communities.

7

Regulating 'Divested' Water Utilities for the Poor

The last two case studies investigating the role of regulation for the poor relate to the two highest-income countries in the sample of ten (though one is still very significantly 'richer' than the other), with the longest experience of economic regulation of water (over 15 years for each), and to the two most 'extreme' forms of privatization by some descriptions, that is divestiture, where the assets have been sold to the private sector (though not necessarily the rights to water), in addition to the licence to operate.

From the research viewpoint, the Chilean case study results from a visit of less than a week and the authors would like to acknowledge with particular thanks Maria Palominos, Chef de Cabinet, SISS who arranged the visits and interviews and to those interviewees from MIDEPLAN, Aguas Andinas, ESVAL, Comision Defensoria, SERNAC, in addition to SISS, who were particularly open and informative. Mention should also be made of Andrew Trevett's very excellent translation skills. The case study from England is filtered through more than ten years of 'participant observation', attempting to represent customers through what is now the Consumer Council for Water, all backed up by the most accessible and extensive public domain information on the performance of the water companies found anywhere in the world.

CASE STUDY 9: SANTIAGO, CHILE

Andrew Trevett and Richard Franceys

> *Regulation applies equally to private and public companies.* (Interview with regulatory staff, 17 May 2004)

During the late 1980s Chile began reforming water and sanitation services. Initially there was a phase of commercialization, focused on the two main cities, Santiago and Valparaiso, followed by the introduction of economic regulation in 1990. Subsequently, in the late 1990s, a process was started in which most urban services were privatized, again starting with the largest providers first. A key point about the urban water sector in Chile is that a high level of access to water has long been achieved. In 1990 urban water supply coverage was already at 98 per cent. However, prior to the reform process tariffs were considerably below operating costs, commonly less than 50 per cent, and in regions where operating costs were very high, the tariff was only covering about 20 per cent of costs. The reform process led to increased efficiency among the water providers but the need to establish cost-reflective tariffs led to concerns about affordability of services. This issue was addressed by developing a nationwide subsidy for water and sanitation services applicable to both urban and rural residents.

The water sector and institutional framework

Coinciding with the tariff reform process was the creation of the national water regulator for urban areas, the Superintendencia de Servicios Sanitarios (SISS), to ensure any tariff increases were justified. The SISS is appointed by the President of Chile with national jurisdiction and a goal of applying uniform criteria across the country. The initial regulator established the organization as it started in 1990, staying for a very short period (two months), the second regulator stayed for six years and the third for nearly ten, having undertaken a significant reform of SISS in 1998 following the Presidential Commission on Reform of Regulation.

Nationally SISS has awarded 45 concessions that between them are responsible for a total of 340 water and wastewater systems. The time period for a concession in Chile is unlimited ('build, operate, transfer' contracts, or BOTs, are limited to 30 years). There are nine relatively large private companies that provide services to 72 per cent of the urban population. Other categories of regulated service providers include state-owned companies, municipal companies and co-operatives. This case study focuses upon the service provider to the capital Santiago, Aguas Andinas, which was divested from the then publicly owned provider, EMOS, in 1999, and also refers to the provider for Valparaiso, ESVAL.

CHILE KEY FACTS

• Human Development Index rank	40 out of 177
• Population living < US$2 per day	5.6 per cent
• GNI per capita at purchasing power parity (2006)	US$11,270
• Country population	16 million
• Urban population	88 per cent
• Urban population growth rate 2005–2010	1.3 per cent
• Urban water coverage	100 per cent
• Water supply by household connection	99 per cent
• Improved urban sanitation coverage	95 per cent
• Research focus location	Santiago
• Research focus population	4.7 million
• Service provider	Aguas Andinas
• Contract form	Divestiture
• Regulator	Superintendencia de Servicios Sanitarios
• Regulatory start date	1990
• Exchange rate to US$ at fieldwork	CLP567
• Implied purchasing power parity conversion rate to US$	CLP313.5
• Implied undervaluation ratio	1.81

In the first tariff-setting process in 1990–1991, the key role of economic regulation and initially undertaken for all companies at the same time (now a staggered process), the average increase was 75.7 per cent though the range was from 7.3 per cent to 463 per cent. For small companies the rates increased very substantially, particularly in the high-cost operating regions of the country. In the second tariff-setting process in 1995–96 the tariff rise was more modest, averaging 6.9 per cent, with a range between -1.2 per cent and 24 per cent, demonstrating that prices can also be driven down through a regulatory process. Note that these rises were for the then public providers. In 2000–2002 tariff increases were again higher, averaging 16 per cent, because of the development of wastewater treatment plants. In addition to the agreed rises there can be price increases due to inflation, under an indexation formula, when inflation reaches more than 3 per cent.

The Ministry of Public Works is responsible for the sector and for letting any concession contracts. It is also responsible for water abstraction rights (tradeable in certain circumstances in Chile) while SISS monitors drinking water quality, industrial effluent and final effluent discharge standards. When there are failures a fine can be imposed; a member of SISS staff said 'we have to notify the company that they are about to be fined, the company has the right to explain, if we continue the company has a right to appeal to the courts. In general companies pay the fine.' The fines are paid to the government treasury. However, SISS was 'protecting' companies during the five-year grace period while the new wastewater treatment standards were achieved.

CORFO, the Chilean Economic Development Agency (established in 1939 and so with a long history of involvement in all sectors of the economy), invests in and promotes PPPs for national development. Being responsible for the shares at the time of divestiture it still retains a 35 per cent shareholding in Aguas Andinas, as one example (Aguas Andinas, 2007).

In the more recent PPPs, following a decision to move away from the divestiture approach ('there were political reasons'), CORFO holds the fixed assets. In the 'new style concession' there is a time-limited licence to serve, 30 years, and for each concession awarded there is an agreed programme of investment and a defined service area. New concession contracts are inclusive of production, distribution, collection, treatment and disposal. Although each of these could be separated with a vertical disintegration of production to promote efficiency, there had only been one separate contract for production as 'it is rather complex in the technical sense because of reservoirs and treatment', said one interviewee. Any company that had bought assets in the past can sell the assets or even sell the operational licence (though the company would have to inform SISS who would have to approve any new operator). In the more recent PPP contracts there is a prohibition of sales or transfers.

The Ministry for Economic Affairs has responsibility and involvement in the law setting the tariffs, and within that actually detailing the process. It can also change what articles say to have influence on how tariffs are calculated. The articles are all about determining or explaining how the law is fulfilled. For example, how should 'capital' be calculated as this might lead to excessive tariffs; however, guidelines cannot be changed too often.

Environmental standards are set by a committee with water quality and wastewater discharge quality standards complying with Chilean and international standards. Although SISS is a member of the committee these standards are not relevant or flexible with regard to price-setting: 'it is as it has to be'.

One telling comment described how 'Influence can be quite personal, with meetings between the minister and the regulator, it is not part of legislation but it happens'. The role of a regulator is to be an intermediary and therefore this level of flexibility is appropriate, presumably taking place within the spirit of and reality of the legal framework. As another example of 'balancing', it was reported that in 2001–2002 the Ministry and SISS proposed changes to articles in the tariff law but the private companies were not in agreement and the proposal went no further.

The legal framework

The laws creating SISS were passed in 1988 and 1989. Between 1990 and 1997 there was 'the first phase of the regulatory system', with assets remaining in the hands of the state. The laws had been passed during the time of President Pinochet and although the first expectation had been for 'crash privatization', after the election of a democratic government, 'the introduction of privatization was much calmer, with a more measured approach', observed one commentator. Between 1990 and 1997 the effectiveness of the laws was evaluated. In 1996, 1997 and 1998, SISS was trying to get a change in the way the laws dictated their approach, to give SISS a stronger voice in the regulation of any private companies. SISS was allowed to present its case to the Congressional Commission before Congress voted. According to one interviewee:

> *The commission would agree with some points, then the commission would add their own points, and reach a compromise in the end. It was a three-year process, always aiming for transparency. In the end a political decision was taken, with political influence supporting the reinforcement of the regulator and the regulatory frameworks.*

Law 19-549 in 1998 modified the earlier 1988 and 1989 laws and, along with changes in various statutory instruments, therefore modified how the regulatory framework functioned. These changes were believed to have led to a more open and effective framework that also allowed greater participation of the private sector but 'restricted the accumulation of capital in private hands'.

SISS described the result as a 'stable legal system that all can observe', believing that as a regulator it is 'independent enough' to develop its own organizational structure. Regulation applies equally to private and public companies with a system for the concession regime, tariff regime, subsidy system, service standards and the system of relations between consumers, governments and concessionaires. The key laws and regulations defining regulation and the subsidy system for the poor are listed and described by Aguas Andinas (2007) as:

- General Law on Sanitation Services (Decree Law No. 382 of 1988). This contains the principal provisions that regulate the treatment of concessions and the activities of the providers of sanitation services.
- Law on Tariffs for Sanitation Services (Decree Law No. 70 of 1988). This establishes the main provisions that rule the setting of tariffs for potable water and sewerage and the reimbursable financing contributions.
- Law on the Subsidies of the payment of the consumption of potable water and sewerage services (Law No. 18,778 of 1989). This establishes a subsidy on the payment of the consumption of potable water and sewerage for low-income clients.
- Services (Law No. 18,902 of 1990). This establishes the functions of the SISS.
- Regulation of the Law on Tariffs for Sanitation Services (Decree No. 453 of 1990). This contains the norms that permit the application of the Law on Tariffs for Sanitation Services.
- Regulation of the Law on the Subsidies (Decree No. 195 of 1998). This contains the provisions for the application of the Law on Subsidies.

- Regulation of the General Law on Sanitation Services (Decree No. 1,199 of 2004, published in November, 2005). This establishes the norms that permit the application of the General Law on Sanitation Services.

Service provider performance and regulatory practice

During the 1990s tariffs doubled for the customers of the service provider in Santiago, Empresa Metropolitana de Obras Sanitarias (EMOS), coverage having already increased significantly in the 1970s and 1980s. EMOS was under pressure to increase efficiency under the new regulatory system, achieving an impressive 2.04 employees per thousand connections even by 1993 (Lee, 1995). EMOS developed a process whereby staff that were laid off were enabled to form out-sourcing businesses, then being contracted back by EMOS for discrete activities such as meter reading.

In 1999 EMOS was privatized when Spain's Grupo Agbar joined forces with France's Suez to pay US$1.1 billion for 51 per cent of the shares. There were 50 per cent staff reductions after one year of the concession, though the company states that redundant workers were generously paid off. By 2002 the company was operating with just over one employee per thousand connections and by 2006 this had 'improved' again to 0.93 employees per thousand (author's analysis of Aguas Andinas, 2007). Initially the newly privatized company continued to be known by its pre-privatization name of EMOS but changed in 2001 to the presumably more 'brandable' name of Aguas Andinas. This was in part intended as a public image measure to give the company a more local-sounding name. By the time the company was privatized Santiago already had almost universal coverage of water and sewerage services but very little capacity for treatment of wastewater. The new owners have invested over US$600 million, much of it in wastewater treatment. Wastewater treatment coverage in Santiago Metropolitan Region was about 3 per cent in 1999 but after major investments in the 380 million litres per day El Trebal plant (operational by 2002) and after the 760 million litres per day La Farfana plant becoming operational in 2004, coverage had reached over 70 per cent by 2006. It is planned that it should be 100 per cent in Santiago by 2009 with the completion of a third major plant.

In 2006 the average tariff for water (including fixed charges) was CLP238.44/m^3 (US$ 0.76) and for sewage CLP204.36/m^3 (US$0.65) (Aguas Andinas, 2007).

In the 2000–2002 tariff revision, Aguas Andinas was only awarded a 2 per cent increase and neighbouring company ESVAL, 0 per cent. In the current price period, running from March 2005 to February 2010, Aguas Andinas was apparently allowed a 9.5 per cent price increase from the previous year and ESVAL 2.7 per cent for 20m^3 consumption (SISS, 2006).

According to the 2006 Aguas Andinas Annual Report (Aguas Andinas, 2007) the company achieved an average return on equity of 21.67 per cent and

---

BOX 7.1 TARIFF SETTING AND INVESTMENT

'We are going to have to reconsider some investment that we need to make', Aguas Andias' Secretary General Joaquin Villarino told local media. Villarino said Aguas Andinas, Chile's biggest water company could still meet its obligations with SISS by using cheaper technology to treat wastewater, although he did not expand further. Building the Los Nogales plant is expected to cost Aguas Andinas US$210 million, but SISS officials say it could be built for as little as US$126 million.

The SISS blames Aguas Andinas for overspending on two wastewater treatment plants – El Trebal, at a cost of US$150 million and La Farfana, at US$315 million, more than the regulator had recommended – but the company says that running the two plants is now not profitable because of low tariffs.

Source: Global Water Intelligence, 2005

---

an average return on assets of 11.3 per cent, having achieved a 9.13 per cent increase in profits compared to the previous year. Revenue from the 1,427,931 customers generated an income of CLP194,507 million (US$620.44 million), an operating profit (after depreciation) of CLP95,116 million (US$303.4 million) from fixed assets of CLP518,371 million (US$1653.0 million) funded by long-term liabilities of CLP266,377 million (US$849.7 million) and equity of CLP391,004 million (US$1247.22 million). The company paid shareholders a dividend of CLP28,208 million (US$ 89.98 million). The researchers calculate that there was a 14.5 per cent return on capital employed.

The company has started the 'Aura Plan' to 'increase our closeness and the satisfaction of the customers' aiming for a 'Close and cordial Attitude, Determination to do things right first time and Never leave a problem unresolved' (Aguas Andinas, 2007).

Before 1990, there were separate domestic, industrial and commercial tariffs along with incremental block tariffs. These have been replaced with a single tariff that SISS determines and makes public, having explained what it is taking into account and allows the companies to respond having shared its tariff calculations. There is then an exchange of calculations and studies, with three weeks for the companies to comment, before SISS considers any disagreements and then negotiates. If there is no agreement then the case goes to the expert commission. The three-person expert commission is convened by SISS and the company who agree a list of three to five people. The company can name one person, the regulator can choose another and the third comes from the list of possible members that was agreed at the beginning. SISS commented that it is difficult to find independent and objective people. As the work involved in setting tariffs is given by both companies and the regulator to consultants, technical and economic, the third person is usually nominated from one of these consultants.

An interesting mechanism used in the tariff-setting process by SISS is known as the Empresa Modelo or model company. The model company is used to judge efficient costs and takes into account operation costs (though not bad debts), investment in capital maintenance and new works and a reasonable profit. The initial rounds of tariff setting simply aimed at establishing average costs and setting tariffs to reflect those costs. Now, however, the real companies must compete against the model company as an incentive to become more efficient. An allowance of 15 per cent is made for unaccounted-for water, which is judged to be 'efficient'. Aguas Andinas criticizes the use of the model company because it assumes that service providers must be self-financing from cash flow. They argue that this assumption is not realistic in the commercial world where companies have to borrow money from the financial markets.

SISS has approximately 140 employees including some based in small regional offices. 'Most have worked for SISS for a long time, there has been a gradual increase, with 40 staff at the start, then 80, with a limit set by the budget. There was a proposal in 1998 that SISS should be paid by the companies, but this was declined by Congress in case of conflicts of interest, so the Treasury is paying for SISS from general taxation', said one informant.

SISS comments that 'the budget is quite adequate, we have a grant from IDB [Inter-American Development Bank] for studies and staff training. Only a few staff are leaving to go to consultants, none have left to go to the water companies.' All staff are civil servants, working to the same pay scale and all regulatory bodies receive extra payments that are common to all, for example the financial regulator as well as the utility regulators. Regulatory bodies have to demonstrate that they have met certain targets and performance standards to justify additional payments, from which the senior staff get greatest share.

Service to the poor and a universal service obligation

Informal housing is now extremely rare in Santiago ('there is only about 1 per cent informal housing', 'there is a minimum of 5 per cent illegal housing') but, as in all societies there are the poor: 'we have 20 per cent poor', said one interviewee. It was described that there are two levels of poverty: the very poor, that is the 4.7 per cent who cannot afford basic nutrition needs as measured by a poverty index and second, the next level of 12.3 per cent who can afford nutrition. There are also those just above the poverty line who are 'vulnerable' to poverty and make up 22 per cent total. Average family size is 4.5. The government has developed a number of ways to serve the poor with a particular target to eliminate illegal housing in cities by 2010. The Chile Solidário programme for the 'very poor' – US$200 (not at purchasing power parity) or less per household per month delivers a starter home and education. Relatively recently a 100 per cent water subsidy for 15m³ per month, 'a law that has been in Congress for three years, has just passed'. The law states that the subsidy could be for up to 20m³ per household per month 'but the process has settled on 15 as that is all that is used'. However, before participation in the Chile Solidário housing programme, people have to demonstrate savings, then to try for a 'social home', with all services provided. The programme has been moving groups in 'blocks' into new housing. For the lowest level of poverty, people pay a one-off small contribution for their social housing and then nothing more; for the next level up, there are monthly payments and then a special payment 'friendly' plan for those in debt; for the middle-class, payment is demanded.

An evaluation was undertaken in 2002, looking at the efficiency of the programme, the cost to the municipality to distribute the subsidies as well as looking at the equity of the programme, whether it is successful in a refocusing on the poorest of the poor. Following this evaluation there were attempts to adjust the focus, trying to ensure that the poorest were not paying 3 per cent of their household incomes on water, whereas the second level of poverty was paying just 1 per cent. This segmentation of poverty levels for better targeting developed after 2002; prior to this date just one level was recognized, and according to one interviewee 'now we are thinking of a third level of poverty'.

Of those receiving benefits, 35.4 per cent of beneficiaries have not completed basic education, 30.7 per cent are retired ('there is a higher proportion of the elderly getting a higher proportion of the subsidy'), 34.4 per cent are daily paid labourers and hawkers, and 26.3 per cent are regular employees but with low pay.

The research found that 'Extreme poverty is recognized as earning under US$150 per household per month, the poverty level is US$300 per household per month', though more sophisticated profiling of poverty by housing, ownership, income, education and employment is also used. 30.2 per cent of poor households are female-headed.

With the significant increases in tariffs in the late 1980s and 1990s, it was realized that there was a need to provide a mechanism that enabled the urban poor to afford a reasonable level of consumption. For those where the cost of water is high so that water represents more than 3 per cent of their income, 25 per cent are above the poverty level of US$300, 51.7 per cent are at the poverty level and 23 per cent are in extreme poverty. This led to the introduction of the subsidy programme in the early 1990s. Essentially the government reimburses the water companies on the basis of the amount of water consumed. The subsidy can cover between 25 per cent and 85 per cent of a household's water and sewerage bill up to a maximum consumption of $15m^3$ per month. Above $15m^3$, households must pay the full amount.

The subsidy programme is organized by the Ministry of Interior and the Ministry of Planning (MIDEPLAN), though it is managed at the municipal level. Funding for the programme comes from central government. Each year MIDEPLAN determines how much subsidy is to be granted to each region of the country. This is done through using household survey information and water and sewerage tariffs from each service provider. This enables MIDEPLAN to calculate how many households will need the subsidy and the overall amount required. The subsidy is intended to cover the shortfall between household ability to pay and actual consumption. The ability to pay is based on the idea that no more than 3 per cent of household income should be spent on water and sewerage. The benchmark figure used by the Pan-American Health Organization is that the water bill should not exceed 5 per cent. In the subsidy programme it was decided to use the 3 per cent figure because of the aim to support the poorest households. Regarding the issues of gender, 56.8 per cent of male-headed households and 43.1 per cent of female-headed households are receiving benefits, relative to 76.7 per cent male-headed households and 23.3 per cent female-headed households in the region generally.

Households apply for the subsidy at their local municipality or water company and as a first step complete an application form that records general household details. Eligibility for the subsidy is based on three main criteria:
- the applicant has to be in economic difficulties and unable to pay the entire service bill;
- the applicant has to be assessed using the Comité de Asistencia Social Comunal (CAS) system and give up-to-date information;
- the applicant has to be up to date in paying water bills.

The CAS score is determined through an interview with the head of household, undertaken by the municipality, and is carried out at the residence. The questionnaire contains 50 questions concerning household size and age, living conditions, occupation and income and other socio-economic indicators. The interview process may be outsourced to private companies but the municipality always calculates the CAS score to reduce the opportunity for collusion between the household and interviewer. The CAS score is valid for two years and can be used as the basis for applying for other subsidized services such as health, family support and pensions. In addition to the CAS interview, the household must demonstrate that it has no arrears with the water company and provide documentation to demonstrate socio-economic circumstances.

Subsidies are issued according to the CAS scores, prioritizing the neediest households, and are normally renewed on an annual basis for up to three years. A household may then reapply for the subsidy. Similarly there are several criteria that will lead to the municipality withdrawing the subsidy from a household. For example, three months arrears means the subsidy to the household is cancelled and they must reapply. Other reasons for withdrawing the subsidy include:

- moving out of the municipality;
- not informing the municipality of change of address (within the same municipality) at least 30 days in advance;
- change in socio-economic circumstances;
- voluntarily giving up the subsidy;
- completion of the three-year subsidy period.

CAS has approximately 1 million registered households and so includes approximately 5 million people out of the 16 million total in Chile. The water subsidy targets segments on the two groups of income level: US$300 and US$150 but the sophistication of CAS 'is useful to determine between two applicants for example at the income level of US$299', said one interviewee. Also, 'Many people are earning less than US$300 so the subsidy has to be focused on those with most need – CAS helps on prioritization of need as overall resources are limited.'

The subsidy reduces a customer's bill by a percentage, leaving the customer to pay the balance. The requirement that a customer must not be in arrears encourages the development of good payment habits. The bill provided to the customer is net of the subsidy, and the municipality pays the water company the subsidized amount. Water companies bill the respective municipalities the cumulative total subsidy. Should the municipality fail to pay on time it can be charged interest, and even more critically the water company can bill the household the full amount in the next payment period. However, the water company cannot cancel the subsidy – this can only be done by the municipality.

The level of subsidy is not the same in all parts of the country. This is because it is recognized that costs of production vary greatly, so subsidies can be higher in one region than another. For example, in Valparaiso there are eight tariff bands, all of which are the highest in the country because of the number of small towns and higher cost of producing water.

Both rural and urban poor have equal rights to the subsidy, though it had been forecast that by the end of 2005 the subsidy will be mostly directed towards rural populations. However, the most recent 2006 figures show that in fact the subsidy was increasing in the metropolitan region.

In July each year MIDEPLAN has to propose to the Treasury the regional budget required for subsidy on a cubic metre per household basis. In December the funds are sent to the regions to then distribute among the municipalities. Another responsibility of MIDEPLAN is to develop methodologies for identifying levels of poverty and discovering ways of trying to avoid favouritism or political parties' capturing the subsidy. There have been cases where money has not been well spent and MIDEPLAN has intervened because it is held responsible for ensuring that funds are directed to the most needy families and for carrying out constant monitoring. In 2006 there were 664,000 households receiving subsidies, that is 6.9 per cent of households were benefiting as a percentage of all customers in the metropolitan region, a 30 per cent increase since 2005 at an average monthly household subsidy of CLP2958 (US$9.44) (as compared with an average tariff at 15m^3 per month of US$21.2), with a total of CLP4,257.3 million (US$13.58 million) spent in the region and CLP32,574.3 million (US$103.91 million) in the country as a whole (SISS, 2007).

In Chile the question of a USO is largely redundant with the exception of the small rural settlements, and they were expected to catch up with urban areas in terms of water supply coverage by 2005. Regulation of PPPs in this particular socio-economic context is delivering. Service providers are making profits and continue to invest in further improvement. It is interesting to speculate to what extent the targeted subsidy programme has contributed to the current high levels of service. Given that the subsidy is funded by central government, and is considerably more economical than a previous universal scheme, it is assumed to be an economically sustainable measure. There is some criticism that the mechanism of transferring subsidy funds from central government to municipalities is slow because of bureaucracy but so far this does not appear to have strained the system.

The advisory unit to the Ministry of Economic Affairs is responsible for analysing the impact the proposed new tariffs will have on the population. During the preparation of new tariffs by SISS, the advisory unit is involved in the discussion of new levels. The advisory unit prepares a commentary on what impact the proposed tariffs would have on the poorest consumers and this information is shared with MIDEPLAN. There is a 30-day period in which the Minister should sign the proposed tariffs. There have been occasions when the Minister has reportedly been 'too busy' to sign off on the new tariffs, which has postponed their introduction. However, service providers can retrospectively charge the new tariff and collect interest.

In addition to the subsidy programme, MIDEPLAN promotes an empowerment programme designed to give skills and information on rights. There is training regarding maintenance and repair of sanitary facilities but, according to one informant, 'it is too male oriented, this is to be changed, to help women and to save money on their bills'. The gender issues inherent in the subsidy are now being recognized. MIDEPLAN is 'helping with bad debt management with water companies, we are helping with plumbing training, we are teaching how to read meters'. It was reported that Region V created the programme, which is subsequently being taken up in other regions, with ESVAL, the private water company serving Valparaiso becoming a very committed proponent of the idea.

A Chilean insurance company now holds the majority of the shares of ESVAL but it describes itself as having 'a strong social interest even though it is a private company'. ESVAL stated: 'We have been working on the social components for the last three years, we recognize the necessity to work in cooperation with the state and in alliances with state institutions as well as neighbourhood committees. We recognize the need for "segmentation of customers" to give the most appropriate service.'

ESVAL's particular programme is called 'Al Día con ESVAL' or 'up-to-date with ESVAL' and it includes the government at regional level, ESVAL and customers. An ESVAL member of staff said:

> *ESVAL is not interested in consumers using lots of water, but in using the right amount. It is aimed at average to low-income customers. The company*

recognized that their language tended to be technical, as an example, talking of reading meters but customers don't understand that, they want to have the same understanding that comes when you go to the supermarket and you only take what you can pay for.

The benefits of the programme were described as:

- being able to pay off debt without having to pay interest;
- initial and monthly payments are decided by the customer, not the company;
- of the money paid, 25 per cent goes to paying off the debt, 75 per cent goes to paying off that month's water charge.

If the customer signs the Al Día con ESVAL agreement for every payment made the company writes off an equal amount. The company believes it knows where households with bad debts are, 'grouped into small neighbourhoods', so an invitation is given to groups of about 15 customers with bad debts who are invited to a workshop where training is given in using 'sensible' amounts of water as well as accessing all possible benefits.

In the two-hour workshops (three hours if signing agreements):

we explain, for example, that $1m^3$ of water is five barrels, we explain that the meter is your friend not the enemy; we have a leak detector in the centre of the meter which shows if there is any usage at all when it spins. We use examples of meter reading calculations with the cubic metre of units translated into pesos. We teach about usage, for example how two and a quarter barrels is 425 litres which represents the usage for a family of five having a ten minute shower each day.

Social workers are involved in the workshop 'who don't know the technical language' to ensure that the terminology used is appropriate: 'we are using simple posters and leaflets, no PowerPoint!' on how to repair leaks. The ESVAL representative also said:

We explain that ten minutes of dish-washing with the tap running is 85 litres, which could mean $1m^3$ per day, $30m^3$ per month, approximately US\$40 per month which would mean US\$480 per year. We teach how to repair and prevent losses. In 'social houses' it is very common for parents not to turn the tap off when going to work – the children left behind don't have the strength to turn it off tight. We teach how to change washers, how to fix PVC and copper pipes using your cooking gas. The teachers are plumbers and it is very hands-on.

After signing, householders have 30 days to go to ESVAL to start the process. At the time of the interview in 2004 they had held 51 workshops in four months and:

- 846 householders were invited representing US$368,757 of bad debt;
- 440 people came representing US $206,705 of bad debt;
- 390 signed the agreement representing US$191,749 of bad debt;
- 251 were fulfilling the agreement representing US$100,646 of bad debt.

200 letters are sent each month to debtors with debts older than six months to invite them to participate in the programme. Another way of capturing special agreements is that when customers who are known as low-income customers come to the office for whatever reason, they are invited to join – but in order to join the programme they have to attend a workshop. They are given two chances, but if customers are invited twice to a workshop and do not turn up they will be disconnected. There is another chance to re-enter the programme for those who have dropped out before disconnection. Of more importance to the company than recouping the debt is recouping the customer!

A major reason for undertaking the programme was the approximately US$2 million of bad debt from low-income customers. Those invited to the workshops had on average six months of arrears on their bills. The alternative of disconnections was seen as bad, 'it physically damages the system and is bad for public health – so the disconnector allows one last chance to a householder to pay before actually disconnecting'. There was an average of 5000 disconnections per month out of a total of 450,000 customers.

Customers who are not on low incomes are given 30 days to pay and then 15 days extra, then they are disconnected. Low-income customers who are known are not disconnected. However, this message is deliberately kept quiet, 'we go out to the *barrios* and tell them they will be disconnected!' in order to ensure involvement.

The reason for the level of bad debts when there is a sophisticated subsidy available is that 'the largest part of the US$2 million debt has been run up by the poorest section of society, the illiterate and marginalized, those who are disconnected from normal society so they have no idea about water and drips; the debt is cumulative over 15 years'. When asked if the debt cannot be written off, the interviewee responded, 'The US$2 million is only from social customers and is only 2 per cent of the annual billing of US$100 million, in line with the total bad debt for all customers of US$8 million'.

The 'Aguas Andinas in your neighborhood' programme has also been developed to promote the responsible use of water and sewage systems in low-income areas. Focusing upon the municipal districts of Quilicura and Puente Alto (supplying 1000 and 2800 homes, respectively) the programme was aiming to benefit 16,000 people with plumbing workshops training 2176 housewives and household heads in 2006 (Aguas Andinas, 2007).

Consumer involvement and perceptions of consumers

Unlike in other countries, no customer committee was contemplated in the laws creating SISS. Although there was some consideration of establishing a customer service committee during the review of the legislation in 1996–1997 in the end it was not incorporated. It is recognized by some that customer rights and representation are generally weak and limited in their scope. SISS does not have the authority to establish a customer service committee so it is an issue that will have to be considered in further legislative developments.

SISS is obliged to deal with customer complaints within ten days and SISS monitors its own performance in this respect. SISS also uses indicators similar to those used by OFWAT, the water and sewerage regulator for England and Wales. There have been complaints surrounding charges made for wastewater treatment on a catchment basis. Some customers are paying for wastewater treatment even though they are not yet served in their district of the catchment. The regulator is not 'accountable' in law and there is no formal procedure for reporting it to another authority, though the President is said to be 'observing' the regulator. It is the President who appoints the regulator and can also remove him at any time.

There are few other entities to which the public may turn for assistance in consumer rights. SERNAC (Servicio Nacional del Consumidor) is the national consumer service and states its mission as being to educate, inform and protect consumers in Chile. SERNAC is linked to the Ministry of Finance and has authority to mediate in disputes between customers and suppliers. There is a view in SERNAC that most people in Chile think consumer protection is a bad thing or does not even exist. Nevertheless SERNAC has arrangements with each regulator and consumers are able to seek help, and it has a weekly spot on television to discuss consumer rights. The whole area of consumer rights appears to be slowly developing in Chilean culture.

MIDEPLAN has undertaken a survey to determine what low-income customers know about the subsidy plan and other means of assistance. They found that 42.6 per cent did not really understand what documents were required to obtain the subsidy, 32.7 per cent knew to some extent and 23 per cent knew very well. When asked if they understood the reasons that might lead to the loss of subsidies, 59.9 per cent did not know and 36 per cent knew a little. Bad debt was the best-known reason for losing the subsidy. Regarding the value of the subsidy, 82.4 per cent thought that the subsidy had helped a lot and they are 'very much in agreement' with the statement that 'the subsidy has been a great help to me and my family'. Recognizing that the poor are benefiting from other social programmes run by the municipality, 57.5 per cent thought that the municipality was doing a good job and 35.8 per cent thought that the water company was doing a good job.

Regulating water and sanitation for the poor?

The water and sewerage sector in Chile has reached very high service standards. The urban population, which represents the vast majority of citizens, has water and sewerage coverage (99 per cent and 98 per cent respectively). The country is pressing forward to provide wastewater treatment, representing very large investments and it is anticipated that in Santiago all wastewater will be treated by 2009. Other Chilean cities are also pursuing similarly ambitious service level targets. Even smaller municipal companies demonstrate an impressive professionalism in providing water and sewerage services.

If there is an issue where further development is warranted, it is customer representation in the regulatory process. Although in theory the ordinary man or woman can participate, in practice this is not the case. The Comision Defensoria, 'not yet an ombudsman but moving in that direction', believes it has a role 'against SISS, on behalf of the public. SISS is not in the middle between the company and the consumer, it is not really taking necessary action, consumers are coming to the commission', said one interviewee. Protecting consumer rights and raising awareness among the public of their existence is a task that will take time.

Economic regulation is performing its role, setting prices, challenging capital cost estimates, fining companies where necessary but delivering the financeability to ensure that water and sanitation services are provided. Separating out the particular responsibilities to serve the poor appears to be a workable and sustainable approach. The poor can access a reasonable amount of water with a significant subsidy. However, that subsidy, being separated from the responsibilities of the water provider, does not distort the overall tariff system and allows for alteration, if economic conditions change, independently and without threatening the viability of water provision. The example of Chile has much to teach other regulatory approaches.

CASE STUDY 10: ENGLAND

Richard Franceys

> *Being regulated is a privilege.* (Severn Trent Managing Director to WaterVoice Central, July 2005)

The water sector and institutional framework

Including a case study on a high-income country in the context of this book might appear inappropriate. However, although there may be 100 per cent service coverage, the challenges of serving those in poverty and ensuring that the needs of poor people are recognized in the regulatory process remain remarkably similar.

Water and sanitation services in the central (or Midlands) region of England have been fully privatized since 1989, though the smaller of the two companies, water-only provider South Staffordshire Water, had been a private provider for over 130 years. Water and sewerage provider Severn Trent Water was privatized in 1989, divested out of the Severn Trent Water Authority when shares were sold on the stock market. The ten Regional Water Authorities, including Severn Trent, had been established in yet another reorganization in 1974, out of '234 local authorities, water boards and other undertakings' (DOE, 1989). At the time, economic regulator OFWAT (the then Office of Water Services, now the Water Services Regulation Authority, with about 200 staff) was established with a primary duty to ensure the financeability of the service providers along with ensuring that water and sewerage functions were properly undertaken.

The earlier duties of the water authorities regarding water resources, rivers, flood and coastal management were separated out at the same time to a newly created National Rivers Authority, which subsequently became, along with additional duties, the Environment Agency in 1996, with now more than 10,000 staff. Although not part of the original privatization proposals it was realized that private companies could not be allowed to remain responsible for monitoring their own water abstractions and treated wastewater returns to the environment, not to mention occasional 'pollution incidents'. Water quality issues related to supply became the responsibility of the Drinking Water Inspectorate in 1990 using an approach based on self-regulation (self-monitoring) by the companies, audited and reported on by the minimally staffed (under 50 staff) Inspectorate. 'The creation of independent drinking water regulators able to openly publish reliable information about the nature of drinking water hazards, and how these are being managed and minimised, restored balance to the public debate about drinking water quality' (DWI, 2007).

Prices were initially set for 10 years by the government, forming, in effect, an agreed contract with a set price and approved service and service enhancement

UK KEY FACTS	
• Human Development Index rank	16 out of 177
• GNI per capita at purchasing power parity (2006)	US$35,580
• Country population	60 million
• Urban population	90 per cent
• Urban population growth rate 2005–2010	0.4 per cent
• Urban water coverage	100 per cent
• Water supply by household connection	100 per cent
• Research focus location	Midlands
• Research focus population	8.5 million
• Service provider	Severn Trent Water and South Staffordshire Water
• Contract form	Divestiture
• Regulator	Water Services Regulation Authority
• Regulatory start date	1989
• Exchange rate to US$ at fieldwork	GBP0.53
• Implied purchasing power parity conversion rate to US$	GBP0.67
• Implied undervaluation ratio	0.79

outputs for those 10 years within the context of the 25-year licence (at that time fixed, now a continually extended licence). However, noting the significant rise in profits under the new agreement ('nobody realized they had been that inefficient', said one interviewee) the new regulator used his powers to revise prices after five years, and that five-yearly price-setting approach has since continued. The ability and flexibility to revise apparently fixed contracts as circumstances change – while maintaining a 'fair' return to the 'efficient' private companies – is the essence of economic regulation. What continues to be debatable is agreement on what is 'fair'.

During the quinquennial price-setting process the water companies prepare their business plans (following their published draft business plans, within the context of their 'Strategic Direction Statements') for the next five years, making necessary assumptions about changes in water demand and customer numbers as well as needs for service enhancement and expansion. The government, through its lead agency the Department for Environment, Food and Rural Affairs (DEFRA) establishes the statutory requirements for water resources and services, heavily influenced by directives agreed through the European Union (the Urban Waste Water Directive being the initial key driver, now the Habitats Directive and shortly the Water Framework Directive) and its own requirements, usually as proposed by the Environment Agency. The task of the regulator is to challenge all these proposals, challenging the companies with regard to their costs and whether sufficient efficiency gains have been built in, also challenging the non-statutory requirements of government with regard to potential benefits. From this analysis comes the annual revenue required to fund operations and investment over the forthcoming five years. When household supplies were only

2 per cent metered, as at the commencement of privatization, the revenue requirements were easily converted into a price cap, thus ensuring the required financeability. With metering now passing 30 per cent and customers beginning to respond to price signals and, more significantly, climate conditions, OFWAT is proposing to convert its price cap into a revenue cap. The key aspect of this approach is that it not only delivers the financeability required for the ever-improving environmental standards but it also gives incentives to the service providers to out-perform their efficiency targets. Any out-performance within the five-year period adds to the profits of the private company – but this also benefits customers in that the benefits of those revealed efficiency gains are shared with them at the next price review.

Where do the interests of low-income customers fit into this elegant (if long-winded in practice) economic regulatory process? Haphazardly is perhaps the best answer. There is significant urban poverty in England and Wales, though of a different kind than in most of the other countries in this series of case studies. There are a significant number of people living on very low incomes, usually on government-provided welfare benefits of various forms. It is reported (ONS, 2008) that 16 per cent of the population in Great Britain lived in low-income households (before deduction of housing costs) in 2004–2005, where 'low income' is defined as 60 per cent of the median household disposable income. Urban slums have not been an issue in England for the past couple of generations though there are signs of their return: significant multiple occupancy as well as 'beds in sheds' in parts of the south-east where recent immigrants can be living several households to a single dwelling or living in rooms ('sheds') hastily built in the gardens of established dwellings.

The poverty figure had reached a peak of 21 per cent in the early 1990s (ONS, 2008), coinciding with the period of most rapid growth in water tariffs following privatization, and the more commercially aware companies were using their powers to disconnect households not paying their bills. As this also coincided with the very significant increase in profitability of the companies, way beyond 'fair', as they learned to take advantage of the underestimate of likely efficiencies, there was a political 'storm' that resulted in the banning of disconnections. The value of economic regulation then came into play again as appropriate allowance for this change was made in the subsequent price review. Whether low-income consumers might have preferred the signal of disconnection rather than being taken to court, with bailiffs subsequently empowered to seize their property to pay off the bad debts, is not known.

The legal framework

The current regime in England and Wales stems from the privatization of the water supply sector that occurred under the Water Act 1989, superseded by the Water Industry Act 1991 and as amended by the Water Industry Act 1999 and the Water Act 2003.

The 1989–1991 legislation established the primary regulator of the privatized water industry as the Director of Water Services in OFWAT, with a remit to operate to a large extent independent of government. The legislation does, however, provide the government (via the Secretary of State) with powers to intervene and give directions to the regulator on matters of social and political importance and that require a democratic mandate. In practice the independence of the regulator relies on minimal corruptibility in the political and administrative systems and full access to the courts by all parties.

The legislation requires the companies, subject to payment of (approved) connection fees and charges, to provide a connection upon request from any owner or occupier. It is the duty of the Secretary of State to ensure that service coverage is available for all areas in England and Wales at all times. Apart from a relatively small number of private water supplies, regulated under different legislation by local authorities, the water companies essentially provide a universal service. While there is no explicit USO in any part of the legal framework, this combination of duties could be construed as one.

With the aim of protecting vulnerable people the 1999 Act introduced a ban on disconnection of service to consumers' principal places of residence following non-payment of charges. The difficult issue for companies now is how to differentiate the 'can't pays' from the 'won't pays'.

Under the Water Act 2003 (HMSO, 2003), the authority of the Director General, OFWAT was in 2006 replaced with a Water Services Regulation Authority, the most notable change being the replacement of the single regulator with a regulatory board. In addition, responsibility was given to take into account sustainability and to:

> *have regard to the interests of:*
> *   *Individuals who are disabled or chronically sick;*
> *   *Individuals of pensionable age;*
> *   *Individuals with low incomes;*
> *   *Individuals residing in rural areas.* (HMSO, 2003)

In addition, the 2003 Act also gave OFWAT powers with respect to promoting competition in the water industry, following on from the Enterprise Act, 2002, with the potential for fines up to 10 per cent of turnover. Competition is allowed for consumers who are likely to use more than 50 million litres of water in a year – currently numbered in the low thousands (out of 24 million customers).

The principles of accountability and transparency are very much enshrined in the Water Act 2003, which requires both the new Authority and the Consumer Council to prepare and make available, for review by stakeholders, all their plans and proposals.

Service provider performance and regulatory practice

OFWAT reports (2007a) that since privatization until the end of the 2005–2010 price period 'more than GBP67 billion (US$100 billion) will have been invested in improved drinking water quality and higher environmental standards' at 2002–2003 prices. Indicators of improved service are that the percentage of billing contacts answered within five working days has increased from 79.8 per cent to 99.6 per cent (with some caveats), properties at risk of low pressure dropped from 1.33 per cent to 0.03 per cent, drinking water quality has now reached 99.96 per cent, river water quality has improved from 47 per cent being considered 'good' to 68 per cent (chemical quality) (and from 62 per cent to 72 per cent for biological quality) and that leakage has fallen from a peak of 228 litres per day to 149 litres per property per day.

However, this has come at a cost of average household bills increasing in real terms (that is removing the effects of inflation) by 42 per cent since 1989. Customers of course have seen those rises as much higher with the effects of inflation added (84 per cent since 1989) and also recognize the very significant variations in the average household bill for water and sewerage of GBP312 (US$466) in 2007–2008, when for one company the average is GBP483 (US$721). This average is necessarily based upon the England and Wales average household size of 2.4 persons. Metered households with children – and households with children are 'disproportionally present in low-income households' (ONS, 2008 – can face much higher bills than the average.

'Average weekly household expenditure in the UK in 2006 was GBP455.90' (US$680); however, the lowest 10 per cent had average weekly household expenditure of GBP155.60 (US$232). Water charges at 1.2 per cent of average weekly expenditure, 21st in line, are not dissimilar to TV, cable and the internet at 1.3 per cent but well below 'package holidays' and 'money spent abroad' at 5.6 per cent (Dunn, 2008).

The two companies in the English 'Central Region' used as a focus for this case study, Severn Trent Water and South Staffordshire Water, serve 7.4 million and 1.3 million people through 3.2 million (29.6 per cent metered) and 0.5 million (20.9 per cent metered) connected properties respectively, at an average tariff of GBP141 (US$210) for water and GBP138 (US$206) for sewerage per customer from water and sewerage company Severn Trent and GBP113 (US$169) from water-only South Staffs. Severn Trent is deemed to be 15th and 9th most efficient (out of 22 companies) for operating and capital maintenance efficiency respectively and South Staffs 5th and 7th, both for water services. OFWAT (2007d) also reports on 'Overall Performance Assessment', which is a compilation of scores on water supply, sewerage (where appropriate), customer services and environmental impact. South Staffs scored 283 relative to the highest score of 288, Severn Trent was lowest at 236. Severn Trent had been placed under formal investigation by OFWAT regarding 'information relating to customer service information' following complaints by a (then) member of the company to the press that reported numbers were inaccurate. 'We are taking formal enforcement action against Severn Trent following evidence of deliberate misreporting, ineffective systems, and clear attempts to manipulate the key data we use to assess and compare company performance within this sector of monopoly suppliers', said OFWAT.

At the time of writing OFWAT had not announced the likely fine that Severn Trent might have to pay but it had earlier announced proposals to fine Thames Water GBP12.5 million (US$18.7 million) for failures in information and service provision following on from an earlier requirement that Thames should also invest an extra GBP150 million (US$224 million) of its shareholders' money to accelerate a reduction in leakage, apparently in lieu of a fine. Along with a GBP8.5 million (US$12.7 million) fine on United Utilities and a GBP20.3 million (US$30 million) fine on Southern Water (OFWAT, 2007e), it is clear that the regulator has significant powers and is prepared to use them.

To achieve the service levels described, Severn Trent with a net debt of GBP3,119.9 million (US$4,657 million) at 55.1 per cent gearing was charging GBP1,195.7 million (US$1,785 million) in turnover in 2006–2007, achieving a current cost operating profit of GBP395.6 million (US$590 million), a return on capital employed of 7.2 per cent, with dividends distributed to shareholders amounting to GBP651.9 million (US$973 million) – significantly higher than the operating profit as the company continues to 'gear up'. Severn Trent had started in 1989 with 353,646,000 'issued and credited as fully paid' shares on 6 October 1989 according to the prospectus (DOE, 1989), with pro-forma indebtedness of just GBP53.2 million (US$79.4 million), pro-forma cash resources of GBP375.4 million (US$560 million) and net assets of GBP1,606.4 million (US$2,398 million). The GBP2.40 share price (US$3.60) at which the company was originally sold equals GBP4.40 today (including inflation at 84 per cent), which can be contrasted with the present share price of approximately GBP14.00 (US$21) – to which benefit can be added a substantial stream of dividends over the years. Shareholders have done extremely well through water privatization and the contributions to the charitable fund, though commendable and very important, are minute compared to those benefits.

The equivalent figures for the much smaller and water-only South Staffs are GBP136.4 million (US$204 million) debt at 59.9 per cent gearing, GBP 72.7 million turnover (US$109million), GBP16.1 million (US$24 million) operating profit, 8.5 per cent return on capital employed and GBP13.1 million (US$20 million) dividends (OFWAT, 2007f). These figures show that although the companies may be delivering services competently they are performing even better for their shareholders. Achieving a return on capital of 7.2 per cent and 8.5 per cent when the regulator had assumed a cost of capital of 5.1 per cent (5.7 per cent for South Staffs with its 'small company premium') but had earlier considered setting a fair cost of capital at 4.2 per cent 'real, post tax' (OFWAT, 2004) shows how well the companies are doing. These excess profits, only partly

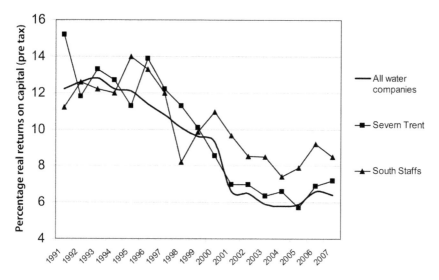

Source: Author's analysis of OFWAT data

Figure 7.1 *Profitability of Severn Trent Water and South Staffs Water, 1991–2007*

due to out-performance of OFWAT's efficiency targets, come at the expense of ordinary customers, particularly poor customers. Simple calculation suggest that the water companies in England and Wales might well be achieving profits over and above what is reasonably required to undertake their functions (as well as financing the admittedly expensive massive enhancement programme) of at least GBP1 million per day (US$1.5 million) over the five-year period.

Over the years the companies have used their new powers to diversify into other activities, Severn Trent, more successfully than most of the newly privatized companies, diversified into solid waste management. Having recently sold that business (and smaller international businesses) to focus again on being a water and sewerage company it is seen as a likely target for takeover by the infrastructure and private equity funds who have become involved in so many UK companies. South Staffs had been spectacularly successful in establishing an insurance and service delivery company to protect against leaks and other plumbing problems in domestic premises. There has been concern at the way in which many of the other water companies have also begun to benefit from this business, providing their customer databases for mailshots to their customers as if the suggestion was coming from the water company itself rather than the insurance business. The insurance arm of South Staffs was demerged and the water company was quickly purchased by a Bahraini investment fund for 'around GBP245 million' (US$366 million) in 2004, at a 27 per cent premium to the share price, only to be sold three years later to another private investment fund for 'an estimated GBP400 million (US$597 million)' (Thompson, 2007).

OFWAT cost GBP11.5 million (US$17.2 million) for 190 staff in 2006–2007 (OFWAT, 2007b), all except GBP0.5 million (US$0.75 million) derived from licence fees that had been approved by government. As a percentage of revenue, the cost of regulation is 0.136 per cent or, by a more customer-oriented approach, GBP0.50 per billed property (US0.75) or GBP0.21 (US$0.31) per person per year.

Service to the poor and a universal service obligation

The key focus of the regulatory regime in England and Wales has been on achieving good water and customer service for the average customer while achieving the required environmental standards. The needs of the poor have been assumed to be taken care of through the universal provision of potable water and the separate welfare services. There is no evidence yet that the specific provisions in the Water Act (2003) regarding 'individuals with low incomes' has had any effect on the regulatory process.

A formal ban on disconnections was brought in by the new government in 1997, following the earlier 'voluntary' reduction in the use of disconnections by the companies in response to the public outcry over their earlier dramatic rise. Also at that time a court order was made indicating that prepayment meters (preferred by so many customers for their gas, electricity and mobile phone charges) were illegal in that households could become disconnected without, at that time, following the appropriate procedures to protect against hardship: 'disconnection without due consideration'. The National Consumer Council (2003) reports that the majority of poor consumers with 'basic skills difficulties' or 'families with young children' use payment cards or token meters for non-water utilities, which are still valued as they enabled consumers to control their expenditure. Water customer committees, who would like to reinstate this option for the people they represent, are advised that there is no chance that government might introduce the necessary legislation.

The government has introduced a 'vulnerable charges' scheme to protect poor consumers on meters, a process now known as 'WaterSure'. This is in response to the gradual introduction of metering, ostensibly to reduce demand, which has begun to affect significantly the bills of low-income families with several children and people with a medical condition that requires the use of more than average amounts of water. The level of poverty in England can best be characterized, relative to the spectrum being used for lower-income countries, as 'vulnerable non-poor'. In addition to the cost of metering, estimated at approximately GBP40 per household per year (US$60), the introduction of metering is leading to the gradual unwinding of the 'progressive taxation' subsidy through the old 'rateable value' system whereby the water bill was some function of the estimated value of the house. Large families in small houses, with some level of correlation to poverty, did best in this system while one or two person households in large houses did worst. Now that those small households can volunteer to receive a 'free' meter and transfer to measured billing they can reduce their bills significantly. However, the companies still require the same amount of revenue (actually a higher level to pay for the cost of metering) and this is redistributed in varying proportions across the entire customer base. An additional 'strange' aspect of the English and Welsh system is that all customers have to pay for 'highway drainage' through their water bills, even poor customers who do not have their own vehicles.

The WaterSure system is therefore designed so that customers who fill in several pages of forms, a process that has to be repeated annually, to prove that they are in the appropriate category of being on approved benefits with three or more children or with a listed medical condition, receive an average measured bill rather than their actual measured bill. Customers who remain on the 'rateable value' unmeasured system are not included in this system.

By mid-2007 just 16,260 customers had successfully applied for assistance under the WaterSure scheme (OFWAT, 2007g) out of over 24 million connected properties – but at least this was higher than the 7200 customers benefiting in 2004–2005 or the 0.4 per cent of the perhaps 440,000 eligible population in 2002 (Fitch and Price, 2002). DEFRA reported that, in the context of water affordability being one of their 'sustainability indicators', the proportion of households spending more than 3 per cent of their income on water fell from its 'fairly constant' 15 per cent to approximately 9 per cent (DEFRA, 2004). This was as a result of the significant price cut introduced at the 1999 price review. However the level is expected to rise again to 12 per cent in 2009–2010 and 'for lower income households the figure will rise from 29 per cent to 40 per cent' (DEFRA, 2004).

It is interesting to consider, recognizing that water bills are only one aspect of low-income household responsibilities, that disconnections are still permissible in the gas and electricity sectors along with the much appreciated 'prepayment meters'. The government has also introduced GBP200 (US$300) winter fuel payments for all pensioners, free TV licences for all those aged over 75 (worth GBP135 or US$200) and also a payment to the over-70s towards council tax bills. Gas and electricity payments can also be deducted before payment of state social benefits, removing the risk of non-payment and subsequent disconnection. There has been no such allowance for water.

In their own attempts to help the poor, and of course maximize revenue, companies have adopted much more flexible payment systems that allow customers to pay small amounts weekly or monthly rather than the established pattern of twice yearly. The companies have also established 'PayPoint' terminals in small shops, where those on low incomes can pay small amounts without expensive bank charges. They have also had to invest significantly in debt collection techniques that include tens of thousands of court summonses for non-payment.

The poor also benefit from the ban on domestic disconnections, although it is uncertain who 'won't' and who 'can't' pay. This leads to perverse incentives such that some Citizen's Advice Bureaux are reportedly recommending that users pay their cable and satellite television bills before their water bills. There is concern that the ban on disconnections is leading to an increase in debt and bad debts that the companies will have to write off at the expense of other customers.

Household revenue outstanding for more than 12 months 'and which is likely to be more difficult to collect' was GBP575 million in 2006–2007 (US$858 million). Of revenue billed, 1.7 per cent or GBP105 million (US$157 million) was written off by water companies in that year. 'The cost of bad debt to the industry represents around GBP11 per year (US$16) for every household billed for water' (OFWAT, 2007h).

To address 'water poverty', now that the private water companies have no right to disconnect, several of them have set up charitable trusts, funded by their donations. Poor customers who run into debt are referred to these charities for advice and for direct financial support. The Severn Trent Trust Fund reports (figures up to November 2007) (STTF, 2007) that out of 73,237 applications received they had been able to help around 47,374 households with grants out of a total of GBP28.3 million (US$42 million) in grants received 'through the generosity of Severn Trent Water' (STTF, 2006). The Severn Trent Trust Fund, which is managed completely independently of the water company, received a grant of GBP3.5 million (US$5.2 million) from Severn Trent Water in 2006–2007. More than 70 per cent of those receiving help are receiving money as well as financial advice, with an average grant in 2005–2006 of GBP509 (US$759) towards water arrears (STTF, 2006). The Fund reports that most people ask for help with water debts from previous years but a substantial proportion also ask for help with present bills and also other utility bills.

The charity, with over 8500 new applications in the most recent reporting year, also has a 'Partnership Payment Scheme' for clients with high water debts. The client agrees to pay an affordable amount each and every week and if they manage to stick to the plan and make all the payments for 13 weeks then the first grant is given. Similarly they pay for the next 13 weeks to receive the second grant and if they make payments for a final 13 weeks, the final grant for the final third of the debt is given. If payments are missed the scheme is cancelled and no further grants awarded. SSTF report a positive response to this scheme.

Eleven water companies formally reported donations to charitable trusts during 2006–2007, totalling GBP7.9 million (US$12 million), and a number of others also make donations to organizations such as Money Advice Centres or offer similar schemes such as 'restart' schemes (OFWAT, 2007h).

The alternative for those who have not asked for help or who are the 'won't pays' is reflected in the number of debt cases threatened with court proceedings, nearly 9 million 'Pre-court action notices being issues in 2006-07, resulting in 200,000 claims in court and 150,000 judgements' (OFWAT, 2007h).

Alternative service providers

Alternative service providers, in the sense the term has been used in other case studies, do not exist in the UK, apart from the ubiquitous bottled water suppliers. However, the requirement to promote competition has been leading to the development of alternative providers directly within the regulatory regime following the 1991 Water Industry Act as extended by the 1992 Competition and Service (Utilities) Act and the Competition Act 1998.

The initial approach to competition has been through what are called 'inset appointments', where a high usage company either setting up and therefore not being currently supplied by any water company or with the agreement of an existing company takes a supply from a new provider. Because of the restrictions on abstraction and the difficulties of obtaining new abstraction licences most of the (very few) inset appointments to date have to take water from the existing supplier through an approach known as 'common carriage'. The challenge has been to agree a fair price for the water supplied.

Regina Finn, Chief Executive of OFWAT reports (Finn, 2007) that 'the combined activities of water and sewerage retailing make up less than 7 per cent of the value chain', which indicates the likely margin for any new entrant to the business who has to take water from an existing supplier. It has been estimated that there are only around 3500 businesses who could achieve the 50 million litres per year threshold for such competition and even if that limit was reduced to 1 million litres per year the likely number of eligible businesses would only increase to around 30,000 out of the more than 24 million customers. Only 11 inset appointments had been completed by the end of 2007. As such, competition would remain irrelevant to low-income consumers. However, late in 2007 some developers began to put in bids for an independent service to new housing developments (OFWAT, 2007i). Promising to take water from (and discharge sewage back to) the existing supplier at 5 per cent less than the current rates having constructed their own distribution and sewerage network on the development site (along with 'all' other utilities), the new entrants can take advantage of bulk water tariffs. Unlike in most other case studies described in this book large industrial and commercial users are charged less on a volumetric basis than domestic consumers because it costs less to supply in bulk. There is no cross-subsidy between commercial and domestic consumers. However, there is a cross-subsidy between urban and rural consumers that allows these new entrants an extra opportunity to pass on savings and (or) make a higher profit.

It appears that the benefits to be gained by any low-income households on a new housing development (unlikely unless they include social housing) will be offset against increases to the other set of customers. OFWAT now has a duty to attend to people living in rural areas.

Consumer involvement and perceptions of consumers

Through the 1983 Water Act, national government, in a presumed attempt to limit the involvement of locally elected representatives on the Regional Water Authorities, reduced the size of the boards (from an average of 40 to a range of 9 to 15), with local authorities losing their right to appoint members. In their place 'consumer consultative committees' were introduced to represent consumers' interests in the regional water authority areas with the 'remit to consider and report on any matter relating to the services provided by a water authority or a water company' (Brandon, 1984).

This pattern was perpetuated when the 1989 Water Act made provision for the OFWAT Director General to establish not more than ten 'consumer services committees' (CSCs) such that every water provider was allocated to a committee on which there would be 'not less than ten nor more than twenty' unpaid members appointed by the Director; the purpose was to ensure 'that the interests of the customers and potential customers of the companies ... are effectively represented' (HMSO, 1989).

With part-time independent chairs and usually a dozen volunteer members, each committee had to work out its own role in its own region, according to its members' various interests, as well as attempting to address national issues.

Supported by OFWAT, which always promoted customer involvement, the CSCs (first renamed WaterVoice, most recently relaunched as the independent (of OFWAT) Consumer Council for Water (CCWater)) actively questioned the performance of private companies in serving all their customers, acted as a place of appeal for customer complaints, and audited private companies' customer complaint procedures. Over the years the CSCs secured many millions of pounds in compensation and rebates for customers.

Membership of WaterVoice is typically competent middle-class professional early retirees. Members therefore are not representative (they were never intended to be) and tend to have a limited 'feel' for the issues regarding low-income customers. Increasingly as the approach to regulation and customer involvement evolves, the role of the 'members' has diminished and the role of the full-time staff and the new Board has increased.

The budget for CCWater during 2006–2007 was set by government at GBP5.85 million, funded by an addition to the water companies' licence fee, to pay for the 81 staff and the approximately 70 regional 'members', all costing customers 25 pence per billed property or 10.8 pence per person per year. The number of members has since been reduced to about 50, presumably to save money. Since its inception in October 2005, the 'watchdog' had obtained over GBP591,176 (US$882,000) in compensation and rebates for consumers (CCWater, 2007c), with a more recent success achieving more than GBP400,000 (US$600,000) of rebates for customers in just one village 'wrongly charged for surface water drainage for many years' (CCWater, 2008).

A simple evaluation undertaken with departing members of WaterVoice Central (average years on committee was five, but with only a limited response) indicated that their reasons for joining were a 'wish to serve', 'interest in utilities', 'interest in a very important utility essential to civilized life' and 'hoped to make a difference'. Limited value was placed on the value to customers of the meetings in public (then held six times a year), 'the meetings themselves were not very effective – it was the work outside the meetings that was of value'; 'It felt uncomfortable to criticize companies in public'. However, the auditing of companies' handling of complaints by members was highly rated: 'companies responded to WaterVoice input', with the value to customers of the work of the secretariat on complaints handling scored by all at the highest possible level.

Members thought that their responses to the many policy consultations were of very limited value: 'I did not have the impression that OFWAT were overly concerned with what we thought!' and 'OFWAT was like an elephant or an oil tanker', and similarly limited on the time-consuming price review: 'probably important for us to be involved, but we were very disappointed in the outcome'. There was deemed to be some benefit to 'disadvantaged' customers with the comment that 'WaterVoice was effective for special needs customers, but not for low-income customers in general', which honestly reflected the type of people involved, or who could be involved, in the committee as reflected in a response to a separate question: '[it was]sometimes difficult to know whether I was representing customers or my own point of view.'

Overall, at the end of almost 15 'man years' of involvement the sense was of being necessary but not particularly effective: 'Generally good, not valued particularly by OFWAT, weak impact on water companies re strategy, financial policy etc'; 'I was less comfortable with the effectiveness of the WaterVoice Central public meetings, although it is likely that they provided the backcloth for the effective sub-groups i.e. without the possibility of the companies being hauled over the coals in public they may have taken less notice of us in private' and 'We were always trying to join a dance between the companies, the government and OFWAT and the other regulators. We were a lone consumer voice. We had little power. I regret that we had little influence'.

A survey of WaterVoice Central meeting minutes undertaken by Narracott (2003) found that over a period of six years and two months, between 20 March 1997 and 15 May 2003, 48 regional CSC meetings were held on a bi-monthly basis. In that time, there were 32 'counts' of low-income customers being brought up and documented as a topic of discussion. Of these 32 'counts', 7 were initiated by the companies. Similarly, from April 1997 to October 2002, 60 regional CSC managers' meetings were held. In that time, 33 'counts' were recorded where the poor are mentioned in the minutes. Throughout the minutes, the poor were referred to in the following terms: low-income customers, needy customers, 'can't pays', customers who struggle to pay their bills, customers declaring hardship, vulnerable customers, poorer customers, the poor, vulnerable households, customers helped by the charitable trust, those in the lower socio-economic group, customers in need and families in financial difficulty.

Reflecting on the 2004 price review the chair of WaterVoice Central's price review sub-group noted (Franceys, 2005b) that:

> *over the two years of price setting we were first advised by one of the companies we oversee to expect single digit price rises over the five year period, then their preliminary draft business plan stunned us with expectations of nearly 30 per cent real, then they published that draft business plan figure as 17.5 per cent, revised it in their final business plan to 27 per cent, were given a draft determination by the regulator of 15.8 per cent and after appropriate final adjustments it came out as a final determination of 20 per cent. All these percentages are in real terms. As customer representatives we not only have to try and make sense of the reasoning behind this apparent 'yo-yoing' (without ever having enough time to delve into the volumes of supporting data) but also to try to communicate with the few customers we have contact with that the final answer is correct – when at present rates of inflation the total price rise they will see over the five years will be approximately 40 per cent. By the end of this price-setting process we were so numbed/neutered by these swings I am not sure we knew which way we were going. Which again illustrates the challenge of delivering useful customer involvement in different settings?*

It is difficult to see how the voices of the poor can be systematically heard in such a process.

The 2004 Periodic Review research into customers' views (MORI, 2002) had undertaken a sophisticated focus group and quantitative survey to determine what customers actually believed and wanted. Quoting verbatim from the MORI survey, MORI reported that satisfaction with both tap water supply and sewerage services was high (87 per cent and 81 per cent, respectively). For both services dissatisfaction was low (7 per cent and 6 per cent respectively). Around two-thirds of respondents were satisfied that they received value for money from the water supply service (67 per cent) and the sewerage service (65 per cent). When asked to choose from a list of quality of life issues facing the UK covering health, crime, education and so on, 6 per cent cited 'water and sewerage services' as in need of urgent attention and improvement, and 20 per cent cited the 'environment'.

Over four in five (83 per cent) agreed that 'the cost of protecting the water environment should be paid for by all who use or benefit, not just by those that pay the water and sewerage bills'. 97 per cent agreed that 'industries that create water-polluting waste should pay to protect the environment'. However, the aspect selected more than any other as being the one in the most urgent need of improvement was tap water taste and smell (despite its overall 'good' rating among the great majority of the sample). It was closely followed by 'maintaining the quality of coastal and bathing waters'. Both were selected as the most urgent by just over one in ten.

An additional survey was undertaken one year later with a focus on those customers who were already in debt, most likely representing lower-income customers. Quoting from the Accent Marketing and Research (2003) 'Paying for Water: Customer Research' undertaken for WaterVoice and OFWAT, it was found that customers with water debt divided into three main groups: those who take the line 'Why should I pay?'; those who are genuinely struggling financially; and the poor money managers (including some strugglers). These water customers did not see their water and sewerage bills differently from their fuel bills. Rent/mortgage and council tax were the priority household bills for payment but gas, electricity and water were then viewed as being equally important. Customers with water debt typically have multiple debts and are continually juggling their bills, trying to decide which to pay next and how much. They will pay whoever is most persistent in contacting them for payment. This is typically not the water company or, indeed, the other utilities. Those creditors who are likely to be paid first are the banks and loan companies. Their stronger and more robust debt recovery approaches often drive people to give their other debts less priority (i.e. rent/mortgage, council tax and utilities).

The Accent study further found that the ban on disconnection of domestic water supplies did not influence payment of the water bill. In fact, most customers remained convinced that they could be disconnected for non-payment of the water bill. For some the fact that the water was turned off at the stop-tap in their street by their water company or in their home by their landlord reinforced the view that disconnection could be carried out even if they felt that, for hygiene reasons, it probably would not be.

The 'strugglers' and 'poor money managers' would have preferred to be able to pay little and often and receive more frequent water bills, preferably on a quarterly basis as for other utilities. Email, text messages and calls to mobile phones were all considered unacceptable forms of contact by the water company. A home visit was thought to be the most effective approach for personal contact in terms of debt recovery. Whichever approach the water company adopted to recover outstanding water debts, customers and money advisers thought it was important that the approach was made in good time to prevent the debt from becoming unmanageable and should be flexible, tailored to the customer's personal situation and their ability to pay. Few respondents said they had personal experience of debt recovery agents for water debt. Those who had thought it had been an unpleasant experience and some had been frightened.

The water regulator continues to consider the extent to which 'the generality of customers' should have to pay for some environmental benefits. On alleviating low flow in rivers, Philip Fletcher (2001) asks: 'What about the effects on those with below average income, who will often coincide with those who have least access to the areas of water concerned?'. Meanwhile, in response to public outcry and a campaign from WaterVoice, the predecessor to the Consumer Council for Water, OFWAT funded the water companies to attempt to limit foul flooding from sewers, when sewage backs up through the toilets and sinks into a customer's home due to limited capacity in nearby sewers. The costs of such flood alleviation grow ever higher, one example being quoted at GBP170,175 (US$254,000) per property (NCE, 2008).

Regulating water and sanitation for the poor

Divestiture in England and Wales has delivered high quality services. The private water providers under pressure from the regulatory process have become much more efficient. However, even with these significant gains, the ever-increasing quality and environmental spend has necessarily led to higher water bills that are creating problems for the poor. The incentive-based regulatory system has made divestiture highly transparent, with reams of information available to drive comparative competition. The inclusion of customer committees as partners may have helped individual complainants, while public meetings held regularly to question the companies may have helped to make private companies more aware of customers' concerns. However, they have not had a significant effect on the needs of the poor.

The involvement of other, non-governmental stakeholders, whether concerned for the environment or for the poor, in addition to the various interests of the media, has perhaps been a more powerful tool for change. The ability of NGOs to experiment and pilot new approaches such as the charitable trust funds based upon the service providers' initiatives and donations, and the ability of lobbying NGOs to promote awareness and transparency, have been a crucial element in the process of improving water and sanitation to all. Perhaps the media, both print and particularly television, have been even more important in challenging the system.

The example of England and Wales suggests that regulated PPPs can deliver improved services. Agreements or contracts between partners can be adjusted after they have been signed. There is always a price to be paid, however, in any such adjustments in reduced regulatory freedom and through a sense of diminishing returns as the companies experience reduced profits and, thus, their freedom to be flexible. However, perhaps crucially, in England and Wales the government, in its new Water Act 2003, has maintained the duty of the regulator to ensure that private water companies can 'secure reasonable returns on their capital to finance the proper carrying out of their functions' as well as enhancing the regulatory duty to 'further the consumer objective, particularly the interests of those on low income' (HMSO, 2003).

At the start of the price review process for the period 2010 to 2015, OFWAT published a consultation paper on 'Framework and approach' (OFWAT, 2007c). Notwithstanding the new Regulation Authority's duty to have regard to the interests of 'individuals with low incomes' the consultation paper makes no mention of that duty. In the entire consultation there is no mention of affordability (except in the context of water companies being able to afford environmental improvements) or of low incomes. Consumers are mentioned mainly in the context of competition or with regard to receiving 'value for money'. The regulatory system in England and Wales remains focused upon the average consumer, not the disadvantaged.

It is not apparent that economic regulation even in a high-income country, even after nearly 20 years of practice and even after a specific addition to the regulator's duties to be 'pro-poor' (at least by this writer's reading of the Act), has delivered anything for the poor.

DEFRA's most recent report (WRc, 2007) places its emphasis on assisting those on low incomes by helping them to reduce their water use and ensure the highest take-up of the welfare credits on offer, while promoting the ineffectual 'vulnerable group tariff' that simply ensures such households do not have to pay more than the average.

The necessarily imperfect process of regulation appears to be giving customers as well as government far more influence and even control over the supply of water and sanitation than was previously possible. However, the extent to which improvement in services and the environment is possible to replicate in an economy where average annual household incomes are US$1000 rather than over US$30,000, is a different issue. Most importantly, can privatization ever be fair? The ban on disconnections and the limits on tariffs for vulnerable customers are measures that promote equity. But the overall price the lowest-income groups are expected to pay, partly to fund wider environmental benefits, partly to rebalance the tariff basket as the rich benefit from savings through metering, is unaffordable for some. The new fashion to move towards rising block tariff systems, an approach now derided in the rest of the world, is unlikely to help much, however many stakeholders initially respond to the apparent 'fairness' of the approach.

The system has always been willing to evolve under pressure from its various stakeholders, particularly the media. OFWAT is now suggesting guaranteed revenues for the next price period, perhaps the best way of avoiding getting into the 'long-term weather forecasting business', not to mention avoiding the revenue uncertainties of rising block tariffs. If the next generation of television programmes starts showing too many bailiffs entering poor homes and removing household goods because of unpaid bills for water and the environment, then we can expect to see the regulatory process adapt again. But it would have been more encouraging to see economic regulation looking for ways to achieve benefits in advance of the next level of pain:

> *Current assistance schemes for customers on low incomes don't go far enough.*
> *Existing measures to help a small category of low-income consumers – those*

> *on benefit who have three children or more, or a specific medical condition requiring them to use more water than average – only helped 13,000 house-holds nationwide in 2005-06. The Consumer Council for Water began 2006-07 by arguing for support to be made available through the tax credits and benefits scheme, as this is a main, high-awareness benefit linked to a customer's ability to pay. However, the government has been resistant to the case for creating such financial support. Therefore we are researching the impact of other support methods, such as so called 'social tariffs'. The evidence suggested that customers reject the idea of cross-subsidies within the water charging system, which would mean the majority of customers pay slightly more to help those who are struggling. The one innovation which enjoys customer support seems to be the 'rising block tariff' – a stepped charging system which would see water charges rising, as more water is used.* (CCWater, 2007a)

The government has declared its interest in the balancing act (DEFRA, 2008) by requiring OFWAT, who it reminds 'is expected to make an important contribution to delivering the government's key priority outcomes', to give 'a renewed focus on affordability and fairness of charging for water'. OFWAT (2008) has eventually recognized its 'new' 2003 Water Act mandate with its 'revised and updated principles that underpin our decisions on charges' by stating that principle 2 on affordability is that 'water companies must have regard to the effects of their charging policies on different consumer groups, including potentially vulnerable consumers'.

8

Regulating Alternative Providers for the Poor

Esther Gerlach

Regulators or agencies in charge of overseeing the delivery of water and sanitation services must have a good understanding of the water and sanitation market if they are to counterbalance its imperfections. As the case studies have shown, in lower-income countries, this market is not limited to a monopoly provider supplying a largely homogeneous customer base with a fairly standard package of services. Inadequate infrastructure, underinvestment and the continuous pressures of rapid population growth and rising poverty levels far exceed the capabilities of conventional public service provision. The result is an irregular, fragmented market with a variety of agents, including a vibrant informal sector composed of dynamic private entrepreneurs. This 'other' private sector (Solo, 1999) occupies the many gaps left vacant by the utilities, and in particular (but not exclusively) caters for lower- and lowest-income households. This chapter investigates these alternative providers and their customers, their operations, the many problems and constraints they are facing along with their survival mechanisms. Having identified arguments for and against small-scale independent provision or utility cooperation with private intermediaries, it then seeks to explore the potential for incorporating alternative providers into the regulatory framework. The term 'alternative providers' is used throughout, encompassing all varieties of small-scale private provider, for which there are many terminologies, often used inconsistently by different authors.

Alternative providers are as diverse as their clientele, offering a wide range of services suited to the requirements of the type of customer that a utility, restricted by high technical standards, inflexible pricing and management structures and legal provisions finds difficult to serve. In the water supply sector, the African Water Utilities Partnership (Plummer, 2003) classifies alternative providers into intermediate and independent service providers. Intermediate providers effectively act as utility extensions by purchasing bulk quantities of water and distributing it, whereas independent providers develop their own sources and supply systems, sometimes in competition with the utility. A small number of 'pioneers' operate independent distribution networks with individual household connections; but vendors and resellers are usually the most commonly found type of alternative provider (Conan, 2003). These may either be working in partnership with the utility (for example stand post operators) or be classified as independent providers. The long list of types of alternative providers ranges from water tankers supplying unserved areas, water carriers providing a door-to-door delivery service, water points or kiosks owned or managed by communities or NGOs and privately managed utility stand posts, to water being sold by neighbours or landlords with a household connection.

There is also an emerging niche market for bottled water for low-income consumers sometimes distributed in plastic bags rather than bottles, with sales on the rise reported from many places, such as Guatemala, India and Shanghai (Conan, 2003; Llorente and Zérah, 2003; Raghupathi, 2003; Foster and Araujo, 2004). While many of the alternative providers' businesses are not officially registered, cases of illegal distribution of utility water have also been reported (WPEP, 2000). The definition of an alternative provider hence becomes somewhat ambiguous: it is difficult to draw boundaries between those simply operating within the informal economy, a common occurrence in developing-country cities, and those engaging in outright theft and fraud.

MARKET SHARE

Alternative providers' market share varies widely. The lowest figures are reported from South Asia, where only about 5–15 per cent of the total population buy water from vendors. This proportion increases to 20–45 per cent in South-East Asia (Conan, 2003) and can be expected to rise. In India, the stronghold of public service provision, about 50 private water businesses have emerged over the last 20 years in the capital city alone (Zérah, 1997). In Latin America, independent providers serve some 25 per cent of urban households (Solo, 1999). In some cities more than half the population may depend on alternative providers, as for example in Guatemala City, where around 200 private providers operate alongside the municipal water utility Empagua (Solo, 1998). The most recent assessment of independent providers in African cities quotes market shares ranging between 30 per cent and 80 per cent (Collignon and Vézina, 2000). It was found that the significance of alternative providers increases outside of major urban centres (Collignon, 1998; Solo, 1999). It should be noted that merely examining volumes of water supplied may be misleading, as low-income consumers tend to purchase the minimum quantities necessary for survival. In Port-au-Prince, Haiti, alternative providers 'produce about 10 per cent of the urban water supplied, distribute about 20 per cent of the city's water,

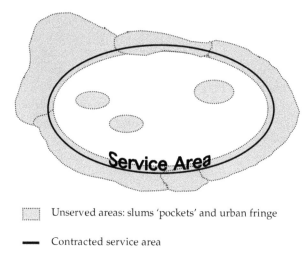

Unserved areas: slums 'pockets' and urban fringe

Contracted service area

Source: Esther Gerlach

Figure 8.1 *A spatial representation of a service area and the unserved*

and reach some 70 per cent of the households' (Solo, 1998). It remains unclear whether all studies included bottled water sales, so that the numbers quoted might still be an underestimate. According to an estimate of the Water Quality Association of the Philippines, for drinking purposes, nearly 45 per cent of households in Metro Manila already choose bottled water over tap water (WPEP, 2000).

STRENGTHS AND WEAKNESSES

Given that some form of alternative provision can be expected to remain a common and essential feature of urban water (and sanitation) markets within the foreseeable future, the quality of service delivered by independent operators or private utility partners needs to be evaluated – from the point of view of their customers. The overriding concern of all opponents and sceptics are the rates charged by alternative providers: 'Exorbitant prices' and 'overcharging' are frequently mentioned in the literature as arguments against small-scale private operators (Zaroff and Okun, 1984; Espinosa and López Rivera, 1994; Vézina, 2002). An overriding profit motive, anti-competitive monopolist behaviour, sometimes with the illegal involvement of corrupt utility staff, and the threat of capture by local elites or mafias are feared to exclude vulnerable groups and reinforce existing inequalities. The safety of alternative and mostly unmonitored drinking water supplies has also been questioned. There are minor secondary concerns about the possible irregularity and unreliability of supplies (Zaroff and Okun, 1984), the lack of qualifications of staff employed by small-scale independent enterprises, and the long-term sustainability of independent providers' activities – for instance, where they are contributing to the over-abstraction of local groundwater resources. As most alternative providers are unregistered informal businesses that do not pay tax, theoretically there are significant losses to the local tax base.

In contrast to these criticisms stands the unanimous agreement on the alternative providers' good understanding of the market, their customer responsiveness and remarkable resourcefulness in finding simple but effective solutions under the most adverse operating conditions. Collignon and Vézina (2000) describe the typical African independent water provider as 'a versatile man, risk and publicity averse; capable of raising important sums of money when necessary, but without a logo or a front office'. The ability of alternative providers to recognize needs, their flexibility in adapting to low-income customers' circumstances and the operational efficiencies they achieve in their businesses put many utilities to shame. Authors positively note the generally good and often personal relationships between suppliers and customers (Raghupathi, 2003); small-scale providers make 'contracts with customers, not with governments' (Solo, 1999). They know customer habits and preferences and the financial situation of households served. When families are experiencing payment difficulties, many independent providers offer non-bureaucratic solutions, adjusting payment plans to customers' income schedules or even delaying payments (Troyano, 1999).

The sometimes considerably higher prices than those charged by the official suppliers are ascribed to basic economics: without access to public subsidies and conventional financing, independent small-scale businesses invest family savings and are consequently forced to achieve full recovery of all costs (Solo, 1999). They simply operate in a competitive market where consumer demand and willingness to pay, existence of competitors, operating costs and seasonal variation of supplies dictate prices. Recent study results indicate that profit margins are in fact low and operators are surviving on modest incomes (Collignon and Vézina, 2000; Vézina, 2002; Conan and Paniagua, 2003). A comparison with official utility tariffs also touches on the subject of often misguided subsidies, which have been exposed as benefiting middle- and higher-income groups rather than supporting the those in need (Foster, 1998). While Llorente and Zérah (2003) criticize alternative suppliers for only providing peripheral solutions, Solo (1999) cites their readiness to see beyond the official city limits and experiment with innovative unconventional technologies as admirable strengths. Probably the most important difference between water utilities and small-scale alternative providers is that utilities are established within political and administrative boundaries, rather than developing naturally along geographic or cultural lines (Troyano, 1999), while alternative private providers cut across geographical, income or even class boundaries.

Irrespective of the various studies' economic assessments and moral judgements on the value of alternative water services, the fact is that small-scale private operators are providing a vital service, and much of their success can be attributed to a thorough understanding and constant observation of a continuously evolving market. Officially their contribution is rarely recognized (Conan, 2003), and where informal business verges upon illegality, the operators face a major obstacle that takes more than technical ingenuity to overcome. Communication with public authorities is likely to be non-existent, and the attitude of formal (private) monopoly providers, protected by exclusivity clauses in their concession agreements, may range from tolerance to outright hostility (Collignon and Vézina, 2000). Obel-Lawson and Njoroge (1999) report that even where official policies have been reformed they are unlikely to accommodate independent providers.

RESEARCH FINDINGS

The country case studies show that alternative providers are indeed a regular feature of water supply (and sanitation) services to the urban poor in the developing world, where they 'provide an indispensable service to those sidelined by the public utility systems'. There are preciously few exceptions, though it must be noted that the sample for the Regulating Public and Private Partnerships for the Poor project is biased in favour of capital and metropolitan cities where economic regulation of various forms of 'partnership' is most developed. Observations may not necessarily hold true for secondary towns, and recommendations based on conclusions drawn from the case studies would have to be treated with caution in this situation.

Even in cities with exceptionally high connection rates, alternative providers were found as vital players in the urban water market, cutting across income boundaries. The case of Amman, where customers resort to tanker truck deliveries to supplement heavily rationed piped water supply, demonstrates that alternative providers are not solely a low-income phenomenon. No water vending in small containers was encountered in the Zambian capital, but Lusaka still relies on alternative models of provision to serve its urban poor. A high level of involvement of international development partners in the city's peri-urban areas explains the absence of the 'conventional' water vending systems. With the exception of Chile, from where no alternative modes of supply were reported in Santiago, even the comparatively well-managed systems in Latin America leave service gaps that are in turn filled by alternative providers, albeit to a much lesser extent than in African or Asian countries.

In none of the cases examined does the present regulatory framework provide for economic regulation of alternative providers' operations. This would of course be expected for a (largely) competitive market, where the main justification for regulatory intervention is absent. In the context of a well-functioning (and thus self-regulating) private provider market the application of fair trading law and water quality regulation would be an adequate level of regulation. However, the case studies present compelling evidence that anti-competitive behaviour and disregard for other regulations can be widespread. This chapter discusses various combinations of regulatory risks and inadequate oversight mechanisms, as well as regulatory attempts to deal with alternative providers. Based on the regulatory challenges identified from the case studies, recommendations are made for incorporating alternative providers into the regulatory framework to minimize potential negative impacts on poor urban consumers. In view of the long-term objectives for the structure and organization of the urban water market, a distinction must be made between independent and intermediate providers in terms of the type and level of regulatory intervention required. This research is based on the presumption that all households should be able to enjoy the convenience of 'better than a stand post supply', that is some form of piped water supply to the home. This long-term objective for urban water services would lead to a gradual phasing out of intermediate providers, as even the poorest households would be given access to the economies of scale derived from a piped distribution system.

INADEQUATE OVERSIGHT MECHANISMS

The case studies show that current oversight systems, where existent, frequently fail to deliver the desired levels of service and consumer protection. Existing rules and regulations need to be re-examined in view of their implications for alternative providers, their conventional (utility) counterparts and, ultimately, service delivery to poor urban households. Economic 'regulation' of the alternative provider market rarely extends beyond abstraction licensing and tanker truck registration. Any further regulations impinging on economic activity of alternative providers frequently result in them operating on the verge of illegality. In Ghana, for instance, customers are required to obtain approval from the water utility in order to on-sell water. Vendors, however, were found to be operating without the utility's consent, and Amman's water tanker drivers admit to exploiting customers' ignorance and the lack of enforcement on the part of the water authorities when exceeding maximum price limits set by the government for their resale activities.

However, legal transgressions may not always occur through malicious behaviour on the part of the alternative providers. Rules may simply go ignored due to the opaqueness and complexity of the regulatory system, where regulations are either unknown or clear lines of responsibility cannot be discerned. Whether disrespect of regulations is blatant and widespread as in the case of some Jordanian tanker drivers or it is rather a matter of lack of information or interest (both on the part of alternative providers and governments as regulators), the cases highlight the importance of monitoring and enforcement by regulatory agencies, as well as the need to strengthen customer protection through readily accessible information, complaints handling and redress mechanisms. Registration, as seen in some case studies, may be a first attempt to provide some level of oversight for alternative providers, with the registration data providing a first point of reference for establishing an information data base on alternative providers.

It is not uncommon for existing regulations to give an (unfair?) competitive advantage to formal utility water providers, in spite of their inability to deliver services to large proportions of the population. Examples for this are exclusivity rights granted to large water utilities, which span the entire service area, even if contractual coverage targets may not envisage the entire population receiving piped water services until the end of the service agreement (or worse still, have been revised to reflect the inability of the utility to reach 100 per cent of a city's residents within the lifetime of the contract – for example Manila and Jakarta). Bulk water may also be supplied by the main provider at less than favourable rates. In Manila independent providers distributing utility water were found to be paying high commercial water prices rather than the cheaper domestic rate. From Uganda the practice of charging value-added tax on water sold to alternative providers was reported. Regulation is called upon to balance the trade-off between avoiding inflated bulk water rates, which hurt end users as on-sellers pass on their costs, and allowing utilities to pursue a commercial pricing policy. Supplying water to intermediate providers at the subsidized domestic rate is likely to threaten the utility's ability to achieve cost reflectivity in order to finance necessary investments.

In defence of any 'utility bias' the large revenue shares currently being diverted into the informal sector (see price comparisons in the next section) must be considered. The size of the alternative market effectively limits the revenue available to the conventional provider and reduces the opportunity to become commercially viable. Of course, before market shares can be adjusted in favour of utilities, the regulatory system must ensure that the main provider is in a position to provide adequate and affordable services to the poorest households in those areas that are traditionally viewed as 'difficult to serve'. Likewise, 'top-up' services such as tanker deliveries cannot be eliminated unless the utility can meet the needs of its entire customer base.

Other inadequacies in current regulatory (and legal) frameworks threaten the continuity of service to urban low-income areas. Successful pro-poor water service programmes implemented by formal providers out-compete small-scale independent providers. Faced with the risk of takeover by a larger and financially better-equipped competitor, small entrepreneurs can be reluctant to continue to invest in much-needed water services for the poor. The lack of an enabling legal framework that would protect independent providers' investments and allow cooperative arrangements between alternative providers and utilities to harness the 'pro-poor service skills' acquired by the former can only be regarded as a serious shortcoming. This is particularly damaging to the under-served poor who continue to settle outside of the utilities' service areas as city boundaries expand to accommodate population growth and in-migration.

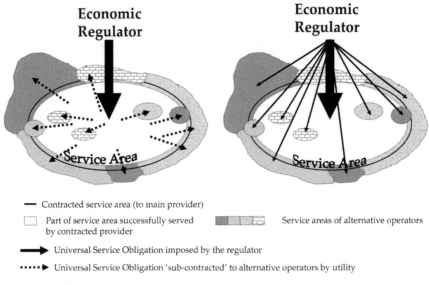

Source: Esther Gerlach

Figure 8.2 *Allocating regulatory oversight to alternative providers*

REGULATORY RISKS

The case studies confirmed the regulatory risks inherent in informal and largely unregulated water markets, where prices fluctuate in response to availability of supply and consumer demands. In addition, water quality as well as environmental impact of alternative providers' operations is a major concern. Alternative providers may be knowingly or unwittingly infringing on existing legislation or exploiting loopholes in the law, such as abstraction, planning and business regulations. In doing so, there is a risk that their activities are contributing to looming environmental crises, such as groundwater over-abstraction and sea-water intrusion into aquifers. Likewise, in the absence of strict water quality controls, the diffuse small-scale provider market can represent a significant public health risk. For regulation of small-scale private water markets to be effective, there may be a strong case for economic, water quality and environmental aspects to be considered jointly.

Given a healthy amount of competition, prices will reflect the cost of provision and respond to consumer demand. However, the case studies demonstrate that due to cartel formation and mafia-like tendencies an oligarchic market structure has developed in some locations, which warrants regulatory intervention in order to control profit-seeking behaviour of some private providers. Compared to the subsidized – usually higher-income – groups able to access piped water from municipal networks, poor households pay significantly more per unit of water.

Relative to the cheapest domestic rate available from the main provider (sometimes designed as a social or 'lifeline' tariff), the poor may be paying as much as 108 times for water delivered to their home, though 10–20 times the lowest tariff seems to be the going rate for alternative supplies. Worst case scenario figures from Jordan are distorted (43.2 times) as the rich frequently resort to tankers during water shortages, but even here the poor end up paying on average 11.5 times more when forced to buy tanker deliveries. The Amman case study demonstrates how effective prices paid by low-income households having to invest in coping strategies and accessing alternative providers reach levels comparable to and higher than those paid by high users and high-income customers. Also notable is the relative stability of formal water tariffs compared with considerable price hikes for alternative suppliers that were observed in some case study locations.

Experiences in regulating alternative providers

Attempts have been made to regulate the alternative small-scale private market to support low-income urban customers who are most at risk from predatory pricing and water quality lapses. The only example of price regulation for alternative providers has been reported from Ghana, where the regulator PURC sets resale prices for stand posts as well as water tankers. Although a Memorandum of Understanding between the tanker operators association and Ghana Water Company Ltd adds a further layer of regulation and encourages self-regulation of members, in practice the system fails with respect to the quality of water delivered to poor customers as effective monitoring systems are not in place. Further regulatory gaps identified by the regulator include complaints handling, mechanisms to reduce prices and counter the development of cartels. The last of these is a major concern of the regulator in Jakarta, who is seeking to disentangle the web of water mafias and vested interests in the status quo by promoting transparent community management practices. The Zambian example cited earlier demonstrates how partnership arrangements can be very effective in reducing opportunistic exploitation of poor communities by some alternative providers or, worse still, corrupt utility staff colluding with private resellers. However, regulators sometimes struggle to find the necessary support. The Jakarta regulator has been encountering legal and political obstacles when seeking to establish community-based partnership arrangements as interim solutions to help the under-served poor. Deregulation measures, intended to ease access for new market entrants and to relieve the financial burden to customers through lower prices associated with greater competition, may be opposed by incumbent small-scale providers. The legalization of household resale in Jakarta allegedly had to be discontinued to prevent perceived profit losses of standpipe operators.

REMAINING CHALLENGES

A number of regulatory challenges remain. One major obstacle to any form of regulation of alternative providers is the major information gap and the limited resources regulators have at their disposal in the face of a large and diffuse market. However, regulators contend that it is the availability of information that determines the quality of regulatory decision-making, and therefore efforts should be made to improve the quality of available data (comments received at the project's Review Workshop). This need not, and should not, go as far as collecting information on each and every alternative provider. The case studies show, however, that it would be beneficial for regulators to have an overview of water sources used by alternative providers, quantities distributed, areas of operation and end-user prices – for customer protection reasons as well as to obtain an estimate of the return on investment achieved by the providers. It was also noted that the required surveying work may exceed capacities of regulators as well as putting additional strains on the regulatory budget. In response to this, a suggestion was to seek partnership arrangements with collaborators on the ground (for example NGOs, community and residents' associations).

Other open questions include how to:

- determine an optimum level of regulation and practicable regulatory arrangements that regularize the informal market but do not undermine its flexibility;
- maintain a light-handed approach to regulation in order to avoid the increase in overheads leading to end-user prices and/or service deterioration associated with an overemphasis on high technical standards and formal procedures;
- offer accessible and responsive customer complaints procedures;
- set up effective monitoring and enforcement mechanisms;

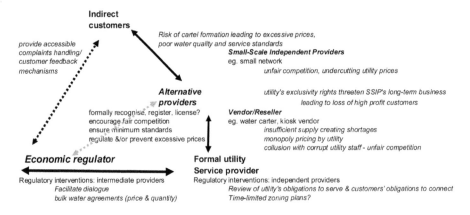

Figure 8.3 *Possible regulatory interventions for alternative providers*

- provide legal/regulatory protection for small-scale private investors;
- increase transparency where price regulation is deemed impractical or unenforceable.

CONCLUSIONS AND RECOMMENDATIONS

Research suggests that in many locations full service coverage through conventional providers (utilities) is unlikely to be achieved in the short or medium term under present arrangements. It is therefore suggested that the vital contribution of alternative providers to urban water service provision be recognized, building upon their strengths and – at some level – incorporating them into the regulatory framework to minimize potential negative impacts on poor households.

The published literature offers very few recommendations on the subject. Most authors put their faith in a loosely regulated market, maintaining that regulation within an adequate legal framework (Conan, 2003) that supports a healthy level of competition will promote expansions, while ensuring affordability for poor households. Components of regulation that receive particular mention are customer protection (Collignon and Vézina, 2000; Raghupathi, 2003), transparency and information-sharing, and performance-based regulation is favoured over technical (input) specifications (Solo, 1999).

The aspects of regulation (price, water quality, market entry and market share) relating to alternative providers have been identified in the literature (for example, Plummer, 2002a), but very few tentative suggestions have been made as to what these future regulatory arrangements would have to be. Plummer recommends relaxing performance standards and exclusivity rights given to utilities, supporting alternative providers in securing legal contracts, revising tariff regimes, addressing land tenure issues and disseminating a 'spirit of inclusion' among the incumbent large-scale service providers. Trémolet and Browning (2002) propose replacing costly 'traditional' regulation through price and quality standards with making performance data publicly available, thus relying on the regulating effects of reputation. 'In any event', they conclude, 'the choice of regulatory instruments should be based on a comparative assessment of the trade-offs between effectiveness, ease of implementation and costs and benefits' (Trémolet and Browning, 2002).

There seems to be universal agreement among the sector professionals questioned during the course of this research that some form of official recognition of alternative providers would be beneficial. Independent small-scale providers could potentially be treated as 'micro-utilities' and issued with an operating licence, which would regulate service provision to end users under similar, though simplified, terms to those specified for utilities. There is less support for licensing of intermediate providers (vendors and resellers who effectively act as an extended arm of the utility), who may be captured more effectively and efficiently through third-party agreements between utilities and individual alternative providers without direct involvement of the regulator. Some experts argue that the potential for successful regulation is severely limited in the case of certain forms of alternative provision, and only public health considerations warrant continued government involvement: 'Truck transportation is generally a business better managed by private enterprises, whose regulation by administration is barely effective' (Collignon, contribution to eConference 2005, cited in Gerlach, 2005).

In light of the occasionally expressed opinion that regulators should concentrate on the (explicitly mandated or perceived) key task of promoting efficiency gains from the main formal providers and making small-scale competitors redundant in the long term, the question remains to what extent economic regulation should integrate alternative providers into the regulatory framework.

Few practical and immediately executable solutions could be derived from case study findings or were proposed by water professionals involved in this research. Consumer education is seen as a key factor in addressing the price regulation problem. One recommendation was to publicize cost and pricing information and thus to exploit the self-regulating effects of making vendors' price mark-ups clearly visible to end users.

However, while some level of price regulation may well be achievable for independent providers (producers), encouraging fair competition could be the best regulatory option for vendors' resale prices at present. A major consideration here should be the cost–benefit ratio of regulatory intervention, as the associated monitoring and enforcement costs appear prohibitive, especially as overheads would have to be passed on to an already overburdened customer base – unless these could be carried out less bureaucratically and efficiently by lower-level administration and/or the main provider (for example through the above-mentioned third party agreements) – and may simply not be practicable from the regulator's as well as the alternative providers' (and consequently the customers') perspectives.

Specific recommendations for preventing monopoly pricing were given with reference to tanker operations. Collignon (1998) sees the role of the regulator in guaranteeing equal access to public water sources, encouraging market entry by enhancing tanker drivers' social status through official recognition of their activities, and reducing overheads by lowering delivery distances and selling bulk water at social rates. Formal bulk water agreements, guaranteeing fixed quantities of treated water to be supplied by the utility at a competitive price, could be overseen by a regulator. In order to achieve maximum impacts in terms of public health, economic regulation of alternative providers cannot be separated from water quality regulation. As with prices, minimum water quality standards are potentially easier to monitor and enforce for independent providers than for vendors and resellers, and the same principles apply. In view of the immediate health hazard, easily accessible complaints procedures need to be in place to report service failures. In line with the demand for fair competition, customer feedback should also be sought on general standards of service delivery for individual alternative providers, and redress mechanisms devised to penalize unacceptable service.

As indicated above, a general framework for regulating alternative providers may have to be set out in legislative terms. The typology of alternative providers in terms of scale of operations, ownership structures and mobility is the determining factor in framing this legislation. Regulators may have to act as facilitators and advisers to policy-makers and demand clarification of the government's position with regard to alternative providers, as strictly speaking some decisions are outside of regulators' remit. A regulator, however, could present a compelling case for refining the regulations with respect to service obligations, both with respect to the obligation of a utility provider to connect new customers and the obligation of residents to subscribe to networked water services, as and when these become available. Geographical zoning or time-limited operating licences may be one approach to solving the problem of competition for high-profit customers and the undermining of cross-subsidy systems. Here it is important to recognize any vested interests in the status quo, as shown by the examples of illegal 'collaborations' between utility staff and alternative providers (Indonesia) or large profit margins for government from abstraction charges, where alternative providers access groundwater resources (Jordan).

In delineating alternative providers' spheres of operation, due regard should be given to the regularity of supply, which is often not guaranteed by the main provider, but which this research has shown to be a major determinant of customer confidence, on a par with water quality issues. Regulators should formally acknowledge the role of alternative providers in providing a vital public service, and facilitate dialogue between utilities and small-scale partners in order to identify opportunities for win-win solutions that ultimately benefit poor urban consumers. There may also be a role for the regulator to lobby for political (and hence regulatory) endorsement of alternative community-based partnership arrangements.

The disproportionately high prices paid for vended water by a large fraction of the urban poor raise questions about equitability within the tariff-setting framework for conventional providers. The research findings point to a huge revenue potential that could be unlocked. The challenge is for formal providers to penetrate the low-income water market and capture revenue flows being 'lost' to the informal market, which could be used to finance network improvements and extensions allowing the under-served poor to access the economies of scale derived from a piped distribution system. This will not necessarily destroy the business of the alternative providers who should easily find opportunities in the always expanding low-density peri-urban areas, in advance of it being economic for the monopoly provider to extend their pipe network.

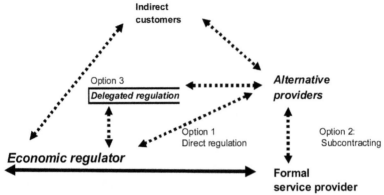

Option 1 Risk: Excessive cost, requires high resource/staff input from regulator
Option 2 Risk: Regulatory burden shifted on to provider who may be struggling with service delivery itself
Option 3 Challenge: Capacity-building and organisation - Risk: Politicisation if local authorities involved

Figure 8.4 *Risks and challenges in regulatory involvement with alternative providers*

Conversely, some cases have highlighted the threat alternative providers can pose to the main providers. Where customers are not legally obliged to remain connected to formal networked services, vendors – mainly tankers – are siphoning off lucrative customers who are happy to switch to a cheaper and sometimes more convenient service alternative. Such unfair competition is not simply an injustice to utilities, but it erodes revenues that are needed to sustain the heavy cross-subsidies between user groups to support the below-cost tariffs offered for the first tariff block and that are in turn intended to benefit the poor.

Figure 8.4 summarizes major regulatory risks associated with service provision by alternative providers that have been identified during the analysis of case study data. In response to these conflicts it also suggests potential regulatory interventions applicable to independent and intermediate providers respectively. These proposals draw on the recommendations formulated for the different case studies as well as discussions with and between regulators, researchers and various water professionals held during the project Review Workshop and eConference (Gerlach, 2005).

The best approach to 'regulating' alternative providers (including whether and to what extent to regulate them at all) will always be highly case specific. This research may not offer definite answers, but it highlights the regulatory risks that justify some level of regulation of alternative providers. Recognizing their role, especially in delivering water services to disadvantaged households, is a first step towards more equitable and sustainable service provision. Furthermore, the case studies give an overview of the kinds of questions that need to be considered in order to extend the benefits of regulation, such as enhanced consumer protection to the often poor urban customers of alternative water service providers, while building on the flexible service approach that the best of the alternative providers can offer.

Regulators face many challenges and may have to temporarily embrace less conventional arrangements in the pursuit of the ultimate goal of an affordable water connection for all households, irrespective of their incomes. Efforts need to be made to give incentives to utilities to take over their small-scale counterparts' customer base, hence enabling the urban poor to benefit financially from large-scale service provision without losing the convenience and flexibility of a small local provider.

9

Involving and Empowering Poor Customers

Richard Franceys and Esther Gerlach

> *I intend that the Customer Service Committees will play a major role in ensuring that the interests of customers get high priority.* (Regulator Ian Byatt, 1989)

The goals for economic regulation of monopoly service providers from a customer perspective are to ensure an effective resilient service delivery at a fair price, taking into account well-targeted subsidies when necessary, ensure service that is equitable and sustainable with adequate incentives for efficiency, and to ensure protection of consumers against monopoly abuse through transparency in price setting and complaints adjudication. These goals require some level of customer involvement in decision-making if they are to be successful over the long term.

WHY CUSTOMER INVOLVEMENT?

Customer involvement is primarily needed for feedback, to maintain and improve services and empowerment in decision-making, to maintain the legitimacy of a monopoly provider. Customers normally give service providers feedback through their purchasing choices, positive and negative, which is used to adjust service levels and options to match user needs and preferences. For a monopoly provider of a product, which everybody has to have every day, this 'natural' feedback is otherwise missing. Customer involvement, through whatever method, acts as a substitute for the absent feedback link between consumers and direct service providers. Regulators similarly need this feedback to inform their pricing and service standards decisions. The challenge for economic regulation for the poor is to ensure that there are adequate mechanisms to receive this feedback from the poorest.

This need complements the other aspect of customer involvement in that it can also empower society in various other ways. There is a significant literature on community involvement in rural water and sanitation in low-income countries which is particularly relevant when those communities are being asked to take direct responsibility for significant elements of their water and sanitation services. Much of this literature refers to the need to empower communities to take responsibility in a manner that supports development in a much broader sense. In urban areas, where economies of scale demand sophisticated pipe networks, beyond the capacity of segments of the population to manage their water supply on their own (always with exceptions), empowerment remains necessary in the face of a monopoly supplier. On their own, individual customers are 'powerless' in the face of a technocratic, monolithic and often inefficient supplier. There needs to be customer involvement beyond the individual level to empower the satisfactory resolution of individual complaints but also to drive sufficient transparency and accountability into the process such that society as a whole is empowered to achieve its wider goals, social and environmental.

Table 9.1 compares the current level and extent of customer involvement in the case study countries relative to Arnstein's 'ladder of citizen participation' (Arnstein, 1969) and more recent variants of the spectrum of public participation published by Wilcox (1994) and Robinson (2003). Techniques should be selected according to the target group (in terms of their understanding of the issues at hand and the number of customers to be involved) and the aims of the involvement exercise.

The aspects of poverty referred to in Chapters 1 and 3 describe how poverty is not only a lack of income or household wealth but also powerlessness. An effective public water supply, even if privately delivered, has to address these issues particularly for the poor, to support the delivery of an inclusive and cohesive society. Securing public support and thereby increasing the chance of

Table 9.1 *Public participation*

Degree of citizen power	Citizen control	Empower	Supporting
	Delegated power		independent community initiatives
	Partnership	Partner	Acting together
Degree of tokenism	Placation	Involve	Deciding together
	Consultation	Consult	Consultation
	Informing	Inform	Information
Non-participation	Therapy (education)	Influence	Information
	Manipulation		
	Arnstein, 1969	Robinson, 2003	Wilcox, 1994

Source: Adapted from Arnstein (1969), Wilcox (1994) and Robinson (2003) in Franceys (2006)

sustainable outcomes, addressing common needs and resolving differences (World Bank, 2004a) is vital, as the Bolivian case study illustrates. Empowering poor customers also minimizes bad debts from customers who are least able to pay – a very practical concern of a water utility. In promoting pro-poor regulator-supported expansion into the slums and shanties, the goal is for those services to be sustainable for both supplier and customers. Increasing access through new styles of connections with subsequent disconnection due to vandalism or non-payment of water tariffs is not the objective. Customer and community involvement and oversight of services and tariffs are ever more important, if also even harder, in the poorest communities.

WHICH CUSTOMERS SHOULD BE INVOLVED?

There is a sense in which all customers are involved in decision-making – through their behaviour in the use of water (or more significantly the waste of water) and their timely payment of bills (or not).

However, beyond the rhetoric that all customers should be consulted, in practice only a very small sample of customers can be involved in any formal contribution to decision-making processes, whether through focus groups, responding to questionnaires or membership of some consumer committee. The challenge then is to ensure that these formal processes capture a representative sample of all segments of customers, domestic, institutional, commercial and industrial users, including even urban agriculturalists in many settings. There is an overriding need to ensure that disadvantaged and vulnerable groups are involved, critically including future and not only existing customers, plus the need, in most societies, to overemphasize the views of women.

In lower- and lower-middle-income countries, where a significant proportion (if not the majority) of the population is currently unserved or under-served by formal water service providers, there is a need to engage with these marginalized groups. In the context of this research programme, ensuring that the views of the peri-urban poor, the slum and shanty dwellers are recognized and acted upon is a priority concern. Giving a voice to the customers of the variety of informal or alternative service providers, recognizing the extent to which they might wish to become customers of the formal provider – helps regulators and utilities to design appropriate formal services and in the meantime provides a mechanism for monitoring prices and quality of this semi-competitive vendor market.

WHAT SHOULD CUSTOMERS BE INVOLVED IN?

The simple answer to what should customers be involved in is 'everything' – but not involved in everything to anything like the same level of detail, and recognizing that while customers will not always be 'correct' (perhaps an understatement in the views of some service providers) their opinions deserve to be heard. The principle is that nothing should be 'off limits', not even 'commercial in confidence' for a monopoly supplier of a 'merit good'. With that principle established, along the lines of governmental freedom of information requirements, it would be normal for most customers to have only very limited areas of interest, often related to service failures in their home or street, the levels of service, particularly in terms of water quality and pressure and responsiveness to any customer contacts. Beyond that, some customers (or their civil society representatives) will want to be involved in understanding the utility's technical competence, levels of tariffs and financial performance and efficiency with a valid view to influencing the 'bigger picture'.

Of particular relevance to this study is involvement of potential customers in planning service extensions and the consequent costs of connection. It is suggested that one of the challenges in Buenos Aires in the early years was the significant, though agreed, increase in connection charges. Existing customers who were most aware of the increase knew it did not concern them and therefore did not speak out against it. Future customers could only get their message across by refusing to connect at the new higher connection charges, leading to subsequent problems of lower than expected revenues.

CUSTOMER INVOLVEMENT AROUND THE WORLD: RESEARCH FINDINGS

In the majority of case study countries the existing level of active customer involvement is low, and UK-style formal customer representation remains the exception. Where regulators are attempting to replicate the England and Wales consumer services committee (CSC) model, there is a tendency to start by establishing links with existing residents' neighbourhood or consumer associations or local customer committees are formed to act as grassroots NGO-type organizations. In Ghana, the regulator's plans to set up formal customer committees have reportedly stalled due to funding shortages and the fear of undue politicization. The Bolivian regulator meets with representatives of FEJUVE on a weekly basis.

ETOSS, the regulator of the Buenos Aires concession, formed a commission from local consumer organizations, who were given full access to all information, particularly in the context of the 2000 review of the five-year plan for future investments. ETOSS Resolution No. 42/00 pointed out the constitutional rights under the Basic Law as public participation in the actions of regulators of public services, and access to adequate and true information about those services.

The regulator explained that a CSC system was copied but with 15 to 18 NGOs forming a Users Commission (Comision de Usuarios) to represent customers rather than individual customers being involved. Subsequently, in a document to ETOSS entitled *Report of the Users Commission (of ETOSS) in Respect of the Renegotiation of the Water Supply and Sewerage Contract Ordered by Law 25.561*, the Users Commission offered their views on the Aguas Argengtinas contract, including advocating termination of the concession contract, placing blame and responsibility totally at the door of the concessionaire. This might not have been particularly constructive.

This approach to customer involvement is seen by some in the city as 'second-best'. In a revised form, the NGOs are required to send one representative to the Users Commission, partly financed by the ETOSS budget, meeting every week with access to all information. 'They can sit in on the board meeting, with no voice or vote, but whatever representations they want can be made. We are obliged to receive them, answer any questions they want, they call me to their meetings to explain and to help them understand', said an interviewee from ETOSS.

As in other regulatory systems it is recognized that customer representatives have to be educated in the realities of the water sector over time. An ETOSS representative said:

> *They are very reactive, but they are not stupid, you have to respect them, be patient, step by step they start learning, start understanding – then their resistance decreases, they enrich the process, they have ideas, they have their own rotation, we don't interfere. ... The Commission has ample access to all the documentation, but it has been proved the commissioners are not sufficiently trained to deal with such an amount of technical information. In some cases their misinterpretations require clarifications from the regulator's staff.*

In an effort to promote nearness and relevance to customers, ETOSS tried to place its representatives in each of the 17 municipal offices. However, 'it didn't work – customers saw them as messengers, not actually those responsible people and they always wanted to talk to the boss. There were no complaints in two years in the district offices, all complaints came to the head office.'

There is no direct compensation system for customer grievances. Any fines imposed on the water company for service deficiencies are paid to a separate account and at the end of the year 'are repaid through tariff adjustments. As an incentive it doesn't work so well', said one interviewee. The example of customer involvement in the Buenos Aires case is included here, even though the full case study for Buenos Aires has been omitted, as it represents a new contribution to this project not previously reported. An earlier view of the role of regulation and service delivery to the poor in Buenos Aires can be found in Weitz and Franceys (2002, Appendix II).

Zambia has developed a unique system where water watch groups (WWGs) serve as a formal link between the regulator and customers and provide valuable feedback on services delivered by the regulated companies. The WWGs have similar complaints-handling functions to the Consumer Council for Water's Regional Committees in England and Wales, but their powers and responsibilities extend beyond a mediator/facilitator role, as the rationale for establishing the WWGs was to directly involve communities in service quality monitoring. Members of the WWGs also play an active role in customer sensitization and education, particularly in peri-urban and low-income areas. In recognition of the WWGs' effectiveness, the Zambian energy and telecommunication regulators are seeking an alliance with the water regulator to expand the scope of WWGs to encompass the three infrastructure areas by adding representatives from the energy and telecommunication regulators. The water regulator, Osward Chanda, welcomes this as a positive step: 'It a first in terms of regulators working together in this manner and we hope further cooperation could be developed' (Chanda, personal communication, 2005).

In Jakarta, following the successful launch of a quarterly Customer and Community Communication Forum (CCCF) by the JWSRB as a formal communication platform between water sector stakeholders, water consumer committees (WCCs) were introduced to facilitate more effective two-way communication between communities and service providers. Besides complaints handling and lobbying for service improvements on behalf of under-served communities, the regulator values the WCCs' role in facilitating acceptance of tariff increases and promoting understanding among customers.

Research from Chile, which features one of the stronger regulatory systems in the developing world, reports the view of the official consumer bodies that consumer protection is rather weak. It is said that the regulator 'SSIS is not in the middle between the company and the consumers'. Presumably the intended criticism refers to the lack of a framework for customer involvement, which is required to validate and inform the regulatory process. (Customer representatives are better placed as intermediaries between customers and providers and can inform the regulator, who should remain independent in order to retain his credibility.)

So-called 'performance cafés' or 'performance corners', designed to provide information for customers on the concessionaires in Metro Manila where there are no formal customer involvement mechanisms, had been developed through external support, but in this research were found to be no longer operational. While the Ugandan 'pre-regulatory' case study remains silent on customer involvement issues, the Jordanian research revealed that to date there is no customer consultation culture in the country, and formal customer representation may not be appropriate at this point in time. India, another 'pre-regulatory' case study describes the newly developed pattern for electricity regulation with an Advisory Committee that includes a customer-focused NGO to advocate consumers' concerns at policy level and that runs customer awareness and capacity-building programmes as precursors to establishing customer committees.

The eleven case studies (including for this chapter only, Buenos Aires) found five examples of formal customer representation (four customer committees, one advisory group), two of which depended upon NGO representation. Two were part of the regulatory office, three were independent (one only recently).

We found therefore that the majority (five out of nine) of regulatory systems support some measure of customer information and consultation, though more often than not information verges on consumer education, which is considered a more limited stage of participation. As long as information and/or education are treated as 'necessary but not sufficient' stages for higher-level involvement, this could be justified by the relative youth of many systems. So far very few allow involvement beyond consultation, and the leap into the top ranges of empowerment or partnership appears to elude all but an enlightened minority and may even represent a 'step too far'.

It is interesting to note that the ratings for customer involvement seem to bear little relationship with the countries' 'voice and accountability' score awarded to the national governance system by the World Bank governance indicator survey (Kaufmann et al, 2005). The regulatory system in Zambia clearly has transcended the barrier that reportedly exists for citizen participation in government matters according to this data. Progress observed in Indonesia, a country that scores equally poorly on 'voice', is remarkable. (The voice and accountability indicator measures political, civil and human rights.)

Risks and constraints, independence and interdependence of customer involvement

The combined experience from the case studies shows that customer groups or committees face a number of constraints that can severely limit the effectiveness of customer involvement. Questions that need to be addressed include membership, resources and remit, capacity and organization, objectives for involvement and how to maintain focus and avoid politicization. The following analysis is biased towards formal customer representation arrangements, but lessons can be learned for other consumer involvement mechanisms, which are discussed subsequently.

The level of independence of (formal) customer representatives from the 'parent' regulator seems to be regarded as a prerequisite for effective customer involvement, as implied by the recent changes in the water regulatory system. After 16 years of successful cooperation the close relationship between OFWAT and the customer committees was deemed by a new national government to be no longer appropriate and discontinued. The Consumer Council for Water now operates as an independent statutory body. An analysis of the case studies can give no definite answer as to which arrangements are most effective and hence would be preferable. If anything, the findings suggest that the non-independent groups and committees enjoy high levels of support from the respective regulators, which contribute to their successful operation rather than diminish their value in the public eye.

Membership, representation and sustainability

In three of the four countries where formal customer representation exists, membership is open to all interested individuals. While customer committees in the UK and WWGs in Zambia are formed following an open recruitment process, Jakarta's customer committees comprise mostly local politicians from the lowest administrative level. The intended benefit of this arrangement is to exploit existing links between administration, customers and providers. In contrast, vacancies are advertised and posts awarded competitively on the basis of experience and motivation in the case of Zambian WWGs. The England and Wales system stresses the importance of bringing lay and particularly local knowledge to the discussions and seeks to appoint a range of members to represent a balance of interests, gender and ethnic backgrounds.

The voluntary nature of customer representation, which is presently the norm, is affecting membership. The average committee member in England and Wales could be described as 'middle-class professional early retiree looking to make a public service contribution'. Small payments have been introduced under the recent reform and are envisaged to encourage a wider membership in order to achieve a more accurate reflection of society and the various customer groups, but initial indications show little change. The absence of allowances for members of WWGs has led to a number of vacancies in Lusaka. The findings seem to suggest that incentives are required to ensure true representativeness and sustain customer involvement at the partnership level, though the nature of incentives (financial, social status, etc.) may depend on the economic conditions and cultural attitudes. Daily wage earners, for instance, cannot afford to commit time to non-essential activities, so that a lack of financial recompense may automatically exclude some of the poorest.

The considerably large proportion of the regulatory budget (14 per cent) allocated to customer involvement reflects the JWSRB's commitment to engaging with consumers. Reports from Zambia suggest that the current level of funding for WWGs is inadequate compared with the workload, and the scope of activities is limited by time and financial resources. Recent reforms in England and Wales have made the customer committees, previously part of and funded by the regulator OFWAT, financially independent by imposing a separate levy on water companies. Worldwide experience to date does not suggest that either mechanism is preferable in terms of allowing customers to inform and influence the regulatory process. Table 9.2 summarizes the findings from the case studies regarding the researchers' perspectives on the different levels of customer involvement.

Table 9.2 *Customer involvement findings from the case studies (1 = low, 5 = high)*

			Lusaka	La Paz	Jakarta	Manila	Central England
Degree of citizen power	Citizen control Delegated power	Empower					1
	Partnership	Partner	2	2	1		1
Degree of tokenism	Placation	Involve	3	2	2		3
	Consultation	Consultation	2	2	4	1	4
	Informing						
Non-participation	Therapy (education) Manipulation	Information	1		1	1	5
	Arnstein,1969						

Source: Author's analysis, partly adapted from Arnstein (1969)

CAPACITY, FOCUS AND THE DANGERS OF POLITICIZATION

As the selection process in Zambia partly indicated, capacity of representatives both in terms of technical and social understanding is essential for successful inputs into the regulatory process. High turnover of members or short tenures can be a significant factor, as new members often require training to perform their assigned tasks. Without strong support, capacity constraints can undermine confidence in the value of customers' contributions, as the following comments illustrate.

There is a need to develop 'strong knowledge' for customer representatives to become competent and respected partners in the regulatory process. Care must be taken not to create an 'enlightened elite', however. In order to be effective, customer representatives need to retain the capacity to access 'weak knowledge' of the average customer, who will not have a detailed understanding of the water industry and the policy-making process.

The England and Wales experience demonstrates how customer pressure can stimulate the evolution of the regulatory and policy framework, which has led to significant improvements for disadvantaged households (for example a ban on domestic disconnections and the new primary duty for the regulator to 'further the consumer objective', giving regard to low-income and vulnerable customers, as per the Water Act 2003). However, it is most likely that these changes resulted from political and civil society involvement separate from the 'official' customer representatives. Civil society pressure in Bolivia has proven similarly powerful, though the eventual retraction of the La Paz and El Alto contract from the private company and the high turnover of water regulators in times of political turmoil arguably will not have the desired effect of enhancing service delivery for the unconnected poor. Both, in different ways, highlight the political nature of economic water regulation. There is a danger of politicization of customer committees, whose close affiliation with local, or indeed national, politics may prevent them from acting as (or being perceived as) independent representatives of consumer interests (for example Indonesia). Research findings suggest a tendency among consumer organizations to adopt either a political profile or alternatively be used as political pawns. There is a risk that in doing so, customer representatives veer from their original objectives or prioritize areas of their own interest. In a low-trust society this may pre-empt the successful introduction of customer representation because the public views its 'representatives' with some suspicion. Alternatively, politicians may prefer to suppress customer involvement to protect their own interest from the 'threats' of community empowerment.

INVOLVING POOR CONSUMERS

Whatever the format of customer involvement, where it is in operation, surveys found that low-income customers and unserved households rarely have any grasp of the existence or functions of regulatory bodies and their customer representatives. Low-income focus group respondents in Manila pointed out that even if they were aware of customer forums or water associations operating in their area, the time, cost and social connections required prevent them from accessing their services. Outreach activities of regulators often fail to target the poor effectively. Internet-based information services are inaccessible to the poor, who also do not appear to be the target audience for newsletters and other published information. The local media is successfully used to reach wide audiences, with radio programmes proving popular with the poor. Furthermore, it appears that without dedicated staff for pro-poor service development and a clear pro-poor mandate, regulators and customer organizations alike rarely tend to make the poor a priority. The Users Commission established by ETOSS in Buenos Aires, for example, was reported to concentrate on quality of service in areas already served by the utility, rather than trying to improve access for poor households in unserved areas.

There are a number of reasons why involvement of poor households would be beneficial, and why involvement should not been seen as an 'add-on activity'. Early engagement helps to match user preferences with available service options, or perhaps to innovate such that services offered match consumers' ability and willingness to pay. Involvement thereafter can be of a very practical nature, as the Latin American cases have shown (and indeed the many self-help schemes that can be found in most countries), with communities making in-kind contributions – mostly labour – towards formal services. From a regulatory perspective this is highly beneficial as it reduces the frequently cited 'barrier to access' connection charges. Consumer involvement, however, should not end at the project implementation stage. Continuous involvement should be the aim as customers may have valuable inputs with respect to further service improvements and need to be informed and consulted in the tariff adjustment process. It may also assist in the process of supporting equitable revenue collection that ultimately benefits all customers as bad debts are necessarily transferred to paying customers, rich or poor alike, through increased tariffs and/or reduced quality of service.

Regulators and service providers may have some reservations regarding involving the urban poor, who end up being labelled as 'hard to reach' (for example in Jordan). Often, however, these are simply due to a lack of capacity to deal with consumers who do not fit standard (imported?) models and a lack of training in participative consultation. Household interviews and focus group discussions undertaken for the research project have indicated considerable interest among poor consumers in regular involvement, provided regulators (and/or service providers) are proactive, giving adequate briefings and feedback on results of any consumer engagement activities. The availability of specifically trained staff would be advantageous for soliciting the views of the urban poor who describe themselves as 'often uneducated, afraid of authorities, lacking time and money to "voice" our opinions'.

TYPES OF CONSUMER INVOLVEMENT

There are varying degrees of formality and sophistication – and cost – for different models of customer involvement. The appropriate degree of participation in terms of influence and decision-making power awarded to customer representatives depends on the complexity of information and the consequences of decisions to be made.

The research indicated the contrasting but complementary needs for accessing the views of customers with a 'weaker' knowledge of the subject area as well as 'stronger' knowledge. Deliberately trying to avoid the terminology of 'low' or 'poor' knowledge, the concept of weaker knowledge is that it represents the average customer level of understanding, based upon everyday experience of accessing, using and disposing of water. This level of knowledge is totally valid and necessary for the regulatory process to understand and reflect in its decision-making on prices and services. It can be assessed most easily through quantitative surveys of large numbers of customers, perhaps through provider 'satisfaction surveys' and also, where budgets allow, through small samples of customers in focus groups. Described in more detail below, these groups are called 'deliberative' where the initial 'weaker' knowledge is reinforced with additional insights or information, and participants are allowed time to reflect on these issues, relative to their own experience, before discussing further.

Regulators have successfully used non-deliberative methods to gather information on the entire customer base and/or specific segments and have also been able to use large public forums for education and stakeholder interaction purposes. Advantages and risks of deliberative methods, which actively engage the lay public in discussion, have been discussed above (in the case of formal customer representation).

Table 9.3 *Appropriate customer involvement mechanisms*

	Involving **large** numbers of customers ('non-deliberative')		Involving **small** samples of customers ('deliberative')	
'Weaker' knowledge related to everyday experience	Questionnaire surveys Quantitative tool		Focus groups Qualitative tool	
	+ standardized information; time series and targeting (location, income groups) possible	– sampling may conceal issues pertaining to certain groups only	+ facilitates detailed understanding of customer perceptions with immediate feedback/ moderation	– costly and time-consuming limited reliability ('snapshot' overview)
'Stronger' knowledge related to exposure to regulatory process and water issues	Consumer forum Large, open meetings to air major issues		Customer committees Proactive complaints' auditors and informed questioners of providers	
	+ interactive (moderately), good for publicity	– agenda likely to be determined by influential/confident speakers; can be superficial	+ direct involvement in complaints auditing and adjudication; educator role	unrepresentative members; needing resources and training; danger of system capture

The concept of customers with 'stronger knowledge' is used with some trepidation in the light of the always ongoing imbalance between the understanding of customers and that of the service providers. 'Water companies [in England and Wales] treat the opinions of committee members as comic illustrations of their lack of understanding of the realities of running a business' (Page, 2003). Good service providers who understand the value of customer involvement do not dismiss customer opinions so lightly but in the context of another commonly used phrase 'a little knowledge is a dangerous thing', the concept of 'stronger' knowledge is not to claim that it is necessarily complete or even high but rather only more than the average customer. It is necessary for any ongoing involvement of customers in decision-making processes to be made aware of issues, whether that refers to the realities of leakage and pipe replacement or the wonders of the cost of capital and servicing debts in such a capital-intensive industry. What does 'capital intensity' even refer to? It is the task of every service provider to educate and continue to educate each new cohort of customer representatives. Then whether through small customer committees or large consumer and stakeholder forums there can be a valid discussion of the issues. Does this lead to 'producer capture' of customers? Yes, to some extent, but it is better to be captured or rather educated in the realities of service provision, but still to have something to contribute, than to end up being ignored as a 'comic illustration'.

In the context of involving poor and disadvantaged customers, there are arguments for and against representation by interested individuals or some form of associations. Proponents view NGOs as facilitators of constructive dialogue and participatory performance monitoring, who can also play a strategic role in identifying communities in need of assistance and educating consumers. However, NGOs are not immune to political influence and may represent a regulatory risk if too influential with regulators. Regulators may succumb to NGO pressure for fear of negative publicity, which is only another form of regulatory capture. Equally NGOs may be so beholden to their stakeholders (and sources of income) that they maintain their 'weaker knowledge' and continue to use that as a basis for their interventions rather than moving on to a more constructive stage.

If 'intermediaries' – whatever their background and affiliation – are chosen to represent customer interests on behalf of poor households or entire communities, they must be chosen carefully, taking into account experience in working with the urban poor and technical competence. More direct interactions between regulators and poor consumers, which were only occasionally observed in the case studies (as for example when one regulator travelled with some participants of a consumer forum directly to a slum area for discussions), could be an opportunity for regulators to gain first-hand information on their most disadvantaged protégés. It was one objective of this research programme to find out if and how such exchanges could be facilitated.

FOCUS GROUP DISCUSSIONS

Focus group discussions and their methodologies were piloted in selected low-income areas in Uganda, Zambia and the Philippines (pilot countries were chosen primarily on the basis of available qualified field staff). The discussions were found to be a useful method for exchanging ideas and the crystallizing of key concerns of poor consumers, which could form the basis of ongoing two-way communication between regulators and the urban poor.

Participants responded positively, expressing an interest in regular focus group discussions provided they would prove to be mutually beneficial. The fairly informal atmosphere in the small groups and the presence of a skilled facilitator allowed all participants to express their views, and were preferred to the public meetings that double as 'customer involvement' in some places (for example Zambia). From a research perspective the focus group discussions were a useful tool to gather facts and opinions and prioritize the key problems affecting a household's level of service, information that would be equally useful for feeding into the regulatory process. The relative simplicity of focus group discussions was noted as positive. Respondents would welcome the direct participation of regulators and service providers, such that the focus group discussion methodology could also serve to increase the 'visibility of regulation' within low-income communities. All three pilot studies stressed the importance of making information available in good time to allow participants to prepare for the meeting and make informed contributions, and subsequently to disseminate information about outcomes of the discussions and next steps to the community. Where the target group includes daily wage earners, a small allowance may need to be paid to compensate for loss of income as an encouragement for the poorest to participate.

There are a number of participatory methodologies and approaches that have been developed for interacting with low-income groups when new service improvements are proposed, such as willingness-to-pay surveys and participation, ranking, experience, perceptions and partnership (Coates et al, 2003). These methods include demand assessment exercises with a view to implementation.

The proposed regulatory focus groups, however, are primarily intended to be used as a monitoring tool once services have been provided, rather than being a tool for planning new services. Rather than simply monitoring opinions on key issues, the proposed 'low-income consultation focus groups' are intended to reinforce or mimic the regulatory customer forums, where key issues or problems are explored in more depth. The outputs from such focus groups when triangulated with other research methods (customer forum, consumer surveys etc.) should enable the regulator and any existing customer forum to adequately consult the low-income people in a particular city. Focus group discussions can be used as part of the ongoing customer involvement process, such that repeat focus group discussions should be planned (yearly intervals).

Where water service provision is a function of municipal departments, local councillors (as part of the same entity and democratically elected direct customer representatives) might reasonably be assumed to have adequate inputs into decision-making on behalf of customers. The shift towards commercial operation of water utilities has removed this 'involvement by default' as it separates operator and regulatory functions. In order to balance the institutional arrangements, where there may be no explicit role for customers except as service recipients, formal customer involvement mechanisms are required to give customers a voice in the regulatory process and hence a means to influence service delivery. To the extent that there is customer power over the formal provider and a citizen voice involvement in policy-making (World Bank, 2003), there has to be similar, with perhaps more immediate effect, citizen and customer involvement in the regulatory process. Formal customer involvement as part of the regulatory process is a way of institutionalizing this right to be heard, for conventional customers of the formal provider, for present customers of informal providers and for future customers of an effective service provider.

The research findings suggest that there is scope for developing this more inclusive framework for consumer involvement, which specifically targets disadvantaged households. The fieldwork undertaken through low-income focus groups gives confirmation that poor, presently unserved, customers are very interested in and willing to be involved in improving their access to a good-enough water supply. This involvement should then be supported by the regulatory process through the years of upgrading of water (and sanitation) services. As and when willingness to pay by low-income and informal customers increases, and thus demands improvements to services, regulators need to be listening such that they can require (and support through price adjustments) the formal providers to meet that need. Customer involvement is crucial. Empowerment for the poorest customers is development.

10

Pro-poor Economic Regulation

Esther Gerlach and Richard Franceys with Peter Howsam

ENABLING EFFECTIVE AND REALISTIC PRO-POOR REGULATION

There are a number of obstacles to and opportunities for effective pro-poor regulation as identified by the case study research. These are in addition to the necessary involvement of customers and alternative providers described in the preceding chapters. The first part of this final chapter proposes legislative requirements as well as technical solutions, the second part outlines the vision for pro-poor regulation and a realistic USO, while the final part offers an inter-pretation of the vision and summarizes practical suggestions for implementation in lower-income economies.

The authors' analysis of the ten case studies is that, to date, economic regulation has apparently delivered remarkably little to directly benefit the poorest people, in rich countries as well as poor countries. Except that, and this point may well be more important than any specific pro-poor activities, economic regulation has begun to facilitate more effective and efficient service provision to the average customer. This is clearly the case in Chile where the regulator ensures efficient service provision that reduces the cost of water, which is then separately subsidized for the poor. Because of the 'spill-over' effect, when more water of better quality at a lower price (or more reflective of efficient costs) is made available to the majority the poor can benefit. The best systems have begun to make an impact on serving the poor, using creative and innovative approaches in the slums. Again, this may be very much more due to improvements from the service provider than anything obviously to do with good regulation but, to revisit an analogy from the Preface, a good referee should never be too obvious.

The other very obvious result of the analysis of the case studies is the extent to which water and sanitation service and the effectiveness of any regulation is related to economic wealth. This is obvious in the sense that everyone 'knows' this to be true, though the development community so often appears to turn a 'blind eye' to the implications of Figure 1.2 in practice.

It is also obvious in that any overall ordering of the case studies considered in this book, according to quality of pro-poor service and regulatory effectiveness for example, is significantly linked to economic wealth. Indeed the order of the case studies in Table 1.2, which lists the case studies according to complexity of any service agreement and length of economic regulation, is highly correlated to economic wealth. It is also correlated to the HDI that, in addition to components also relating to wealth, considers adult literacy and enrolment in education.

To recognize this challenge and to attempt to ensure an element of realism in the recommendations from the research, recognizing the 'recency bias' in our understanding of service delivery, the lead researcher investigated the development of water supply in a secondary city in what is now described as a 'high-income country'. Figure 10.1 illustrates the rate of progress in a 'genuine' demand-responsive approach where there were no external providers or enablers. The changes in service standards show a steady progression according to the growth in economic wealth, with services and transitions between service levels that seem quite familiar to what is happening in many countries in the world today. It is not apparent in this example that any technological change might have dramatically reduced costs (apart from electric pumps?) or enhanced demand since that period. The present average economic wealth of low-income and lower-middle-income countries is shown to indicate the challenge facing those countries as they try to accelerate service provision to achieve the desired MDGs. However, the challenge is not solely economic. Just as the HDI incorporates aspects of educational attainment, so the achievement of the development of a sustainable and almost cost-reflectively priced water supply in the secondary city is also a function of the development of 'institutional capital', that is the 'coevolution of economic institutions, social developments and technological innovation' (Kay, 2004). Proposals for economic regulation to act as an additional driver to support the acceleration of service provision have to recognize the very real limits of economic and institutional capital.

At the beginning of this final chapter on pro-poor regulation it is also appropriate to try to summarize the main issues that poor people said that they faced during the interviews and focus groups. For the very poor the biggest challenge was obviously finding and keeping work to maintain some sort of income. In that context all costs have to be minimized and it was better for water to be of low quality and difficult to access than to entail any financial cost at all.

For the coping and developing poor, many researchers reported on concerns over water quality and the cost of having to boil or buy bottled water to avoid illness. This was true whether they had access to piped water or were using alter-

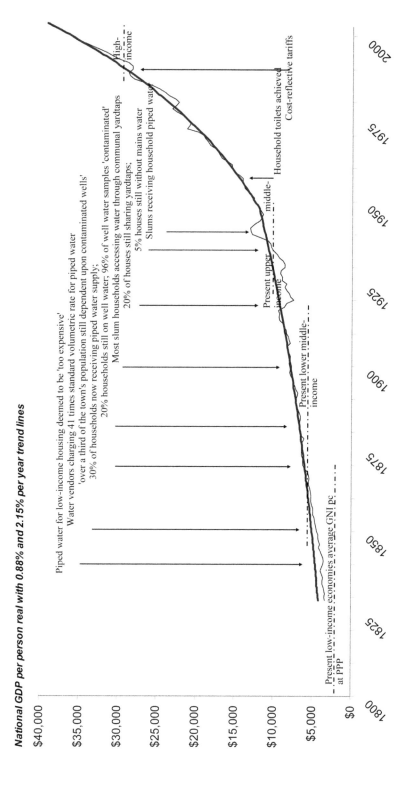

Figure 10.1 *Economic development and water supply in a 'secondary city' 1800–2000*

Source: Compilation and analysis by Franceys from Skill (1983); Ewen (2003); Anderton (2004); Harman and Showell (2004); Upton (2005); Officer (2006); World Bank (2007); and various others

native, usually groundwater, sources. If they were accessing the piped network, frequent and lengthy supply interruptions and low pressure in the distribution network were experienced by many. Water quantity was only an issue in one specific situation.

There was significant use of alternative sources and vended water, primarily tankered water. Surprisingly perhaps, quality and not price appears to be the main concern of tanker customers, even though the vended water was always much more expensive than the network supply and there were no appropriate avenues to direct any complaints. 'Borrowing' from neighbours was also very common. There was also an apparent willingness and ability to pay over the odds for high quality bottled drinking water even among 'the coping poor', though much less so among those representing 'the poorest of the poor'. Consumers tend to buy purified water for drinking. The prohibitive cost of medical care and hospitalization justifies this extra expenditure.

A large number of people were using sources such as hand-dug wells or self-supply bore wells, even in peri-urban areas, or were forced to use them in case of low pressure or water shortage. In the context of accessing alternative supplies, sexual harassment, suspicions of infidelity and even cases of rape were concerns during the longer time it takes to collect this water. The privately owned public baths that exist in some areas were also recognized to be notorious for crime and prostitution.

Accessing conventional connections was extremely difficult because of the high connection charge and the costs associated with road excavation and distance from the mains. Affordable tariffs, considered a major pro-poor measure among policy-makers and service providers, are of less concern to poor households. Much more important are affordable options to connect to the piped water supply in the first place, with 'easy-payment' plans being requested.

Others know that as tenants it is not possible to install connections and for those renting one room a 'house connection with inside plumbing is obviously out of the question'. A yard connection would be a possibility 'but the price should not be high'.

For those who had achieved a connection there were fewer complaints about the actual tariff though there was real fear in some locations of needing to use more water than allowed for in the 'lifeline block' or when there were abrupt changes in monthly water bills. Paying little and often was the preferred mode, including the in high-income country and some believe that 'pre-paid water services would promote fairness and ease', and remove the fear of corruption and lack of accountability for funds collected by the stand post attendants.

Disconnection for non-payment was common in one focus group. Where that option had been banned as a pro-poor measure the alternative experience of debt recovery agents had 'been an unpleasant experience and some had been frightened'.

There was general agreement that there was no mechanism to channel their complaints and concerns to the water utility and that 'community members are never consulted on issues concerning service delivery in their area', 'it is only existing customers who have clear channels to complain and make their voice heard'. Respondents described themselves as being 'often uneducated, afraid of authorities, lacking time and money to "voice" our opinions'. They describe how they are used to having to cope with very bad conditions and are not used to voicing their grievances.

Finally from one group there was the perception that regulators protect water companies, not the consumers, which, in the approach to regulation described by the authors, is correct. Regulators have a primary duty to require and facilitate adequate and fair tariffs such that the utility has the resources to deliver a better quality, regular and efficient supply of water that will be accessible and affordable, even by the poor. It is the failure of the water utilities to deliver adequately that causes so many of the problems described by the respondents in the focus groups. Pro-poor regulation requires above all a clear legal framework to enable and require good-enough performance from the key providers, the water utilities.

Prerequisites to pro-poor regulation

The legal framework

The key legal issue is to ensure that the economic regulator is given a primary duty and obligation to ensure financeability of service provision and that service levels, within the understanding of what has to be financeable, include meeting a USO, as discussed in detail below, within a reasonable timeframe.

The legal framework includes not only the core component of the legislation itself, but also the institutional, administrative, political, social and economic conditions or arrangements, which make the legislation available, accessible, enforceable and therefore effective.

A legal framework is 'good' only if it helps to achieve a particular objective; it will fail for a whole number of different reasons, for example:

- where sound legislation exists on paper but the regulator is weak and ineffective and/or poorly resourced;
- where the judicial system is not strong and independent; and
- where legislation exists but few if any of the key stakeholders are aware of its existence or understand what it means.

The legal framework must also embrace inter-related sectors, i.e. not only the regulation of water supply and sanitation providers but also pollution control, resource management, public and environmental health, land-use planning and development control, social services, education and so on. This involves a wider range of people and institutions. However, for this project the primary focus has been on the service providers and the service recipients.

The starting point for the legal framework, and it seems to be a critical element, is the national constitution. Where water supply and sanitation are explicitly declared as the right of every citizen then this enables incorporation of the objective in the primary and secondary legislation, as in the case of South Africa. In India where the right to life is enshrined in the Constitution, this has been taken in the courts as incorporating essential needs of life, such as a water supply and sanitation. This process of public interest litigation has been used to reinforce the obligations of local authorities (commonly the primary service provider) to provide an adequate and safe water supply.

This model is quite common, whereby central government has a decentralizing policy and delegates via legislation the responsibility for water supply and sanitation provision to local authorities. The same or other legislation may then permit the authority to delegate the actual provision to other, often commercial/private, entities. While in these latter cases the legislation provides for often quite robust overseeing and regulation of the service provider, it does not provide for the equivalent overseeing of public authority provision. Or where it does it is often ineffective.

Some other observations on legal frameworks, based on both general and the case study materials, are that there is some substance to the legal frameworks for water supply and sanitation provision; much of this has emerged in the last decade. It can be difficult to, first, identify and obtain all the relevant legislation, and second, identify which piece(s) of legislation provide the answers to the questions being asked. There can be discrepancies between non-binding policy statements that advocate or imply universal service and specific duties as defined in the operating legislation and/or service contracts. Governments seem to be reluctant to enshrine USOs (for example those advocated in UNCESCR's General Comment No. 15, 2002) in legislation.

Regardless of whether providers are public sector, private sector or a PPP provider, the key questions to be addressed are: who are they, are they a legal entity (what status do small-scale service providers have), what are their legal obligations, is universal service delivery defined as an objective and if so, how is it defined, what can they do (i.e. what, if any, powers do they have with respect to charging and disconnecting customers, for example), what do they do in practice, who regulates them, what mechanisms exist if they fail to meet their obligations and what relationship do they have with those they serve?

With respect to the legislation, there may be a number of different and not necessarily coordinated pieces of legislation that contribute to the legal framework in which service providers operate; i.e. legislation that governs how they operate – sets out their duties, obligations and rights, which provides them with authorization to operate (for example with respect to water supply infrastructure, water abstraction, wastewater disposal) and that governs the authority(ies) that has the power to grant, attach conditions to, refuse, revoke or modify any such authorizations.

With regard to service recipients again there are a number of key questions to be addressed: who are they (all citizens, all of the registered population), are they defined, and if so, how and by whom, what are they entitled to, what if any obligations do they have (for example with respect to payment, use and conservation), who protects those entitlements, what, if any, redress mechanisms exist if rights are breached/entitlements not received, and what is their relationship with service providers (for example is there any requirement or mechanism for stakeholder/consumer involvement in the process of service delivery)?

With respect to the legislation, there may be a number of different and not necessarily coordinated pieces of legislation that contribute to the legal framework in which service recipients exist, namely legislation that defines who are the legitimate service recipients, what are their rights and obligations, how they may gain redress if a right is breached, and the rights of those who do not have entitlement to services.

While governments have generally been reluctant to impose specific public service obligations on themselves, they seem less reluctant to impose statutory requirements when water supply and sanitation services are provided via the private sector. As such the legislation, and the regulatory framework established under it, would appear generally to be more robust with respect to private sector service provision than it is for public sector service provision, although in reality governments and public authorities still retain legal obligations (responsibilities and duties). Service to the poor is being addressed in some cases, but it seems to be dependent on good will and socially aware practice, rather than on explicit legal obligations.

Generally the legislation does not appear to provide for or facilitate provision by community groups or the SSISPs who currently operate informally.

Practical recommendations for a pro-poor regulatory framework

Based upon an analysis of the country case studies and the academic literature, practical recommendations are made for a pro-poor regulatory framework. This framework should be regarded as providing the underpinnings of the regulatory framework, which defines, explicitly or implicitly, the formal and informal rules for water service provision and the allocation of regulatory functions among the various actors and stakeholders. While the term 'legal framework' suggests an emphasis on formal constraints (applicable legislation, contracts and specific regulations), these have important informal counterparts (such as norms and conventions, commitments, incentives and expectations), all of which influence 'regulation' as a process. We make this distinction in recognition of the fact that all water service providers are more or less formally regulated, irrespective of ownership and the institutional model of regulation in place.

A good legal framework is one that has essential components and that is developed to suit local circumstances (political, social, cultural, physical, environmental and economic). In other words, an effective regulatory framework considers the 'institutional endowment' of any country and respects the constitutional context as well as existing administrative capacities. It does not need to be complex and comprehensive and will be more effective if simple, workable and accessible. Of course even if a properly structured system of essential components is created, it will not be effective without the necessary political will and without common social values.

It should also be recognized that a legal framework cannot be got right in one go – all examples reviewed exhibit varying degrees of evolution, responding to lessons learned and changing circumstances. The legislation has to create the right balance between creating a sense of certainty and allowing a degree of flexibility. The latter is often provided via discretionary powers, which is acceptable providing there is transparency and accountability over any decision taken and corruption is constrained. The legal framework should make room for feedback mechanisms that allow governments as the 'guardian' of the regulatory framework to identify and respond to conflicts and inconsistencies.

The core of the legal framework governs the status, rights and responsibilities (duties/obligations/liabilities) of the service providers and the service recipients. However, the relationship between these two parties does not exist in a vacuum. It is governed by relationships between each party and a range of other key parties: the regulator, government and the courts. These relationships and the rights and responsibilities need to be clearly defined in law, as do the powers and procedures required.

It should normally be the case that the establishment, operation and maintenance of water supply and sanitation systems is supervised and controlled by the state. However, some roles and responsibilities need to be devolved to autonomous or semi-autonomous authorities. Economic regulators should therefore be regarded as part of the institutional framework that is set up to implement the law and help the government achieve its policy objectives with regard to water and sanitation services provision.

As this research has demonstrated, access, equity and distributional aspects, as well as the public health and environmental externalities of water services, introduce a significant social dimension to economic regulation, such that economic regulators are no longer simply technocratic agencies, faced with the challenge of having to balance politically sensitive and frequently conflicting financing and service objectives. Ideally, social and water policies should be well integrated, and the law should provide a clear rationale for regulatory interventions. For instance, it is widely argued that it is the responsibility of democratically elected governments to develop effective mechanisms to protect vulnerable groups in society. If this responsibility is partly delegated to an (economic) regulator, it would then remain a government responsibility to clearly define the regulatory mandate (providing the regulator with authority to legitimately make decisions that extend beyond its original technical remit) and to formulate laws so that the constellation of regulatory duties is such that different tasks and objectives do not contradict each other, and that regulators are awarded sufficient powers to achieve both social and economic objectives. In some instances it was found that governments failed to recognize or act upon the problems arising from commercial operation of services (based on the full cost-recovery principle), increasing access to services (through capital-intensive service extensions) and a desire to protect affordability (through low tariffs for an overwhelmingly large customer base on low incomes).

A set of basic considerations for governments wishing to create or adapt regulatory frameworks would include legal considerations for serving the poor, an understanding of what is meant by universal service, the role and responsibilities of utilities and small-scale providers all within the context of institutional roles.

A regulatory framework will not become 'pro-poor' unless it succeeds in delivering improved access to water and sanitation services for the under-served poor, many of whom may be found in urban slums or informal settlements or on the peri-urban fringe. Having clarified the institutional set-up of regulation and its combination of social and economic functions, it then becomes necessary to clearly define the regulator's responsibilities vis-à-vis poor consumers, who may or may not be served by the formal main provider. The following recommendations assume that the resources and mechanisms to enable duties to be carried out, liabilities to be met and rights to be protected, are in place. It must be stressed that it is not appropriate for the legislation to impose duties and responsibilities that cannot be met under the prevailing circumstances. It is, however, recognized that new legislation can induce beneficial social change in difficult circumstances.

The legislation should contain an explicit USO or a number of requirements that together result in universal service provision. Where necessary, delivery of universal service can be delegated and imposed, in appropriate forms, as a primary duty on both the regulator and the regulated (service provider). The legislation should clarify who is entitled to the service – it should not be at the discretion of the service provider. This USO must consider all people, regardless of legal status (for example citizenship, residency, land or property rights), i.e. it should include visitors, migrants, refugees, people living in illegal settlements. However, it should be realistic, taking into account existing service gaps and the time and finance required to close them. Likewise, it should not impose unnecessary burdens onto the regulator and service provider (and ultimately, the customers).

There is a risk of failure to acknowledge the persistent inability to pay of some groups of society, which require a level of support that necessitate interventions beyond what the regulatory model can realistically be expected to deliver. The USO should be consistent and explicit throughout the legal framework, for example from the constitution, through primary and secondary implementing legislation, to specific service contracts/agreements.

The definition of 'universal service' and any accompanying service obligations must be worded such that its interpretation can evolve in a positive sense, i.e. a USO should not be seen as a static target, but one that can become increasingly ambitious in line with social expectations and technical/financial feasibility. However, the legislation should give sufficient guidance for regulators to arrive at this socially efficient interpretation without giving the impression of consistently 'moving the goalposts', which could be seen as discriminating against an increasingly efficient provider.

Any USO must give regard to the financial implications of making such a target a legal obligation. Where affordability is a primary concern, this should not be prioritized at the expense of the financial health of the main provider. In the first instance, the regulator must be enabled to secure funding by setting cost-reflective tariffs. Where the investment requirements exceed the potential funding that can be generated without undue negative impact on all or poor/vulnerable consumers (and this is likely to be the case in many of the case study countries), the law must consider placing financial obligations on government and the social security system.

The legislation should acknowledge the various models of service provision in a particular setting, and enable the regulation of any type and scale of provider. It should specifically include provisions for a level of formalization of small-scale alternative providers, which frequently operate in the informal sector and/or in a more or less unregulated (and, where regulations do exist, unenforced) market. Rules should clearly set out the powers, duties and rights of any service provider, whether it be public, private or some form of partnership, irrespective of its size – with respect to its service recipients and potential competitors.

As far as relationships between the various providers (especially between the main utility provider and comparatively small private or community-managed providers) are concerned, exclusivity rights emerge as a major bottleneck to universal service provision. Especially in the case of large-scale concession contracts, utilities are protected from competition by exclusivity clauses in their contracts, ignoring the reality that they are unable or unwilling to offer services in some parts of their service area or to adapt their service portfolio to meet the needs of a certain type of consumer. Legislation should carefully balance the needs of all providers to protect their investments against the need of all residents to be served and define the conditions for market access and share.

Confining alternative providers' activities to the fringes of the law or declaring them illegal in primary legislation or contracts is an overly simplistic approach that fails to account for the reality that alternative providers – independently or in cooperation with the main provider – will remain a part of the service solution at least in the medium term. The legislation should be inclusive, but not apply uniform rules to all types of provider. A measure of flexibility is required to balance the necessary control of smaller-scale activities against the operators' capacities, otherwise workable (though by no means 'perfect') solutions may be excluded by default. In the case of utility providers, inflexible contract clauses and high service standards and performance targets could have a similar effect. Minimum service levels should be defined such as to allow acceptable trade-offs in price and service standards, enabling affordable solutions for the 'difficult-to-serve', which may differ from conventional techno-logical choices. The legislation should also consider the various possible models for delegation of responsibilities, providing this is done in a transparent and accountable manner; for example subcontracting to alternative/local service providers or use of local NGOs to engage on behalf of vulnerable people/communities who are not in a position to help themselves.

Conversely, there is a risk of not protecting a utility against willing and highly adaptable competition, especially where customers in low-cost parts of a service area have an incentive to switch to cheaper alternatives. In such a case the legisla-tion must consider the immediate implications of allowing competition, including self-supply. Pricing policy objectives, such as the cross-subsidization of domestic and/or lower-income users, may be undermined if the customers providing the subsidy are allowed to opt out of the utility services. Other consid-erations, in many locations, are the environmental and public health risks associated with cheaper and/or unregulated alternatives, such as the possible overexploitation of fragile groundwater resources and a potential lack of water quality monitoring.

The legislation must also consider the legal impediments that need to be lifted in order to enable providers to realize the service objectives. Some of these relate to routine functions, such as access rights for the provision (installation and maintenance) of services. Similarly, the legislation must also provide a mechanism for dealing with (i.e. authorizing) access to, use of and purchase of land for the purpose of carrying out statutory duties (for example required infra-structure installation/maintenance). Another set of considerations, such as land tenure issues in slums and peri-urban areas or presently informal resale activities, may require amendments to existing legal provisions that are not directly related to water law, such as planning, property and business law.

As far as regulation is concerned, the legislation must provide effective penalties for, and enforcement of, any failures to meet obligations or carry out duties, which are the fault of the service provider. At the same time it should clearly set out the rights and responsibilities of service recipients, for example the right to receive services and the responsibility to pay for them. Note that the issue of ability to pay will need to be dealt with outside this regime alongside other social/economic measures to deal with poverty and low-income recipi-ents, unless any specific measures can be absorbed within the regulatory system.

The legislation should clearly set out the powers and duties of any regulator and its relationship with government and where necessary with other regulators and agencies, where their responsibilities relate to water and sanitation services provision. In view of the frequently observed fragmentation of responsibilities between a variety of national-, regional- and local-level organizations, the clear allocation and, where appropriate, separation of institutional roles and delineation of functions is essential. Especially where economic regulators are expected to take on social responsibilities, the legitimacy of regulatory decision-making must be anchored in the law and translated into the regulatory mandate. The law should also shield the regulator(s) from undue political influence, and any subsequently introduced legislation that affects the financial balance (as some social protection measures do, such as a ban on disconnections for reason of non-payment) should be accompanied by provisions to restore that balance, without placing an unreasonable burden on any party (for example paying customers effectively having to subsidize non-payers).

The legislation should require the actions of the government, the regulator and the service provider to be transparent and accountable. This will include establishing the necessary procedures, standards and administration. It should establish a transparent and accountable body that serves (by clearly defined powers and duties) to protect the interests of all service recipients. Various models exist, for example an ombudsman or citizen advisory bureau. Particular provisions may be necessary to facilitate accessibility for vulnerable (poor, inarticulate, disabled) people. Similar appeals mechanisms should be accessible for all other parties, mainly the service providers.

The legislation should provide for access to the courts for all parties, as a mechanism of last resort, where any part of the system fails to deliver. The judicial system can only apply the law as is. There are arguments for and against involving the courts in regulation and dispute resolution. In the UK experience, negotiation between the regulator combining adjudicative and investigative functions and the regulated companies, subject to scrutiny by the Competition Commission (formerly Monopolies and Mergers Commission), has limited the use of the courts, saving public expense and time in reaching final decisions (McEldowney, 1995). Likewise, the House of Lords ruled that the regulator is best placed to deal with disputes between individual customers and water companies, especially where expert consideration of technical/financial issues is required to strike a fair balance between the rights of an individual and the community as a whole (for example *Marcic vs Thames Water*, 2003). Minimal use of the courts will prevail where the legislation provides clarity over powers, duties and rights. The law must therefore be qualified to suit prevailing conditions/circumstances, i.e. it must generate reasonable expectations on behalf of service recipients and reasonable performance on behalf of service providers.

In order to achieve the required flexibility, and in consideration of the likely need to make some adjustments to rules and regulations once more experience has been gained with the implementation of new water laws and new policy objectives, a recommendation is to ensure that the legislation is clear on these objectives and in the broad regulatory framework that is intended to achieve them, but at the same time untested rules should not be fixed in primary legislation, which is difficult to change. The legal framework should therefore consist of an appropriate mixture of laws, secondary legislation or statutory guidance, which is implementation oriented, and more flexible and detailed contracts, which can be amended in response to new insights with the consent of the parties to the contract.

To achieve universal service the regulatory framework must include:

- sufficient independence and length of tenure of regulator and/or regulatory board to promote cost-reflective tariffs for higher-income consumers, particularly for sewerage;
- transparent and fair appointment/selection process of regulators;
- sufficient resources: personnel with the capacity to deal with poverty-related consumer issues, and an independent budget;
- primary duty for the regulator to achieve universal service as well as the equally critical financeability;
- inclusive definition of regulatory remit (in terms of regulated entities, area of jurisdiction, social/economic aspects of decision-making);
- legitimacy for the regulator to make decisions that are not strictly of an economic nature.

It must include regulatory powers to:

- access and request information (from providers and other organizations);
- license suppliers and develop appropriate tools for the regulation of alternative providers;
- monitor and audit (require monitoring and auditing);
- define and adapt performance indicators to current circumstances (for example minimum service levels, coverage targets);
- set tariffs;
- make regulations (for example setting flexible technical/service standards, accountability of service providers, anti-corruption measures, allowing on-selling, if only temporarily);
- abolish exclusivity clauses of service provision by monopoly direct provider; the 'legal concept is non-exclusivity of service provision';
- enforce decisions, including powers to fine utility providers for failing to provide distribution mains to high-density urban slums;
- involve consumers/stakeholders in the regulatory process, possibly empowering existing consumers' organizations to participate.

It must include regulatory duties to:

- give regard to the needs and special circumstances of the poor and vulnerable;
- ensure providers have sufficient finance to meet their obligations;
- review implications of subsidies built into the current tariff structure;
- recognize an 'acceptable process' towards USO without penalizing direct providers inappropriately as long as 'reasonable steps' are taken towards meeting obligations, recognizing that 'targets are not absolutes' and legal restrictions may be in place to prevent their achievement (for example, land tenure issues);
- recognize the competition implications for main utility and alternative (independent) providers;
- make decisions in a transparent manner;
- consult with consumers and stakeholders.

Some legal restrictions outside of the regulator's authority that may need addressing are:

- entitlements for citizens/residents;
- accessibility of public services/legal system for the poor and vulnerable;
- legality of 'differentiated service standards';
- business laws affecting alternative providers;
- overlap of regulatory authority;
- rights to lay 'tertiary distribution lines' across landlords'/customary land;
- legality/implications of 'temporary mains' access to 'illegal' slums;
- legality of requiring a utility to serve areas that contravene planning laws – permanently or temporarily;
- service to areas that are not only informal/illegal but a public health risk (for example squatters on solid waste tips).

Reliable information is at the heart of effective economic regulation. It is not possible for a regulator to determine appropriate tariffs relative to desired service levels without the detailed information necessary to populate the financial model. Considerable effort is spent on balancing the effects of information asymmetries between providers and regulators in mature regulatory systems. In addition to information requirements mandated by licence or contract, incentive systems are used to induce firms to reveal their efficiency potential over time, thus adding to the quality as well as the quantity of available information with the added value of leading to cost reductions for the benefit of customers and society as a whole. Water regulators in developing economies, faced with the challenge of facilitating service provision to a large and overwhelmingly poor proportion of consumers, who are currently excluded from the convenience of networked water services, are frequently constrained by the lack of basic information about who is actually being served, over and above the technical and financial information advantages held by service providers.

Obstacle 1: Lack of reliable information on existing and potential customers
While modern information management is revolutionizing administration in many water companies, the customer data held by formal service providers falls short of meeting the requirements of 'regulating for the poor'. Census data and independent (for example government) poverty assessments, which might complement available customer data, may contain significant statistical errors. Nevertheless, in order to develop an approach to pro-poor regulation appropriate to a particular country (or even city) context, regulators need comprehensive information on existing and potential customers within their area of authority. Background information on social and cultural attitudes, which influence customer expectations and preparedness to take responsibility for certain aspects of the service, are as important as accurate data on poverty incidence and segmentation among consumers.

Obstacle 2: Lack of reliable information on water service options for existing and potential customers
Authoritative access data for different water service options can be equally scarce, and inconsistencies between different data sets are not uncommon. While information on formal networked services is most readily available (figures for non-networked services less so), coverage data for formal providers must be viewed with caution. Generous assumptions for the number of persons using a household connection or public standpipes may exaggerate success. The picture is much less clear for alternative service options. Comprehensive databases on alternative providers, for instance, are virtually non-existent. Likewise, access statistics have rarely been linked with socio-economic data.

Target groups for special consideration must be assessed based on their vulnerability and location with respect to existing service areas. The different aspects of poverty other than low income must be taken into account. Vulnerable groups frequently include single parent families, female-headed households, the sick and disabled, pensioners, the unemployed or underemployed, larger than average households, slum settlement tenants or groups excluded from welfare assistance on the grounds of residential status. Social mapping can be a useful tool to combine water service and consumer data, which when overlaid can help select priority areas for service improvement, or indeed service extension into new areas.

At the same time it is essential to recognize the limitations of water regulation, as certain groups of society may require a level of assistance that is beyond the capabilities of regulated water service providers. It is therefore recommended to establish the likely candidates for formal networked water services whose demands will need to be taken into account in the preparation of future investment programmes. Basic minimum services, closely matched to households' willingness and ability to pay, should be offered to poor customer groups at the lower end of the poverty spectrum. Due to the delicate financial situation in most cases, those with no means to make contributions to ongoing service provision in cash must be taken care of under welfare programmes so as to not jeopardize service for all. Detailed indicators describing the categories shown in Table 1.1 are highly context specific. Care should be taken to avoid demeaning terminologies, which the public may be very sensitive to.

It is not the role of a regulator to collect and continuously update the information required for regulatory decision-making. Accurate water service information, explicitly linked with socio-economic data, should be the responsibility of formal providers as part of good demand management practice and system development projections. Experience in higher-income countries has demonstrated that all utilities need to know who their customers are, present and potential, with information technology available to overcome the challenges faced by larger utilities whose customers should benefit from economies of scale. As a starting point coverage statistics should be disaggregated by customer categories and/or location. Likewise, monitoring of active connections would shed light on the operator's efficiency in maintaining customer satisfaction and hence actual success rates in improving access and encouraging water service uptake.

Alternative means of data collection and maintenance must be sought in areas where the utility fails to provide acceptable services, i.e. certain 'pockets' within the service area (slums, illegal settlements) or the peri-urban fringe outside of the contracted service area. Data collection in those areas – likely to comprise the target groups for pro-poor regulation – can be subcontracted, for example to NGOs, community associations or other social intermediaries, but could nonetheless remain the responsibility of the main provider; under-served pockets within the service area unquestionably are within its remit, irrespective of the 'legality' of settlements, while a proactive approach to service area definition (i.e. reclassification once certain conditions are met, such as automatic review in line with municipal growth and adjustment of administrative boundaries, or inclusion of peripheral areas that have reached critical size and/or housing density) would capture fringe areas. Understanding areas of potential demand sooner rather than later must always be beneficial to utilities' long-term planning process. The costs of undertaking this work in advance of service provision (and therefore allied revenue generation) can be funded through the regulatory process by adjusting tariffs to suit.

A second important set of constraints arises from the fact that economic regulators, though often expected to deliver socially desirable outcomes, are not policy-makers. Regulators may stretch to imaginative interpretation of existing rules and regulations, but ultimately the ground rules are set by political decision-makers. Unfortunately, this may lead to the regulator being required to perform a delicate balancing act as contradictory demands are placed on service providers and the regulatory system alike.

Obstacle 3: Ambiguous or contradictory strategic sector targets

Unreliable access statistics, especially in informal areas and regarding services catering for low-income customers, represent a first and serious impediment to the formulation of realistic (achievable) and pro-poor sector targets. As lack of knowledge, compounded by misconceptions about 'the poor', prevails among many planners and decision-makers, targets may exceed what even the most efficient system could be reasonably expected to deliver in the given timeframes. Moreover, policy-makers often fail to associate the financial implications of any requested connection targets and below-cost tariffs for low-income customers deemed essential to safeguard affordability. Cost recovery is increasingly recognized as essential for the sustainability of the water industry and thus declared a primary policy objective. However, in few cases are cost-recovery objectives synchronized with social protection objectives with the two left to coexist in spite of mutual exclusivity in their existing form.

Obstacle 4: Conflicting objectives and high risk of interference

An incomplete separation of operator, regulator and policy-making function has been a common observation in the case studies undertaken for this research. Regulators often find themselves in the midst of a power struggle between influential vested interests, which can seriously impede the regulator's effectiveness in securing support for and compliance with regulatory decisions. Problems are most likely to arise where there is an imbalance between responsibilities given to regulatory authorities (and high expectations are to be met) and the powers available to regulators to carry out their functions. Tariff setting, one of the critical tools of economic regulation, is a prime example. In some locations tariff decisions remain firmly vested in political hands. The consequences of governments' 'unwillingness to charge' for political reasons – service failure and desperate need among the low-income population – are the very reasons for water sector reform and the introduction of regulation.

Proposal: Embrace a mediator/facilitator role

As water regulators are facilitating governments' duty to serve the public, a guiding concept and a supporting set of regulations – not to be confused with the process of regulation itself – need to be provided by the legislature. A mandate providing legal clarity and a mission in the form of a set of clear and achievable objectives allow the regulatory authorities to carry out their work effectively and purposefully. The third supporting 'm' on the wish list of regulators, it emerged during the course of this research, was money made available by governments in the form of grants and subsidies where cost recovery and social objectives conflict. As this research has shown, imprecise legal mandates can (to a certain extent) be compensated for by increased accountability on the part of the regulator and legitimacy gained through special regard to consumer involvement in order to secure public support.

There is a vital role for the expert regulator to facilitate understanding among leading decision-makers, especially where governments have failed to recognize links between sector targets and funding required to meet these targets, or where expectations exceed what public or private utilities – even under a demanding regulatory system – can reasonably deliver without the government accepting a share of the financial commitments. Besides, even where they are denied ultimate tariff-setting powers, there can be a meaningful role for regulators. Their expertise enables them to evaluate different technical options vis-à-vis financial and social implications, making impartial recommendations to (political) decision-makers who are likely to lack the required level of insight and neutrality.

A VISION OF UNIVERSAL SERVICE UNDER PRO-POOR REGULATION

The vision for water services regulation in lower-income economies includes a pro-poor bias in support of national and international development goals and the achievement of universal service – adequate and sustainable water services for all. A special regard to poor and vulnerable people is deemed justified in terms of the potential public health benefits to society as a whole in addition to the goal of poverty alleviation. That regard is also necessary in view of the high capital intensity of the water business and generally weak governance systems in many target countries, which have led to the failure to meet the most basic requirements of the poor. The proposal is to give regulatory authorities a primary duty to oversee and facilitate a USO on water service providers in addition to their primary duty of ensuring the financeability of operations, capital maintenance and capital enhancement.

As Chapter 3 has shown the use of the term 'universal service' frequently confuses its economic and social meanings, ignoring its historical development with reference to competitive markets rather than through regulatory intervention and deliberate social policy. Within the water sector the notion of 'universal access' is underpinned by an ambition to promote socially desirable consumption levels based on strong public health and social welfare imperatives. However, a clear definition of 'universal water service', crucial for pro-poor regulation, is needed – though precise indicators may differ depending on individual regulatory systems.

The concept of 'universal water service' underpins household water security, which refers to a reliable and safe water supply of sufficient quantity accessible for use within the home. It encompasses notions of access, adequacy, sustainability as well as equity and fairness in the guise of affordability. There continues to be a widespread overemphasis on technical aspects of 'adequate access', misinterpreting service levels (i.e. available water source, such as springs, public taps, household connections and so on) as 'access to water services'. The sustainability criterion of universal water service links with the financeability requirement in that finance must be secured to make services available and ensure their continuing availability, and stresses the fact that any USO must not destroy the financial sustainability of the service provider. It also touches upon the need to consider natural resource availability and protection and wider governance issues. Sustainable, universally accessible and affordable water services cannot be achieved simply by stipulating a USO for providers and instating a regulator to oversee its implementation. By demanding a universal water service, society – government and individual consumers – must accept responsibility and strive to meet the complementary obligations arising from the USO on the provider. This is why a USO should be harmonized with other sector targets, or else it will descend into bureaucratic irrelevance as 'just another sector target'. To some extent this reiterates an earlier point: the regulatory framework, including legal provisions to this effect, is critical to the success of pro-poor regulation and the achievement of universal water service.

Considerations for 'adequate access' include:

- facilities must be convenient and responsive to actual needs so as to encourage optimum water service uptake/use;
- ideally the need for consumers to adopt coping strategies would be eliminated – benefits will accrue predominantly to the poor and vulnerable;
- equivalent, not identical, services should be available to customers within the same category;
- service levels should be matched to customer categories.

TECHNICAL OPTIONS

In lower-income countries, and particularly among lower-income communities, the regulatory process needs to recognize alternative means of delivering 'adequate access' to clean water and sanitation in order to achieve the USO and to match service levels to different segments of customers. Achieving the USO should not default to the level of a stand post serving a hundred families. There are many variations of service differentiation for the poor, to be reflected in pricing differentiation, which can be considered by economic regulators in agreeing assessment management plans (AMPs) for peri-urban areas. These are described in more detail in Sansom et al (2004). Although apparently requiring a 'lowering' in technical standards all these methods have been used and have enabled the delivery of effective water and sanitation services to the poor at a level that householders report is much more satisfactory than queuing at 3a.m. for water from a stand post.

The premise of economic regulation is that services provided should be cost-reflective to the greatest extent possible (unless supported by ongoing sustainable subsidies). The goal therefore is to match a level of service provision to the affordability of the majority of consumers and, most critically, their willingness to pay for that service, which is the demand. This is the demand-responsive approach that has been long recommended in the water sector though rarely made to work in practice.

The approach proposed is that to the greatest extent possible, piped water should be delivered direct to the household. Stand posts, water access points some distance from the home, remain important as 'fall-back' options, particularly important for low-income households with very uncertain incomes, the 'coping poor' or as the direct point of access for the 'very poor'. But to every extent possible a direct pipe connection will not only deliver convenience, time savings and potentially higher quality water (though has the downside of potentially limiting social interaction around the water point) but also a more certain stream of revenue to the service provider, all at a lower volumetric cost to the customer. The higher costs associated with water carrying and trucking should only be acceptable where peri-urban housing density cannot immediately justify pipeline extensions.

If some form of piped network is a goal of a USO this does not mean that it has to be a conventional connection. Originally pipes were buried beneath the ground so as to avoid the effects of frost in those, usually northern, countries where piped systems developed (in the modern era that is, recognizing Roman successes in a previous era). Burying pipes also gives protection against accidental damage and particularly nowadays against damage or loading from road vehicles.

In many very low-income urban communities frost is not often a threat to the pipes and the access widths may preclude vehicles and therefore vehicular damage. Running pipes along the surface of the ground can facilitate leakage detection with leaks being immediately visible. Similarly illegal connections are also visible, but in both situations this is only valuable if the community of consumers have a sense of responsibility and a mechanism to arrange for mending of leaks and restricting of illegal connections.

In an informal housing area installing water supply pipes on the surface means that existing drainage paths, whether surface water or grey water, are not disrupted, which reduces costs. Burying pipes in narrow access-ways can require complete reconstruction of drains and pavement to a higher standard than was previously there – a benefit to slum dwellers but an expensive one that could restrict the installation of piped supplies.

Above-ground pipes are well suited to community construction. The advantage of self-connection, perhaps from a delivery point on the edge of a (smaller) slum, is that it reduces costs to the utility by transferring the responsibility for negotiating rights-of-way and easements to the householder. The reduction in bureaucracy can lead to significant savings, making such systems affordable. Similarly, where it is appropriate to bury connection pipes, householders (groups of householders) can excavate and reinstate more cheaply than utility employees.

Surface pipes with flexible household-managed connecting pipes to yard taps and/or surface yard tanks are highlighted as being the cheapest means of achieving the convenience and low cost of piped water supply in low-income high-density housing areas – far better than stand posts but cheaper (and therefore more affordable if the utility recognizes those savings) than conventional distribution systems.

The most common form of charging is by volume consumed as measured by a water meter. Frustratingly the larger part of the costs of water supply is not variable according to volume consumed but is fixed, that is related to the investment in and maintenance of the fixed assets that treat and deliver the water. Water meters, of which the installation, maintenance, repairing, replacing, reading, billing and resulting complaints resolution, can add one quarter to one third to the water bill are an expensive solution. Some societies, having achieved almost universal coverage and community acceptance, have ensured reduced costs for consumers by not having meters. Instead they charge for water through a fixed payment for access, which might vary according to perceived housing value as a proxy for wealth and presumed use. This solution is definitely unfashionable but is widely practised, as an unacknowledged default, by utilities that only supply water for one or two hours per day (thereby limiting all in that area to a similar consumption) and by utilities that fail to maintain their meters (remarkably common) and then charge a fixed amount.

Meter costs, particularly where installed meters cannot be used in any acceptable way for the reasons described above, can therefore be removed by design through the use of flow restrictors and volumetric controllers. Flow restrictors, sometimes know as trickle devices, allow a limited flow and therefore avoid excess use by some consumers making it possible to charge fairly a fixed tariff to all. However, flow restrictors come with the need for household storage, which adds to the cost and in areas where supplies are intermittent and/or pressures are low the inability to access sufficient water usually leads to householders arranging to bypass the flow restrictor.

Alternative devices include the use of ground tanks with float valves and limited supply hours during each day so that customers receive a fixed amount for which they can pay an adequate tariff but without the expense of a meter. An intermediate approach is a volumetric controller, in effect a meter but one that does not need to be read and billed separately. Both these systems can be used where water is paid for in cash in advance, very appropriate in slums where there are no addresses to send bills to and little means of enforcing payment. This reinforces the point that none of these technologies works in isolation from the acceptance of the community of customers – these cannot be technical solutions to social problems, only aids to enabling fair customer involvement and responsibility.

Some low-income households actually value having their own personal water meter and even more surprisingly their own personal bill. As in richer countries, where utility bills are seen as proof of identity and/or residence, slum dwellers also value that recognition. To reduce costs of metering one technique is to install rows of household water meters at the edge of, or in a convenient location in, the low-income housing area. Householders make their own flexible pipe connections to their own distant meter (or on occasion collect water from their meter by bucket), while the utility reduces costs by not having to provide individual house connections in difficult areas and reduces the costs of meter reading.

A variation on remote metering is group or street metering where a group of householders share out the bill from a single meter, taking responsibility for equitable payments by whatever mechanisms they choose, thereby reducing costs. This approach depends upon the utility allowing for reduced tariffs as a result of reduced costs and not using the incremental block tariff approach that would quickly disadvantage groups of households. There is a similar challenge when stand posts are metered with tariffs collected through 'kiosk vendors' or community-appointed on-sellers. If no allowance is made within the incremental block system the poor end up paying commercial/industrial rates for water. As ever, the technology is only effective in conjunction with suitable approaches. One variation on this idea for stand posts is for householders to agree to buy tokens from a local shopkeeper adjacent to the metered stand post, contributing a token per container filled. This ensures that cash is received in advance and removes the expensive (time-consuming) task of trying to get poor households to contribute towards a monthly group water bill long after that water has been consumed.

A further metering development is the use of prepaid meters. Originally using some form of coin-in-the-slot mechanical device, electronic versions are now available and have been well-received by customers (if not by NGOs) in, for example, South Africa. Householders value the opportunity to manage their spending on water, buying top-ups as they can afford it and, just as for their similar popularity in mobile phones, being able to prevent excess use (and unaffordable bills) by accident or theft.

The problems of selling water in slums that regulators have to understand, within any AMP by service providers for regulatory price setting, are: limited pipe networks, limited access to supplies, lengthy queuing and carrying (of limited quantities or high charges for limited quantity vended stand posts), necessarily expensive vendors/carriers, where there are connections the use of incremental block tariffs that discriminate against multi-households (one water board finding a single connection compound 'house' with 99 rooms, each representing a household), bad debts on attempts at piped supply, significant ferrule leakage as well as illegal connections, the temptation to use polluted alternatives, all in the context of vulnerable 'tenancies', very low incomes, often changing circumstances and therefore wildly fluctuating incomes, the inability to save to invest in improved services and exceptionally high borrowing costs.

If this list reflects reality, how can conventional suppliers, let alone economic regulators, make a difference? From considering the range of types of slum supply explained in the case studies, as well as other experiences from around the world, the researchers have developed a concept of water supply that is 'beyond stand posts' but cheaper and more accessible than a conventional pipe supply. It is designed to meet the needs of the 'developing' and the 'coping' poor while enabling access by the 'very poor' and the 'destitute.'

The concept is to develop an existing stand post with the addition of a valve or meter chamber. Heightening part of the stand post to allow for more convenient head-carrying by women also serves the purpose of creating additional space within the structure for an above-ground valve chamber. This facilitates easy access to valves and meters that do not then become submerged or covered in dirt. From the valve chamber it is possible to run flexible above-ground pipes, though buried under crossings where necessary, direct to a 200 litre plastic barrel on a small stand outside a nearby house or even a rented room. When the customer has paid for their day's water in advance, the valve can be opened and the tank filled – giving the convenience of household water even inside the house (through a short pipe extension) though at low pressure. Mcleod (1997) describes how such systems were developed in Durban. The variation on the theme suggested here is that the system is managed by a stand post vendor who has additional opportunities to sell.

If the daily filled-tank customer cannot afford payment one day, either the vendor knows that customer well enough to allow a level of credit, or the tank is simply not filled that day and the customer can buy water by the bucket as previously. The above-ground valve chamber offers further opportunities in that it could include a 'meter bank', similar to those developed in Manila. The suggestion though is that this bank of meters is accessed with new connection charges and also without disconnection charges for non-payment. Giving the stand post operator the responsibility for the main connection, with a master meter for all usage according to which the utility is fully reimbursed for water sold, there is no need for unaffordable connection fees. Households pay according to their 'flexible pipe' connection use direct to the home. As the vendor recognizes that the bill is not being paid at regular enough intervals they can simple cease supply until it has been paid. But that household still has the option of accessing water from the stand post by the bucket. If financial circumstances have changed such that the household can no longer afford a household connection they can easily be reconnected to a daily filled tank or even come off direct supply altogether, but without having to have wasted scarce finance on then unusable connection fees. Similarly if the daily filled tank customer wants to upgrade to a full pressure metered connection, that change can be undertaken within the stand post chamber at zero connection cost.

The aim in such a design is, by taking advantage of best practice ideas from around the world, to promote customer choice and flexibility while ensuring revenue, even from the poor, for sustainable service provision. The system could be extended further through the inclusion of prepaid meters as an option, never mandatory, but only we stress as an option for a service provider and their customers to consider.

Approaches of this sort can deliver the type of 'consumer experience' that is evident in other utilities now, particularly mobile phones. It is especially valuable for all those on the spectrum of poverty described earlier because that spectrum is a dynamic reality for many households. They can move up and down according to jobs, health incidents, slum bulldozing and for many other reasons. Serving the poor needs to allow for customer choice and the ability to swap between those alternatives.

In addition, where appropriately managed, it can guarantee prepayment to the utility, reduce or remove bad debts, reduce leakage as there are no ferrules on any distribution lines, with local leakage risk transferred to customers, and it can avoid or minimize the costs and challenges to the utility of managing pipe networks in slums. The closeness to the customers of the vendor/stand post operator also minimizes illegal connections as it would be costing the local operators money. All of these advantages, where appropriately regulated, should therefore also deliver a reduced charge for the water. This is pro-poor regulation in action. Ideas such as this are viable for tenants and room-renters. The flexible pipes and water tanks can all be moved, removed and reused as circumstances and locations change.

Options therefore include:

- buy by the bucket;
- buy by daily filled household tank;
- buy by metered household connection;
- buy by prepaid meter;
- buy by volumetric controller;
- change between these alternatives, free of capital charges, as circumstances change.

It is the task of pro-poor pipe-networked water providers to invent their own versions of a 'WaterChoice point' such as is illustrated in Figure 10.2, all in conjunction with their alternative service providers who might operate them, and through discussions with the community, find out what customers are willing and want to pay for. It is the task of the economic regulator to expect and require service to all in the business plans of the service providers and to expect tariff adjustments to suit the means of distribution.

Differentiating sanitation for USO in peri-urban areas

As explained in the Foreword, the urgent requirement for improved sanitation has not been addressed in this study on the understanding that monopolistic networked sewerage, which would be the focus of any economic regulation, is

Source: Design by Franceys

Figure 10.2 *Facilitating flexible access for the poor and revenue generation: a possible 'WaterChoice' point*

not usually a viable solution for slums and shanties. Where sewers are present, usually for the higher-income or commercial areas, there is a role for a regulator to ensure that tariffs, usually charged as an add-on to water charges, are cost-reflective. If not, it is the poor who gain access to piped water who end up subsidizing the rich with sewers.

Economic regulation in partnership with the environmental regulators also has to recognize the validity of on-site solutions for improved sanitation. Both have to resist the temptation to require, and attempt to finance through tariffs, piped sanitation in advance of affordability.

With the reminder that even in the impressive city of Jakarta with a population of 10 million there is only 2 per cent sewerage coverage, on-site solutions to sanitation have to be recognized for some time to come. There is an overwhelming imperative to get excreta off the streets in densely populated urban areas to protect inhabitants against any resulting pathogens and disease. Defecating directly into open drains or into bags and newspaper for 'wrap and throw' may meet the first criteria of removing faeces from the street but are not an acceptable alternative. There are various forms of 'pit latrine' that serve the purpose well, giving, where well designed and constructed, convenience and privacy that are often the drivers for households to invest in their own sanitation, as well as to ensure health protection.

There is a key difference between types of latrines based upon the method used for anal cleansing, whether water or solid materials (see Franceys et al, 1992, for further information). The spectrum of choice ranges from conventional septic tanks through to various types of pit latrines, pour flush or ventilated improved, to plastic urine-diverting 'eco-toilets'. This last being eminently saleable as a consumer product to temporary 'room renters', the 'very poor' and perhaps including the 'coping poor', who would otherwise be unable to access any in-home facilities, this point being critical for convenience at night in an unpaved, unlit, insecure slum.

Where housing density is exceptionally high, 'hyper dense' by one description, pay for use communal toilets, perhaps with attached shower facilities, are a suitable option. Experience of communal toilets has been that they are extremely difficult to manage communally with no one wanting to take responsibility for cleaning and users gradually fouling the toilet area and approach areas until they becomes unusable.

The approach that has worked most effectively is therefore 'pay and use' whereby an NGO or community group obtain funds (sometimes from local government or donors) to construct a facility and then employ a full-time caretaker to ensure it remains clean and in good condition. The caretaker's salary being paid through small amounts given by users, either monthly as a household or daily as it is used. Soap can be provided as part of the service and some of the Sulabh toilets in India, for example, also provide bathing and locker facilities.

Where appropriate topography and economic conditions coincide, conventional sewerage can be appropriate – even though it usually remains too expensive in very poor communities. An intermediate level, 'condominial sewerage' or 'reduced cost sewerage' (though now also being used in some high-income areas) is to design the pipe network more carefully to minimize the pipe lengths, also often running the pipes through the backs of properties to minimize the depths of sewer pipe where no cover under roads is required for protection, and using shallower gradients, particularly where small interceptor tanks are used for settling out solids outside each house. Additional approaches use 'rodding eyes' rather than more expensive 'manholes' to provide access for when the sewer becomes blocked. It is necessary to ensure the involvement of the community in deciding pipe routes, perhaps in trench-digging to reduce costs but also to agree or rather accept a temporary discharge point for the smaller sewer where it cannot connect directly into a conventional drain (see Reed, 1995, for further information) .

The key points for regulatory understanding of peri-urban sanitation within any asset management planning for price setting are the need to:

- recognize the need for community involvement in achieving total sanitation where sanitation is primarily to be undertaken by households;
- accept possible short-term groundwater pollution to ensure immediate sanitation for health within a phased approach (recognizing that it is more economic in the short term to pipe in clean water than pipe out wastewater);
- recommend sanitation approaches that minimize grey water, storm water and solid waste challenges in the short term;
- assess environmentally sensitive means of excreta disposal (eco-sanitation, composting, reed beds);
- avoid 'Rolls-Royce' sanitation solutions that demand unaffordable standards and require almost total slum and shanty upgrading through the need for straight pipe runs (as is standard for gravity sewers) and subsequent reconstruction of surface drainage.

DEFINING UNIVERSAL WATER SERVICE AND USO

A definition of universal water service must recognize the corollary of the 'adequacy' requirement. If the aim is to encourage an acceptable consumption level, the emphasis must be on water use, not simply access. It is worth noting that equity considerations do not necessarily require the 'same services for everyone'. Case study research has shown that under certain conditions equivalent services would be the rational choice. For instance, in distant parts of a provider's service area, beyond the provider efficiency frontier (see below), a regular tanker service in combination with sound household storage facilities will provide a more economical service and technical problems associated with long pipelines (for example physical losses, low pressure, high chlorination levels) can be avoided, ultimately to the benefit of the customer.

Nevertheless, the ultimate aim should be to provide household-level services, which equates to a private household water connection with a continuous supply of potable water. No doubt this appears to be a distant goal for many urban low-income communities in the developing world, though the WaterChoice point described earlier demonstrates one way of achieving it. For this reason, the definition of a USO should reflect the evolutionary nature of its constituent targets: space, time, service types and levels.

If universal service is thus to be regarded as a dynamic concept, policymakers are called upon to set the direction of evolution, while regulators drive the pace, relative to costs and potential revenue. The USO on the service provider therefore does not exclusively refer to any specific point within the spectrum. It will at first have to be set to an initial set of parameters, but will subsequently be continually adjusted in pursuit of the next incarnation of 'universal service'.

Such a definition acknowledges the fact that '100 per cent coverage', a common assumption, cannot constitute the single criterion for achievement of a

USO, as it does not account for service quality aspects, such as reliability of supply, which this research has confirmed to be equally important to existing and potential customers. Equating 'universal service' with '100 per cent coverage' also creates difficulties with small minorities that simply cannot be served under conventional service models (as discussed above).

Figure 10.3 is adapted from Stern et al (2006) who investigated universal access programmes for telecommunications. In the context of mobile phones the grey area is described as a 'market gap', while the white area is called the 'access gap.' In our reinterpretation for the water sector it is suggested that the grey area is not so much a market gap but more of a service provider failure area where the monopoly provider has failed to extend their pipe networks fast enough (if at all). The researchers recognize, a critical point in the context of economic regulation for sustainability, that there is a network efficiency frontier. The desire for a USO has to recognize technical, social and economic realities. It also has to recognize that universal might not mean 100 per cent coverage, hence the distinction between a USO and a universal service frontier.

In the new peri-urban areas with limited housing density there may become an obligation for service through tankers, as described above, but it need not be subsidized for those with a higher willingness to pay, that is those middle-income households who are taking advantage of lower land costs by establishing homes on the urban fringes. For the poor with limited ability to pay, stranded for whatever reason beyond the network efficiency frontier, subsidized tanks and stand posts are required.

Figure 10.3 can be further adapted to recognize that the provider efficiency frontier can be extended by facilitating demand, as through the WaterChoice

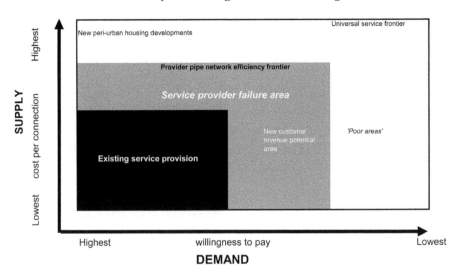

Source: Author's adaptation from Stern et al, 2006

Figure 10.3 *The boundaries of service provision*

point or its equivalent described above. As with the time variability of poverty there is a 'moving target' element of this supply and demand diagram.

There is the 'moving target' of the spatial dimension – needing to capture natural growth and expansion of the service area relative to housing expansion into new areas, as well as the level of densification that determines the network efficiency area. Initially, this will account for failures to provide adequate (or any) service in certain parts of the service area – alternative arrangements (for examples partnership with NGOs/community associations, subcontracting to other operators/alternative providers) will need to be sought.

Similarly the spectrum of service types and levels described will lead to a regular revision of various service targets as the demand side, critically linked to willingness to pay and therefore to service provider revenue, adapts and develops. It will also take into account quality of service aspects, not simply the physical availability of service options. Pulling this number of unserved into the potential revenue base by recognizing alternative delivery modes is a vital facilitation role of the regulator.

Service delivery to the poor, as shown earlier, is significantly dependent upon levels of economic wealth and growth. Addressing the supply-side and demand-side factors through regulation can only improve services so far. The next level of improvement, particularly regarding any networked sanitation, is dependent upon economic growth. The challenge to regulation is to be able to respond to that growth as it happens so as to capture the potential benefits as soon as possible and before the wealth is diverted elsewhere.

Finally the precise definition of the USO will necessarily change with time, in recognition of the fact that the goal of continuous potable household service (Franceys, 2002) and high-specification sanitation facilities take time to achieve. Further changes will occur in response to further spatial adaptation (changes to the contracted service area) and the evolution of service options in line with the gradual improvement of network capacity and customer preferences as well as, eventually, technological innovation and ecological demands. For the USO to have tangible and long-term benefits for low-income households it is critical to recognize standpipes for instance as only temporary solutions, however long 'temporary' might last.

Figure 10.3 has been expanded further in Figure 10.4 to attempt to capture the complexity and the potential of regulating for the poor by expanding demand and the customer potential revenue area through service and pricing differentiating (WaterChoice points and others), demonstrating that regulatory influence and requirements span the entire supply and demand map, and trying to illustrate how the needs of the spectrum of poverty can best be met by differentiated levels of supply. It is the task of the regulator to require and facilitate the monopoly providers to behave as if they are in a competitive market place in terms of innovation and creative service delivery to create an 'extended service delivery area' that is self-sustaining through tariffs. Similarly regulators need to

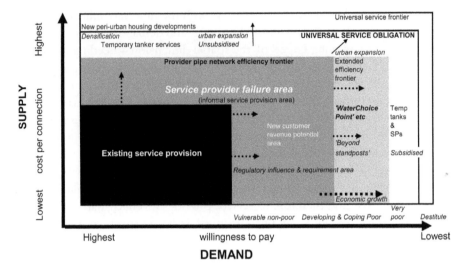

Source: Author's adaptation from Stern et al, 2006

Figure 10.4 *Targeting a universal service obligation*

ensure that there are no exclusivity arrangements that limit the ability of alternative providers to serve the affording peri-urban areas with cost-reflective prices. The subsidies for the very poor and the destitute are ideally met through government payment rather than cross-subsidies within the water sector – however, those cross-subsidies should be enabled by the regulator where there is no alternative. And the regulator has to be able to access sufficient information to be able to adjust both requirements and enabling instruments as these boundaries move, more rapidly than usually assumed, for example due to economic development or spatial expansion.

GUIDELINES FOR PRO-POOR REGULATION: IMPLEMENTING AN EVOLVING USO

In highly simplified terms, the process of pro-poor regulation entails driving the continuous evolution of a USO towards higher – but always realistic and financeable – goals, so as to accrue progressively the benefits of improved water services to disadvantaged households and communities. The regulatory problem, implementation of the 'moving target' USO, can be divided into four main aspects: requiring a USO, defining and redefining/adjusting the USO, allocating USOs, and finally sustaining/funding universal service.

1) Requiring a USO

The legislation empowering the economic regulator must specify that in addition to ensuring service delivery and the financeability of that service in the long term, there is an equal 'primary duty' to require the regulator to 'referee' the urgent move towards achieving a USO.

2a) Defining USO

With tariffs very rarely approaching cost reflectivity, creating universal access, not affordability, will be the priority concern in the majority of situations. However, the purpose of addressing this issue through the 'lens' of economic regulation is to facilitate a move towards financially viable service providers who are also serving the poor. Choosing the right initial set of parameters for a USO is closely related to the information problems discussed earlier.

Consumer involvement at a level appropriate to the various consumer groups identified is an appropriate regulatory response. Identifying and involving all existing and potential customers, especially the low-income communities labelled as 'hard-to-reach' and unserved by conventional water service providers, requires a level of skill that may not be readily available among technically oriented regulatory staff (and indeed among many operators). Chapter 9 outlines lessons from worldwide experience and suggest strategies to develop effective two-way communication and direct links between regulators and protégés. In defining and developing the USO, regulation must recognize the vital role of civil society as well as the explicit and implicit contributions it can make to empowering the poor by formalizing arrangements at an appropriate level. Consumer involvement can also help with assessing real demand for services and match the right service with specific customer groups and/or areas. The idea behind service differentiation is to allow some flexibility in meeting minimum service targets (that is, bypassing the tight bounds of conventional, 'first world' technical service standards) and reflecting the savings in lower prices for the poor while achieving the desired convenience of service.

The challenge lies in aiming high enough to make significant improvements, but low enough to make the USO achievable – the latter primarily to avoid disappointing unreasonable expectations, be they held by customers or governments. While exact definitions will necessarily have to be context-dependent, so that no generic standard can be suggested at this point, a USO should be specific and indicators measurable. Of course, close cooperation will also be required with service providers and other (government) agencies. Targets are not simply 'good' if they are socially responsive, they must also recognize external constraints, such as situational water resources.

2b) Adjusting USO

If continuous improvement is the aim, the question then becomes how and when to adjust USOs. For example, a challenge in capturing the 'space' dimension is the problem of fluid and ill-defined administrative or municipal boundaries, which may rapidly outgrow contractually agreed service areas. Likewise, the USO should encourage transitions from 'good enough' to 'better' services, i.e. differentiated service standards are not to be understood as permanent solutions

While this may not be a problem, at least initially, in low-income communities, customers' expectations can be generally expected to rise with increasing economic wealth. Again, customer involvement will remain a crucial tool for distinguishing between (individuals' and society's) needs and expectations and managing demand and expectations. In the initial stages of pro-poor regulation, objective needs may actually exceed subjective expectations, an issue that regulators need to handle with sensitivity, negotiating affordable minimum service standards in support of public health.

Transparency in the evolution and redefinition of USO is paramount, or the regulator could be justifiably exposed to the criticism of continuously 'moving the goalposts'. Adjustment could be conveniently incorporated in a process similar to the 'rolling incentive mechanism' used by regulators such as OFWAT (England and Wales) to promote the early achievement of greater efficiency. In terms of timing of adjustments, the process might be similar to tariff adjustments, for which there are basically three options: periodic reviews, partial or 'extraordinary' reviews and automatic adjustment. Contrary to preferred tariff-setting procedures as observed in the case studies, a 'periodic USO review' based on wide consultation with consumers and providers might be the better choice.

3a) Allocating USOs

As outlined above, USOs will necessarily have a spatial component. Under conventional contract arrangements, performance indicators usually refer to a specified service area. However, as the prevalence of various types of alternative provider indicates, utilities or main providers often fail to provide the required service in all parts of the service area (notwithstanding the fact that there might be a mismatch between service areas and actual settled areas), as illustrated in Figure 10.5.

This failure must be recognized in allocating USOs to providers – by acknowledging the role of alternative providers and the various possible partnerships (for example between the utility and community associations, NGOs and/or small-scale providers) and incorporating them into the regulatory framework. Depending on the situation (level of organization of the alternative water services sector, monitoring capacity of the regulator, management capacity of the main provider and so on), two basic options can be envisaged.

First, a USO is imposed on the main provider. The responsibility for achieving the set targets rests this with the main provider, who is encouraged to subcontract service delivery in 'difficult-to-serve' areas, taking advantage of alternative providers' (including NGOs' and communities' own skills in working with the poor). Second, the service area is divided into sub-areas and different operators assigned to achieve a USO in their respective service areas. This practice would be consistent with contractual clauses allowing operating licences

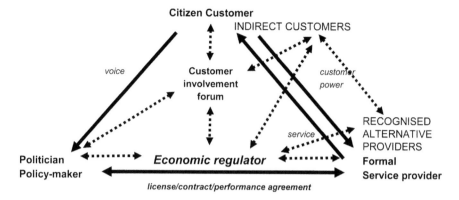

Figure 10.5 *Economic regulation for all providers, empowering all urban customers*

to be revoked in case of default. However, in order to fully exploit the economies of scale achievable by one major service provider, licences for sub-areas may be time-limited. It is proposed that periodic price reviews should automatically consider and redefine the service areas appropriate to each utility, in addition to negotiating prices and investments.

3b) Facilitating, monitoring and enforcing USO

Meeting the USO is going to be a tremendous challenge for providers and will require skilful facilitation on the part of the regulator. As intimated in the 'prerequisites' section, facilitation may need to extend beyond direct interactions with service providers and their customers. Expert regulators may need to press policy-makers to supply the policy instruments that will enable the acceleration of service to marginal areas. A tangible tool would be a set of service obligations and connection targets specifically designed to prioritize formal service provision to poor households. Where the poor and vulnerable are most likely to be found in informal housing areas where land title cannot necessarily be proven, or slums where settlement has occurred illegally, regulators need to be empowered to negotiate – and eventually require – utility service coverage. The affordability imperative almost invariably requires some form of subsidy mechanism to be employed. Special care must be taken to refine targeting mechanisms and maintain efficiency incentives on the provider. Particular challenges arise when regulating the public sector, where incentive mechanisms are less well defined.

Asset management planning assumes new dimensions in the context of the pro-poor, universal service goal. The economic regulator needs to demand viable AMPs within strategic business plans that include early achievement of a USO. While AMPs must emphasize and even prioritize service coverage to the poor, regulators must seek to retain a suitable balance of those pro-poor objectives with maintaining (or improving, where appropriate) quality of conventional services to all, such that a sustainable revenue flow can be maintained. Reasonableness vis-à-vis demand and sustainable outcomes must be a guiding consideration in evaluating providers' technical and financial proposals. In the definition of 'reasonable expenditure' much depends on local circumstances, but incentive mechanisms need to ensure that 'reasonableness' is constantly challenged in line with the evolving universal service paradigm. Any required utility efficiency improvements must uphold the affordability principle, i.e. regulators must ensure that tariffs, though necessarily cost-reflective for sustainability reasons, are least cost. Research findings indicate that appropriate low-income customer payment facilities and differentiated connection charges are readily implementable solutions to facilitate universal service.

4) Sustaining/funding universal water service

Without going into the details of the financing problem, a subject on which a substantial literature exists, there are a few points worth mentioning in view of funding universal water services. As it is imperative that any USO must not destroy the financial sustainability of providers, regulators will be using a mixture of tariffs and subsidies to fund service extension to the poor. Subsidy allocation must be optimized to ensure benefits are indeed delivered to the poor and vulnerable, minimizing errors of inclusion and/or exclusion. International best practice shows this is possible. At the same time, the public needs to be sensitized to appreciate the cost of the water service, that is home delivery of what may otherwise be perceived as a 'free good'. Consumer education is important to counter any existing culture of non-payment, which undermines effective service provision and regulation. While the extent of subsidization remains a government responsibility, as indicated previously, it becomes the regulator's responsibility to monitor and report on the use of subsidies, preferably in combination with some form of output-based approach to service provision for the poor.

PRO-POOR ECONOMIC REGULATION

The sustainability of a universal water service does not solely depend on financial matters. Although good financial management (under an efficient and effective regulatory regime) is a significant initial driver towards serving the disadvantaged groups, the case study evidence shows that good governance is the key to its long-term sustainability. Good governance entails every party accepting responsibilities that arise from society's goal of adequate water services for all. As such, there is not only a USO on providers imposed by the regulator to serve all urban consumers. There are a whole range of corresponding and complementary obligations on the remaining key actors, customers and policy-makers. The development and maintenance of the institutional capital required to deliver this additional level of regulatory enabling or refereeing requires long-term societal and professional capacity building.

Transforming 'informal customers', from Figure 1.6, into viable utility customers, albeit served through recognized alternative provider intermediaries, with a suitable level of customer empowerment, is a significant goal. The evidence from the case studies investigated here show that so far it is only happening in a haphazard way. If global society is to achieve the desired sustainability and extension of the MDGs (beyond the initial halving, that is serving 'the easiest half'), it will have to recognize the centrality of the conventional public utility in urban areas and seek to strengthen it through long-term capacity building of the staff within that utility as well as the supporting institutional and legislative framework. The short-cut 'heart transplant' of international private sector involvement is no longer available. The donor 'life-support system' is too likely to be switched off at less than a moment's notice. The long-term 'pacemaker' of effective pro-poor economic regulation is an important driver and facilitator for improved service delivery to all, though remaining 'necessary but not sufficient'. The patient, the utilities commonly failing to meet the needs of their customers in low-income countries, current and potential, have to be enabled to start exercising hard. To switch metaphors yet again, the referee can only ever improve the game, while the players, most importantly the service providers, still have to be trained up to actually score on behalf of all urban consumers.

References

Abdalla, H., Naber, H., Quossous, R. and Asad, T. (2004) *Pricing as a Tool for Water Demand Management in Water Scarcity*, Conference Proceedings, International Water Demand Management Conference, 30 May–3 June, Dead Sea, Jordan

Accent Marketing and Research (2003) *Paying for Water: Customer Research*, Birmingham, London for WaterVoice and OFWAT

Aguas Andinas (2007) *Annual Report 2006*, Santiago, Aguas Andinas

Anderton, T. (2004) *A Tale of One City: The New Birmingham*, Project Gutenberg Ebook

Almansi, F., Hardoy, A., Pandiella, G., Schusterman, R., Urquiza, G. and Gutierrez, E. (2003) *Everyday Water Struggles in Buenos Aires: The Problem of Land Tenure in the Expansion of Potable Water and Sanitation Service to Informal Settlements*, London, WaterAid and Tearfund

ARD (2005) *Case Studies of Bankable Water and Sewerage Utilities, Volume I: Uganda*, Washington DC, United States Agency for International Development

Armstrong, M., Cowan, S. and Vickers, J. (1994) *Regulatory Reform: Economic Analysis and British Experience*, Cambridge, MA, MIT Press

Arnstein, S. (1969) 'A ladder of citizen participation', *Journal of the American Institute of Planners*, vol 35, pp216–224

Asian Development Bank (2001) *Regulatory Systems and Networking: Water Utilities and Regulatory Bodies*, Proceedings of the Regional Forum, 26–28 March, Manila

Asian Development Bank (2005) *Connecting East Asia: A New Framework for Infrastructure*, Manila, The World Bank, Japan Bank for International Cooperation, Asian Development Bank

Baker, B. and Trémolet, S. (2000) 'Utility reform: Regulating quality standards to improve access to the poor', *Public Policy for the Private Sector*, vol 219

Baldwin, R. and Cave, M. (1999) *Understanding Regulation*, Oxford, Oxford University Press

Barja, G. and Urquiola, M. (2001) *Capitalization, Regulation and the Poor. Access to Basic Services in Bolivia*, WIDER Discussion Paper No 2001/34, Helsinki, Finland, UNU/WIDER

Bayliss, K. (2002) *Privatisation and Poverty: The Distributional Impact of Utility Privatisation*, CRC Working Paper No 16, Manchester, CRC

Berg, S. V. (2000) 'Sustainable regulatory systems: Laws, resources, and values', *Utilities Policy*, vol 9, pp159–170

Better Regulation Task Force (2003) *Principles of Good Regulation*, London, Better Regulation Task Force

Bishop, M., Kay, J. and Mayer, C. (1995) 'Introduction', in Bishop, M., Kay, J. and Mayer, C. (eds) *The Regulatory Challenge*, Oxford, Oxford University Press

Black, J. (2002) *Critical Reflections in Regulation*, CARR Discussion Paper Series DP 4, London, Centre for Analysis of Risk and Regulation, London School of Economics

Boland, J. and Whittington, D. (2000) 'The political economy of water tariff design: Increasing block tariffs versus uniform price with rebate', in Dinar, A. (ed) *Political Economy of Water Pricing Reforms*, Oxford, Oxford University Press

Brandon, T. (1984) *Water Distribution Systems*, London, Institution of Water Engineers and Scientists

Brocklehurst, C. (2002) *New Designs for Water and Sanitation Transactions. Making Private Sector Participation Work for the Poor*, Washington, DC, PPIAF, WSP

Budds, J. and McGranahan, G. (2003) *Privatization and the Provision of Urban Water and Sanitation in Africa, Asia and Latin America*, Human Settlements Discussion Paper Series, London, IIED

Burra, S., Patel, S. and Kerr, T. (2003) 'Community-designed, built and managed toilet blocks in Indian cities', *Environment and Urbanization*, vol 15, pp11–32

Byatt, I. (1989) *CSC Members Conference*, Proceedings, Birmingham, OFWAT

CCWater (2007a) *A Fair Deal for Customers, Review 2007*, Birmingham, Consumer Council for Water

CCWater (2007b) *Consumer Council for Water Annual Report and Accounts 2006–07*, London, The Stationery Office

CCWater (2007c) 'About CCWater: Providing a strong voice for water consumers', www.ccwater.org.uk/server.php?show=ConWebDoc.158, accessed April 2008

CCWater (2008) 'Staffordshire village receives landmark water rebate', Press Release 9 January, Birmingham, Consumer Council for Water

Chisari, O., Estache, A. and Waddams Price, C. (2003) 'Access by the poor in Latin America's utility reform: Subsidies and service obligations', in Ugaz, C. and Waddams Price, C. (eds) *Utility Privatization and Regulation: A Fair Deal for Consumers?*, Cheltenham, Edward Elgar

Choné, P., Flochel, L. and Perrot, A. (2000) 'Universal service obligations and competition', *Information Economics and Policy*, vol 12, pp249–259

Clarke, G. R. G. and Wallsten, S. J. (2002) *Universal(ly bad) Service: Providing Infrastructure to Urban and Poor Urban Consumers*, Washington DC, World Bank

Coates, S., Sansom, K., Kayaga, S., Chary, S., Narendar, A. and Njiru, C. (2003) *Serving All Urban Consumers: Volume 3*, Loughborough, PREPP, WEDC, Loughborough University

Cohen, M. and Sebstad, J. (1999) *Microfinance Impact Evaluation: Going Down Market*, paper prepared for Conference on Evaluation and Poverty Reduction, World Bank, 14–15 June, Washington DC, World Bank, http://rrojasdatabank.net/wpover/evalfin1.pdf accessed 5 July 2005

Collignon, B. (1998) 'The public water service for disadvantaged people', *Villes en développement: Efficiency of Urban Services*, vol 42, pp6–7

Collignon, B. and Vézina, M. (2000) *Independent Water and Sanitation Providers in African Cities. Full Report of a Ten-country Study*, Washington DC, UNDP–World Bank Water and Sanitation Programme

Conan, H. (2003) *Scope and Scale of Small Scale Independent Private Water Providers in 8 Asian Cities: Preliminary Findings*, Manila, Asian Development Bank

Conan, H. and Paniagua, M. (2003) *The Role of Small Scale Private Providers in Serving the Poor: Summary Paper and Recommendations*, Manila, Asian Development Bank

Cook, P. (1999) 'Privatization and utility regulation in developing countries: The lessons so far', *Annals of Public and Cooperative Economics*, vol 70, pp549–587

Cook, P. and Minogue, M. (2003) 'Regulating for development', *Insights*, vol 49, pp1–2

Cook, P., Kirkpatrick, C., Minogue, M. and Parker, D. (2003) *Competition, Regulation and Regulatory Governance in Developing Countries: An Overview of the Research Issues*, Manchester, CRC, IDPM, University of Manchester

Courmont, V. (2001) 'Poverty, a few definitions', *Villes en développement: Exclusion and Urban Poverty*, vol 53, p4

Crane, R. (1994) 'Water markets, market reform and the urban poor: Results from Jakarta, Indonesia', *World Devlopment*, vol 22, pp71–83

Darmame, K. (2004) 'Gestion de la rareté: Le service d'eau potable d'Amman entre la gestion publiquie et priveé', www.iwmi.cgiar.org/Assessment/FILES/word/ProjectDocuments/Jordan/RapportDarmame(1).pdf

DEFRA (Department for Environment, Food and Rural Affairs) (2004) *Cross-government Review of Water Affordability Report*, London, DEFRA

DEFRA (2008) *Consultation on Draft Statutory Social and Environmental Guidance to the Water Services Regulation Authority (OFWAT)*, London, DEFRA

Department of Statistics (2004) *Jordan in Figures*, Issue 6, Amman, Department of Statistics

DESA (Department of Economic and Social Affairs) (2006) *2005 Revision of World Urbanization Prospects*, New York, DESA, Population Division, United Nations

DOE (Department of the Environment) (1989) *Prospectus: Offers for Sale*, London, DOE and Secretary of State for Wales, London

Drafting Group (2002) *Guidance on Public Participation in Relation to the Water Framework Directive*, Water directors of the European Union, Norway, Switzerland and the countries applying for accession to the European Union meeting under the Danish Presidency in Copenhagen (21/22 November 2002), EC Report, Brussels

Drangaert, P., Melgarejo, S., Kemper, K. and Bakalian, A. (1998) 'Aguaterias: Small entrepreneurs bring competition to Paraguay's small town water sector', Paper presented at the Community Water Supply and Sanitation Conference, 5–8 May, Washington DC, World Bank

Dunn, E. (2008) *Family Spending*, 2007 edition, Office for National Statistics, Basingstoke, Palgrave Macmillan

DWI (Drinking Water Inspectorate) (2007) *Drinking Water in England and Wales 2006*, London, DWI

Ear-Dupuy, H. (2003) Comment submitted to the electronic discussion forum on the Draft World Development Report 2004, http://econ.worldbank.org/WBSITE/EXTERNAL/EXTDEC/EXTRESEARCH/EXTWDRS/EXTWDR2004/0,,contentMDK:20318077~isCURL:Y~menuPK:613303~pagePK:64167689~piPK:64167673~theSitePK:477688,00.html, accessed April 2008

ECLAC (2003) *Regulation of the Private Provision Public Water-related Services*, Santiago, Economic Commission for Latin America and the Caribbean

EPA (Environmental Protection Agency) (1998) *Information for States Developing Affordability Criteria for Drinking Water*, Washington DC, EPA, www.epa.gov/safewater/smallsys/afforddh.html

Espinosa, L. and López Rivera, O. A. (1994) 'UNICEF's urban basic services programme in illegal settlements in Guatemala City', *Environment and Urbanization*, vol 6, pp9–29

Estache A. (2005) *PPI Partnerships Versus PPI Divorces in LDCs*, World Bank Policy Research Working Paper 3470, Washington DC, World Bank

Estache, A., Gomez-Lobo, A. and Leipziger, D. (2000) 'Utility privatization and the needs of the poor in Latin America: Have we learned enough to get it right?', paper presented at Infrastructure for Development: Private Solutions and the Poor', 31 May–2 June, London

Evison, L. and Sunna, N. (2001) 'Microbial regrowth in household storage tanks', *Journal of the American Water Works Association*, vol 93, pp85–94

Ewen, S. (2003) 'Networks of power in the British police and fire services, c1870–1938', paper presented at the Economic History Society Annual Conference, Durham, 4–6 April

Finn, R. (2007) *Competition and Regulation in Water: Striking the Right Balance*, Birmingham, Water Services Regulation Authority

Fitch, M. (2003a) *Unaffordable Water*, Leicester, Centre for Utility Consumer Law

Fitch, M. (2003b) *Deep Waters*, Sutton Coldfield, Severn Trent Trust Fund

Fitch, M. and Price, H. (2002) *Water Poverty in England and Wales*, Newcastle upon Tyne, Centre for Utility Consumer Law and CIEH

Fletcher, P. (2001) *Regulating for Sustainability*, speech given at Wessex Water Forum for the Future, 7 November, www.ofwat.gov.uk.

Foster, V. (1998) *Considerations for Regulating Water Services While Reinforcing Social Interests*, Washington DC, UNDP–World Bank Water and Sanitation Program

Foster, V. (2003) 'What role for consumers in the regulatory process?', paper presented at the International Conference on Financing Water and Sanitation Services: Options and Constraints, 10–11 November, Washington DC

Foster, V. and Araujo, M. C. (2004) *Does Infrastructure Reform Work for the Poor? A Case Study from Guatemala*, World Bank Policy Research Working Paper 3185, Washington DC, World Bank.

Franceys, R. (2002) 'Change Management Times – World', Policy Makers Study Tour Brief, Change Management Forum, Hyderabad, ASCI

Franceys, R. (2005a) 'Charging to enter the water shop? The costs of urban water connections for the poor', *Water Science and Technology: Water Supply*, vol 5, no 6, pp209–216

Franceys, R. (2005b) 'Regulating P&PPs for the Poor', unpublished newsletter, Cranfield University

Franceys, R. (2006) 'Customer committees, economic regulation and the Water Framework Directive', *Journal of Water Supply: Research and Technology – Aqua*, vol 39, pp430–455

Franceys, R. (2008) 'GATS, "privatisation" and institutional development for urban water provision: Future postponed?', *Progress in Development Studies*, vol 8, pp45–58

Franceys R., Pickford, J. and Reed, R. (1992) *A Guide to the Development of On-Site Sanitation*, Geneva, WHO

Friedmann, J. (1996) 'Rethinking poverty: Empowerment and citizen rights', *International Social Science Journal*, vol 148, pp161–172

Gasmi, F., Laffont, J. and Sharkey, W. (2000) 'Competition, universal service and telecommunications policy in developing countries', *Information Economics and Policy*, vol 12, pp221–248

Gerlach, E. (2004) 'Literature review', in R. Franceys (ed) *Charging to enter the Water Shop?*, Research Report KaR 8319, London, DFID

Gerlach, E. (2005) *Regulating P&PPs for the Poor Global eConference*, Cranfield, Cranfield University

Ghana Statistical Service (2000) *Poverty Trends in Ghana in the 1990s*, Accra, Ghana Statistical Service

Global Water Intelligence (2005) *News*, March, London, Global Water Intelligence

Government of Ghana (1992) *Constitution of Ghana*, Accra, Government Printer, Assembly press

Government of India (2002) *National Water Policy 2002*, Delhi, Government of India

Government of Uganda (2004) *Water and Sanitation Sector Performance Report*, Kampala, Government of Uganda

Graham, S. and Marvin, S. (1994) 'Cherry picking and social dumping: Utilities in the 1990s', *Utilities Policy*, vol 4, pp113–119

GTZ (2004) *Sharing the Experience in Regulation in the Water Sector (SOWAS, sub-Saharan Africa)*, Lusaka, GTZ

GTZ and MWI (2004) *National Water Master Plan*, Digital Summary Version, Jordan

Gutierrez, E., Calaguas, B., Green, J. and Roaf, V. (2003) *New Rules, New Roles: Does PSP Benefit the Poor?*, synthesis report, London, WaterAid and Tearfund

Halcrow (2002) *Private Sector Participation and the Poor 3: Regulation*, Loughborough, WEDC

Hanchett, S., Akhter, S. and Hoque Khan, M. (2003) 'Water, sanitation and hygiene in Bangladeshi slums: An evaluation of the WaterAid-Bangladesh Urban Programme', *Environment and Urbanization*, vol 15, pp43–55

Harman, T. and Showell, W. (2004) *Showells Dictionary of Birmingham 1888*, Electronic Library Book 14472

Hasan, M. E. (2003) 'Implications of financial innovations for the poorest of the poor in the rural area: Experience from Northern Bagladesh', *Journal of Microfinance*, vol 5, pp101–134

HMSO (1989) *Water Act 1989*, London, Her Majesty's Stationery Office

HMSO (2003) *Water Act 2003*, London, Her Majesty's Stationery Office

Hossain, N. and Moore, M. (2002) *Arguing for the Poor: Elites and Poverty in Developing Countries*, IDS Working Paper 148, Brighton, IDS

Inocencio, A. B. (2001) *Serving the Urban Poor through Public-Private-Community Partnerships in Water Supply*, PIDS Policy Notes 10, Makati, Philippine Institute for Development Studies

Iskandarani, M. (2001) 'Water market participation and effective water prices in Jordan. Globalization and water resources management: The changing value of water', paper presented at AWRA/IWLRI - University of Dundee International Specialty Conference 6–8 August, University of Dundee

IWES (1977) *Symposium on Water Services: Financial, Engineering and Scientific Planning*, Institution of Water Engineers and Scientists, London

JNNURM (undated) *Jawaharlal Nehru National Urban Renewal Mission*, http://jnnurm.nic.in/jnnurm_hupa/jnnurm/Overview.pdf, accessed 10 January 2008

Jordana, J. and Levi-Faur, D. (2004) *The Politics of Regulation in the Age of Governance*, Cheltenham, Edward Elgar

Kay, J. (2004) *The Truth About Markets: Why Some Countries are Rich and Others Remain Poor*, London, Penguin

Katakura, Y. and Bakalian, A. (1998) *PROSANEAR. People, Poverty and Pipes*, WSP Working Paper, Washington DC, World Bank

Kaufmann, D., Kraay, A. and Mastruzzi, M. (2005) *Governance Matters IV Governance Indicators for 1996–2004*, Washington DC, World Bank

Kjellén, M. and McGranahan, G. (1997) *Comprehensive Assessment of the Freshwater Resources of the World*, Stockholm Environment Institute, Stockholm, Sweden

Klein, M. (1996) *Economic Regulation of Water Companies*, World Bank Policy Research Paper 1649, Washington DC, World Bank

Komives, K. (1999) *Designing Pro-poor Water and Sewer Concessions: Early Lessons From Bolivia*, World Bank Policy Research Working Paper 2243, Washington DC, World Bank

Komives, K. (2001) 'Designing pro-poor water and sewer concessions: Early lessons from Bolivia', *Water Policy*, vol 1, no 3, pp61–79

König, A., Taylor, A. and Ballance, T. (2003) *Infrastructure Regulation: An Introduction to Fundamental Concepts and Key Issues*, GTZ Working Paper No 10, Eschborn, GTZ

Laffont, J.-J. (2005) *Regulation and Development*, Cambridge, Cambridge University Press

Laffont, J.-J. and Tirole, J. (1991) 'The politics of government decision-making: A theory of regulatory capture', *Quarterly Journal of Economics*, vol 106, pp1089–1127

Laurie, N. and Crespo, C. (2002) 'An examination of the changing contexts for developing pro-poor water initiatives via concessions' final report on SSR Project R7895, Newcastle upon Tyne, Institute for Research on Environment and Sustainability, Newcastle University

Lee, T. (1995) *Improving the Management of Water Supply and Sanitation Systems in Latin America*, ECLAC, www.africanwater.org/ppp_debate_5_terence_lee.htm, accessed 4 February 2008

Lewin, K. (1997) 'Field theory in social sciences', in Moorhead, G. and Griffin, R. W. (eds) *Organizational Behavior*, Boston, MA, Houghton Mifflin

Llorente, M. and Zérah, M.-H. (2003) 'The urban water sector: Formal versus informal suppliers in India', *Urban India*, vol 12

Lovei, L. and Whittington, D. (1993) 'Rent-extracting behaviour by multiple agents in the provision of municipal water supply: A study of Jakarta, Indonesia', *Water Resources Research*, vol 29, pp1965–1974

Macleod, N. (1997) 'The Durban water tank system', paper presented at 23rd WEDC Conference, Water And Sanitation for All: Partnerships and Innovations, Durban, South Africa, 1–5 September

Manila Water (2006) *Annual Report 2006*, Manila, Manila Water Company Incorporated

Manila Water (2008) 'Investor relations', www.manilawater.com, accessed 16 January 2008

Matthews, R. (2006) 'Water: The quantum elixir', *New Scientist*, 8 April, pp32–37

Maynilad (2008) 'Corporate profile' and 'News and events', www.mayniladwater.com.ph, accessed 16 January 2008

McEldowney, J. (1995) 'Law and regulation: Current issues and future directions', in Bishop, M., Kay, J. and Mayer, C. (eds) *The Regulatory Challenge*, Oxford, Oxford University Press

McIntosh, A. C. (2003) *Asian Water Supplies: Reaching the Urban Poor*, London, ADB and IWA

McPhail, A. (1993) 'Overlooked market for water connections in Rabat's shantytowns', *Journal of Water Resources Development*, vol 119, pp388–405

Ministry of Planning and UN (2004) *The Millennium Development Goals, Jordan Report 2004*, Amman, Hashemite Kingdom of Jordan

Minogue, M. (2002) 'Governance-based analysis of regulation', *Annals of Public and Cooperative Economics*, vol 73, pp649–666

Minogue, M. (2003) 'Back to the state?', *Insights*, vol 49, p2

Minogue, M. (2004) 'Accountability and transparency in regulation: Critiques, doctrines and instruments', in Jordana, J. and Levi-Faur, D. (eds) *The Politics of Regulation*, Cheltenham, Edward Elgar

Mitlin, D. (2002) *Competition, Regulation and the Urban Poor: A Case Study of Water*, Centre on Regulation and Competition, Manchester, University of Manchester

MORI (2002) *The 2004 Periodic Review: Research into Customers' Views*, for WaterVoice, OFWAT, the Department for Environment, Food and Rural Affairs, Welsh Assembly Government, Water UK, Environment Agency, Drinking Water Inspectorate, English Nature and Wildlife and Countryside Link

MoWLE (2003) *Urban Water and Sanitation Strategy Report*, Ministry of Water, Land and Environment, Kampala, Government of Uganda

Mueller, M. L. (1997) *Universal Service: Competition, Interconnection, and Monopoly in the Making of the American Telephone System*, Cambridge, MA, MIT Press and AEI Press

Muhairwe, W. (2006) *Improving Performance: Case of National Water and Sewerage Corporation*, UN Sustainable Development Issues, Water Workshop, December, www.un.org/esa/sustdev/sdissues/water/workshop_africa/presentations/ muhairwe.pdf, accessed 17 January 2008

MWE (2006) *Water and Sanitation Sector Performance Report 2006*, Ministry of Water and Environment, Kampala, Government of Uganda

MWH (2004) *Draft Water Supply Policy*, Ministry of Works and Housing, Accra, Republic of Ghana

MWI (1997a) *Jordan's Water Strategy and Policies*, Ministry of Water and Irrigation, Amman, Hashemite Kingdom of Jordan

MWI (1997b) *Water Utility Policy*, Ministry of Water and Irrigation, Amman, Hashemite Kingdom of Jordan

MWI and WAJ (2001) *Programme Management Unit Charter of Operations*, Revision 1 – approved by EMB, Ministry of Water and Irrigation and Water Authority of Jordan, Amman, Hashemite Kingdom of Jordan

MWSS-RO (2007) *Tariff Matrix*, Manila, Metropolitan Waterworks and Sewerage System Regulatory System

Narayan, D., Chambers, R., Shah, M. and Petesch, P. (1999) *Global Synthesis Consultations with the Poor*, 20 September, Poverty Group, Washington DC, World Bank

Narracott, A. (2003) 'Regulating public private partnerships for the poor', unpublished MSc Thesis, Cranfield, Cranfield University

NCC (National Consumer Council) (2002) *Involving Consumers: Everyone Benefits*, London, NCC.

NCC (2003) *Everyday Essentials: Meeting Basic Needs*, London, NCC

NCE (2008) 'New tunnel to clear 57 properties from the flood register', *New Civil Engineer*, 4 February, p28, London, EMAP

Nickson, A. and Franceys, R. (2003) *Tapping the Market: The Challenge of Institutional Reform in the Urban Water Sector*, Houndmills, Basingstoke, Palgrave

Nickson, A. and Vargas, C. (2002) 'The limitations of water regulation: The failure of the Cochabamba concession in Bolivia', *Bulletin of Latin American Research*, vol 21, pp128–149

NWASCO (2000) *Guidelines on Required Minimum Service Level*, Lusaka, National Water Supply and Sanitation Council

NWASCO (2006) 'Consumer groups', National Water Supply and Sanitation Council, Lusaka, www.nwasco.org.zm, accessed 16 January 2008

NWSC (2008) 'Home page', National Water and Sewerage Corporation, www.nwsc.co.ug/modules/pagewrap/ accessed 16 January 2008

Nyarko, K. B., Oduro-kwarteng, S. and Adusei, K. (2004) 'Water pricing in Ghana Urban Water Utility: A case study of GWCL operations in Kumasi', Proceedings of the 12th Congress of the Union of African Water Suppliers, 16–19 February 2004, Accra International Conference Centre (AICC), Accra, Ghana

Obel-Lawson, E. and Njoroge, B. K. (1999) *Small Service Providers Make a Big Difference*, Field Note 5, UNDP–World Bank Water and Sanitation Program - Eastern and Southern Africa Region, Nairobi

Officer, L. (2006) *The Annual Real and Nominal GDP for the United Kingdom, 1086–2005*, Economic History Services, September, http://eh.net

OFWAT (1996) *1995–96 Report on the financial performance and expenditure of the water companies in England and Wales*, OFWAT, Birmingham

OFWAT (1999) *1998–1999 Report on Financial Performance and Expenditure of the Water Companies in England and Wales*, OFWAT, Birmingham

OFWAT (2003) *Financial performance and expenditure of the water companies in England and Wales 2002–2003 report*, OFWAT, Birmingham

OFWAT (2004) *Future Water and Sewerage Charges 2005–10*, Final determinations, Birmingham, Office of Water Services

OFWAT (2007a) *OFWAT Facts and Figures*, May, Birmingham, Water Services Regulation Authority

OFWAT (2007b) *Annual Report 2006–07*, OFWAT, London, The Stationery Office

OFWAT (2007c) *Setting Price Limits for 2010–15: Framework and Approach – a Consultation Paper*, Birmingham, Water Services Regulation Authority

OFWAT (2007d) *Levels of Service for the Water Industry in England and Wales 2006–07 Report*, Birmingham, Water Services Regulation Authority

OFWAT (2007e) 'OFWAT confirms/proposes fines', Press Notices 19, 33 and 42/07, Birmingham, Water Services Regulation Authority

OFWAT (2007f) *Financial Performance and Expenditure of the Water Companies in England and Wales 2006–07 Report*, Birmingham, Water Services Regulation Authority

OFWAT, (2007g) 'More water customers receive help', Press Notice 31/07, Water Services Regulation Authority, Birmingham

OFWAT (2007h) *Regulatory Director Letter 18/07*, 18 September 2007, Birmingham, Water Services Regulation Authority

OFWAT (2007i) 'Expansion sought', Press Notice 38/07, Birmingham, Water Services Regulation Authority

OFWAT (2008) *OFWAT's Future Strategy for Customer Charges for Water and Sewerage Services: A Consultation*, Birmingham, Water Services Regulation Authority

Ogus, A. I. (2001) 'Introduction', in Ogus, A. I. (ed) *Regulation, Economics and the Law*, Cheltenham, Edward Elgar

Ogus, A. I. and Veljanovski, C. G. (1984) *Readings in the Economics of Law and Regulation*, Oxford, Oxford University Press

ONS (2008) 'Society: Low Income, fewer children in poverty in recent years', Office of National Statistics, www.statistics.gov.uk/CCI/nugget.asp?ID=333&Pos=6&ColRank=2&Rank=208, accessed 17 January 2008

Page, B. (2003) 'Has widening stakeholder participation in decision-making produced sustainable and innovative water policy in the UK?', *Water Policy*, vol 5, pp313–329

Parker, D. (1999) 'Regulating public utilities: What other countries can learn from the UK experience', *Public Management*, vol 1, pp93–120

Parker, D. and Kirkpatrick, C. (2002) *Researching Economic Regulation in Developing Countries: Developing a Methodology for Critical Analysis*, CRC Working Paper No 34. Manchester, CRC

Plummer, J. (2002a) *Focusing Partnerships: A Sourcebook for Municipal Capacity Building in Public–Private Partnerships*, London, Earthscan

Plummer, J. (2002b) 'Developing inclusive public-private partnerships: The role of small-scale independent providers in the delivery of water and sanitation services', paper presented at World Development Report 2003/04 Workshop, 4–5 November 2002, Oxford.

Plummer, J. (ed) (2003) *Better Water and Sanitation for the Urban Poor: Good Practice from sub-Saharan Africa*, Abidjan and Washington DC, Water Utility Partnership and Water and Sanitation Program

PMU (2002) 'Vision and mission', website of the Programme Management Unit (PMU) of the Ministry of Water and Irrigation (MWI), Hashemite Kingdom of Jordan, www.pmu.gov.jo/Home/AboutUs/VisionMission/tabid/63/Default.aspx, accessed June 2004

Posner, R. A. (1984) 'Theories of economic regulation', in Ogus, A. I. and Veljanovski, C. G. (eds) *Readings in the Economics of Law and Regulation*, Oxford, Clarendon Press

Prosser, T. (1994) 'Utilities and social regulation', *Utilities Law Review*, vol 5, p156

Prosser, T. (1997) 'What should the regulators be doing?', in Prosser, T. (ed) *Law and the Regulators*, Oxford, Oxford University Press

Prosser, T. (1999) 'Theorising utility regulation', *Modern Law Review*, vol 62, pp196–217

PURC (2005a) *Review of the Performance of Ghana Water Company Limited 1998–2003*, Accra, Public Utilities Regulatory Commission, Cantonments

PURC (2005b) *Social Policy and Strategy for Water Regulation*, Accra, Public Utilities Regulatory Commission, Cantonments

PURC (2005c) *Urban Water Tariff Policy*, Accra, Public Utilities Regulatory Commission, Cantonments

Raghupathi, U. P. (2003) 'Small-scale private water providers: A growing reality', *Urban Finance*, vol 6, no 3, pp1–3, New Delhi, National Institute of Urban Affairs

Reed, R. (1995) *Sustainable Sewerage*, London, Intermediate Technology

Rees, R. and Vickers, J. (1995) 'RPI-X price cap regulation', in Bishop, M., Kay, J. and Mayer, C. (eds) *The Regulatory Challenge*, Oxford, Oxford University Press

RERC (2003) *Distribution Licensee's Standards of Performance – Regulations*, Jaipur, Rajasthan Electricity Regulatory Commission

RERC (2004) *Annual Report 2003–2004*, Jaipur, Rajasthan Electricity Regulatory Commission

Robinson, L. (2003) 'Consultation: What works', presentation to Local Government Public Relations Conference, February, Wollongong

SAFEGE (2000) *Feasibility Study: Jaipur Water Supply and Sanitation Project*, Jaipur, Public Health Engineering Department

Sansom. K., Franceys R., Njiru, C. and Morales-Reyes, J. (2003) *Contracting Out Water and Sanitation Services – Volume 1*, WEDC, Loughborough, Loughborough University

Sansom. K., Franceys R., Njiru, C., Kayaga, S., Coates, S. and Chary, S. (2004) *Serving All Urban Consumers – Book 2: Guidance Notes for Managers*, WEDC, Loughborough, Loughborough University

SAPI (2004) 'Special assistance for project implementation for Bisalpur', mimeo

Satterthwaite, D. (2003) 'The Millennium Development Goals and urban poverty reduction: Great expectations and nonsense statistics', *Environment and Urbanization*, vol 15, pp181–190

Shirley, M. M. and Ménard, C. (2002) 'Cities awash: A synthesis of the country cases', in Shirley, M. M. (ed) *Thirsting for Efficiency: The Economics and Politics of Urban Water System Reform*, London, Pergamon

Shourie, A. (2004) *Governance and the Sclerosis that has Set in*, New Delhi, ASA Publications

Simanowitz, A. (2004) 'Ensuring impact: Reaching the poorest while building financially self-sufficient institutions, and showing improvement in the lives of the poorest families', paper delivered at Asia Pacific Region Microcredit Summit Meeting of Councils (APRMS), Dhaka, 16–19 February

Simmonds, G. (2002) *Consumer Representation in the UK*, Bath, CRI

Simmonds, G. (2003) *Universal and Public Service Obligations in Europe*, Bath, CRI

Simpson, R. (2002) 'Should consumers demand higher water prices?', *Consumer 21*, newsletter of Consumers International, London

Simpson, R. and Shallat, L. (2004) *WaterWorks: A Consumer Advocacy Guide to Water and Sanitation*, London, Consumers International

SISS (Superintendencia de Servicios Sanitarios) (2006) *Memoria 2005*, Santiago, SISS

SISS (2007) *Memoria 2006*, Santiago, SISS

Skill, V. (1983) *The Making of Victorian Birmingham*, Studley, Brewin Books

Smith, W. (2000) 'Regulating infrastructure for the poor: Perspectives on regulatory system design', paper presented at Infrastructure for Development: Private Solutions and the Poor, London, World Bank, 31 May–2 June

Social Exclusion Unit (2006) Social Exclusion, www.cabinetoffice.gov.uk/social_exclusion_task_force/context.aspx

Solo, T. M. (1998) 'Competition in water and sanitation: The role of small-scale entrepreneurs', *Public Policy for the Private Sector*, Note No. 165, Washington DC, World Bank

Solo, T. M. (1999) 'Small-scale entrepreneurs in the urban water and sanitation market', *Environment and Urbanization*, vol 11, pp117–131

Stallard, K. and Ehrhardt, D. (2004) *Private Sector Participation in Infrastructure for the Benefit of the Poor*, Frankfurt, KfW

Stern, J. and Holder, S. (1999) 'Regulatory governance: Criteria for assessing the performance of regulatory systems. An application to infrastructure industries in the developing countries in Asia', *Utilities Policy*, vol 8, pp33–50

Stern, P., Townsend, D. and Stephens, R. (2006) *Telecommunications Universal Access Programs in Latin America*, Regulatel, Bogota

STTF (Severn Trent Trust Fund) (2006) *Annual Review 2006*, Birmingham, STTF

STTF (2007) 'Latest News', www.sttf.org.uk/Latest_News.htm accessed 19 January 2008

Suez (2005) *Aguas Del Illimani – La Paz Background and Facts*, Paris, Suez Environment

Thompson, S. (2007) 'Bahrain firm sells South Staffs water', *The Times*, 29 October, London

Trémolet, S. (2002) 'Pro-poor regulation', paper presented at the PPIAF/ADB Conference on Infrastructure Development – Private Solutions for the Poor: The Asian Perspective, Manila, 28–30 October

Trémolet, S. and Browning, S. (2002) *Research and Surveys Series: The Interface between Regulatory Frameworks and Tri-sector Partnerships*, London, BPD Water and Sanitation Cluster, BPD Water and Sanitation

Troyano, F. (1999) *Small Scale Water Providers in Paraguay*, *WSP Working Paper*, Washington DC, UNDP/World Bank Water and Sanitation Program

Ugaz, C. (2002) *Consumer Participation and Pro-poor Regulation in Latin America*, WIDER Discussion Paper No 2002/121, Helsinki, Finland, UNU/WIDER

Ugaz, C. and Waddams Price, C. (2003) *Utility Privatization and Regulation: A Fair Deal for Consumers?*, Cheltenham, Edward Elgar

UN (2006) *The Millennium Development Goals Report 2006*, New York, United Nations

UNDP (2008) *Human Development Report 2007/08*, New York, UNDP

UNFPA (2007) *State of the World Population 2007: Unleashing the Potential of Urban Growth*, New York, United Nations Population Fund

UN-HABITAT (2003a) *The Challenge of Slums: Global Report on Human Settlements 2003*, London, Earthscan

UN-HABITAT (2003b) *Water and Sanitation in the World's Cities: Local Action for Global Goals*, London, Earthscan

Upton, C. (2005) *Living Back-to-Back*, Chichester, Phillimore

Utilities Reform Unit (2003) 'Performance contract between Government of the Republic of Uganda and National Water and Sewerage Corporation 2004–2006', Kampala, Utilities Reform Unit, Ministry of Water, Lands and Environment and Ministry of Finance, Planning and Economic Development

van Ryneveld, M. B. (1995) 'Costs and affordability of water supply and sanitation provision in the urban areas of South Africa', *Water SA*, vol 21, pp1–14

Vass, P. (2003a) 'Profit sharing and incentive regulation', in Vass, P. (ed) *Regulatory Practice and Design*, Bath, Centre for the study of Regulated Industries

Vass, P. (2003b) 'The principles of "better regulation": Separating roles and responsibilities', in Vass, P. (ed) *Regulatory Practice and Design*, Bath, Centre for the study of Regulated Industries

Verhoest, P. (2000) 'The myth of universal service: Hermeneutic considerations and political considerations', *Media, Culture and Society*, vol 22, pp595–610

Vézina, M. (2002) 'Water services in small towns in Africa: The role of small and medium-sized organisations', Field Note 12, August, Nairobi, UNDP/World Bank Water and Sanitation Program Africa Region

Waddams Price, C. and Young, A. (2003) 'UK utility reforms: Distributional implications and government response', in Ugaz, C. and Waddams Price, C. (eds) *Utility Privatization and Regulation: A Fair Deal for Consumers?*, Cheltenham, Edward Elgar

WASA (2005) *Annual Report*, Vientiane, Water Supply Authority of Lao PDR

WASH (1992) *Working Paper 102*, Arlington, VA, Camp Dresser McKee for USAID

WaterAid (2001) *Land Tenure*, London, WaterAid

Webb, P. and Iskandarani, M. (1998) *Water Insecurity and the Poor: Issues and Research Needs*, ZEF – Discussion Papers on Development Policy No 2, Bonn, Center for Development Research

Weitz, A. and Franceys, R. (2002) *Beyond Boundaries, Extending Services to the Urban Poor*, Manila, Asian Development Bank

Whittington, D., Boland, J. and Foster, V. (2002) *Water Tariffs and Subsidies in South Asia: Understanding the Basics*, Washington DC, World Bank.

WHO (2005) *Water for Life: Making it Happen*, Geneva, WHO

WHO and UNICEF (2000) *Global Water Supply and Sanitation Assessment 2000 Report*, Geneva and New York, WHO and UNICEF

WHO and UNICEF (2006) *Meeting the MDG Drinking Water and Sanitation Target: The Urban and Rural Challenge of the Decade*, Geneva and New York, WHO and UNICEF

Wilcox, D. (1994) *The Guide to Effective Participation*, London, Partnership Books

Winayanti, L. and Lang, H. C. (2004) 'Provision of urban services in an informal settlement: A case study of Kampung Penas Tanggul, Jakarta', *Habitat International*, vol 28, pp41–65

World Bank (1997) *The Hashemite Kingdom of Jordan Water Sector Review*, Washington DC, World Bank

World Bank (2001) *World Development Report 2001: Attacking Poverty*, Oxford, World Bank and Oxford University Press

World Bank (2003) *World Development Report 2003: Sustainable Development in a Dynamic World*, Oxford, World Bank and Oxford University Press

World Bank (2004a) *Social Development in World Bank Operations: Results and Way Forward*, Draft Strategy Paper, 12 February, Washington DC, World Bank Social Development Department

World Bank (2004b) *World Development Report 2004: Making Services Work for Poor People*, Oxford, World Bank and Oxford University Press

World Bank (2007) *World Development Report 2007*, Washington DC, World Bank

World Bank (2008) *World Development Report 2008*, Washington DC, World Bank

WPEP (2000) *Small-scale Independent Providers: 30 Years of Urban Experiences in the Philippines*, Manila, Water Supply And Sanitation Performance Enhancement Project

WRc (2007) South West Pilot Scheme on Water Affordability Final Report from WRc, London, DEFRA

Young, A. (2001) *The Politics of Regulation: Privatized Utilities in Britain*, Basingstoke, Palgrave

Zaroff, B. and Okun, D. A. (1984) 'Water vending in developing countries', *Aqua*, vol 5, 289–295

Zérah, M.-H. (1997) 'The real price of water', *Villes en développement: India*, vol 38, p2

Index

Page numbers in *italic* refer to boxes, figures or tables.

For Product Safety Concerns and Information please contact our EU
representative GPSR@taylorandfrancis.com
Taylor & Francis Verlag GmbH, Kaufingerstraße 24, 80331 München, Germany

www.ingramcontent.com/pod-product-compliance
Ingram Content Group UK Ltd.
Pitfield, Milton Keynes, MK11 3LW, UK
UKHW021620240425
457818UK00018B/655